1

JulieRenee.com

Your Divine Human Blueprint

Your best guide to creating and maintaining your 100% healthy happy life using the quantum field and your original blueprint to restore and renew health vitality momentum clarity and joy here and now!

Julie Renee Doering

February 2014

Bringing Heavenly Knowledge to an Awakening Human Community

JulieRenee.com

Also by Julie Renee Doering

Books

- *100% You Formula*

- *Awakening the Healthy American*

- *Balance Your Life Now E book*

- *Your Divine Human Blueprint Protocals*

- *Breaking Through (Poetry)*

Programs

- *Activate Masters Program*

- *Accelerate Wealth 7 Day Jumpstart Challenge*

- *Accelerate Wealth 21 Day Activation*

- *Balance Your Life 12 Week Program*

- *Beautiful From the Inside Out (look 10 years younger in 60 days naturally)*

- *The Definitive Guide to Meditation Series*

- *Illumination; Rosary for a New Era and (Instructors Guide)*

- *The Sound Of Truth; Himalayan Mantras for health and transformation*

- *Secret Keys: 18 Core Teachings with Guided Mediations*

- *Unlimited Love*

- *Your Divine Human Blueprint Audio series*

Music

- *Gratitude; India classical influence harp and vocals*

- *Pleasures; Celtic harp and vocals*

- *The Message; Rumi Love Poetry*

- *Illumination; Harp*

Video

- *Regeneration; Healing the Glands of the Brain*

- *Birth Massage Training Video*

All are available and you may order by visiting

www.julierenee.com

Your Divine Human Blueprint

Published By: T. Allen Hanes & Associates

Cover Design: T. Allen Hanes & Associates

Printed February 2014 Printed in the U.S.A.

ISBN-978-0-9915558-2-6

Visit Julie Renee on the World Wide Web
http://www.julierenee.com

Terms of Use – Disclaimer

The purpose of this book is to educate and entertain. The author and/or publisher does not guarantee that anyone following the techniques, suggestions, tips, ideas or strategies will become successful. The author and/or publisher shall have neither liability nor responsibility to anyone with respect to any loss or damage caused, or alleged to be caused, directly by the information in this book.

Warning – Disclaimer

Reference herein to any specific commercial products, process, or service by trade name, trademark, manufacturer, or otherwise, in no manner

Table of Contents

Preface

I'm so excited you've decided to delve into Learning about your own magnificent Divine Human Blueprint. This manuscript represents literally thousands of hours of research and documentation over a seven-year period. I could hold onto the material for another seven years and would likely still not feel like I had documented everything but my commitment to you is to get you a workable usable guide so you too can start accessing your grand design and get on with the process of living your 100% healthy life.

I wrote this book to translate heavenly information to a ready and eager human community. In the beginning, finding words to describe what I was seeing and experiencing came slowly, but eventually I was able to find my voice and the language of the blueprint I hope you will resonate with and cherish.

Being Human is a wonderful experience. When we shift from the idea of survival to living a 100% healthy fully engaged life we will have reclaimed our birthright.

At the urging of my students I have included many stories to illustrate each of the concepts and ideas so that this new way of thinking might be simple and easy to comprehend.

I have also included specific protocols and techniques for you to practice and use in your daily life so that you too can access the quantum field and be fully empowered to live your best life now!

For your convenience I have also created a companion book of just the protocols for you to refer to once you have completed studying this book.

If the content of this heavenly manuscript inspires and delights you I encourage you to considered joining in our yearlong study of the Divine Human Blueprint. You can learn more about this and the home study programs by visiting us at JulieRenee.com

Here's what people are saying about Your Divine Human Blueprint working with Julie Renee's system

"Julie Renee Doering has written an absolutely fascinating book on 'transformational healing'. Her miraculous and indomitable spirit is everywhere in the book. And yet, the book is about more than healing or 'energy'. The reader comes away with a deep and transforming understanding of the Divine Human Blueprint for health, personal wholeness and success. She offers the reader a fresh look at how to find access to, and become, a 'super star' in your own life and community. I have personally worked with Julie Renee and have been a part of her fabulous workshops. This book captures so much of the magic of those moments. It is not only well-written and inspiring, but it touches the deep places in your soul that have been crying out for a way to escape the mundane and all those limiting circumstances in your life, so that you can fly with the deep aspirations of your soul and heart. The book is more than a 'good read'. It is a doorway and an opportunity to redesign your life in ways that begin on the physical level but quickly affect all the ways you energetically show up in life. If you want to play the game of life at 100% capacity in many ways and levels, this is the book to buy."

Safe to Love Again Workshop- **Gary D. Salyer, Ph.D**

"Julie Renee is the most extraordinary healer alive today. And I say to everyone, run to Julie Renee versus walk – Run!"

Founder of CEO Space 9- **Berny Dorhman**

"Clients have been generating with effortless ease. I seem to possess magical abilities. My phone is ringing. I'm receiving checks and commissions in the mail. Money is multiplying literally overnight. I'm so excited. I literally find checks in the mail. I get calls from clients who want to use my services and are ready now. I'm noticing grace and ease throughout my life. I am receiving bigger acknowledgements on stages and invitations to speak have multiplied. One just came in from New Zealand. Additionally, a cruise just got offered to me. Life is very good. I give credit to Julie Renee for developing this course, for helping me get grounded in my life. Thank you, Julie Renee."

Author of the New York Times Best Seller "Guerrilla Publicity" and "Publicity Crash Course"- **Jill Lublin**

"Julie-Renee is a global thought leader in the field of quantum level healing. What makes her work so extraordinary is that her system is so masterful and her results are so rapid. You are in for a luscious treat when you open yourself to the tremendous healing of her work. She is indeed a precious treasure."

Speaker & Coach- **Eli Davidson**

"I have been working on Julie Renee's program. The process I have been going through day by day is nothing short of a miracle. Things are really starting to open up. I am getting real clarity and connections to people I have never spoken with before. There is an energy in the air around me that says whatever it is I am doing, I am doing the right thing. Thank you, Julie Renee"

Author of "The Fearless Factor", "When the Crow Sings"

10- Jacquliene Wales

"Before working with Julie Renee I was feeling tired, burnt out and older than my years. After working with Julie Renee's program I had the same energy level I remember having when I was fourteen years old! Julie has been able to clear and heal emotional and physical patterns that no other practitioner has ever been able to heal. I highly recommend working with Julie if you struggle with fatigue and chronic health issues that are holding you back from experiencing incredible health."

Health and Business Coach and Owner
www.holisticmba.com

- Cary Peters

"My 12-year speaking business was booming until I hit a dry spell this past year. Despite many marketing campaigns, I was struggling to get booked and my attitude and mindset weren't good. I connected with Julie Renee and she was able to activate my healthy brain and thoughts. Within 5 days of the session, I booked 2 events and I know there are many more to come!"

Speaker, Trainer MLM

- Karen Phelps

"Just when you think you have heard it all, you haven't. Not until you read and experience Julie Renee. Her unique and powerful formula for designing your life, for your greatest expression, is in your hands. What a gift! Julie Renee is a leading edge teacher connecting with thought and business leaders who are ready to finally say YES!"

Host of the radio show 'Everyday Attraction' on Unity.fm

The Beginning

Before

Before the time of legends
Before Mythology began
Before elements, time, space and matter
I am.
I exist in all
As the very essence of truth
My knowledge is limitless
I am the record of all
I am infinity
I am breath, life, hope and joy
I am surrender
I am all that is pure and true

Do you know how extraordinary you and your body are? Have you actually stopped to consider that you have come with a miraculous system? When you get a cut on your hand you heal. When you come down with a cold you do indeed return to health. When you bruise a muscle, it does return to ease. Imagine if you got a headache and it never went away or scratched your skin and it never mended. Life would be very different. We would all need to live in a bubble if we could not regenerate.

The good news for all of us in human bodies, is that we come into this world with an innate ability heal. Our bodies are meant to live hundreds of years. In order to accomplish this we need to learn how to care for the spiritual and cellular body.

When we are young we learn to brush our teeth and comb our hair, but we are not shown how to care for our miraculous system.

Through my Miraculous Living programs, and specifically through the technique of Cellular Neo-Genesis, I am now teaching how to care for your cells and live your life in health, vitality and vibrant longevity.

I would like you to imagine being gifted a most amazing flying car. It has arrived at your doorstep and is ready to use. It is all fuelled up with tons of neat gadgets. The only trouble is, you haven't been trained to operate this thing, so you pretty much just drive it around the neighborhood without really understanding what it's capable of.

Well my friend, what if that was an analogy for your relationship with your amazing human body? There are a bunch of gadgets you haven't yet discovered, and which I'll introduce to you in the following pages.

Have you ever wondered where the amazing design of human spirit in body came from?

What if the beginning of Humankind was as simple as this?

Genesis

I exist not out of some desire or will
Rather, I exist in truth

You can find me hiding in the
belly of the biggest lie
I eagerly await your discovery

As I exist in everything
Who could not know me?

And yet you gaze past me
Your dearest friend and ally
Your own truth

In a land of great riches and abundant resources, earthly life evolved. Reptiles, birds and mammals lived in harmony, exploring the physical world. The fertility of this blue planet truly provided an idyllic environment for all the creatures that inhabited the Garden of Eden. In a natural progression, new inhabitants came in to share this great good earth and intelligent life arrived.

Spirit had long desired the chance for a mortal life, and was finally given the opportunity for an earthly body of flesh and blood. However even before there were humans on earth, the Divine Human Blueprint existed.

The Divine Human Blueprint was eloquent: truly a masterpiece. We looked beyond the legends of the Biblical Genesis, where Cane and Able, sons of Adam and Eve, married girls from a neighboring village.

Small discrepancies notwithstanding, perhaps respectfully we might set aside the rib and clay mythos and open to the idea of a benevolent group of biological engineers operating under the care of the our planetary Supreme Being (God).

The human blueprint took sixty earth years to develop. It involved thousands of these benevolent biological engineers we will refer to as designers, who worked together to provide the birth of human animal. This allowed for human spirit to actually live in the physical realm. Human spirit existed well before the Divine Human Blueprint. These spirits had experimented with inhabiting the dynamic physical realm, and imagined the pleasure of a full physical experience.

We can imagine the designers being the right hand guardians of the Divine. They did not embody physical form. They were not of the human spirit realm. Perhaps they, 'The Elohim', (a group of divine beings found in ancient scriptural legend) were the caretakers of our human realm.

As time progressed enhancements were added to the Divine Human Blueprint. These improved elements adjusted the developing species of humans. With each alteration, humans enjoyed more possibilities and new challenges.

The DNA is an exquisite factor found in the lusciously rich design. This complex DNA program was not part of the original scheme, yet as time progressed and human spirit enjoyed use of the physical body, the designers were able to identify improvements that would help provide a fulfilling corporeal experience for human spirit. This made the magnificent human anatomy and fabulous brain a perfect vessel for the advancing human.

Once the model was dramatically improved, the brain advanced and allowed for significantly more processing than we are currently using. The last improvements to this model were made 20,000 years ago. It appears the Divine Human Blueprint designers meant to gift us all their full improvements to complete the 'Human Project.'

There are currently forty-two designs of humans and many, many variations and mutations of the original designs as humans mate cross culturally. The multitudes of design versions were created with the intention of cross-pollination. As the designs meld together with interracial coupling a vibrant beauty and structural strength advances with the excellent qualities of each design.

I honor all creation stories as accurate and an important part of the overall truth. I ask that you make a little room for the possibility that this additional story may have great validity and explain much of our incredibly complex and astonishing make-up.

Before we begin delving into the science of the Divine Human Blueprint I would like to tell you of my journey and how I came to have the information and skill I now embody.

When you come to me
See me
Joy, Truth, Clarity and Divine Vision
Are my fruits

I am the messenger
I am the message

I am all that is and
All that can be
All that is hoped for

Past, present and future blend
Into oneness
There is no separation

Time, eternity is all and nothing

Weep not my beloved
For the echoing voice
Resounds in the hearts
Of the people who come to me

Come for your healing
Come for your light
Come for your truth

Come into yourself
I await your recognition

I love you
I am you.

1989 Julie Renee Doering

My Story

I was born during the era of military super powers and nuclear threat. War and biological weapons were in full swing. The American dream rested on the notion that the people with the most possessions were the winners. Patriarchal systems ruled, usurping the role of divine connection.

I literally survived the atomic underground bomb testing in the Nevada desert when I was a child. Our family traveled, something my father was able to provide for our pleasure and education and a fact my parents were very proud of. We slept in forty-eight states during my childhood, saw all the national monuments and parks, hundreds of forts and learned first hand about the history of our nation.

What I didn't know was that the trip to Nevada would completely alter my life trajectory and set me on a path that would lead me to the Divine Human Blueprint.

Unlike many of the nuclear down-winders, I was just a tourist. I went home completely unaware of the tumors that

17

were growing in my body. It wasn't until I was twenty-four and pregnant with my third child that I learned I had a 'terminal' thyroid cancer.

From that moment to this, I have traversed many lifetimes; from the worst of suffering to the most incredible ecstasy; from utter isolation (to the point of believing God was dead) to a rich and deep connection with the Divine.

The cellular quantum mechanics outlined in the coming chapters began coming through to me after I had been profoundly ill for many years. I was suffering from overwhelming pain, could barely walk, and had difficulty breathing. I felt I could not continue with my life in this pain.

I wrote my will and health care directive and spoke to my family about my desire not to continue if any additional complications showed up. However after a week of thinking there was no choice, I awoke to the promise of a great life.

I went to my garden declaring to God that He should take me or make me well. Day after day I chanted and prayed and meditated. As I went into a high state of ecstasy I begin receiving the images of the Divine Human Blueprint. Over the coming days, information poured in about the miraculous system and how to heal myself.

After two weeks I emerged from the garden without pain and many symptoms alleviated. As the years have progressed I have seen more and more of the Divine Human Blueprint while looking for the answers to health concerns of my clients.

This book is filled with the design and the stories of the wonderful people I have journeyed with and been blessed to serve.

If I had world enough and time
1986

If I had world enough and time
Loves sweet fragrance I would define
Yet amber glows of heart in troughs
Again to gather baskets of posies
While children play ring round rosie

I am not so wise to know
these things of material and clay
Waiting is but impossible
Yet I do wait
For she calls to me and I stay
Again and again I stay
Like the nine lived cat
I stay

Though not by my choice
I'd abandon this cause
For pleasure is fleeting in this dimension
Yet I stay because she asks for so little
Still in clay I feel so much

Pursue me not sweet lady
Ask me only of human things

A shoe
A bath
Now this I could respond
I know these things well

But this flame needing re-sparking
'tis not a human call

Chapter 1: The Human Spirit

Soft the light and sweet the spirit
Gentle voices call our song
We are magic we are wonder
When we live beyond the veil

Human kind, please raise your thoughts
Bring a plane of peace and love
We the guardians of the pilgrims
We the authors of the play.

"Human Spirit" is the essence of our individuality.

Our spirit, though not technically immortal, exists long beyond what our mind can conceive.

Our spirit functions in many ways. It is the carrier of our information and accumulated wisdom. It provides challenges we have yet to resolve and understand. It assembles the entanglements with others that we've left unresolved, waiting for the understanding to release them. Without human spirit being fully engaged in the body, many maladies can appear, as you will read in the upcoming chapters. Here we seek to understand how it is connected to us and why it is so important.

The human spirit consists of light and the absence of color, as we understand it.

Human spirit has substance

When the spirit leaves the body at the end of one's life, the body loses eight ounces on the deathbed. A tiny amount of that, about one eighth of an ounce, is from spirit and the rest of the weight loss is attributed to the soul, which is described in detail in Chapter 2.

Since we cannot see human spirit, for many, it is a mystery or even a legend. However without a human spirit animating the body at birth, the body becomes an empty shell with no possibility for breath, heartbeat or any other signs of life. Human spirit must be present and/or connected to the body for life as we know it.

If you have known a person in a coma, you may feel the presence of the person around the body. They may even be able to trigger a squeeze reflex in the hand, but it will be very apparent they are not occupying their body.

Remembering the birth of my daughter Becky is like remembering a hilarious comedy. I was almost two weeks overdue and had been dilated for four weeks. The Doctor kept saying, "Any time now," and another day would pass with no B-A-B-Y. This had not been the easiest pregnancy as I had developed toxemia and had also taken a bad spill down thirteen steps, providing me with a very fancy boot and a broken ankle to help make the last three months of gestation a little more exciting.

I had been dilated for a few days and I think the nurses were making bets on when I would deliver. Becky had a mind of her own, and one fine day, later in the evening, she said, "NOW!" That was when the fireworks began.

My husband, Phil, had just come in from doing his chores. He was tired so he said he would clean up and join me later. I was downstairs, lying on the sofa in full-blown labor, and with my two year-old climbing all over me. Arg@#%@@?!!! Where was Phil? I was going to deliver any minute.

I yelled upstairs, but Phil (who had some hearing loss) did not respond. I was minutes from delivery, and yet I had to climb up those thirteen steps with the boot on my ankle only to find that Phil had shut the bedroom door and gone to sleep (it took me two contractions to get up those steps, so you know I was ready to deliver).

I thought Becky would be born in the back seat of the car, however we finally did get to the local community hospital. I ran in saying, "I'm having a baby!" It seemed unbelievable now that Becky was crowning.

I was ushered towards the labor ward for delivery. When the nurse saw my baby's crowning head, she screamed, "Oh my God, get the doctor!"

Moments later the most perfect baby you have ever seen was in my arms.

A human spirit with all its wonder and complexity had come into my life. Her personality was already clear and pronounced, announcing her uniqueness from the way she came in, to the way she now does everything. Her time her way, and oh so beautiful!

If you are a mother you will always say that the most important thing you did in this lifetime was give birth to your children. You can do other extraordinary things, however the miracle of birth and the miracle of connection of human spirit to the little baby body and what you provide for that child through infancy (and beyond) is truly extraordinary!

In this chapter we will explore the nature of the relationship of human spirit to human body (animal) and how sport provides a multitude of key components for the successful operation of the body and the energy body. I've included a lot of new never before seen material, which will help you fill out a more complete picture of the dynamic human experience.

Human spirit, when animating a human body, stimulates many of the operating systems of the physical body.

Human Spirit Provides Systems Support as follows:

System	Function
Cardio-vascular	Stimulation
Respiratory	Activation
Digestive	Operation
Nervous	Stimulation
Sense Perception; Touch, Auditory, Taste, Visual, Smell	Activation
Lymphatic	Stimulation
DNA programs (related to body function)	Activation
Chakra and Nadis	Development, Operations
Mental Body & Brain Including Pituitary Gland & Hypothalamus	Stimulation
Golden Rings	Pattern

Other aspects of the human body and human incarnation influence or are affected by Human spirit:

- The thymus provides operation information for this director of the immune system.

- The pancreas stabilizes the human spirit in the physical body connection.

23

Every part of the human body is somehow touched by human spirit. Improving the connection between the human spirit and these important systems in the body can vitalize our lives and bring about a fully embodied human experience.

The process of human incarnation

Before conception, when you were just a twinkle in your father's eye, you existed. You were in a family spirit group, which could be experienced as Heaven, Nirvana, Shangri-La or another version of Paradise, based on your tribal or religious program.

Some of you worked out a path of learning and challenges for your and highest and fastest path of growth, while others entered human incarnation with karma or incomplete complications from a previous life that you were given the opportunity to resolve.

Upon your mother's successful impregnation, cells begin to divide, creating the beginnings of a physical human body. At any time between two hours after implantation and five months gestation the human spirit takes ownership of the developing physical body. In so doing, it begins the journey of human incarnation.

While in the womb, the body movements are reflexive and instinctive. The earlier the human spirit connects to the forming body during gestation, the more influence the spirit has in the development of the physical body. Then, upon first breath at the miraculous event of birth, the human spirit begins to animate its body.

While the baby's body is developing inside the womb, the

spirit often dwells inside the mother's physical body, causing endless problems. Ideally (and what we teach in our Miraculous Living programs) the spirit needs to live in the outer layer of the mother's aura through the nine-month gestation period. This is the easiest location on the mother for baby's spirit to participate in the connection while waiting for the body to develop enough so it can be occupied. Very few human spirits have this helpful information.

Spirit to baby connection in the womb

Michelle and Mike came to me desperate for assistance. Michelle, in her fourth month of pregnancy, was overtaken by the worst inhabitation of an incoming spirit in a mother's body.

Michelle's symptoms included massive gum infection, a constant headache and severe nausea and vomiting, along with intestinal problems and diarrhea. Michelle had a hypnotherapy practice until besieged with these intense symptoms, and Mike was a corporate trainer. They were a really awesome couple who were truly suffering. Michelle's yoga instructor, Kari, sent them in to me for spiritual triage.

What I initially discovered was that the spirit connection was a battlefield. With such fantastic parents, there were a number of baby spirits who wanted them as parents. In this case, none of them were willing to wait. Five spirits brawled it out until one made the ownership bond by forging a new path through mommy's mouth and throat, down through the stomach and intestines connecting into the womb.

The battle for ownership of the body had taken six hours.

When I told Michelle what had happened, she could put a date to it and now understood more clearly why she was so sick. I directed the baby spirit to remove its energy from the mother's digestive tract and gums and assisted it in connecting through the base of mommy's spine and into the womb from the back. Then I showed it how to keep peaceful and to rest in the seventh layer of the aura rather than dominating the middle of mommy's body (which had been the cause of her unending nausea).

To the baby spirit, this was all news. We, as human spirit, set aside much of our accumulated information when we start life anew as an infant. Typically, the strongest spirit wins in a battle for an incarnation. While I have never seen another such situation this bad, I have from time to time seen two, or sometimes three, spirits attempting to gain control of and ownership of a developing body.

Michelle's infections were the result of left over fight energy, which had totally kicked her own spirit out of her gums. We were able to help her tremendously in the first session and restore much more in the second and third session. Part of the therapy for Michelle was to communicate with the baby while *in utero*. As you might imagine, the violence of her illness combined with her feelings of being overtaken had caused a rift in her affection for the child. Doing a number of sessions after the clearing helped her to find neutrality. She used her skills as a hypnotherapist to develop a loving dialogue with the gestating infant. At birth, ready for motherhood, her heart was wide open to welcome her new child into her arms.

Michelle and Mike are the most amazing parents and are now raising two wonderful little humans.

Human spirit - body connection

The definition of spirit is that which animates and infuses life in body. According to Wikipedia, the *human spirit* can be seen as the heavenly component of human's non-material makeup in contrast to the **psyche,** which can refer to the ego or lower element.

How I see it, is that the human spirit is the light that carries our information for eons from the very beginning of our being and continues on after the physical body passes. The physical body itself, which is human animal, begins at the time of conception and lives only one incarnation. It supports human life on planet Earth.

I have been present for a number of human spirit passages and have witnessed the spirit leaving its human body behind as it launches into a world of freedom, away from an ailing or elderly body, which can no longer provide an enjoyable journey.

Nic, a real Estate mogul and longtime client-friend, passed in a powerfully memorable way. While alone at home he had experienced a massive stroke and was left without care for nineteen hours. Much of the damage to his brain function and paralysis happened because of this prolonged time without care. I had come to work with him for in home care and therapeutic massage.

When I treated Nic, my 'miraculous' healing abilities had not yet fully blossomed, yet I was still able to provide a calm enjoyable experience for Nic, whose very nature was agitated and rajasic (aggressive and irritable).

His stroke had left his spirit mostly out of his body; he had paralysis and a significant loss of brain function. On several occasions, I had Nic share my auric field in order to assist him in accessing his brain and memories. Those were happy days for him. We sat and laughed as he told one story after another, joyous to feel himself present once again.

On one occasion, his family decided to have a Catholic priest come in to do prayers for the sick and dying (essentially last rites) with his family present. He pleaded with me to be there, afraid the priest would pray him out of his body and end his life. He told me, "I am not done yet; I need you here to help me."

When the end finally came, I had been treating Nic with daily therapeutic massage for six years. I had noticed a few weeks earlier that, first, one toe was going black, then a second. As it turns out, this blackening was gangrene. Because of many other serious extenuating health conditions, his doctors choose not to treat the condition.

In the hospital, Nic pleaded with me to help him escape the hospital. He knew that if he stayed, it would be his end. He scolded me when I told him we would have to wait. I remember this clearly, "I am so disappointed in you," he said, "You have never let me down before." The next day, he choked on vomit and died. They put him on a respirator to keep the appearance of life within his body while they called relatives to come for their last goodbyes.

To his family Nic was a wealthy "King." The passing of the King meant wealth distributed amongst his heirs.

It was interesting to be part of this passing. I was the only one touching him, singing to him as he left. His daughter then had the family sing a show tune together since Nic loved Sinatra type songs. After all he was a "cool dude" in his day.

The nurse pulled the respirator plug and the life had left his body. Nic rose up from his body and looked at me to say, "Is that it?" I didn't have time to answer. I and his other caretakers were immediately ushered out while his family stayed and said their goodbyes to his vacant body. I went to the waiting room, sat down and he then joined me as a spirit to talk.

A human spirit will often stay "earthbound" to see the affairs of loved ones until all their loose ends are tied up. It is possible to ascend to a heavenly realm immediately. About one in thirty human spirits do just that. However, it is more typical for a spirit to stay on the earthly realm without a body for six weeks or longer.

Nic did hang out for weeks, showing up at the oddest times to talk. I told him I couldn't have him popping in like that, so he said he would pay me. I assured him he could not do that since he no longer had his body. He disappeared then, but the following day he popped in to say, "You were right!" I offered to help him ascend to the Catholic version of heaven but he was not ready. Where was he most happy? He said Las Vegas. He loved the scene there. So we sent him to Vegas to have fun with the other human spirits who had left their bodies but loved the game.

When the body is done and can no longer support life, human spirit automatically detaches.

The role of spirit in human incarnation

We have now talked about two births; the birth into human existence and the birth into the spirit realm after a life well-lived. What is the role of spirit in the incarnation of an individual?

During waking hours, usually in the daytime, a spirit inhabits their body. The extent to which the spirit and body are bonded will influence how much the spirit can be a support to the body.

Here's a personal example of what can happen when spirit and body are not fully bonded:

One morning, I awoke early and made sweet passionate love to my new Sikh paramour. He, on a tight schedule, rushed off to the city to help change the world in his supporting role with Landmark Education. I moved from the bed to play my harp and when the moment was right, I dressed in workout clothes and went for my daily walk. I strolled in the sweet little Gerstle Park neighborhood of San Rafael. For me, all these activities celebrate life and joy.

As I walked, I experienced such bliss and ecstasy; my feet hardly touched the ground as I crossed the street at the corner, smiling inside. I had barely walked about three-quarters of the way across in the crosswalk, when a car came careening around the corner, not noticing me. The violent, life-changing impact was eminent.

I have no visual memory of impact. I heard a loud thud and then it became very dark. I had been thrown out of my body as a spirit. I had literally lost touch with my body. Moments later when I became aware of my body, I was on the ground far from the point of impact. I had been out of my body for about three minutes. I felt no pain. I had literally no physical sensations. I was looking out of my eyes with blood streaming over them. The world was pink.
I remember having an urgent sense that I needed to get to work. I had the feeling of, "Let's get the show on the road." But I could not feel my body. At the time, I didn't realize this, so it was an odd feeling of needing to get on with life

30

without the capacity to do so.

One of my neighbors was holding my head and neck very still. It took twenty minutes for the ambulance to arrive. During that time, the fellow kept asking me my name and my address. After asking me for what seemed like the tenth time, I said, "Could you please just get a pen and write it down?" I thought, "Oh brother, this guy has a terrible memory." I still could not feel my body and remained unaware of this fact. A male voice, one of my angels, kept speaking in a soft gentle tone, "Stay close to your body, honey. We will help you. Stay close to your body, honey. It's not your time."

My neighbor's voice, during this traumatic injury, helped my spirit stay with my body. There is a quality in the human voice, which delivers human spirit and is an important tool to preserve life in such situations.

I finally felt my body when the EMTs arrived and began pressing their hands on me to see what was broken. The brain injury was obvious with definite problems in the right leg.

What could have been a fatal accident became a long journey of recovery.

The frontal lobe and rear cortex brain injuries from this right side impact amplified the other problems. My right knee was broken, my right hip was pulled out of its socket, I had nerve damage on the right side and I was covered with cuts and bruises. My spirit no longer occupied the right side of my body. Unable to use my legs for walking, my spirit no longer inhabited either of my legs. The related energy centers at the feet and knees had turned off.

Years later, when I was finally able to get spirit permanently back in my legs, I could fully own my legs and use them again as they were meant to be used.

If you really think about it, this concept of spirit animating body will become apparent to you. You may have friends or relatives who have only a partial relationship of their spirit to body. The parts where spirit is absent will not be animated. That's a great way to imagine it.

Spiritual illness

You might be wondering if spirit can get sick, injured or die. Spirit can definitely develop a spiritual illness. And yes, it can be injured, suffer illness and it can indeed die.

All of these can happen to you in this life, but more likely the injury or illness began in another lifetime. Death of the spirit will not happen in a single lifetime. It happens when a human spirit incarnates one time and decides it never wants another incarnation. Then, over perhaps millions of years, the spirit loses connection to its humanity and eventually ceases to exist. As I scan over the eons, it has happened less than three hundred times since man's beginning. Considering the humongous number of human spirits, this is a miniscule number and should put to rest any concern of your spirit coming to an end.
Spiritual illness often begins with the impact of a confusing piece of information that does not have time to be understood prior to the untimely death of the individual.

Before we go into a longer definition of this situation I would like to give you a good understanding of very real spiritual body intelligence.

Eight spiritual super brains

From the time of our spirit's first incarnation, we are accumulating memorable information. Our profound experiential information, including scientific, spiritual, emotional and mental, which includes our lives' research and studies, is stored in eight "super brains." What I mean by *super brains* is that these storage minds do not require a physical body to exist but instead transcend physical existence.

1. **Communal Spirit DNA Brain** – This aspect of the super brain provides individual access to the information the spirit group has gathered.

2. **Anatomy of Spirit in the Structure of Light** - Information about the individual exists throughout the entirety of the spirit in its light structure. The light structure provides information to others, such as the leaders of the spirit group, about the path and direction of each individual spirit, with the purpose of supporting course correction if the spirit journey has veered off its trajectory.

3. **Soul Mind** - A complete explanation of the function of the *soul* is included in Chapter 11. The human soul appears with each physical incarnation and stops existing once the physical body that it provided for dies. Although it will not consist of the same elements as in the previous incarnation, the pattern of *soul* specific to the individual's spirit still continues to exist. The specific job of the soul is to protect the light of spirit. Soul mind provides all structure and protection details for the soul.

4. **Nucleus of Spirit**–This nucleus serves to produce embodiment. It provides all information for vitality.

5. **Miraculous System, including Golden Rings and Human Frequency** – The *Golden rings* and *human frequency* are directly related to mastery of human spirit in the body. They provide the essential intelligence to recreate health.

6. **Spirit DNA**– Similar to our human DNA, it provides programs for running the spiritual body, in and out of incarnation.

7. **Spiritual Timeline** – This is primary essential storage for historical data that will continue to affect future incarnations until final resolution of an event and/or entanglements. Timeline events become virtually imperceptible beyond nine incarnations following the event.

8. **God Particle** – This provides source origins for all human life.

If you are struggling with a spiritual illness, the outer world may diagnose it as a mental illness or a psychological abnormality. One of the characteristics of a spiritual illness is its relentless looping and constant dead-end thinking that takes you nowhere.

An example of a spiritual illness is the experience of believing you are alone and that you are not able to receive assistance from the Divine realm.

Imagine yourself having been a spiritual leader or perhaps a cantor in the Jewish faith during the time of the holocaust. Your role in life was to inspire and point direction to the Divine through your astonishing and pure connection and your authentic voice of devotion. Thousands upon thousands of ears have been lifted to the heights of spiritual bliss as a result of your pure voice and passion for the Divine.

Now, you are held captive in the prison camp. Yet, you do not give up your voice of love and connection. To the end you are telling others God will save and protect them. Then all at once, you are gassed and you all die of a horrible death.

Your mind did not have time to resolve this crisis and you left feeling betrayed for the loving God of whom you sang. You did not have the chance to reach into the situation and alter it to what you thought it should be.

Imagine now you are now in your next life as a young person. You still lead and are passionate about God, but now you have deeply impressed on your timeline an unresolved betrayal issue. Since this is an internal spiritual picture you are working with, it will keep presenting itself in various forms for resolution until you are able to clear the idea of betrayal (which, by the way, will read as a true betrayal, thus making it a spiritual illness).

Resolution of spiritual illness

The following procedures are explained in detail in the Appendix. Here are instructions for their use to clear spiritual illness.

You can easily muscle test on a few issues you might suspect to be a spiritual illness. You can then clear this illness by pumping gold into the concept and getting a new positive loving picture, thus replacing the illness picture.

You can also remove this from the timeline once you have understood what you wanted to learn from this situation.

Imagine a timeline shooting out the back of you far into the distance. Then imagine a golden vacuum sweeping through the spiritual timeline, removing anything negative related to this event. Once the timeline has been cleared, pump gold energy through the time line with your right hand.

Damage or injury to the spiritual body is rare. It can happen in or out of the body, and you are responsible for the injury by what you leave undone. It can only happen with a blatant disregard for spirit, placing your spirit in harm's way while expressing a high level of self-loathing. Damage or injury to the spiritual body has happened less than four thousand times since the advent of the human race, a minuscule yet possible outcome. This is not related to suicide.

Akashic records

As a spirit, in addition to the eight super brains, you have a personal encyclopedia referred to as Akashic records. Akashic records serve to store your important lessons that will be accessed through out your incarnation. This way you don't need to repeat the same experience of challenge to resolution more than once. You can store what you are learning here to reduce the impact on your body of any event. This allows you to move beyond it.

For example, once a serious issue, such as a brutal rape, is cleared from the physical, emotional, mental and spiritual body, you will still have the information without the damaging impact it can have on your life. This is valuable information and should not be erased, but instead can be stored away from the physical body. I see that the purpose of the Akashic records is to store all the research and development that you have accumulated from lifetime to lifetime.

Chapter 2: Recessive DNA Obliteration

Surely goodness and mercy shall follow me
All the days of my life
And I shall dwell in the house of the lord
Forever and ever amen

All that I am
And all I will ever be

Is expanding from this mystery
Surely goodness and mercy shall follow me
All the days of my life
And I shall dwell in the house of the lord
Forever and ever amen

DNA programs are an amazing gift in the human blueprint. It is from DNA direction and instruction that we humans are able to enjoy life. The unending miracles that are generated from our tiny, complex, central program give us cause for celebration.

The core DNA structure is phenomenal. What we address in this protocol is the small three percent of DNA programs that do not serve our overall wellness and sense of health, vitality, wealth, and connection.

To clarify, this process is meant to give access to (and enables us to correct) the DNA programs that are causing problematic issues. By using this protocol you will be able to experience your life in full self-expression. In this chapter we will not address how to correct or improve congenital or birth defects. Instead, we will focus on the improvement and correction of programs that cause illness, poor health, wealth, and love issues.

Many of the new thought leaders are now speaking of the possibility of reprogramming DNA. I love that this has become a consciousness among the new thought leaders and spiritual thinkers. My intention here is to provide the real life blueprint for permanently and fully altering the DNA that is causing challenges.

Altering DNA starts with the awareness that there is a recurring challenge, whether it is a repetitive problem in your life or in your family history. You cannot, however, deeply alter your DNA through your mental body, that is, by just thinking about it.

Who can benefit from recessive DNA obliteration?

Examples of DNA Obliterations I have assisted with:

- Removal of cancer gene and activation of the DNA program for healthy cells (e.g. breast cancer).

- Removal of a mental illness program and activation of a program for vibrant stability and mental wellness.

- Removal of criminal activities gene: This DNA program runs in many amazing leaders who, once cleared, experience the freedom to be able to sync up with their own desired full self-expression.

You might think this is a gene that only folks in jail could benefit from however, that notion is not true. I had the privilege of assisting a top mid-western health-conscious woman leader in shifting the energy signature that prevented her from gaining the trusted following she so deserved.

Tamara's Story

Tamara was approaching seventy and was still raring to go with love and contribution. She sought me out privately however, for two reasons: Firstly she wanted answers about why certain things were the way they were; secondly, she wanted help clearing up the limiting cellular messages so she could lead powerfully from a place of honor and trust.

When she came to me she had already been instrumental in bringing a farmers market to the town, she was actively mentoring young and underprivileged women, and had the respect of her community. What was missing, however, was the trusted following, the deeper level of her work. The image that comes to mind is that of her standing in a field of flowers, sounding a gong. She was filling the space with lovely sound, but was not speeding the flowers' growth.

While getting to know Tamara, I learned that she was the beloved daughter of a single mother who had conceived her during a rape. "A child is a gift from God," was the family's attitude, and they turned sour milk into delicious buttermilk by bringing into the world a daughter who was loved and cherished.

The biological father had criminal behavior running through both the paternal and the maternal DNA. This included jail time, robbery, untrustworthy activities and violence. As we explored each piece of information, she began to understand the source of her current issues, and we were quickly able to remove the core cellular problems.

After two hours of 'forensic' research during her session, she could return to her life. At this age so many people know her with the previous cellular information she had, so her actions would need to open up new channels for them to perceive her in her new DNA clothing. However, the good news was that the weight of the criminal information in her cellular body had permanently been transformed.

Tamara is an amazing woman and she has used her strengths extremely well. Here is how we approached the transformation.

- Poor organ or gland function to a full restoration of healthy function: This typically will require several types of healing, including Cellular Neo-Genesis, that bring the body to full wellness. Without clearing the DNA program, all the other processes will eventually (in months or years) revert back to the original DNA program. Clearing the DNA program is a necessary process for permanent wellness.

Time and time again, what I have seen is that the program for deterioration is set up to go off like a time bomb, and the previously normal functioning organ now becomes a poor performer.

George's Story

George is a great example of this. He developed diabetes four years ago. Now at retirement age after working for years in PG&E upper level management, his pancreas, (directed by the DNA) had reduced in function enough to cause him some trouble. Unlike many who suffer from poor pancreatic performance (who add excess pounds) George, at 6'3' was struggling to keep weight on and was literally a beanpole at only 175 pounds. By using the DNA protocols George has the possibility of returning to a healthy functioning pancreas and life without diabetes.

- Brain malfunction to brain wellness: Great progress has been made in understanding Dementia as well as Attention Deficit Disorder, or ADD. If done early enough, the DNA obliteration process can have a huge influence on the health of the brain.

Charlene's Story

Charlene contacted me to get some healing. As we spoke, she mentioned one of her greater stressors was the care of her husband, Earl, who was in an advanced stage of Alzheimer's. This kind of illness involves both the DNA and emotional body.

After several sessions, he enjoyed a reversal of the symptoms that had plagued him for four years. He shifted from a state of having no memory from moment to moment, to being able to recall the experiences of the day. Earl and Charlene enjoy a connection that was not formerly possible.

- Love and relationship challenges: Since these are imprinted in DNA this process can dramatically improve an individual's experience of love and connection if the DNA landscape is especially troubling.

I address this topic deeply in my book: *The Seven Stages of Love*.

To understand this concept better, imagine yourself having a family history that includes slavery and impoverishment. Imagine this stretches back for as many generations as you know, where bonding to another was required for survival. Companionship was based literally on the fact that two can navigate a dangerous world better than one.

Feel what such a survival program feels like in your cells. Is there room for divine companionship? Probably not. Is there a relationship that is based on mutual spiritual evolvement?

You get the picture.

If you are not in a relationship but wish you were, it is likely that your DNA programs aren't yet upgraded to support the physical foundation of enlightened love and relationship.

- Wealth and Abundance challenges: These can either prevent full realization of the dream of a fulfilling life. When they are cleared, it creates the freedom to soar.

These are several of the common recessive DNA upgrades I have routinely improved.

Deep DNA alterations should only be carried out by a wise elder who understands the impact of the shifts on the person's growth process and how their life will play out. Also, a healer should never alter DNA without the go ahead from their Divine connection and the permission of the person receiving the healing.

Warning on DNA Clearings

Do not, under any circumstances, think you automatically have permission to perform such clearings just because the person being healed is a family member, close friend or spouse. You will create potential problems for them and, more importantly, for yourself.

You could deplete your life force and possibly take on their health issues. Worse yet, you could take on their incomplete karma issues. They brought these issues into their life for their own growth and for the resolution of their human spirit. These are not the challenges you came in to deal with.

The impact of altering DNA

For many individuals, the gift you give them by altering the recessive DNA programs will mean the difference between health and vitality, or illness, suffering, and early death. For others, it will allow them to embody the life for which they have carefully studied and trained, but as yet have not been able to realize. This is because, up until now, the cellular body was programmed for a less than desirable situation.

Katie and Barbara's Stories

One year I worked with a well-loved and respected Pilates instructor, Barbara, who was going through radical treatment for breast cancer. That same year, I was also approached by a Scottish-born artist, Katie, whose mother had died of breast cancer. She "knew" that death was just around the corner for her as well.

For both Barbara and Katie there's a common thread of breast cancer DNA, and yet the protocols I used for each of them were very different. When doing miraculous healings, the healer will care for each individual based on their possibility for wellness. It's vital to honor their desires and limitations.

Barbara chose hands on healing and some intuitive guidance, even though I offered her the advanced deeper healing. Sadly, I watched her choose a path of extreme suffering, which included chemotherapy. It was her choice to make. She had literally become a walking skeleton since she could no longer hold her food down.

As we worked together, I was able to help her visualize colors that calmed the body. Sadly her need to direct the movement of recovery and her inability to step into the next level of wellness dominated her mindset.

We eventually stopped working together. The last time I saw her she looked like a twig. She was fragile and brittle, holding on for life in what she perceived to be a barbaric system. Her doctor said she would likely not survive past the five-year mark because of the type and stage of cancer she had.

Quite the contrary, Katie, the Scottish artist, approached her breast cancer DNA very differently. She had not yet become ill and, although she was challenged with some significant health issues, she was open-hearted. She knew that a "recessive DNA process" would yield her a prolonged and happy life with her young son and husband.

In one session, we were able to remove the massive cancer programs in her DNA and reprogram a new life story with her authentic God-health experience.
Years later, happy, healthy and glowing with a sense of ease and with a long life ahead of her, she is experiencing a kind of freedom and future anticipation she could not have enjoyed prior to the clearing process.

Joanna's Story

We found a solution for Joanna; a St. Louis event planner who was losing the use of her legs from neuropathy. With further research into her family health history, we discovered numerous elders in her direct family line (such as parents and grandparents) had their legs or feet amputated in later life.

Most of the time, she was unable to feel her feet and had numbness running up her legs, especially above the right knee. Back then, despite being new to DNA work, our efforts to heal her were absolutely remarkable. She regained full feeling and use of her legs and was able to return to a normal, active life in just four short months.

After the recessive DNA program was obliterated, we re-grew the nerves through cellular regeneration and removed a significant amount of unwanted and undesirable 'information.'

She is now living a happy and active life with full use of legs. She is an amazing woman living out her legacy in the world, finally able to fulfill her human spirit mission!

Your fat may not be your fault

Many years ago I discovered I could alter my DNA. I wondered why I was on a perpetual diet and why it seemed like I was always fighting to maintain my youthful slender shape. As I investigated further, I saw that both sides of the family DNA were programmed for significant weight gain after age thirty-five.

Since both sides of the family were programmed with servitude and poverty pictures in the DNA, our family members were programmed to gain weight so we would have the capacity to survive a serious illness, such as scarlet fever or the plague.

Thankfully, I was able to remove this recessive

programming for weight gain as well as DNA programs for servitude or slavery. Since that time, I have consistently maintained weight below 139 lbs, which is a good weight for me at 5'6" tall. Previously my weight had climbed up to 152 lbs, which felt uncomfortably plump. As for the slave and servitude DNA, since then, I have constantly maintained a six figure income, something I had only done briefly twice before.

When DNA changes, your mindset naturally upgrades and you begin to explore a world and a life free from the constraints that previously limited you.

Now that you have a good idea of what we are up to in the DNA Obliteration process, here are the specific steps you will follow to create change in your life, permanently.

In the genes

What is a family?
A genetic strand
That hurls us together
Linking us hand in hand

Or an intellectual tick
That makes us click
Our shared past
Does that make us last?

Could it be our choice?
Do we have a voice?

Recessive DNA obliteration protocol

1. Connect with the Divine.

46

2. Connect with the individual, human spirit to human spirit.

3. Ask permission to heal them.

4. Identify the core issue through kinesiology (See Appendix). Our Miraculous Living Apprentice training guides you to gain skill and understanding to effectively ask the right questions so you can get to the bottom of the core issues.

5. Identify the location of the recessive DNA program. If it is in the nerves, locate the "master cell" that is directing that area. If it is an overall program (for example, a slave program) identifies the master cell that you will use to effectively alter their situation.

6. Inform the individual with whom you are working that you are preparing to work on the recessive DNA. Let them inform you whether they are ready for it. If they have changed their mind, do not proceed.

If you have received the message from them to proceed:
7. This is an energetic process. In your mind's eye, see the DNA strand extended like a clothes line with forty-six towels hanging down that represent the chromosomes. Have the recessive DNA appears on the extended DNA strand (towels) as black spots.
8. You can count and identify the number of pieces of recessive DNA from the mother's side and the father's side, but it is not entirely necessary. The recipient might verify that they knew this was there.
There are forty-six chromosomes: twenty-two from the mother's programming, twenty-two from the father's programming and two authentic God strands. Surprisingly, there is rarely something in the DNA the individual is

unaware of.

9. Suction off the black recessive DNA. A simple way to expedite this process is to imagine using a golden shop vacuum to suction off the black dots.

10. When all the black is removed from the DNA strand, using gold energy, activate the highest, healthy DNA programs which exist in the human blueprint.

11. Pulse a golden wave, like a radio wave, through the DNA strand to seal up the newly established DNA.

12. Mirror the master cell with the new DNA information to all the surrounding cells. The master cell is like a college professor, able to teach all the other cells how to function and how healthy to be. For example if you go to Harvard Law School you'll experience a top-notch professor with amazing information. You're unlikely to experience this at your local community college. What we're doing here with this process is activating the Divine Human Blueprint. Even better than a Harvard Law professor, we've activated the perfection of humanity. The master cell in its highest expression is able to teach all the other cells how to be healthy through a mirroring process.

13. This process is amplified by filling the area with gold light. Continue amplifying this until all cells are able to receive the new program.

14. Use kinesiology to measure the percentage of cells that are able to respond to the new DNA program. A good result is 70% or more.

Final steps

Next, include a family bubble DNA clearing and finally a

reset adjustment. These additional procedures allow for a permanent and lasting solution.

15. Identify the family DNA bubble. You're looking for the information that's streaming towards you (if you're healing yourself) or the individual who's being healed (namely the information that's no longer serving that person). We're not changing DNA for any other family members, only that which relates to the person being healed.

16. Have the undesirable program (that's streaming towards you or the person being healed) light up from the family bubble as black spots.

17. Vacuum off all the black points.

18. Send a golden pulse through the stream to seal up the healing.

19. Identify the reset program in the healed individual. This is a physical body program also located in the DNA.

20. To prevent the body and program from resetting itself after a night's sleep, remove the old recessive program and set the new DNA program as the waking program.
Note, when the spirit returns after sleeping, the body will now be reset to maintain the healthy new DNA programs and will not revert to the old patterns.

This completes the Recessive DNA Obliteration procedure.

It is true that anyone following these steps can alter DNA. I highly advise you be trained in the wise elder knowledge so you know why, when and how to use this life-giving and life-changing process.

You are a radiant being of light. You were meant to have this knowledge. For generations this knowledge has been hidden. What you might have naturally learned as a child is now being shown to you. Understand that there is a love-wisdom culture that provides the space for unparalleled shifts and changes.

From: In the Genes
Or

Is being together with love
The 'family' sanctioned from above?

Are family's true friends
We rely on and depend?

Can I by myself make a bond
and find it to live on and on?

Or is support from friends to come and go?
On this question I must know.

If I love you as my clan
Can I count on you to be in my life next
may?
Can I trust you not to leave?
Can I trust you with my love?
Can I Trust

Chapter 3: The Process Of Cellular Neo-Genesis

All is found

Just when I think that all is lost
And there's nothing more that I can do
When the pain in my heart gets to great
And I feel that I will explode

When all is lost and hope is nowhere
And find myself screaming in terror
I find my depth, my center, my light
While surrendering to my soul

Grace finds a way to melt away the tears
And a soothing gentle trust reappears

When all is calm and I find myself at one
When chaos is transformed into clarity
I find my depth, my center, my light
While surrendering to my soul

The foundation of regeneration in the Miraculous Healing program is the specific regeneration of the master cell. Without the ability to either entirely reestablishes a cell that is missing, in all its glory, or to massively improve the health of the existing sick master cell, we could not then regenerate the glands and organs. Our healing requires that the basic structure and health of the cell is sound and true. We create new life to the larger organ or gland by making one cell perfect, whole, complete and healthy. When one cell is well, the surrounding cells can now match that perfect health and rise up to wholeness once again.

If the master cell has been surgically removed, then our job is to activate the human blueprint and cause the cell to reappear in its perfected health. And literally we will progress over time to grow back the surrounding cells through the activation of the human blueprint.

The blueprint for a lizard's tail exists whether the tail is there, or has been bitten off (in which case it will re-grow its tail).

Why would we not have the same capacity? We come equipped with the reptilian brain, why would regeneration be reserved just for lizards?

Growing back cells is an exciting process. After Cellular Neo-Genesis you must just rest enough and drink plenty of clean water and nourishment to have cell growth for many days to come.

When Martin attended the 100% Healthy Immersion weekend, he needed a lot of healing. As we did hours and hours of concentrated Cellular Neo-Genesis on the brain, nervous system and endocrine system, a remarkable thing happened. His body got into a miraculous state and began to radically transform in other areas. As we got to the third day of healing, his dark purple angry scars had faded away. We did not specifically work on his feet, but low and behold, after a healing of the nervous system and brain, he could feel his feet, and the overwhelming pain in his body disappeared.

When you are fortunate to get into a deep supportive space of healing (such as that in our miraculous weekends) or some intensive one-to-one time with a master healer, your body is literally able to regenerate at a rapid pace. Once you have turned the corner from illness to health, these same regeneration tools can restore your youthful vibrancy and appearance.

Annabelle, now a radiant 100% You Immersion Program at age sixty-five, claims literally a youthing affect overcame her in her first weekend. Months later she is looking twenty years younger, and, after some effort, her eyes are restored to clear, focused vision. This is a direct result of Cellular Neo-Genesis.

I believe this will be one of the most important healing concepts for restoring health and reversing aging. In the years to come, products and potions, as well as cosmetic surgery, will play second fiddle to the deep inner work that literally restores you and then regenerates you.

Then the question will be what age body do I want to live in? If I live four hundred years, do I want to live in a thirty-two or a forty-two year-old body? And eventually even that conversation falls away as we chose to live in our most healthy radiantly beautiful or strong, or fit body and the conversation of aging is irrelevant.

In the following pages I reveal the secret formula for youth, health and vitality. You will want to read the instructional chapters over many times to allow them to become part of your new longevity information.

If this touches your heart and you want to go deeper, come study and work with me. The technology revelation has already had its hay day. We are revealing the new way. Longevity and vitality are the wave of the future, and at 100% You we provide the most complete guidance to restoring your wellness and vitality.

What is cellular neo-genesis?

Cellular Neo-Genesis is the process that is initiated by rebuilding/restoring a "stem" or master cell in order to generate new healthy cells. Cellular Neo-Genesis can be, and is, performed on nearly all body systems, glands, and organs, with the exception of bones or carrier fluid.

Preparation

1. **Connect with the Divine** to raise your energy vibration above the state of unconditional love, which is 500 on the kinesiology scale of human expression. See table 3-?? to review the numerical human vibrational energy chart.

2. **Identify the area of illness**. For example, ask the body for the first place to address. You may be presented with any number (from five to more than one hundred) steps to prepare the body for a successful cellular neo-genesis. If you skip the preparation work you will have a less effective result.

Examples of preparation for cellular neo-genesis steps (not a definitive or complete list):

- Chakra activation
- Aura healing
- Deprogramming of death energy
- Restoring life force
- Restoring spirit body access portal
- Activating the 'Miraculous System'
- Improving function of affected area, e.g. from 20% function to 90% function
- Removing memes (group mind) thoughts that lock illness in from the mental body
- Removing wins or benefits to stay in the illness from the mental body

- Correcting other areas of the physical body that support the area you are healing

If a person is very ill, you still have to clear and prepare, growing new cells without this step is a mute point. Why? Because without proper preparation and clearing you are growing new cells into a death pattern.

For example, had I not cleared the DNA of fear and anxiety patterns from Julie, she never would have been able to hold the healing in the restored nervous system. She would also not have been able to permanently hold a healing and clear the anxiety and panic that she had struggled with her entire life.

Once you have thoroughly prepared the body, proceed to the next step:

3. **Secure the "Master Cell" in the affected area.** Connect the cell to its divine state. You can do this either by connecting it to God or the scientific expression of truth. They are the same.

4. **Cellular membrane neo-genesis**. Observe the membrane. Notice the color and strength. When a cell is sick, it will appear grey, black, white or brown.

5. **Golden halo activation**. Activate the golden rings over your head and run gold energy down into the back of the head through the spirit body portal, one inch above where the spine meets the skull. Bring this gold energy through the right shoulder and down through the right hand, sending gold energy out your fingertips.
Direct the gold energy to the membrane (outer skin of the cell). Continue applying gold energy to the membrane until the color shifts to a color from the light spectrum meaning

colors of brilliance verses colors containing gray and black.

The membrane serves to gather environmental information, encompass and contain the cell.

5.**Nucleus/neo-genesis**: Observe whether the nucleus still exists in this compromised cell. If it does, identify the color and percentage of function.

About 8% of the time, the nucleus is entirely gone. About 92% of the time, there is at least some small remnant of the nucleus remaining.

Procedure for restoring existing low-functioning nucleus:

- Observe the nucleus: is it grey, black, brown or white? What is the percentage of functionality?

- Run gold energy, as explained above, into the nucleus until you are reading 100% function and a light spectrum color.

6. **Absorption organelle/neo-genesis:** Observe whether the absorption organelle still exists in this compromised cell. If it does, identify the color and percentage of function. About 3% of the time the absorption organelle is entirely gone. About 97% of the time there is at least some small remnant of the absorption organelle remaining.

Procedure for existing low-functioning absorption organelle:

- Is the absorption organelle grey, black, brown or white? What is the percentage of functionality?
- Run gold energy as explained above into the absorption organelle until you are reading 100%

function and a light spectrum color.

Procedure for restoring missing absorption organelle:

- Pump gold energy to the place where the absorption organelle used to exist. The blueprint of the absorption organelle continues to exist in the physical body; directing gold energy allows it to reappear as a functional organelle.

The absorption organelle serves as the 'stomach' of the cell and allows nutrients to enter and nourish the cell.

7. **Elimination organelle/Neo-Genesis:** Observe whether the elimination organelle still exists in this compromised cell. If it does, identify the color and percentage of function. About 5% of the time the elimination organelle is entirely gone. About 95% of the time there is at least some small remnant of the elimination organelle remaining.

Procedure for restoring existing low-functioning elimination organelle:

- Is the elimination organelle grey, black, brown or white? What is the percentage of functionality? Direct gold energy into the elimination organelle until you are reading 100% functionality and a light spectrum color.

Procedure for restoring missing elimination organelle:

- Pump gold energy to the place where the elimination organelle used to exist. The blueprint of the nucleus continues to exist in the physical body. Directing gold energy allows it to reappear as a functional organelle.

8. **DNA strand Neo-Genesis:** 78% percent of the time, the DNA strand is in one piece in the cell. Missing DNA strand in the cell happens about 3% of the time. The severity of the illness can be comprehended by the amount of breaks in the DNA cell. 19% of the time the DNA is damaged.

- If the DNA strand is intact, do nothing else to it. Leave it as is.

Note, healing recessive DNA programs is a separate and unique procedure covered in the *Miraculous Living* program. The process we cover here applies to the cell DNA organelle itself. We are restoring the physical health and structure of the organelle.

- **DNA Neo-Genesis and repair.** Observe the number of breaks in the DNA strand. Place yourself in the cell and pull each broken piece of the strand to connect with its matching piece. Plug each broken piece into the appropriate matching end until all pieces are reattached. Once you have connected all broken pieces, seal the strand up and restore it to its God state by flowing a golden liquid from the top of the strand to the bottom of the strand. (Pumping gold healing energy also works but it takes longer. Use this process if you are not able to do the golden liquid process.)

For me, the phenomenon of DNA repair is both challenging and fun. In the last step, I ride the golden liquid down the spiral DNA strand like a water slide. When I slide off the end of the DNA, I know the process is complete. The water slide process isn't necessary in this step. However, it is a joyful and fun movement in this otherwise surgical procedure.

If your energy is under 700, do not do this; it will leave a heavy and unpleasant feeling in the DNA.

- **DNA Neo-Genesis restoration**. Direct gold energy through the right hand to the former DNA strand location. The blueprint for the original DNA strand will begin to resurface until it is fully restored. Restoring the DNA strand takes time and a lot of gold energy. Be patient and continue until it is fully restored.

9. Light of Cell Illumination

- Amplify gold light in the cell
- Mirror the healthy cell to all cells in the area with gold energy.

Each cell, when healthy, has light resembling the light of the spirit in the human body. This light animates and feeds the cell. The light in our cells is just like human spirit animating the human body. The cell can be alive without the light and continue unanimated for a short period of time just as the body without spirit can continue unanimated. Without spirit, we call the body dead and bury or cremate it. Our interpretation, and rightly so, is that the body does not live without spirit. A person in a coma that is, unanimated by spirit is casually referred to as a vegetable. Over time, if the spirit is unable to get back into its body and if life support is removed, the physical body will cease to exist.

10. **Mirroring.** Once you have mirrored the healthy master cell to all other cells in the body, flood gold energy into the master cell to enhance the process.

11. **Measure the percentage of cells improved** by the

process and you will discover 70-100% of the cells have just upgraded. Anything above 70% is considered a good percentage for healing.

12. **The Cellular Neo-Genesis is a powerful spiritual upgrade.** The process of new cell growth will continue for several days.

What to know and disclose:

It is important to mention what to expect during this growth period to people who are receiving the healing so they are not surprised. Remember being a child and having a growth spurt? Your legs ached as you grew an inch in two days. The Cellular Neo-Genesis is a growth spurt of healthy cells replacing sick and dead cells.

- The area will potentially ache.
- You may be tired and sleepy. The cells grow when you are asleep. The body will naturally want the new cell growth, so you will feel good but need a lot of rest for up to 72 hours.
- Occasionally the body will warm slightly while the cells are growing.
- Hydration and good nutrition help the process. If you chose to go out and party, drink alcohol, or somehow contaminate your body while you are in the Neo-Genesis process, you will revert to where you were prior to the healing. You are telling the body you are unable to care for the new state of wellness and it will return to its aging and 'death' cycle. NO alcohol pain medications or recreational drugs after regeneration.

Jody and William (names changed because they definitely

learned from their mistake) had scheduled three hours of healing together. They were excited to get started and squeezed it into their busy schedule.

After some very, very deep work including several cell regeneration we competed their sessions. I recommended that they have a light meal, drink lots of clean water and go to bed early, as the Cellular Neo-Genesis process was in full force. They told me they would do what they could but they already had evening plans. They were out past one in the morning, and though the renewal with friends was wonderful, they had both experienced a tremendous drop of in the new cell growth. Later they confided to me they had really regretted going out and since then have always created time to incorporate the session.

To really amplify the time your cells regenerate you also want to add in the meditations from the Miraculous Healing guided meditation menu. These are specifically designed to lower the cellular stress you accumulate during the day, as well as clear the energy channels. Through a very specific sequence of spiritual clearings, your body is perfectly retuned morning and night, providing you with the best environment for regeneration.

I occasionally hear people in the one-to-ones tell me they meditated this week. My response is "Great which one?" They often say they used some other technique. It's not all the same, however. Meditation and the specific sequences you progress through (or not) make a huge difference with your body's ability to regenerate and for you to move forward.
Think of it like this: it would be like taking the directions you received on how to operate your Blackberry smart phone, and instead using those same directions to help you learn use your new Mac book pro. You would never think

that that was going to work, right? They are great directions for the Blackberry, but are useless for the Apple computer.

Another step I highly recommend in the days following the healing is for you to be in nature as much as possible, relaxed and unplugged from the stressors of life. I often find people who are in need of healing are out of touch with their natural rhythms. To suggest listening to what their body is telling them may be a puzzling instruction. Being in nature, without the stressful influence of technology, and being away from work/family will allow you to sink into the natural rhythms of the natural world. In time you may find yourself placing a greater priority on understanding yourself, and being in nature consciously is an excellent beginning.

Using your mind to help the progression of the healing is a fundamental. Heidi is such a great example of positive self-talk. A few months back Heidi received word from her medical practitioner that she had stage four untreatable lung cancer.

When Heidi and I met she had felt she would die soon, and was winding down her life. I her first healing weekend Heidi was able to experience a complete healing of the death energy and group mind that was causing her to experience the hopelessness of her situation. Since then Heidi's number and attitude have improved dramatically. She is alive and well and it is blowing her doctors minds that she appears to be living not dying. Heidi is getting better!

Miraculous healing which I refer to as Cellular Quantum Mechanics can be sudden and instant, but more often it is gradual and happens over a periods of days weeks or even months. This is not a magic show, or a science fiction thriller, the work of regeneration is beautiful amazing and extraordinary. Think of your healing in comparison to a fast food restaurant. You get what you pay for. If what you order is a hamburger, fries and a coke, you'll get that pretty fast. However if you go to a five star restaurant and order a seven course meal, you are prepared to have the experience of a lifetime, enjoy every wonderful treat as it appears before you, and it just keeps getting better until you are satiated.

Cellular Quantum Mechanics is the crème de la crème of healings.

The journey of healing also supports you in discovering what actions thoughts and behaviors allowed illness and aging to take root, and provides the time for you to shift and grow. Your Miracle starts today, and continues for the rest of your life!

The beauty of the Cellular Neo-Genesis process is that it is efficient and has all kinds of positive lasting affects for the recipient.

Western medicine always discloses the side effects and possible complication of drugs and procedures. Here is the Miraculous Healing disclosure for the procedure of Cellular Neo-Genesis
What clients report after Cellular Neo-Genesis:

- More energy and often more physical strength

- Improved health and vitality, often needing rest for the first 36 hours, however there is no 'tired feeling' just a strong awareness the body wants to rest.

- Noticeable improvement in mood,

occasionally a few days of euphoric bliss

- Calm and peace in the nervous system

- Compromised glands and organs return to full function

- Heart normalizes, Blood pressure issues often dissolves

- Breath becomes deeper

- Scar tissue is reduced or entirely disappears

- Neurotransmitters return to high function

- Dramatically improved brain chemistry

- Improved memory and mental clarity

- Improved muscle tone

- Improved skin, both the disappearance of rashes and the plumping rosy healthy appearance of the tissue.

- Improved vision

- And a host of many additional bonuses based on the location of the Cellular Neo-Genesis

Every day I use the extraordinary process of Cellular Neo-Genesis to assist my clients and students in securing the health and vitality they had only dreamed possible and is now for them become a reality.

Six years ago I went to my garden in prayer and meditation. I was a woman on a mission. My declaration to the Divine, "God take me home or make me well! You promised me the Garden of Eden, but I have been living in some version of hell, with all this pain and suffering. I am ready, show me what to do, or take me!"

At that moment life changed forever for me. I have never been the same. To stand up and say 'no more' is an important part of healing. 'I don't agree to be sick any more God, I don't agree to be in a nine on the pain scale one more day, I don't agree to another cancer or another horrendous surgery.'

We can stand up and claim our divinity. We can call on the power of the Divine to show us the way. I can honestly say that I didn't realize I didn't have to suffer until I had reached my absolute limit. It's not really pushing back, it's saying I've learned everything I want to from that old pattern and am not in agreement to another day.

Maybe some of you are at the end of your rope. Earlier in my life, during the cancer treatments I attempted suicide twice. I overdosed, and both times was found and had my stomach pumped, so I got to live another day. I don't think I wanted to die. I took pills that would not end my physical life but which would just make me miserable. I was simply looking for a way out of the unbearable pain and suffering.
I have grown so much in this journey of discovery and understand what it is to be hopeless, facing with no way out, and with the prospect of more suffering for as long as I could imagine being alive.

It doesn't have to be this way anymore. There are answers for those of you who truly want to heal, and for those of you who have a contribution to make and who can see living a few hundred years. Life is meant to be filled with love, and joy with many moments of blissful connection and celebration.

The potency of the Cellular Neo-Genesis is that it was the first of many revelations in the garden. As I prayed, God sent me a vision of a cell. I saw my cell. I saw it in its perfection. What I was seeing was the stem cell for my thyroid. In the Divine Human Blueprint it appeared in it's perfected state. At that moment I began to grow a new thyroid. News cells appeared replacing the death energy surrounding the area that had been surgically altered.

Then I was working with a congenital heart defect. My heart had never quite worked right, and in addition, my lungs had been troubled by reduced function and asthma.

As I started the healing work, my legs and knees began to regain strength, and I could feel a new resilience in my step. Was it all this easy? Did I just need to slow down and listen?

Be still and know that I am God.

In the stillness
In the quiet
In the open heart
There I am
I am essence
I am breath
I am light of God
I am I am

I felt the presence of Jesus in the Garden, like a big brother sharing in my revelry.
And his words were echoing in my ears, as if he were

whispering to me and to all of us in this new era.

These and greater works than these you shall also do.

I experienced an East-meets-West Garden of Eden. My time in India, chanting and praying, serve to skyrocket my energy of devotion and love. I sang my favorite chants and called in the Yogic Deities as helpful spirit guides to join in my celebration and resolve. I felt the legions of divine beings supporting the movement of a new era and a new awareness.

Are you waiting to call health into you? Are you waiting for a health crisis and then maybe, you will make a change in your lifestyle, thoughts and habits? I ask you now, If not now when? When are you going to turn your health and vitality around and become the living-breathing spark of God you were always meant to be? I invite you to join me on the miraculous path of life!

Chapter 4: Relationships And Love

Breath
I cry the tears of lost love
...and breathe...
I let you in
All I hoped for is gone
Yet there you are loving me.
I am in need of your devotion
...waves of emotion...
I feel unable to hide a moment longer.
Feelings of loneliness surround me
Like gray fog on a cold day.
I weary of being strong and brave
In this dreary climate

You offer me your willingness,
I am grateful
...breathe...
I inhale you into my being.

Grandmother Grace was a Catholic woman. She and her two sisters were sold off to families as indentured servants. They somehow managed to keep in touch even though they had all been sent to different families. I honestly think their mother Katherine (Kennedy) Petite, who was an immigrant from Ireland, could see no other way to feed them and put a roof over their heads. Their younger brother stayed on with Great Grandmother Katherine.

Grace had had a difficult start to life; the patterns were set for struggle and striving for her adult life. She married young to a military man, my grandfather Frank Gable. In short order, they had produced a batch of children. Military life was hard. Grandfather was always stationed somewhere other than where his family lived; Grace was left in the lurch with six children, one of whom sadly died at a young age as a result of a cough syrup overdose.

Frank was stationed in Germany. Since Grace wanted to keep the family together, she loaded the children onto a ship. With the hope of a better life together, they endured rough seas and horrendous seasickness over a two-week period. As you might have guessed, my grandfather was a member of the troops occupying Germany. The family set up in Hamburg, but no sooner had they settled, when Frank received a transfer order to Frankfurt. When they could, the family followed.

As the years progressed, Frank was always stationed in different ports, which made it virtually impossible for a devoted Catholic wife to follow. Whatever romantic hopes and dreams she had for her relationship with Frank were dashed. He was really no more than a mate and financial provider. Grace had to face the challenge of effectively being a single parent under extremely difficult circumstances, with virtually no support. To make matters worse, Frank was prone to infidelity.

The idea of family, which had been such a hopeful ideal for Grace, became the bane of her life. The grand finale played out as Frank partnered with a Korean woman my mother's age and had children with her, giving them the same names as his children with Grace.

There was of course no annulment and I do not know the details of the divorce, but I can tell you with absolute certainty that the aftermath of the divorce left my grandmother deemed as an unforgivable sinner by her church. She was never again allowed to receive the sacrament of communion because of the infidelity of her husband and their eventual divorce.

As you can see, Grace married a man who had virtually no loyalty to her or their children.

Predestined for failure, or so it seems

We come into this life with a set of internal programs that guide our decisions. The internal programs that attracted the situation that Grace was dealing with were held in four aspects of her body: the cellular body, the DNA, the mental body and the lungs. Grace was up against so many failing pictures within her body's field, there was actually no possibility for a cherished love relationship unless she could clear a lot of these programs.

It's not so easy sometimes. You can do all the right things, take all the right classes, read all the right books and yet it can still feel like there's some secret you're not privy to or even some habit of self-sabotage you can't stop. It's as if you are not in control of the fact that you're thwarting all attempts to love and be loved.

We are so much more than our thoughts or our bodies. Many people experience a real handicap from their DNA: these relationship patterns are embedded in the cellular information and play out as archaic or dysfunctional.

In the past the normal recourse for these kinds of problems was prayer and a gradual shifting through lifetimes to a more palatable or even enjoyable love life. The great news is that we can now get to the bottom of love and relationship failures and transform them. We can reach into the DNA to remove the problematic programs, and activate successful patterns for aspects of love.

70

Is it only our DNA programming?

DNA is not the only place we find hidden patterns related to relationships. What follows is a list of places 'failure' patterns have been discovered and from which they can be removed:

- Group mind and viruses: memes and miasms
- Glands and organs
- Timelines: spiritual emotional, mental
- Mental body and the human brain
- Early emotional entrainment, largely formed in the amygdala
- DNA as mentioned above
- Bloodline
- Nurture; love wisdom
- Chakra system
- Gestation-womb pictures
- Failed love and relationships; residual energy and karma

As you can imagine, it is a big job to rebuild a love system where there is significant dysfunction. I recommend a lifestyle of balance. Take out of the love-renewal equation things related to high drama and unhappiness.

Included in this book are the guidelines to follow for living life in balance. In addition, on the website you'll find a valuable home-study program that was originally created for a women's coaching program (geared towards women aged 26 to 42) yet it is appropriate for everyone.

Make a commitment to:

- Be loving

- Allow love in
- Fill yourself up first
- Be a good listener
- Listen through the other person's point of view
- Be compassionate with yourself
- Turn off self-criticism and harsh self-judgment
- Be responsible for things when they don't work out
- Step back, learn from the behaviors that you repeat but yield poor results.

I will give you the tools to be more loving and fulfilled than you ever thought possible. At the same time, you will want to begin the journey of becoming the wise-elder, embodying love wisdom. Your goal is to be the safe abode for yourself and all others. Your job is to become love; your version of love.

Memes (group mind) and miasms (group viruses)

In my thirties, I lived in India for a half year. During that time, I witnessed an extraordinary meme among the women and, especially, the mothers of India.

Picture the scene. You are in a typical Indian home, a movie is playing on the TV and all family members are present. They are glued to their seats as the story unfolds. The two main characters (who are not from the same caste) fall in love. Then the parental scene comes, the mother cries out; *"My son how could you do this to me; how could you betray us all? I forbid you to love this slut; she is nothing to us. You must disavow any ties to her here and now*!'

There are two examples of 'group mind' influence here. This movie is like every other in the depiction of the mother who feels she is being betrayed by her son or daughter not loving the person he or she should according to "societal rules." This is an example of a ***meme***. Certainly well over ninety percent of Indian mothers experience this group thinking or meme. Since everyone in the Indian culture is thinking this, it is a societal fact. A meme is a group agreement: we will all think this way and we will create a thought form of control for everyone to conform to this thought. On higher planes, however, this does not resonate with Truth.

Typically memes are stimulated by emotions and drama; they serve to control and make others conform or they become wrong.

Here, the ***miasm*** or group virus is the idea that someone is more or less worthy because of caste, color or creed. It is a virus of a kind, typically prejudicial in some way. I meme or miasm always excludes someone or something and causes pain.

Removing memes and miasms

Using kinesiology, muscle test for a meme or miasm affecting the full expression of love.

If you get a yes:

- For a meme, look for a concept that is from family or church. An example of a meme: *"I must be married to have value and importance."*
- There are literally thousands of possibilities. Test until you find what's right. A good clue will be to look at how love is thwarted.

- When you find the meme and get a *"Yes, this is it,"* use your right hand to pump gold energy into the concept of the meme forty times to clear it. When it is cleared, it will no longer be an influence.

Test again, *"Am I/are they being influenced by a meme or miasm?"*

If this time, you get a yes on miasm:

- Look for wrong thinking that is exerting an invisible control or causing mental pain. A meme is exclusive to the mental body, whereas a miasm has an emotional charge as well as coming from the mental body. A meme may feel logical (even though it is not); a miasm will feel screwy (that's a technical term). It will feel like there is something wrong or the person experiencing it is really messed up.

- With a miasm, follow the same procedure, but, since the emotional body is also involved, pump sixty times instead. Remember to muscle test if it is clear. I am giving you a general average; it can clear faster or it may take more pumping time. When your kinesiology reads a 'no' you can check what has cleared in percentages. Say you are 85% clear, you can pump a little more and be complete.

My clients are absolutely blown away by the freedom they've experienced once the clearing is complete.

Glands and organs

Bobbie was full of grief. Her husband, fifteen years her senior, had recently passed. While he was eighty-one years old and ready to go, she, at sixty-five years old, was still needed by her family and students. After becoming profoundly ill, she called me. She was filled with guilt over the way her husband passed. In addition, she was also left with no money and a mountain of debt, without even life insurance money for house payments. She collapsed into an emotional funk.

The physical ailments became overwhelming. First came an uncontrolled asthma, then pneumonia took over her lungs. She confided, *"I would be better off dead than with all this debt and no way out."*

The lung illness was directly related to the feelings of not having a 'right to take up space.' She no longer felt she should occupy space on planet Earth. With her moral and religious background, she saw no other options. Later, as we talked, she could begin to see a way out: a bankruptcy with a restructuring of her home loan and family situation, moving in with her sister for a while, and renting the home to her grown children.

The first thing to do when clearing a gland or organ is to just clear the black, grey or brown energy by pumping gold. The gland or organ may have white energy, which represents someone with a body (in other words, a live person) exerting control on them.

If the gland or organ is experiencing illness, for example, an infection, you will need to go through the protocols forhealing. It is important to restore color and function, as well as restore the energy source. For example, if the lung

75

function is down, you will need to check the fourth and fifth chakras to insure they are functioning properly, both in front and in back.

Table 4-1 Relationship of Organs to Emotions

Organ	Symptom of malfunction	Vitality Affirmation
Heart	Lack of self-love, disconnection with God, inability to receive live, broken hearted	Self love, appreciation (God connection) receiving love
Lungs	Emotional constriction, inability to breathe deeply, unsafe	I have a right to take up space, I have a right to be alive and to love
Spleen	Betrayal, back stabbing	Everyone supports me and I live in a friendly world
Liver	Anger, jealousy	I am relaxed and at peace in all my connections. I am enough
Kidneys	Hurt, underdog, inability	I am a compassionate self-actuated individual
Stomach	Overwhelm, out of balance, too much	I naturally find my balance in
Pancreas	Poor personal connections outer focused	Relationship, self-love, in balance
Gallbladder	Slave, anger, injustice	I am the authority in my life and am well respected
Intestines	Parts of life difficult to digest	I have enough time to learn from my life's difficulties
Appendix	Out of phase, spiritual body elsewhere	I love being in my life here and now
Pineal	Sneaky, omitting parts of the truth, fudging	Integrity
Pituitary	Grudge	I am able to forgive and let it go
Thyroid	Overly responsible for others	I enjoy going in and learning the secret longings of my heart
Thymus	Endure and survive	I am consistently strong and vibrant
Adrenals	Misunderstood role, responding to everything with high priority	I have awareness naturally by taking time to check in with myself
Ovaries	Drained, depleted, abused	I enjoy fueling my spiritual emotional mental and physical reserves and when I choose to share, I share from strength.
Uterus	Lacking divine acceptance, guilt, shame	Compassion and tenderness flow to all my parts
Testicles	Strangled suffocated, shame	I naturally take the time and space I need and successfully breath life into my male body
Prostate	Guilt	I choose the thoughts I think and the emotions I feel. I easily recognize my own authentic emotions as opposed to those borrowed from others

When you remove the dark energy from the affected area in the body, use kinesiology to find out if these same issues are in the DNA and/or spiritual timeline. If so, keep clearing until the harmful energy found originally in the organ is entirely removed.

The above list is by no means complete. If there is an area not explained above, questions are welcomed on our contact page: www.julierenee.com/contact/.

Lungs have been one of my issues. As a long distance runner, my legs would carry me long distances and never complain. However, my lungs and heart were another story. If you have a lung issue you will understand. I would feel a pull in my chest to slow it down and never allowing me finish first in my race category. Typically, I was in the top ten as my legs were strong, but I never could to make it to the top.

I can attribute this to a sense of not having a right to take up space personally. I felt my mission was to take care of everyone else's needs. Ideally, this would lead to someone coming in who would make sure I was also taken care of. However, if you have this pattern, you will eventually realize that if you always take care of others and put your own needs on the back burner, you will always draw folks to you who will 'need' and 'take' from you. You will not draw in givers because that is not what you are sending out as a signal to the universe.

The higher expression of this, and the step up, is to shift from a reality of over-giving to a realm of filling yourself up well. Then you can offer your gifts to healthy individuals in terms of them receiving rather than taking from you. The process is led by you; you teach those around you how to receive. It feels tangibly different.

rare (and profoundly bad) circumstances, the source could begin as many as nine lifetimes ago.

This circumstance is wired into the *Human Blueprint* to give us the opportunity to discover that we have power and the ability to restore and heal even the worst of life's challenges. All illness is an opportunity to discover your magnificent God self.

Clearing recurring illness from the timeline*

* It is not important to identify the specific timeline for any of these clearing, i.e. spiritual, emotional, mental, or physical.

Identify, using kinesiology: "Is this recurring illness caused from a past life?"
If the answer is 'yes,' then ask: "From what lifetime?"
Query 9,8,7,6,5,4,3,2,1 and present.

With my lungs as an example, prior lifetimes five and three as well as the present lifetime came up as positive for influencing my lungs. The present time read is important, as it has already set itself to influence a future lifetime.

Now that you have identified the original lifetime there are two choices:

    a. Identify the age of the problem occurred in that original lifetime.
        or
    b. Clear directly without doing more research.

Curiosity may be the motivation for learning more, and that is all right if this is part of your learning process and you feel it would be helpful to know. However, for a complete clearing, it is unnecessary to know the time or age in the first lifetime where the challenge appears, and learning this will take extra time.

Judy came to me with extreme anxiety. Given her family background and her wonderful match for a partner, the level of anxiety did not match he present time information. As we researched her spiritual timeline we discovered that the original anxiety and panic issues started five lifetimes ago. It played out in lifetimes three, two, one and in this lifetime skipping her fourth lifetime back. While this is enough information to clear the issue, sometimes there is the question, what happened to make this so awful for so long?

At that point we can look back and see what got it started. Five lifetimes ago, as a young woman of twenty-two she witnessed a violent attack of her husband and thus the cycle started.

An example of spiritual illness a present life is Mathew, age fourteen, who has suffered from a mysterious fatigue and depression virtually untreatable for about three years. His Doctor referred him to me. It was a pleasant surprise to his mom and the whole family that after four sessions Mathew was again laughing and responding to life like a young fella this age would.

We did many healings, but the healing that seemed to unhook the pattern was the removal of a piece of information about an incident with an older boy who acted inappropriately two years seven months prior. By removing the impact of this incident, the post-traumatic stress melted away and he returned to his natural emotional response to life.

Path A: Discovery

1. Start with the first lifetime affected and muscle test from birth; age 10 age 20, 30, 40, and so on. When you get the range, so stop at age 20 then go down 3; age 19, 18, 17 or go up 7; 20, 21, 22, 23, 24, 25, 26 (In my case my lungs were affected five lifetimes back and I read that the problem started at age nineteen).

2. Next, pump gold into that specific lifetime and age to clear the health issue.

*Pay special attention to the fact that we are not looking at personality or life details. We are literally going in and finding the source of the condition and then moving on.
3. Next, clear all other lives affected, repeating the process above.

Path B: Streamline Clearings

1. Using kinesiology, identify which lifetimes initiated the issue, and are still affecting the recurring illness: 9,8,7,6,5,4,3,2,1 and present.

2. Pumping gold into the timeline, clear from the farthest back to present time.

For example, for my lungs, I cleared prior lifetime five first, then prior lifetime three, then finally my present life (which would be lifetime zero). Confirm each clearing using kinesiology.

The discovery of this super simple healing is one of the main components that prevents the recurrence of illnesses and poor emotional and mental patterns once cell regeneration or other healings have been completed. This is vital to producing incredible results.

Mental body and the human brain

Many people 'think' that their emotions are the cause of their relationship trials and tribulations and, sometimes, this is the case. However, what I have discovered is the mental body and the thoughts we think (rather than emotions) are a larger contributor to the problematic issues in matters of relationship. This is why a lot of 'therapeutic models' are successful as they lean heavily on behavior modification, which results from a decision not a feeling.

Common conversations about being stuck are "I can't change how I feel." For example, in the old movie, "*South Pacific*," they deal with issues like these. The Young woman falls in love with a mature gentleman and then after she accepts a proposal of marriage she discovers he has Polynesian children from a Polynesian wife who passed away. Several songs are devoted to this feeling of prejudice, hate and fear for people who are different from you. She was from Iowa, and everyone thought that way.

At the completion of the story she shifts out of the miasm (group virus) and takes on the role of a loving mother to the beautiful children as they wait for their father to return home from war.

Miasms and failures (or illnesses) related to love and relationships stem from the same place. *You have to learn how to hate and fear, you are not born this way.*

Clearing the mental body and brain may require 'DNA obliteration.' This will remove the cellular program or the memes and miasms influencing the faulty thought process.

88

If these processes don't fully release the challenge, I encourage you to look for unwanted squatters. These can be 'entities' that have a stake in keeping you stuck in your negative mindset. You'll find the removal process in Chapter 29, "All Things of Spirit," helpful if this test results in a 'yes.'

Test with kinesiology: "Are there evil spirits, spirits, demons, aliens, entities, spiders, or snakes affecting thinking around relationships and love? If this answer is 'yes,' use kinesiology again to discover what type.

When I clear folks, and this is an issue, I might read that there are a number of spirits. Let's say, for example, there are three. Once I have cleared the three spirits with the process laid out in the protocols, I will again ask the question: "Are there evil spirits, spirits, demons, aliens, entities, spiders or snakes affecting thoughts and beliefs around relationships and love?" Don't be surprised if get another answer that you didn't get before because this is a layered and multifaceted healing.

If you needed this healing, once you have successfully cleared all unwanted 'spiritual parasites' from your mental body and brain, you will feel fresh, relaxed and more peaceful than you have in many moons.

Do not attempt to battle with them. Aggressive energy from you can give them ground to hold on more tightly, making them more difficult to clear. Move them out in neutrality and authority. Do not expect to be perfect at this, be patient and persistent. Slow and steady wins the race. Practice being the tortoise and avoid the behaviors of the hare. No jumping, darting or erratic movements.

Early emotional entrainment

Jesus said; *"It would be easier for a camel to go through the eye of a needle than for a rich man to attain the kingdom of heaven."*

The difficulty of sending a camel through the eye of a needle is similar to the concept of willing or mentally trying to change the early pre-three year old emotional training. The amygdala in the brain contains and stores the emotional background from which you will understand and interpret the rest of your emotional interactions and experiences. Much of that information is stored before the age of three.

It also helps you understand a safe or unsafe world based on how you began your first three years of life. This programming is considered by the medical community to be virtually impossible to shift. Basically the thought is: what you start with is what you end up with.

The medical community is correct: you cannot, by thought or action, alter the early emotional training. Just like the rich man who wanted to attain the kingdom of heaven through mental knowledge or physical attainment and yet could not, the emotional programs are not altered by ways of man but, rather, by ways of the spirit.

'You must become like a child.' In other words, you must let go of the mind and become present to what is. You need to be present to the essence and the nature of things in order to effectively address and alter the programs of the amygdala.

If you had a loving safe, nurturing experience during your first three years, this will need no altering. If, on the other hand, you had parents who were struggling with self worth and self love, you will not have the foundation you need to generate the deep honoring sense of self and love. This means that of the experience of true authentic love through the fifth seventh stages will elude you. I am referring to the love of 'soul mate' and above.

The concepts of the seven stages of love are covered in my upcoming book with the same title. For now let us look at and address how to prepare your emotional nature to support deeper levels of connection if this is a challenge for you.

Since there are endless versions of interruption to the serene emotional brain, I have selected five statements that address many of those disturbances. Feel free to create your own that offer solutions to issues unique to your situation.

> I am whole, perfect and complete.
> I am loved and cherished.
> I am respected and cared for.
> I am comfortable and safe in myself.
> I easily connect and am safe with others.
> I take my place of honor in my life and the world.

Say statement one. If, with kinesiology, it reads as true, you have this one perfected. Move to statement two. If statement two reads as false, pump gold energy fifty times from the right hand into this statement. As you pump in gold energy, you allow the statement to become true for you in your emotional brain and your cellular body.

Once you have a 'yes,' test to see if any other factors would prevent you from experiencing this as completely true.

Check DNA, memes, and miasms; clear any other negative concepts the same way.

Move to statement number three and proceed until you have completed the six self-love and acceptance statements I have provided you. Once you understand how simply and easily this works, you can alter any interruption as it surfaces.

If you surround yourself with people who have a challenge with knowing they are whole, perfect, and complete, you may have to reestablish this clearing on yourself a number of times until you no longer match their 'pain' pictures.

DNA

DNA and its role in the interruption of the full and free expression of love and honoring relationships lies at the heart of the programs that have permeated generations of your family's history. There are endless possibilities for malfunction and wrong thinking as you move up the evolutionary ladder from survival love to a fully-honoring and expressive love.

I will give you some examples for locating and identifying DNA challenges around love and relationship. This will serve to help you discover your personal lower programs and show you how to resolve them so you can move into the fuller expression of love without being held back by DNA.

Below is the guide for love and DNA programming:

Test for a 'yes' to each of these. For example, "My DNA is programmed to support me in this level of love."

Table 4-2 Seven Stages of Love and Their Vibration Levels

Level	Stage of Love	Vibration Level
1	Obligation	0-130
2	Obligation and Morality	110-190
3	Companionship Basic	170-255
4	Fun Context Partnership Mutual Respect	230-450
5	Mutual Honor and Devotion	370-480
6	Joy is the basis of the relationship Knowing Awareness	470-720
7	Cellular Harmony	630-1000

You can begin to see where your DNA patterns are on this hierarchy of love and relatedness. My upcoming book, *The Seven Stages of Love,* will give you all the processes to allow you to move up to level seven and use guided meditations to keep you at your highest level once you have achieved it. In the meantime, you can begin to clear the DNA patterns that you are aware of in the categories to you have not yet risen.

This is a process of transformation. It should not be thought of as a quick fix to jump you up to higher levels prior to your understanding and embodying the truth found in each level of love.

I realize I have given you enormous possibilities with little to support your process. I promise to give you everything you are looking for in the upcoming book. Needless to say it is a gigantic transformation. I could not do the subject justice in just a few paragraphs.

Bloodline

Your bloodline will influence the have chemistry you have with others, and the kind of people who appear as a good mate for you.

A shining example of bloodline and love is my dear friend, Katherine, from Scotland and her African American rock star husband, Kevin, from Oakland, CA. It may not seem obvious why a Scottish lass would end up with an African-American rock and roller, but they do indeed fit together perfectly.

The Scottish bloodline is one of clans. Clans are very resonant with the tribal nature of the African history. Both cultures endured suppression by another: the Scottish were ruled over by the English Lords and the Africans were taken into slavery by American aristocracy.

In order to ensure safety to her family, a woman would look for the attributes in a man who is both a hard worker and who would not cause problems with the powers that be in order to ensure the safety of her family. These bloodline survival attitudes ensured that another generation would survive.

Though Katherine is from a level of Scottish Aristocracy, here in America she likes to think of herself as challenging the system and living in an honorable way. Community is incredibly important to her.

Kevin is the perfect match for her. As a back-up singer to many famous rock stars, he effectively supported rock and roll royalty. The attraction, even though not the same bloodline, ran deep and a lifetime bond quickly formed with these two meant-to-be partners.

Bloodlines can also interfere with love, however. The Middle Eastern bloodlines prevent marriage to one of another class or caste. Although it is not entirely apparent in the West, these invisible bloodline decisions get made every day. In the aristocracy of the Mayans, Egyptians and European cultures, bluebloods only mated to other bluebloods, and this inbreeding created offspring with genetic anomalies.

Although I do not give protocols for clearing bloodlines, you will want to look to memes and miasms if you find these issues interfering with your freedom to love in the way that you are wishing to love in this lifetime.

Nurture; love wisdom

Although there may exist a strong chemical attraction to a very macho strong male, a man who is very caveman-ish will not provide the tenderness and emotional intelligence many women are ultimately seeking.

The chemical attraction, that is, chemistry, is the language of human animal and will not provide the glue for a loving, long-term relationship. A wise woman or man will understand the difference between the chemical attraction and real affection: you must like the person you are considering bonding with.

Some basics: *men are not women*. They do not think like women or experience the world the way women think they do.

If you see a man sitting quietly staring into space and ask him what he was thinking, he will answer, "*Nothing*," and has quite honestly has given her a truthful answer. He was literally thinking *'nothing.'*

A woman, however, is never thinking "nothing." Her brain never stops, and so she will think he is being evasive and may even be hurt or offended by his answer.

Since a woman's brain is largely social, she will want to be involved in community and in planning and organizing events where relationships can be nurtured and expanded.

A man's brain is focused and directed; he is a good strategist and will want to provide and protect his woman. If she wants him to listen as she presents all the challenges she went through during the day, he will naturally want to provide the solution to these problems. She, however, may just want to have him listen to her as she winds her way around to getting to the present moment. When she finally feels like she has caught him up, she is ready to get into present time.

A man is largely in present time.

A good solution for this mismatch is for the couple to have an agreement about how he listens to her catch-up conversations. She could say to him I would like to just have you listen to this or I would like you to help me resolve this issue. Either way, he can now 'win' because he knows what is being asked of him and can provide that for her.

Do not assume ever, ladies, that he should know this. Be generous and help him win.

John Gray in his book, *Men are from Mars, women are from Venus*, talks about men going to their cave. This is incredibly important to understand. When a man needs time to be by himself, so as to not have to think or have demands on him, it is extremely important to gift that time to him.

Women, understand that this is not going to get better with processing. He will just get more irritable and flustered. It is **not** about "not loving you" or about "getting away from you" or "avoiding" anything. It **is** about getting grounded and finding his own equilibrium.

If you appreciate him and thank him for the things he brings to the table, he will bring more of the goodies. If you are in his face about the apparent deficiencies that you feel you must cram down his throat until he has changed his ways, you will never win.

Men feel happy when their woman understands them, supports them and enhances their life.

As women come into their own as CEOs and leaders, they are finding it more difficult to partner. The nature of our brain is such that we can hold both the male and female role. As a leader, we can provide and protect for our employees. Our brain is capable of doing both. Men, on the other hand, have a male brain, not a female brain. Men's brains are not marinating in estrogen every day of their lives, providing them with all the bonding and socializing aspects of the female brain.

In the age of equality, ladies, you will still need to find a way to support and enhance your partner and let go of the provide-protect role in relationship, even if that is what you do all day long in your career. We may evolve over thousands of years into something new. But the blueprint we currently work from is still defined by brain chemistry roles that we each supply for relationship to really work.

Understand that a man is king in his world when a woman has his back. And a woman is queen in her world when her man listens to and protects her.

There are many studies and discussions of the stages women go through. Men also have their own evolutionary stages. I recommend Alison Armstrong's excellent books, *"The Amazing Development of Men"* and *"Keys to the Kingdom,"* for providing excellent insights into being successful in understanding and loving each other.

Love wisdom comes from genuinely getting out of your own way and learning from the mistakes you have made. This wisdom comes from letting go of ever being in the right again: you can be 'right' or you can be 'loving' but you can't be both at the same time. Understanding the other's point of view and why or how they do things can be vital to making the shifts needed to transform love to the highest elevations.

Chakra System

Chakras provide the necessary energy for the body and the projects of your physical nature. In the yogic system, which provides us with the science of chakras and nadis, we discover that healthy blending of chakra energy can enhance many areas of life, including the arena of love and relationships. If the chakras are not functioning or are missing altogether, relationship or love may not have the energetic fuel needed to progress.

Consider chakras an enhancement to loving rather then the main dish. They are the frosting on the cake.

For love to survive, chakra one must be on and functioning well. Love will manifest even better if the chakras of two lovers are lined up in harmony with each other.

Marl and Cindy's Story

Marl and Cindy really wanted children. They had been married a number of years and had been trying for most of that time. Cindy was a home birth midwife. With every baby she delivered, her body got more agitated and anxious about her inability to conceive. Marl worked for the Environmental Protection Agency and was one of the good guys. He was a "granola" man if ever I met one.

With Marl and Cindy, being out of sync with each other seemed to be the 'way of things.' When they finally came to me for assistance they were literally fighting every day. They even fought in the car on the way over to see me.
The air was thick with tension as we sat down to explore the nature of the interruption of fertility and possibly correct it.

Cindy had done a couple of preparatory sessions with me but I felt the missing piece would be discovered if Marl attended a session with her. They were both tense and in emotional pain, both wanting to please the other. Marl was utterly confused about what to do; Cindy was angry that he couldn't read her mind. She was probably most angry with herself, and her own body, for betraying her and not producing the child she longed for.

After some chatting I set out to bring them together in a safe harmonious space where a baby spirit could find a safe and loving home with the two parents she had always wanted. I restored and cleaned up the couple's auras, creating room for another family member. I then set about matching up the chakras, front and back, to each other. Thus, for a 72-hour period, the couple would share the same energy and their chakras one through seven were linked and spinning together.

During this process, I discovered that chakras were broken off and even repelling the other person. It wasn't a pretty picture. Thankfully, by the end of the session, all chakras were spinning in harmony, energetically balanced, and at peace rather than in pieces.

They relayed the events of the next six hours as personalities still having to have drama. They then settled down with each other, finding an ease and natural comfort. They made love in the most connected and beautiful way, even feeling their daughter June join them. Within days, they received the confirmation they had successfully conceived. Nine months later, they brought little June home to finally be the family they had always imagined possible.

In most cases, I would not recommend linking up seven chakras as this could be all consuming after a time. However, to get in sync with each other, really in a harmonious connection, was exactly the healing balm this couple needed to produce the miracle they had longed for.

At the end of the chapter on chakras, I have listed a few combinations for using the energy of two or more chakras as a healing vehicle to enhance an area in need of enrichment or fulfillment.

Gestation-Womb Matches with Mother

Eight years ago 'gestation-womb matches with mother' was my big project. This was prior to my discovery of the Divine Human Blueprint and it was providing a lot of material for me to assist women who had taken on difficult emotional and mental challenges their own mothers were experiencing during their gestation period.

In a 200-page manuscript on my research and findings of the time, I wrote about 'parental gunk' that we pick up while we are forming. Most of it is irrelevant to our life, yet some of it forms our self-concepts and our role in life. These patterns emerge not from our own challenges, but rather challenges our mothers, and sometimes our fathers were experiencing during our fetal development. Until we unhook from these patterns, we can actually stay trapped in a life we weren't even planning to live, working on projects we never planned to work on.

Sally's Story

Sally was always sad. She never felt loved or wanted and had a terribly difficult time in life. She was constantly over-extended and was never sure if she was loved and doubted that her boyfriend really loved her. She was never sure if she was lovable and didn't know how to feel love. It became more of a maneuvering puzzle to her, and a painful one at that.

I could help her get out of the deepest and worst of the emotional valleys, yet there was a breakthrough she had not yet accomplished. We were both looking for a way to find her path to emotional health.

Sally had been conceived after her parents had lost the baby girl they had loved and cherished to sudden infant death in the crib. While her parents were in grief and mourning, their family and friends had suggested they get pregnant and have another child as soon as possible.

Conception happened but the grieving was not over. There was no happiness or joy during the pregnancy. Sally did not feel cherished and wanted while in the womb. Instead she felt sad, lost, and lonely. She had wondered why she was developing a body when her sister (about whom she heard through the emotions and conversations of her parents) was no longer there.

Her parents were not ready for her, and as a finicky infant with a fragile sensitive nature, Sally cried a lot and was often inconsolable. As a result, her parents blamed her for their stress and unhappiness, and rejected her. They wanted a happy baby to replace the daughter they lost; they didn't know what to do with Sally.

Years later, Sally steadfastly worked with me in healing sessions spread six weeks apart. She was routinely experiencing a sense of balance, yet the feelings of contentment eluded her. The breakthrough opportunity came with the conception of her daughter Jade. I was able to provide Sally with guided meditations that she used during her pregnancy to establish a healthy and easy dynamic with her daughter and unhook the negative patterns she experienced while in her mother's womb.

The transformation was utterly remarkable as Sally was able to step into the role of loving mother. The feeling of being an unwanted little girl left her completely. She made an extraordinary and beautiful transition using the pregnancy and birth of her own daughter to unwire the negative gestation experience.

Gestation matches are easy enough to clear once you have found them. However, a person coming through this experience will often form an attachment to being wronged. In other words the ego formed in this particular dysfunctional gestation period can make it challenging to fully remove the negative patterns.

The wise view is to see that whatever challenges your mother was going through while you were in the womb are not those that you chose to learn and grow from. By simply saying, "This is not mine," you are ready to make everyone right, understand their point of view and move on. With that attitude and a little pumping of gold energy, voila and presto change-o, you are complete.

Later in this chapter, I will teach you how to detach from energy and contracts that may apply to gestation imprints. If a little gold healing energy doesn't move them out, then following the complete love clearing process will.

Failed love and other relationships: residual energy and karma

Turning Up the Ashes

I thought there would be more.
I am left with emptiness.
Like ash after the roaring blaze is long
extinguished,
Desperately, I search for the remnants of the
spark to rekindle my fire.

Searching goes on in vain.
I recognize ash is sacred.
Complete in it's own existence.
I hunger for fires of passion to restore the
Brilliant flame to me.

It happens to everyone who has ever lived or loved, that things just don't always work out and you are left with baggage. In the following pages, I will show you, step-by-step. how to clear negative energy and karma with every person you have ever known. You can get free of painful baggage and live a life of ease and connection if you so choose to.

Strangely enough, this process came to me while going through morphine withdrawals nine years ago. This was after probably the most difficult year of my life. The pain and suffering I went through in that year catapulted me into a whole new dimension in the area of love and relationship.

On Thanksgiving day the previous Autumn, I had been given a date rape drug and had been brutally violated. It took months of therapy to regain the ability to get up and walk, sing, even play harp for the first time. And then, right when I had just begun a fresh chapter with a new boyfriend and I was starting to think the world was safe, without warning while crossing a street in my neighborhood, a car hit me. Life became even worse than I could have imagined.

The new boyfriend was more of a fantasy than a reality, as he had fidelity and loyalty issues that were not a match for me. I was now confined to my bed and a wheel chair with a serious brain injury. The pain in my body was off the charts. Nothing seemed to help. At one point, they tried a combination of 2000 mg of time-release anti-inflammatory drugs, nine Morphine tablets, a Fentanyl patch, and three Xanex tranquilizers daily.

As crazy as it sounds, even with this high-level chemical cocktail, I was still in a significant amount of pain, but now I also felt like a blithering idiot. After a relatively short time on this protocol, I had had enough. I went cold turkey off all the drugs on my own locked in my house. For eleven days, I went through the withdrawal symptoms of shakes, hallucinations and panic attacks. I knew it would soon end, however. I used warm baths, many daily, to calm my body down as I transitioned off all pain meds.

Both of the experiences the previous year had been the worst of human violence. This excruciating physical pain, with nothing to help me get through my day but willpower, magnified by the mental and emotional anguish of a lifetime of adversity, forced a transformation in me.

In my pain, which I welcomed, I asked to see the purpose of these and many other atrocities. What became clear to me was that I was creating a reality that was connected toan earlier violence. I understood that if I did not absolutely develop an entirely new emotional landscape, I would perish from the worst of human behaviors.

I had a revelation: Jesus experienced the worst of humanity when his own disciple betrayed him. He was then tortured and hung on the cross.
What if He had actually agreed to all of it? What if Jesus were the director of this show and He told father God prior to coming into this incarnation that He wanted to touch, move, and inspire people to do good and be light in the world? Because He wanted to make such a big impact and that there were so many forces on the planet working for darkness, the way to leave a lasting and permanent impression was to suffer and to die publicly and horribly. All humans would remember Him for centuries to come for His life, His works, and the purity and goodness He was.

What if He said "Yes"? And what if Judas, prior to birth, said, "I want to help you with this project, and I will play the role of the villain"? What if Jesus, with the big impact He wanted to make, had those who could step up and stand with him take the roles necessary to play out His story?

I thought about these concepts in terms of my own experience; that *my life was my design*. What if I said "yes" to the early abuse and violence so I could grow, learn, and discover the full human experience? What if everyone were simply playing their roles to help me accomplish this task? What if I was the director of this show?

I felt a sense of rightness when I thought this way. I discovered a sense of power that I could now change my path. I could let the people off the hook who I had held accountable all these years for my challenges (in other words all the people I blamed). *I could build myself a life in the Garden of Eden.*

This is how I gained the capacity to love and forgive everyone. I now understood that I had been directing the show and creating the roles everyone was playing. I needed to create some better roles. I could let those who wanted violent or harmful roles to move on to others who might benefit from learning on that energy of vibration.

The first step in this process was to call all fifty-six family members to tell them I loved and appreciated them. If I had been making them wrong for something, I also apologized for making them wrong for things that happened in the past and promised never to do it again. Then, as often as possible I would say to each of these family members something I loved about them or that I loved something that they gifted me in my personality.

If I broke my word and said something negative about a family member or friend, I forced myself (not fun) to call and apologize to the person I had blamed or spoken badly about. In addition to that I called the person with whom I had had the conversation in order to make it right. I kept my word and things began to change rapidly.

I had another revelation. Anything I was saying against a family member was creating a kind of darkness around them and preventing them from healing or letting go of that issue. I became aware that I was causing them harm in their energetic space. I was creating a group miasm of negativity towards one of my family members. Wow. This had to stop and it was urgent. I was on fire to clear my mind of these negative thought forms and become the loving person I knew myself to be.

This amazing work, piece by piece, became clear to me. I transformed from victim to powerful compassionate leader. In between, I practiced being the energy of unconditional love.

How to pull your energy back

1. Begin by grounding and clearing your energy. An excellent way to get started and do this process from a neutral space is to meditate using "The Definitive Guide to Meditation."

2. Once you have completed the meditation, reinforce your grounding to the center of the Earth.

3. Picture the person you are clearing energy with ten feet in front of you, also grounded to the center of the Earth.

4. Place two roses, a red one and a blue one, between you. Ground the two roses to the center of the earth so they do not float away.

5. These two roses serve as magnets; they have the power to magnetize energy out of the body. The red rose is the magnet that suctions your energy out of the other person. Understand that it is natural while in any kind of

relationship to exchange energy. This process is just to restore your energy back to you.

6. The blue rose serves to magnetize the other person's energy out of your body.

7. Set the roses to 'on' and allow them to remove energy appropriately from one another until all of this relationship energy has been removed.

8. Use kinesiology to test when this process is complete. The entire process can take from five to ten minutes. If you are sensitive to energy, you will feel different, lighter and more positive.

9. Each step can be done on its own. But the complete healing follows all the steps below.

You can also use this healing to clear energy from places, things, ideas, work, communities, banks, religions etc.

How to clear energy cords

One cold day you'll look outside your
window and
Find me still,
Turning up the ashes with my cane.
Restlessly seeking an unanswerable quest,
To find the life we once knew.

I remember you my beloved.
In my memories live the soaring flames
Of the love we bore.
Our glory shall light my long dark night.

Energy cords are formed naturally between a mother and her newborn infant. This provides a direct channel between mother and child. From that cord, information is passed as well as the connection to each other is enforced.

The mother-child cord is the healthy human-spirit cording connection.

When in a relationship, cords typically form between the two parties. Connection is enforced and awareness of the other will be amplified. Cords are not formed without consent. In other words, you have to somehow agree to the connection. Even if you have never heard of cords prior to reading this, you will have consciously agreed to any cords you now have wired into you.

Cords may also form between family members, friends and work associates. People who are very insecure or concerned about control tend to form cords to many people while those who are independent and self-confident tend to form fewer cords.

There is also the "guru cord phenomenon." It is a very specific kind of cord plugged into the devotee's right brain from the guru. It gives the guru access to the devotee's energy, allows both the ability to quickly connect and assist the follower, or to rapidly use all his devotees' energies to direct in the area the guru chooses.

This is a very old system and was extremely important thousands of years back when access to the Divine and the power of creation was limited. The issue was that the overall average group energy was so low, that little in the way of miracles or inspiration could happen without this ancient tool.

We are now in a new era. The days of the guru to be corded to so many followers is falling away quickly. Instead, individuals are turning to teachers who can show them the way to their own power and connection with 'God.' Just as political structures from the patriarchal era are falling away and new dynamics are emerging, this 'guru' arrangement is also rapidly disappearing and will not be found for much longer on Earth.

The cord clearing process:

1. Once the energy clearing process is complete, sit quietly in a comfortable seated position spine erect, feet on the floor.

2. Become aware of your body and feel into the areas where cords between the other person and you exist.

3. If you are not sensitive to energy, you can use kinesiology to identify cords;
   - Ask how many cords you have plugged into you connected to the other person: 1? 2? Keep working up till you get a yes.
   - Ask for the location: torso, limbs or head/neck.
   - If torso ask front or back, upper or lower torso.
   - This is enough information to remove the cords.

4. Imagine pulling the cords out, just like pulling an electric cord out of the wall. Remove all the cords to the outside edge of your aura. Important to note: the edge of your aura after doing our guided meditation should be between 18 inches and 36 inches away from your body.

5. Once the cord is outside your aura, fill in any holes in the aura to prevent further access. This can be done by

pumping gold energy into the aura or, for fun, you can use the image of auric spray paint.

Note: it is not your job to remove cords from the other unless you know you stuck them there. You can test with kinesiology to discover this. Once removed from you, the cords are no longer are active, even if you do not remove them from the other person. Our general rule is to not alter or heal anyone who has not directly, verbally asked for our help. The less you disturb their space in the process the better and more complete your healing is.

How to clear contracts and agreements

1. Identify with kinesiology if there are any contracts, or agreements still outstanding with the other person. Contracts are different from agreements so be sure to check both.

> A contract is something that is more of a legal arrangement between the two of you. It may have to do with your relationship, money, possession or perhaps property.

> An agreement is something that, at one point, you had both consented to creating together. For example: "When we retire let's spend a year in the outback and study kangaroos." Here there was never anything written down, however it is something that lives in the astral as an agreement till you clear it. Don't assume these go away just because you have gotten a divorce.

2. If 'yes,' it is good to have a sense of what that might be so using kinesiology test:

- **Is it physical?** Money, home, property, and even clothing are possible unfulfilled contracts or agreements.
- **Is it emotional?** Promised to love, honor and cherish, and the agreement didn't end even though you are divorced. Promised to support them during difficult times. Things like this are in this category.
- **Is it mental?** In this category, I look at logistical things: legal contracts and issues related to justice and righteousness.

You can clear agreements by just pumping gold energy into the space of the agreements. With contracts, I use imagery that unlocks the energetic contract from all realms.

3. Again, sit with spine erect, feet on the floor, and picture the other person seated six feet in front of you. Picture that you are bound to each other with chains and shackles. See these at the minimum around ankles and wrists. You might also see a chastity belt, a color or even a chain around your brain.

4. In your mind's eye, reach in your pocket and discover a key. Take the key and unlock both the chains and shackles from yourself and, in this case, you must remove the chains and shackles from the other. You are freeing them and yourself and, in so doing, there can be no residual resentments towards you, fueled by your left over control energy in their space.

5. See the chains and shackles sucked down into a vortex between the two of you, making any residual negative energy from the chains and shackles in your space permanently disappear.

Note: The other person may still experience a mental malady and ruminate on you, but it will not affect your energy because you have cleaned it all up from your side. They may sit with their own 'hot potato in hand,' with resentment being the hot potato. It cannot hurt you because you have let go.

How to clear karma

The final step in this very thorough clearing is karma clearing. Karma is any unresolved problem energy that needs completion or resolution. Unresolved energy attaches you to the other over many lifetimes until the lessons are learned and problems are resolved. Unless you do this final step, even with all the clearing you have done, you may still end up living out this problem again in a future life.

There actually is great value in clearing with this method, even with the ones you love and have an easy time with. The freedom to operate with no unresolved past problems allow you the joy of discovering each other in this life, without a preconceived notion of who they are.

1. Imagine half a gold ring, like a half new moon, filled in on top and with nothing yet on the bottom. This half gold ring represents the half of the karma you have already both lived out with each other.

2. Pump gold energy into the ring to fill it in entirely, having it become a complete golden circle. As it fills in, you are witnessing the fulfillment of unfinished karma.

3. When the golden ring is 100% complete, place a large white rose under the karma ring and ground it to the center of the earth. The white rose represents both purity and finality.

4. Drop the gold ring into the white rose blossom and toss cartoon bombs on to the white rose until the rose has disappeared.

5. When the white rose is gone, your karma has been cleared. You are free to create new fresh loving karma with them or to walk away completely unattached and free.

I have observed hundreds of lives change for the better with this process. This process is incredibly powerful andsupports you in bringing a fresh new you to a relationship free of baggage of the past.

Getting unhooked from everyone and everything, and being free to consciously choose how you show up in life can be amazing! You get to rewrite your own script, step up to higher levels of expression and pace your own personal growth process. Stepping up is easier from a free space.

Chapter 5: Light of Cell

Breaking through

Rain keeps falling.
I feel God grieving with me.
Crying the tears of loss,
We wash away the stains of absent love.

Our tears nourish a fertile ground.
We ready the earth and her seeds
for their inevitable duty.

Bringing forth new life,
Again and again.
Each time with no less pain
The sprout breaks through
Her protective shell.

With the first breath of life the human spirit animates the body. Likewise, the light of each and every cell imbues these cells with the ability to heal, regenerate and recover. Unlike the animation of the body by the human spirit (which occurs at birth) the light of cell is established *in utero* early in the development of the embryo-fetus, as soon as the healthy cells have divided and differentiated.

Mother's and father's contribution to light of cell

The mother provides an 'enlightened egg.' Not all eggs are enlightened, only those that are successfully fertilized to begin the development of a human body. The sperm starts the program running for the human body to begin its development. If sperm were to hit the 'program button' in an egg without light, nothing would begin. Sperm does not deliver light: it is like a programmer setting up the program for 'game on.' The egg with light will initiate the 'game,' not the programmer.

The light of the first egg, in its perfection, teaches the dividing cells how to have and be light. The enlightened egg gives the first blueprint of life and the second blueprint of light.

The survival of the developing egg has much to do with the program that supports life. If this program is very strong, life continues. If the program for life is weak to begin with, the light of the cell will go out. From hours to months after conception, human life will end. This is the challenge some mothers repeat with multiple miscarriages.

Master or stem cells

Master cells provide the blueprint of light as the body merges with human spirit at birth. This enlightenment allows the master-cell (stem cell) to be an intelligent guide and an effective mirror to assist in restoring ailing cells.

It is exquisite for the body to have eighty percent of its cells being enlightened cells. The bone structure does not use light for healing, so we do not see light of cell in bones. Incidentally, you can rapidly heal bones by pumping gold energy from your golden rings into the affected area and watch a process of new bone growth resembling plant roots intertwining from both sides of the break.

Because the fluid surrounding our cells does not consist of cells, it also is not infused with light.

Though this light doesn't have a human visual color, it is similar to the light of the sun. I sketch it in as yellow when I am demonstrating on a white board, but it does not 'wear' a color.

What is 'normal' in a healthy baby is to have the light activated in all stem cells and up to sixty percent of the remaining cells having no light. Light is specifically for **regeneration.** A healthy birth does not require 'cell regeneration' because an embryo's cells are new. In other words, no regeneration is needed in new cells at birth.

Changing DNA programming in compromised birth

In a compromised birth, where the child is born with an illness or congenital flaw, there will be even fewer cells with their light activated. This is because the stem cells that allowed the glitch to exist in the newborn did not have their light on or activated. Healthy stem cells do not teach unhealthy patterns.

In this case, using miraculous healing protocols to build new cells where flawed cell programs exist is the best choice.

The DNA programs that supported a breakdown from healthy development will also need to be removed and perfected. No-one in a human body is born 'perfect'. Thirty percent of individuals have great, exceptionally strong patterns, while many of us have been born with some, or even numerous, challenges in our programming.

I would like to suggest to you that instead of asking what went wrong with the program deficiencies, consider the question, "What went right?" You or the person you are

117

helping to heal had so many healthy patterns that supported life that they have accomplished the miracle of life. That is no small feat.

If you develop the attitude of gratitude and appreciation for your miraculous human body and see it as your friend and a benevolent cooperative assistant in the process of greater wellness, the body will give you all its got and will rise to the occasion. See the body as perfect and the challenges as temporary. After all, you did come with a divine human blueprint plus all the information necessary to correct inadequacy.

If, on the other hand, you are spending much of your time focusing on the errors, mistakes and defective things you came into the world with, then you will manifest struggle, difficulty and additional challenges for yourself instead healing and becoming healthy.

Cheryl was an interesting person to work with. She was a very, very sick woman who lived close enough that she would literally come in to see me. I think she looked forward to the time we spent together. When you are that sick there is no social life, just conversations with doctors and loved ones about how bad you feel.

As she walked through the door she would exclaim with breathless enthusiasm, "Hi Julie Renee you wouldn't believe what happened to me!" Finding her place on my sofa, a steady stream of rapid complaints, symptoms and disturbances would ensue. Every now and again she would pause for just a moment to ask what I thought, but would barely give me time to respond before she'd barrage me with more problems.

Unfortunately, the benefit of much of the healing work we

did in the sessions was undone by her constant obsession with illness and death when she was at home.

I liked her very much and really wanted to help her out. I began to coach her about her attitude. Whenever she would have a setback, I helped her see how she had created it by her negativity at home. It has been an amazing transformation to see her come out of the darkness and into the light.

She really did want her health and vitality back and with her steady prayers and improvements in conversations and decision to let go of drama she is actively using her thoughts to help herself heal.

She was very ill when we began our work together with life threatening condition of the entire digestive system. She eventually was completely cured of this condition and of the many infections that had taken over her body.

Re-growth of organs

The seedling grows, flowers,
And at long last bears the fruit of love.
She offers her fruit freely to anyone
who would accept this gift.

Breaking through is a painful thing,
with no guarantee of success.
Yet the seedling must forge ahead,
its quest for life too strong to repress.

'Light of cell' teaches the unhealthy cells how to be healthy or, when necessary, to grow new cells even when a part has been surgically removed. For example, my tonsils and adenoids were both surgically removed but I have re-grown both back to full size.

Current genetic research experiments are exploring ways to grow glands or organs outside the body using stem cells. The scientific community knows organ re-growth is possible because, for example, the liver is programmed to re-grow. Scientists are attempting to re-grow other organs but since they have not yet achieved it, such organ re-growth is met with mixed reactions, even in the face of a large body of evidence.

At Miraculous Living, we are able to (anecdotally) produce results, such as re-growing organs, that the religious community considers miraculous. The medical community greets the news with statements ranging from "that's not possible" to "sign me up for the program. I want to learn how you do this!"

Light of cell activations are most effective following Cellular Neo-Genesis.

1. After you have restored the membrane, nucleus absorption and elimination organelle as well as restoring the DNA Organelle.

2. Pump gold energy into the cell to activate the light of the cell.

3. Once the light of cell in the stem cell/master cell is activated, continue pumping gold into the master cell to amplify its reach to the surrounding cells as it mirrors the new healthy upgrades to the surrounding cells.

4. As a last step you will test for the percentage of cells that took the upgrade

5. Test for how many days of new cell growth.

The light of cell is our ace in the hole. It is the secret sauce that supports the needed environment of light to literally regenerate. It's not a Band-Aid. It is a new beginning.
I think of the light of cell as the gift of regeneration God wired into me so that I could always choose life!

Chapter 6: Golden Rings

Exploring Love, Light and Power 1989

What is the difference between Power, Love and Light?
They are clearly parts of God
And yet they can be accessed separately

Power is tapping into universal source
It is transient; it comes and goes like the wind
It is useful to create momentum and inertia
But you are cautioned not to depend on it in the long run
Like a flint when struck properly it will ignite a spark
But a moment later if it hasn't made a good connection
It disappears. Power can exist without love or light.

Light is the essence of matter
Without light matter would not exist

There was no need for love at first
Because the existence of light in its purity
Functioned in perfect harmony
In perfect harmony there was
No need for the nature of love
Because everything was in divine perfection

Love came in with a powerful force
Available to heal
Before love, all that was
Existed in a state of perfection
There was no need for the healing power of love

It came only after the event of disharmony
As a response to disharmony
In love there is Karma
In light there is no Karma

Introduction

As we enter the 'dawning' of the Age of Aquarius and leave behind the Piscean Age, distinct gifts and markers begin to appear and become the new standard for transformation. The old Piscean age, defined by a patriarchal reign and a submissive acquiescing culture ruled by a few, is being ushered out. The new Age of Aquarius standard, which includes androgyny, representing true equality in the spiritual realm, replaces the old patriarchal standard. Furthermore, previously obscured and unavailable knowledge is now accessible to the general population. The uncovering of these mysteries levels the playing field enabling all to experience the power that was once only imagined and held by a select few. This leads to transformation on a global scale.

Our *'human halo'* or *'golden rings'* is one such marker. Though knowledge of our halo has been around for thousands of years, this new era defines a shift in both the understanding and the use of this divine tool, bringing its power now to our fingertips.

Golden rings or human halo

Individuals have zero to ten rings, starting three inches from the base of the crown chakra and extending upwards like a funnel or cone. Our golden rings belong with the physical body and are not part of human spirit. They disappear with the death of the physical body. The physical DNA provides the information for the halo or golden rings, which is available to every spirit incarnating in a physical body.

The energy signature of the spirit incarnate provides the details of when and how developed the human halo appears.

Think of the story of baby Jesus as he lays in the manger surrounded by his loving parents and the adoring shepherds who have come in from watching their flocks. There is a glow emanating from the holy child. For dear baby Jesus, who was an advanced and enlightened spirit, his halo comes online within hours of birth.

This beautiful condition is a result of the extremely high-energy signature he as a spirit embodies. 'Christ Consciousness' vibrates at one thousand; Master Jesus came with spiritual tools awake and activated, available to create miracles even in childhood.

And we are told of the miracles he created as a child. There was also a reverence and a respect that he commanded among the elders as a young boy, due to the vibratory rate of his body and his heavenly glow.

There are stories of holy births in many traditions that share this golden presence. It is as if the sun has been born with the child, and all present feel awe and wonder when witnessing 'God Presence.'

The miracle of childbirth

Gather your children oh mommies today
And bind them close to you and love them I pray

And give them your heart, your time and your ways

Singing oh bonnie mommy I love you this way

Give them the confidence, the care and the play

Talk to the daily about their new world
And share with them light from the mystical
plans

Singing oh bonne mommy I love you this
way!

The story of any child born on earth to average human parents is wondrous. For each child born, legions of divine helpers assist in the birth and the person's orientation from the spirit to the physical world. I share here the details of the Judeo/Islamic and Christian traditions, as these were the experiences of my culture.

I was nineteen years old when my daughter Britta was born, She was not my first pregnancy; I had experienced a seven-week pregnancy prior to conceiving her. Britta was strong and held fast for the challenging ride of pregnancy in my young, already compromised body.

I felt weak throughout, but also had the happy sense a female body experiences with the pregnancy hormones, knowing my body was doing what it was meant to do. Think about the anatomy of a woman: everything about us, from breasts to belly and our social brain marinating with estrogen, is wired to create children.

Although I had had a mysterious illness around age twelve and pulled through, Britta's birth was the first close call with death I experienced. During the birth, I felt a kind of pain I did not feel in my subsequent births. This resulted from a tearing away of the placenta from the uterus wall and an open hemorrhage with massive blood loss.

As Britta was born, three guardian angels supported her birth. At some point, we had an emergency: her heart rate dropped and I was hemorrhaging. To save her, she was pulled out rapidly with forceps. I saw the reflection in the birthing mirror as a massive red flood of blood left me. While her guardian angels cared helped her spirit's integration into her body, I had a team of medical professionals working to save my life. I, of course, was in prayer. Clearly, since I am still here, my prayer was answered with, "yes."

Britta had angelic helpers to get her oriented into her body, which is the case with children like her born to a mother that may not be healthy, or who could even die. She was born with the blueprint of golden rings but not the appearance. The heavenly feeling around the birth of each of my children was the presence of the angelic helpers.

Infants who are enlightened masters that choose to incarnate, and children born to enlightened masters (namely a mother who is awake to her mastery at the time of the child birth) experience a birth with golden rings on.

Children born to enlightened masters may experience the activation of their rings up to about age seven where the responsibility for their energetic signature now rests entirely on them.

In our ongoing apprentice training, students are given the opportunity to have their rings routinely activated.

How do our golden rings appear and activate?

The actual purpose of the golden rings is to assist in the betterment of humanity, and for that reason they appear or activate when the individual is well-steeped in wise elder love wisdom. The rings begin to make an appearance at a vibrational energy of 500, lighting and extinguishing when energy rises above or falls below that of compassion.

Our golden rings stay on at around 680, which is the condition of 'enlightened master.'

The number of rings an individual will have access to is related to their energy vibration. For example, a woman I am training consistently comes in around 475 and this will give her access to five golden rings.

Table 6-1 Number of Golden Rings Related to Energy of Vibration

Number of Golden Rings	Lowest Energy of Vibration	Highest Energy of Vibration
1	90	180
2	180	263
3	263	355
4	355	460
5	460	530
6	530	610
7	610	705
8 - 10	705	1000

Appearance of ten active golden rings

Our halo can appear differently depending upon the Enlightened Master you are observing.

- *Ring one* is the base or bottom of the funnel, appearing 1-4 inches above the head with an outside diameter of 10 inches.

- *Ring two* is 7 inches above the head with an outside diameter of 20 inches.

127

- *Ring three* is 40 inches above the head with an outside diameter of 4 feet.

- *Ring four* is 5 feet above the head with an outside diameter of 5 feet 8 inches.

- Ring five is 8 feet 6 inches above the head with a diameter of 15 feet.

- *Ring six* is 12 feet above the head with a diameter of 23 feet.

- *Ring seven* is 16 feet above the head with a 30-foot diameter.

- *Ring eight* is 20 feet above the head with a 38-foot diameter.

- *Ring nine* is 27 feet above the head with 46-foot diameter.

- *Ring ten* is 36 feet above the head with a 70-foot diameter

Average human being ring appearance

The average human being shows three inactive rings:

- *Ring one* is 1-4 inches above the head with a 6-inch diameter.

- *Ring two* is 7 inches above the head with an 11-inch diameter.

- *Ring three* is 14 inches above the head with an18-inch diameter.

Years ago I dated a fellow who had ring envy. He was a funny sort of fellow on his own path, had a spiritual nature and loved the color purple. Peter, seeing my energy vibration, set out to wow me by determining, through force of will and mind, that he would meditate himself up 200 points. He went into seclusion and focused on doing just that.

You know that whatever the mind can conceive and believe it will achieve. He did lift his energy vibration and rings to the higher number, but only temporarily. We are where we are vibrationally because we have set up a series of challenges and circumstances to assist us in our growth process as human spirits.

What did Peter gain by forcing his energy up while passing by the opportunities to learn and grow? Virtually nothing, as without having gained the wisdom he needed to hold the vibration, his energy returned to a lower setting. But hoorah for him! He took on a grand spiritual experiment and learned many things in the process.

Bikram Yoga methods do something similar for muscles. The practice is performed in a very warm room so your muscles are able to stretch more easily. You can than, without injury, stretch into more difficult yoga poses than are possible in a regular or cool room. It's the fast track to a number of postures. However, the muscles have not reveled in the joys of gaining agility in a natural way. I do know there are many wonderful benefits from this hot yoga. I'm just pointing out the limited mastery.

The quality and nature of golden rings

The nature of the golden rings is that of creation and of destruction. When accessing the energy of the rings, you can amplify your power and ability to be a positive force for good and for change.

The presence of gold is warm, potent, intelligent, healing and powerful. In the yogic tradition, a yogi harnesses the golden energy to master a siddha. When used by a master, this energy can control the course of the weather, the conditions of the earth and geometric plates, as well as alter the thoughts and minds of humanity, shifting group consciousness.

In the Miraculous Living experience, we teach how to access the golden rings for health, wellbeing, love, DNA shifts and curative qualities for the full experience of being human. Prayer, communion with the Divine, and merging with that energy for a prolonged period can produce the experience of a vibrating active halo.

Once the golden rings are on, for the healing process we bring the gold energy through the **human spirit access portal** (see Chapter 7) located the back of the head, one inch above where the spine meets the skull.

From there you direct the flow of golden energy down through the neck right shoulder and arm, through the elbow, wrist, palm, through the fingers and out the fingertips. With a pumping action from all five fingers, send the golden energy out the fingertips towards the area in need of healing.

While I am healing from the toxic exposure to nuclear radiation, I imagine sitting in my golden rings, as a golden pyramid, supported and engulfed by this miraculous Golden God energy. In this energy I see my entire body bathed in a rich supply of golden curative energy.

Distance Is Not Important

The flow of energy from the halo into the spiritual access portal, down the arm and out the fingertips is an extremely powerful mode of healing. In recent years, I have healed thousands of people using this technique. It does not require the one being healed to be in the same room or even the same country as the healer.

Healing someone in another country is no less powerful than healing someone in the same room. If you consider that there's no limitation in terms of distance, it also means that there's no limit to the number of people who can receive the healing simultaneously.

In my experience, as the number of people being simultaneously healed increases, at a certain point it feels like a blast furnace and my whole body heats up. In contrast, if it is a group emotional healing, it might feel like an energy build-up, such as a stress/tension, leading to a sudden release that almost pops, leaving them feeling very liberated and free. After this type of healing, the air is crisp and pure. The minds or brains of everyone in the room are clear and lucid.

Richard's Story

Roland, the husband of my student Anna, is an Austrian fellow around eighty years old. He has had difficulties with his vision; he came into a healing weekend really unable to open his droopy lids and unable to see clearly. Richard's doctor had reported a number of problems including macular degeneration.

In one simple healing using the golden energy from the halo, in a number of ways, we were able to improve his vision and his lids held a new strength allowing for his eyes to open.

When giving a healing of this type, the healer begins by

- Activating their own golden rings
- Ask the recipients body what it needs through the questions provided in the Miraculous Healing protocols.

In his case, his body 'told us' it needed a physical healing. With focused intention, gold energy cleared his eyeballs, optic nerve, visual cortex and lids that were all presenting grey and black energy.

When we see black and grey energies we know that this area has failed significantly and we refer to this condition as death energy. Not because in portends death, but rather because of the inability to improve or heal.

When we clear the dark colors saturating the physical body we restore the natural healthy colors and once hidden health begins to resurface. When the dark energy is cleared, the healthy energy appears in its place.

After the first three clearings, our next step was to ask:

- Is Cellular Neo-Genesis (cell regeneration) appropriate for his body now?

His body gave us important information needed to complete a successful healing of his eyes: a significant alteration in the visual programming of the eyes that is stored in the DNA needed attention prior to growing new cells. (See Chapter 2: DNA Obliterations for specific details to this procedure.)

We removed many difficult programs in his DNA around healthy eyes and clear vision. These were replaced with excellent eye health and vision programs. It is important to also look at the family DNA group bubble to see if the program will be reset into his cellular body from that familial energy. Before moving to another procedure, reset the DNA program. This reset will return the old program if it is not corrected.

Note: The DNA has a reset system, very uncomplicated and easy to move. Essentially there is a reboot program wired into the human body that will reset a person to the former *status quo.* This is a fail-safe mechanism preventing loss of important information to the body. Only a very tiny amount of the DNA should ever be altered, as your DNA is an amazing and complex gift. When human spirit leaves the body during sleep, the body is at rest/sleeping. Upon waking in the morning, the old pre-altered programs will reboot, very much like a computer after the battery has been removed and later replaced. It basically restores the old programs. Simply pumping gold energy into the reset of the DNA will inform the body of its new set position; the individual will wake up maintaining the healing instead of reverting to the *status quo.*

As Richard's healing progressed prior to generating new cells, we were led to the emotional body where some painful family pictures were preventing a full vision recovery. To accomplish this healing, using gold energy we cleared the emotional body of blocks.

Finally the thumbs-up for the Cellular Neo-Genesis was given. We stimulated new cell growth as laid out in the cellular neo-genesis protocols as in Chapter 3.

Complete a miraculous healing by:

- Filling the person receiving the healing with gold energy. You do this by pumping gold energy towards them and by assisting the human spirit back into their physical body.

A nice visual to assist in the process is to put a golden sun on the top of their head and set them as a spirit in the golden sun. Then bring spirit into the body to fill in every cell all the way to the outer edge of the skin. This visual and the pumping action of gold energy will aid the spirit to get fully into their body after the healing.

Golden ring activation

The 'Miraculous Healing System,' with all its power to shift and improve life, relies entirely on the *golden rings*. The human halo for Christians is part of Christ consciousness. However you define them, these *golden rings* are warm, potent, healing and powerful. They are a major power source. *Golden rings* for humans, as a species, make us extraordinary and give us a unique position on our planet. Golden rings can transform humankind and the rest of the planet, as we awaken to the new era, the Age of Aquarius.

When new to the experience of accessing the energy of the golden rings, activating and drawing from your own golden rings may not be consistent. It is perfectly appropriate to access the universal source gold energy while you are unable to access your own. With practice, this step will become unnecessary.

You may be one of the few who had their golden rings active in another life. This life, you choose to experience growth, setting up a lack of access to the rings until you have experienced the steps you designed for yourself to grow in wisdom and understanding. This is my circumstance.

I have, throughout my life, been able to access great power for no apparent reason. During the 'death watches', friends and partners were being told there was no way I would survive a week. To their surprise by some miracle, I would strengthen and come through. Frequently, I would pull a rabbit out of a hat to save other's lives. These miracles came from the golden rings without human awareness.

Super-human feats stem from the golden rings

Many, many years ago while studying herbal medicine with Adam Seller and the Pacific School of Herbal Medicine, one such incident occurred. While out collecting live specimens for drying and creating tinctures, we, as a group, came across a large patch of evening primrose in a ditch off a seldom-traveled highway. While we stopped to collect the primrose for use in female health and balancing formulas, two young women in our group, aged twenty-three and +
+twenty-seven, slowed to wave at us from their car, then pulled out onto the freeway. They apparently didn't notice a large semi-truck barreling down the road.

The semi-truck hit the car full on, dragging it down the freeway a third of a mile before it came to a stop. I ran towards their car and found the driver side door was bent well into the driver's seat. Amy, the driver, was in shock with four fractured ribs, a punctured kidney, and other internal damage. The passenger, Adriana, had a broken nose that was spurting blood as well as having internal bruising.

I yelled to passer-bys for ice while I started running gold energy and my own life force into the girls as both moved quickly into shock. I began using my voice as a soothing balm keeping them calm and serene as they began slowly returning to their bodies.

Finally, after what seemed liked hours, the jaws-of-life cut the driver out of the car and I joined the girls in the ambulance. Once we arrived at the hospital, the doctor who examined them said it was highly unusual that they would still be alive after such a severe accident and thanked me for helping them.

Because I did not know anything about what I was doing, I used a great deal of my own energy to assist them. Once everyone was safely tucked in their hospital beds I went into shock myself and took a few weeks to recover my own energy and feel my own strength. Regardless of where I was at with my spiritual awakening, I still had a clear understanding of the *force* available to me. So even if I was in a stage of learning and challenge and had not yet stepped into my awakened state, I could still draw on my *golden rings*.

Golden rings can appear

My golden rings became visible to one of the ministers at the Lake Harriet church on Ash Wednesday, twenty-five years ago. This occurred as I felt myself slip into spiritual ecstasy; I lit up the room. The Pastor, who passed from cancer just three weeks later, spoke to me following the service. She said, "I watched you from the pulpit as we read the scripture of the Last Supper. As I observed you, you seemed to emanate a heavenly glow and were radiantly transported into another realm with the angels surrounding you. I am sure you participated in the First Communion."

A few months later, traveling in India at the Mirabai

136

temple, Guruji mentioned a similar appearance, that of a glow and an awareness of a past incarnation related to Mirabia and Krishna.

In extraordinary blessed moments, golden rings activate as special high spiritual memories that amalgamate into present life. At these times, the golden rings become visible to exalt the bearer and those who witness the spiritual manifestation.

Our Lady of Guadalupe, The Image of Jesus Sacred heart, St Francis and other saints are always painted with a full golden halo. We somehow sense it in the enlightened ones. Seers throughout the ages have reported this phenomenon in their recounted descriptions.

Doctoral level golden ring

There are times when more is provided for those committed to doing the work of healing and love with communities and groups of seekers needing profound healing. As I had largely been a one to one healer for many years, I have learned so much about the golden rings as I have delved into the next part of my journey healing larger groups both in person at my events, and on teleconferences.

What I have discovered is the ability to use golden energy to heal is fueled by skill as well as by supply and demand.

About four months ago we started doing a monthly free tele-class called, Your Health Can't Wait. In the call twelve to sixty people would receive a healing on the three glands that help with improving energy and sleep. These glands were the pineal gland, the adrenals and the pancreas. While I was vacationing down on the island of Cozumel, I led one of these calls. We had many sick people on that particular call with life-threatening conditions each were hearing my voice and receiving their first miraculous healing.

When I completed the call and for a day or so later I noticed I was experience extreme fatigue. I had drawn on my own energy for the volume and depth of illness, and my own physical body was depleted.

Since I know this is my calling, I realized there was something I still needed to learn about administering this golden balm to the masses. I took my questions into prayer and rapidly received the answer. I would need to shift the one to one style of healing to a mass style.

Two significant changes for a large group were; I would not run the gold energy into my own human spirit access portal or through my right shoulder, arm and hand, and I would have access to more golden rings.

With the additional golden rings I was easily able to handle large groups. The rings appear for me only when I am working with groups and provide a fervent strength. One of my participants mentioned it felt like a blast furnace coming out of my hand.

Now that you have been excited and awakened to the possibility of using creator God force energy for healing you are likely wondering how, Julie Renee, do you turn your rings on? It is important to raise your energy vibration to that of unconditional love. As I mentioned earlier in the chapter, prayer and contemplation, raising your voice in devotion and chant, communion, and spiritual ritual are the top-notch ways of getting elevated.

I help my Miraculous Healing apprentices over the course of a year to consistently access their rings until it becomes effortless. Then they are able to raise their vibration to love and have their golden rings dependably turn on as needed.

I invite you to come into our community and receive the support needed for the consistent creation of miraculous healing.

If you are unable at this point to access your golden rings, use the universal gold energy for your healing fuel until you are able to take your next step up!

Illumination and the sound of truth provide an extremely high energy match. These are spiritual programs we have provided for students to explore the vibratory rates from 500 to 1000 as the prayers and mantras provided here are resonating at that vibration. As you speak the words and feel the feeling of pure truth, your energy matches the energy of the prayers and mantras for a time.

In the Beginning was the Word, and the Word was with God and the Word was GOD. Genesis

During the afterglow is a fabulous time to embark on your healing projects.

In the immortal sentiments of St. Francis (interpreted by Donavan)

> *If you want your dreams to be*
> *Take your time go slowly*
> *Do a few things, but do them well*
> *Heart felt work grows purely*
>
> *If you want to live life free*
> *Take your time go slowly*
> *Do a few things but do them well*

139

Heart felt work grows truly

Day by day, Stone by stone
Build your secret slowly
Day by day, You'll know too
You'll know heavens door way!

In this chapter you have been gifted a treasured secret. Now that you understand the power you yield, how will your life change? What will you do with this information? What good could you do accessing the secret of the golden rings?

Chapter 7: Human Spirit Access Portal

Angels Call *2003*

Angels call while we are sleeping
Riding through the waves of dreams
Keeping safe our mortal bodies
While we play in astral streams

Beams of light flow from their bodies
Showing us a glimmering mirror
Waking to the world of wonder
Leaves behind all doubt and fear

Ever wonder how everything works in relationship to your spirit and physical body? It is fun to discover the access point and the incredibly well-designed connection of the embodied human to its spirit. When the portal is clear and open, a person is free to live a fully self-expressed and active life. But when the portal is damaged or blocked, a person's experience is that of a life half-lived.

The human spirit access portal to the physical body is located in the back of the head, three-quarters of an inch above where the spine meets the skull. The opening is oblong in shape, an inch and a quarter long and three-quarters of an inch wide.

This human spirit access portal begins to develop in the fetus at an age of 142 days in the womb and continues to develop until full access is obtained. It becomes fully useable around 582 days from the start of development. The human spirit access portal grows until the child reaches about age ten, when the portal has fully developed.

The purpose of this access portal is to provide a doorway for the spirit to readily gain access to the body. Like the unique fingerprint identifying an individual, this entry is unique to each spirit, allowing access only to the spirit who grew and developed the body, that is, the owner of the body.

The blueprint for this access point is maintained in the spiritual body. Growth and development of the body is directed from human spirit. Knowing this gives us strong cues on how to approach healing and repairing the doorway to the human body.

Causes for closures and reduced access

Illness and aging are on the top of the list for "access clogs." As the spirit returns to the body after its separation during sleep and meditation, spiritual "gunk" can be scraped off onto the portal during re-entry. Imagine paraffin wax collecting time after time on the entry of a bottle, as a thin layer left behind. After hundreds of times, the access can become significantly blocked.

Benjamin, Marty, and Bill are mature men who all came to be healed for the first time in a live 'Miraculous Living' event. As the weekend progressed, they connected with each other and started comparing stories. All of them had, at some point, experienced serious brain trauma. They all had the best that Western medicine could have offered them, but little awareness that anything else could be done to improve their situation. The weekend of healing for each of them was very eye-opening.

Before I did the big brain healing, which involved clearing all 'five brains,' (See Chapter 16.) I did a human access portal clearing, opening up each of their portals. What I

142

discovered is each had significant blockages in the portal, preventing easy access to the brain: Benjamin who, thirty-six years prior, had survived a horrendous car accident was 60% blocked; Marty who had been in a coma after a near fatal motorcycle crash eight years prior was 70% blocked; and Bill who had survived the Viet Nam war and had since suffered with PTSD was 54% blocked.

To me, it is amazing that having so little access of their spirits to their bodies that these fellows had any life at all. When the spirit cannot get into the body, the body does not have the proper foundation that allows fulfillment. Imagine a baseball with the nice leather exterior and well sewn treads which only has 30% or 40% of the stuffing inside. A baseball player would be hard pressed to get any 'life' or game out of the ball. This ball is a D-U-D, dud. In the same way, the spirit that is largely absent from the body can wreak all kinds of havoc. Without the spirit being fully embodied, pain can take over, emotions can turn flat and a person may become 'deadpan'.

The extent to which the spirit occupies the body is largely responsible for the health of the body. I once treated a newborn, named Colin. Colin had only partially gotten into his body. After a week in the hospital, he still had a critical lung and heart issue. Medical professionals offered no help other than to say they expected the child to die within a year.

Desperate for assistance Kate remembered me and how much I had helped her during her pregnancy. She called me from her car, asking if I could help her little one. As I greeted her at the door later that day, I saw the eyes of a mother on a mission, weary worn that her precious child was suffering. She told me of the constant little cuts on his heel and all the tears everyone had shed because their little king was in danger.

Together we all went into the healing room, and laid little Colin on the table in his little bunting. Using a hyper state of awareness I felt into him, I could feel he had no access as a spirit to his chest. I was able to resolve the issue in fifteen minutes, after which the child had great heart and lung health function.

What I did was show Colin's spirit how to get into his chest cavity. I held the doorway open for him allowing him to access what was previously inaccessible to his spirit. I also showed him how to 'own' his physical body and maintain the area. Twelve years later I still get Christmas cards with photos of him healthy and strong. He's never since had a challenge with ownership of his chest cavity.

Owning the body: the purpose of the incarnated spirit

After opening the spirit access portal for Marty, Benjamin and Bill, they were now able to own their bodies. After their brain healings, many additional awakenings happened but these would not have been possible if we had not first cleared their human spirit access portals.

In these cases related to injury and limitation in the flexibility and movement of the neck, once the human spirit access portal is open and spirit again owns the body the neck becomes supple and flexible. That was the case with these gentlemen. Years of pain and stiffness dissolved, allowing them to easily turn their necks from side to side.
What is blocking the human spirit access portal? That 'gunk' (that's a technical term, by the way) is residue that comes from the mental body.

Where does the mental residue come from and how do you avoid its negative affects?

Negative group mind or *memes* play a major role in this residue. When the human spirit plays in a field of negative group mind, a build-up of "that which is not true" attaches to the outer edges of the spirit. Imagine playing football in a muddy field and then squeezing through a door that resonates with your energetic signature. The mud has no access to your authentic signature and is left behind on the entryway to the body. Daily residue deposits build to significant levels as a person ages.

Restoring access

The process of cleaning and clearing is a simple one, but will not happen without intervention. Think about a person who doesn't realize they can wash their winter parka. The coat eventually gets filthy and eventually will need to be replaced. In the case of the human access portal, however, since it is the main access point and can't be replaced, it will continue to build up residue until the death of the body.

Cleaning the opening can be done with a number of unique and effective processes.

Five effective ways to restore your human access portal

1. Repetitive action

  a. Connect with the Divine.

  b. Begin repetitive action using violet light from the hands to the human spirit access portal. (Note: violet light emitted from the fingertips will not disturb the person's spirit-body link. It will be comfortable and easy for them to experience.)

Continue this action until you read 100% access.

2. Vacuum

    a. Connect with the Divine.

    b. Set a vacuum energy four inches from the human spirit access portal, behind the head. This technique requires a twirling hand movement to activate the vacuum momentum. Continue until reading is at100% access.

3. Light process

    a. Connect with the Divine.

    b. See the blocked area light up from the inside as pink. This process is done without using hands to emit energy. This is a self-healing technique so the pink originates from the individual who is healing themselves by accessing universal light. Continue amplifying pink light until the residue has moved out of existence.

4. Perfection alignment

    a. Connect with the Divine.

    b. A healer's energy needs to resonate at 1000 or Christ consciousness in order to heal in this way. Raise your energy, if not already there, to Christ consciousness.

    c. Connect with the individual's past experiences or history for a blueprint of perfect access. Restore 100% open access by instilling the former state of perfection over the compromised opening until the opening is 100% clear. This happens rapidly using gold light by using a light pumping action with the right hand. The maximum number of pumps is five for restoration while you're at Christ consciousness energy.

5. Self Restoration

a. Connect with the Divine.

b. Follow the clearing meditation process. (Use one of our program meditations, such as the Definitive Guide to Meditation.)

c. When you have completed the meditation, return to the center of the head and activate the halo over your head. Every individual has golden rings. These allow you to access your miraculous God energy to assist you in healing yourself and others.

If you have never accessed these rings they may be dormant. The Miraculous Living spiritual tools can help activate the rings. If you have difficulty accessing them, it may require having a spiritual master turn them on for you.

Once your golden miracle rings are vibrating, use this gold energy to purify the human spirit access portal opening until the residue is completely cleared.

d. This process may take up to six months of daily clearings to affect a complete restoration of the access point.

This clearing is an important part of many healing procedures in the Miraculous Healing process. Restoring the human spirit and body to wellness is a complex journey. We are asking the body what is needed next. By closely following the Miraculous Healing protocols, we are able to bring lasting health and wellness to those who for years, and even a lifetime, have suffered from illness and poor health.

If this chapter has caught your attention, I would also like to direct you to the chapter on Autism. In that chapter to a very large extent we explore the full impact of human spirit being unable to access the body, and the steps to take towards gaining full access. There is a tremendous amount of detail in this chapter and will give you a great deal of information that you will find useful in fully connecting, filling out and owning your body in the most powerful way.

Chapter 8: Chakras and Nadis

Thanks to the science of ancient times, India has blessed us with the knowledge of both *chakras* and *nadis*. Most folks these days have some notion of chakras, though they will likely not understand their appearance or function. Contrary to common belief, chakras are not seven colorful circles lined up the front of your body. They are surprisingly often colors that not only differ from what most people expect, but also vary from one person to the next. Further, a chakra attunement meditation will rarely help someone attune chakras that are damaged or missing.

In this chapter, we will clear up many misconceptions about the chakras that support your body and how you can access them to heal yourself and others.

The energy systems that develop along with our physical body include the chakras and nadis, the human spirit access portal and the meridians. They exist solely to support the physical organism and cease to exist within ninety minutes of the passing of spirit from body at the end of one's life.

A healthy individual enjoys the energetic support of seven major body chakras as well as numerous lesser chakras (nadis). There are 278 nadis and they support every joint, gland, organ and system making life possible.

Although it is obvious to us that we need to fuel the physical body with food, few realize that without the spiritual energy sourced by this system, their body would no longer function.

My brother, Marty, who was in a serious accident several years ago, is a good example of this. Marty could not feel the bottom of his right foot. Both feet and knee chakras, which play a very important role in healthy feet and the ability to walk, were missing. Once I rebuilt the four missing chakras, the pain in his feet dissipated and he could feel them again. The angry purple scars on his knees disappeared and he began walking with greater ease. Within a couple days of the healing, he was using his legs to carry himself miles on mountain trails, traversing the hills with little effort and enjoying the ache of newly reestablishing leg muscles being used for the first time in years.

If you have a friend in a wheel chair, it is almost certain their feet and knee chakras are gone. If you know someone suffering from a mental illness or dementia, check to see if the sixth chakra is missing.

In the following pages, we'll explore in depth the influence and support the chakras provide for the body. You will also gain a good understanding of the healthy colors in the seven chakras and how to loop energy between two chakras to create strength and healing for an individual.

How chakras develop

When a child is born, they arrive without the appearance of chakras. Newborns come without the presence of chakras having their blueprint beautifully laid out for the perfect timing and development of the energy systems. There are two layers to the aura at the moment of incarnation. Up to this point, the infant has relied entirely on their mother's energy systems to feed and protect them.

By day ten, a child begins to sprout a chakra bud, which is essentially the third chakra. This chakra supports the energy of will. Ever notice how babies can control and even rule their environment? Well, now you know why.

Will, which is the energy of the third chakra, is the first energy system to kick into gear. It is incidentally not about "survival," which is supported by the first chakra. Chakra one will take another six years to develop. Human children are supremely dependent on their parents to help them survive and thrive.

At about thirty days after the birth the child's fourth chakra begins to emerge as a little love bud. Thus, the next level of enchantment begins. The parents, who bonded upon their first glance of their infant, are now truly and completely in love with the little one and will be for a lifetime.

The infant's connection with God through the seventh chakra begins to emerge in the third month. Until then, parents temporarily exist as God for the child.

At around the two-year mark, the child begins to activate the area supporting speech and the fifth chakra bud grows in at the base of the neck. Communication rapidly accelerates as the child's voice is fueled by the energy from the growing fifth chakra. So begins a massive campaign to rapidly increase vocabulary and to understand as the seemingly unending 'why' question becomes part of every experience.

At about the twenty-sixth month, the second chakra appears as a little bud, this chakra supports creativity and motor skills. Ever see a little two-year old going at it with a dance routine or singing in front of a mirror? This action is funded from the second chakra, which provides the energy to develop and use physical creative energy.

At age five, the sixth chakra begins to develop, as does the advent of self-awareness. Prior to this, the process of higher learning is supported by the seventh chakra, which is the

God connection. Once the sixth chakra is fully developed, wisdom and knowledge will be sourced by this chakra.

As the child becomes self-aware, the first chakra, 'survival,' is now necessary. This chakra begins to bud at age six.

Age seven is the dawning of a fully supported and developed chakra system. Think about this stage of development and how the baby qualities fall away around age seven. A child can even appear as a wise sage. This physical change reflects the full development of the chakra system.

Description of the chakras

Chakra 1 is approximately eight inches in length, half an inch at the narrow end, starting about one inch inside the body. It extends down towards the knees and is four inches in circumference on the wide end. Looking at the wide end straight on reveals seven smaller spinning disks that extend into the chakra two inches with three central disks and four exterior disks, appearing like a flower.

Chakras 2-5 appear on the torso of the body in front and back. The narrow end of the funnel shaped energy center is against the surface of the skin, extending out five inches with a four-inch diameter. Chakras two, three, four and five have the seven disks in the same configuration as chakra one. For 98% of humans, chakra four is also like its siblings. For 2.2% of people, individuals we think of as love masters, their fourth chakra can extend seven inches out the front and back of their body and have up to eleven spinning disks with a diameter of six and a half inches.

Chakra 6 appears between the eyebrows and out the back of the head at two and three quarter inches above where the spine meets the skull. It extends six inches out the front and four inches out the back. Discs range from five to fifteen in number with this extraordinary chakra that supports mental activity and brain function.

Chakra 7 is beautifully positioned over our head, extending upwards. It appears like a pillar rather than a cone shape. The top is still larger (eight to nine inches in diameter at its opening) than the bottom of the chakra (four to five inches diameter close to the top of the head). It provides energy of the highest essence for human growth in all areas of physical, emotional, mental and spiritual.

Nature and characteristics of the seven chakras and their role in supporting the human biological systems

Chakra 1

The first chakra provides energy to support survival; this chakra provides the ability to breathe, eat, and have the ability to keep a roof over one's head. It is located at the perineum extending down towards the knees. It provides the best area from which to ground and sources the energy of birth and death. It provides energy to the legs allowing for movement, which again relates to survival, such as being able to run away from the saber tooth tiger as needed.

Chakras can appear with different colors at different times and the colors are neither fixed nor wrong. Let me explain a little further. A chakra may for a time be blue as the energy needed at that time was peace or calm, and then at another time will be green as a person is developing a greater need for consistent health of financial flow. I have gone into detail below to help you understand what a color appearing in a chakra may mean. When you have fulfilled the energy of the lower color say blue, you will move up to a stronger color.

There are articles and books by people that show the first or root chakra (as well as other charkas) just holding or being just one color. Here, however, I present you with a more accurate concept of chakras. The nature of a human is to be creative and constantly changing. Our aura at any given time can be a rainbow of brilliant colors, and at other times a fog of black and grey. So too it is with the chakras. As we change, grow and move through our life, chakras will appear as different colors, become damaged, and even be broken off entirely. The nature of the first chakra is male, characterized by action and providing safety from which to live life.

Best to worst on the color scale for Chakra 1 supporting the nature of survival:

- **Red 100%**: In this chakra red provides capacity to be and to exist. When I see red in Chakra 1, I know this person is a strong yes to life. Red in the root or base chakra provides energy and action.

- **Green 90%**: Green provides a capacity for wealth. It represents slightly less balance in Chakra 1 because the focus is primarily on the aspect of wealth rather than survival. Green is a very good and strong color in the root chakra and can provide happiness.

- **Pink 80%**: Pink in the root chakra provides the capacity for love. This continues to be a good color for this chakra, though the color pink does not line up with the male nature of the chakra, and loses some capacity of strength.

- **Purple 57%**: Purple in the base chakra aligns survival with spirituality. Chakra 1 is weakened by this color.

- **Orange 30%:** Orange is misplaced in the root chakra, although orange is often associated with happiness. That does not apply in this chakra.

- **Yellow 5%**: Yellow is misplaced in this chakra by attempting to bring the higher aspects of God into survival.

- **Blue 3%:** Blue causes stillness in a chakra known for action.

I have worked with individuals with no first chakra and they are unable to walk. When healing a missing chakra, a gold healing with a spinning motion of the right hand will activate the former blueprint of the chakra and eventually restore it. Whenever you are restoring a missing chakra, ask what caused the chakra to go missing. For many, you will find this is a problem on the spiritual timeline. This refers to injuries and accidents that happened prior to coming into this body. You will need to clear these issues for the healthy chakra to take root and stay. You must also remember to reset the program in the energetic body at the completion of the healing just like you would for a DNA reset.

Chakra 1 spins both clockwise and counter clockwise simultaneously.

Chakra 1, the 'survival' chakra, can be missing from birth; 80% of the time this condition is related to trauma in a past life. Illness and accident can also be the causes of the missing or damaged chakra.

Reasons for a missing or damaged Chakra 1 are:
- Cancer
- Cardio-vascular system failure
- Accidents/physical injury
- Decapitation (Chakras 1 and 6)

Chakra 1 fuels much of the physical body, immune system, skeletal system, digestive system, liver, kidney, stomach, spleen, gallbladder and DNA survival programs.

Debbie's Story

Debbie was an amazing woman. She was a literary professor and had raised a healthy strong son. Through apparent illness she lost the ability to walk and was wheel chair bound. When she noticed I was speaking in her community through an article in a spiritual magazine, she enthusiastically came to hear me speak about miracles. The audience was engaged. I felt the palpable shift in the room as I explained reality. You can reverse illness and live a long healthy life. These were good-hearted mid-westerners who were in need of the possibility of something more than what they knew from the medical community.

Debbie approached me after my talk and asked if I could help her. I got a strong yes and began working with her that very week. I discovered many oddities in her energetic make-up. Half her chakras were missing and she only had a partial aura. As we virtually built her from scratch, calling on the Divine Human Blueprint to direct the upgrades, something amazing was happening. Debbie got out of her chair daily and would walk a few steps at a time. At one point she had left her wheel chair and walked forty-seven steps. How awesome is that?!

On that day her son came in to discover what she had done. Instead of being happy to see the evidence of her walking he told her not to do that again. Her friends also wanted her to go back to who they knew her to be in the chair, and alas she retreated to the chair and gave up walking.

After not walking for seventeen years, I can assure you her first steps were much like a toddler. Her atrophied muscles and grown up body were put to the test. If however she had stayed with the program she would be out of her chair and enjoying an upright life.

Group mind can be so powerful it can take you down, and if your mind resonates with group mind, you can altogether lose your miracle.

She has continued to have the chakras I lovingly built her and energy now into her lower legs and feet but will not walk.

Chakra 2

Chakra 2 provides creativity on a physical level, sensuality for both genders, and sexuality for women. The nature of this chakra is receptive with feminine qualities. Fine artists and dancers are well versed in the attributes of this marvelous energy source. The manifestation of this chakra's energy in the world includes the creativity of painters, sculptors, jewelers, dancers, musicians who play instruments, and lovers.

Sensuality for both sexes is fueled by a healthy second chakra, that is, the specific enjoyment of the senses related to human procreation and love making activities. Sensuality supporting sensual pleasures can be improved by the tune up of this chakra and the removal of dark energy in the related glands and organs.

The second chakra supports sexuality for women. Think about the location of the chakra, three inches above the pubic bone, and out the back of the body, four inches up from the base of the spine. Internally, this area is where all her baby making equipment is located. For a woman who has never experienced an orgasm, a tuned and spinning second chakra can be exactly the healing this woman needs. The greatest blessing you could give this woman is to turn the second chakra energy on or up from a still or non-existent chakra.

Chakra 2 supports female reproductive organs, lungs, and muscles.

Best to worst on the color scale for chakra two supporting the nature of physical creativity:

- **Pink 100% women, 60% men:** Pink is the color of divine female love and is the strongest color for most women in expressing creativity on a physical level.

- **Green 100% men and 97% women:** In the second chakra, green is the essential nature of divine male love. Green provides fuel for a healthy, creative life as well as health and vitality.

- **Red 80%:** Red provides passion, intention, enthusiasm and drive. Though the second chakra is, by nature, female and receptive, this color turns the chakra to a male-natured chakra.

- **Purple 50%:** In the second chakra, purple is a fairy color supporting other worldly creativity often found in fine art.

- **Orange 40%:** Orange provides joy to the creative

chakra and a child-like expression. The painter, Chagal, with his free-flowing expressive paintings would have had an orange second chakra providing the proper fuel for his work.

- **Yellow 10%**: Yellow serves as a protection, as the person is veiled from their experience of that area. It provides mental energy to the chakra, stopping the flow of difficult emotions in the second chakra.

- **Blue 1%**: Blue provides blocked access for the owner of the chakra.

On a physical level the second chakra spins counter clockwise in front and clockwise in back. Reasons for a missing second chakra include violent assault on the area, a physical injury in past life, and cancer.

I recently tuned up a fourteen year old girl Angel with chakra 2 problems. Angel had started having 'bladder control' issues a couple years back and even had symptoms of vagina problems. It's unusual in a young person but not unheard of. Without the chakra working in front and back, her female parts as well as her bladder and urethra were functioning at a very low energy. This circumstance also affected her glands and organ which had shifted to a black, death energy (not good at any age, but really upsetting to her and her parents at this extremely young age).

Activating the Divine Human Blueprint and 'creating' a second chakra has and will do a world of good for Angel as we work together to restore 100% function to all the cells fueled by the second chakra.

Chakra 3

The third chakra provides the energy of personal will. It is located an inch above the belly button out the front, and at the waistline out the back. The expression of will is outward, forceful, and male in nature. Accomplishment and fulfillment are supported by having an active and fully-funded will. It is the secret power that dynamic leaders access to drive them to the heights mere mortals find impossible to reach.

I have heard others teach that Chakra 1 is the fuel for male sexual energy. In actuality, a combination of both Chakra 1 at 30% and Chakra 3 at 70% fuels male sexuality. Chakra 1 provides the energy of survival of the species with sexuality for men, and Chakra 3 provides compassion and power. Think about the power a man uses to drive sexuality and love making. It makes sense that will energy from Chakra 3 is an important player in male sexuality.

An individual who suffers from adrenal fatigue will undoubtedly have a crashed third chakra. The third chakra is an important support for physical energy as well as the pancreas and adrenals.

My story of adrenal fatigue

I had adrenal failure during a difficult romantic engagement. Each day was miserable. I was exhausted all the time and unable to enjoy my life. My physician informed me that my adrenals had failed and there was no hope for recovery. I managed to turn that all around, however, and am happy to say that I am remarkably healthier and younger-looking than I was back then. I followed a number of important steps to return to vibrant health.

Did you know that people who lack humor in their lives tend to have less protective immune responses? That means no joy and laughter weakens your system dramatically.

Since adrenal fatigue syndrome is a collapsing of the adrenal response if you are to recover you must reduce all unhealthy stress as an important element in your recovery protocols.

I didn't really recover until my fiancé left. He was always massively stressed out, a pediatrician with a lot of debt and little emotional landscape for fun. But before we separated we really tried to get him into his own happiness. We went to Mexico where I rested on the beach in a lawn chair for hours while he windsurfed. But it just wasn't enough. He was in such a rut of unhappiness and the mindset of lack that when the opportunity for joy and full self-expression came up, he would miss it, dropping back into the grumpy fella he was used to being.

Having tried all avenues, I was convinced that the engagement should end, and that my very life and the enjoyment of the days I had here in paradise depended on it.

I got better. But it took a while. First I grieved. I allowed myself to grieve for all the unexpressed grief of my life. I didn't wallow in it, I courageously welcomed the sadness and as the grief was allowed its voice, my adrenals began to heal. Prayer was a steady partner for me during this very challenging passage.
Not long after, in prayer I asked God to be my business partner and things changed dramatically.

In the Miraculous Healing program you are taught how to restore the light of the cell (Chapter 5) and bring the adrenals back from shriveled raisin-like glands to plump, healthy glands (Chapter 26). To fully recover from adrenal failure and fatigue you must also live life in balance and love and appreciate the little things. Make sure to add laughter into your daily routine. A very, very important part of healing the adrenals is keeping the third chakra on and healthy. You will need to reset the adrenals daily for some time until your systems are able to hold the healthy program.

Chakra 3 is also a key player in outer world accomplishment and wealth building.

Chakra 3 fuels the appendix, adrenals, stomach, and 80% of the cellular body. What that means is that this chakra is providing energy to a majority of your cells. Chakra 3 also provides life force.

Best to worst on the color scale for Chakra 3 supporting the nature of will:

- **Green 100%:** The 'will' chakra, best supported with the color green, provides strength, health, and wealth. Green is the expression of divine male love. The color is particularly useful here where 'will' incorporates the strong and beautiful qualities attributed to divine male love: protection, watching out for the tribe, and providing.

- **Red 90%:** Also a very strong color, red provides force and vitality.

- **Pink 50%:** A will that is monitored and functioning at 50% is pink. It is sometimes extremely helpful for a person wanting to learn how to incorporate love and compassion into will but has been running on force. Once the love lessons are gained, the individual can ascend to green, which is also the aspect of love in its male expression.

- **Purple 40%:** When purple is the color of the will, chakra magic is required to manifest in the world. Will governed by the color purple is creative and less interested in worldly accomplishments.

- **Yellow 20%:** In the third chakra, yellow is mental energy. A person who has yellow here thinks obsessively and believes thinking will shift the circumstances they find themselves in. Mental energy in itself is not an effective fuel for will; it cannot manifest in the physical realm. This is not to be confused with clear focused direction, "As a man thinketh, so shall he live." or "What the mind conceives and believes, it will achieve." These ideas, when effective, represent focus and clarity, directing will and action.

- **Orange 4%:** The color orange brings happiness to will and may restore hope in a will that is said to have been broken.

- **Blue .2%:** A frozen will, unable to move forward, may provide a sense of peace for an individual known to strive and overwork. Blue is stillness and peace and frozen.

Chakra 3 spins in front counter clockwise and in back clock wise.

Missing Chakra 3 can be caused by: crucifixion of some sort in a past life, such as being burned at the stake, being betrayed and killed by followers, and includes being rightly and wrongly killed. A murderer who is crucified can also have Chakra 3 missing. Likewise, a person who did good and was killed off by the church can also be missing the third chakra.

In addition, poison in present lifetime such as radiation or chemical poisoning, attacks the physical body can cause a broken or missing third chakra.

Chakra 4

The nature of the fourth chakra is expansive appreciation and love for yourself, feeling loved and cared for by the universe. You experience the benevolent, divine connection. When love for self is healthy and strong, generosity and love for others flow easily.

The opposite of this is narcissism: self-obsession, selfishness and lack of connection or compassion to a benevolent divinity or awareness of others.

The fourth chakra is located two inches above the sternum in front and directly out the back of the body. Because of the self-love aspect of the healthy chakra, to be full and filled up with love, it is inward in nature and therefore female. True love for self is a 'Jupiter' experience. In other words, having a healthy fourth chakra manifests as the expanding universe for the embodied human spirit into the Divine.

For example, in Buddhism, the essential nature of the goddess, Kuan Yin, is exactly that fourth chakra embodiment, expanded into the Divine. Kuan Yin is a compassionate goddess who is love eternal, permeating beauty and peace to the world. She is entirely complete in herself, capable of loving and overflowing compassion for all others.

The fourth chakra supports the love organs and systems, including the heart, cardio-vascular and circulatory system.

Best to worst on the color scale for Chakra 4 for supporting the nature of love includes:

- **Red 100%:** In the heart chakra, red provides the 'yes' to love and connection. For men and women alike, red is the strongest energy for the heart chakra. Red here is ancient, wired into the embodied human spirit since time began. It is said that love is the most powerful force on the planet and that with love you can move mountains. We create miracles with red as the power of love. When the heart chakra is in this purest form of red, the energy of the human resonates way beyond unconditional love and joy, which is between five and six hundred on the vibrational scale. This kind of love will have us resonate at a vibration of 700 or as an enlightened master.

  Love energy in its red form can mirror to others and create a revolution of compassion. It is potent, and blissful to match.

- **Pink 99%for women and 40% for men:** For a woman, pink in the love chakra evokes nurturing female love. It will expand into her home family and immediate community. For a man, the pink identifies him as soft or gentle, as 'yin' or female energy. Women will read this signal from a man as an inability to provide and protect. He will often find himself as a friend to women, like a girl friend, rather than a lover of the opposite sex.

- **Green 97%for men and 70% for women**: For a man, green provides activation for his loving, divine self. His nature to protect and provide will rule his love interaction. For a woman, green often provides 'yang' or male energy that brings balanced love.

- **Peach 91%:** This is the color of love and happiness combined a fun and nurturing version of healthy heart chakra.

- **Orange 85%:** The color orange in the heart chakra provides happiness in the love center. The individual experiences love from self-actualization and self-affinity rather than a lover's companionship.

- **Blue 24%:** Variations of blue provide peace and stillness to the fourth chakra. These are good for a peacemaker, but not good for long-term love and companionship.

- **Yellow 20%:** Yellow provides the process of thought or mental energy to the heart, preventing the outflow of unconditional love. The wisdom of the 'heart brain' is in the neurons of the heart, amplifying love, rather than strategizing and over thinking. Yellow in the heart shows us the nature of this individual is fear.

- **Purple 10%:** Purple in the fourth chakra provides a spiritual essence in the expression of love. The experience of love is physical in nature. Therefore when one embodied human spirit relates to another, purple in the fourth chakra directs an individual away from the experience of fully embodied love.

Chakra 4 spins counter-clockwise in front and spins clockwise in back.
The heart chakra can be broken. When this happens, a person can exist but not live a quality life without a heart chakra. In some cases they can commit spiritual offenses or become a morally bad or even an evil person.

You can expand the heart energy and raise the function of the heart chakra to its highest energetic delivery by blessing and appreciating all the wonderful people in your life, and by getting off the blaming and unhappy with others track.

Love the Ones You're With 1995

The answers are not in the questions you ask.
Sense cannot be made of them.
You must ask new questions.
Till the answers bring you
Divine peace and contentment

Why hope, when all you need awaits your call?
Why grieve when life has given you more than your share?

Be happy with the simple things
The tender touch of a loved one as you sleep
The caress of misty rain on your cheek and
the call of the ocean waves beckoning you to dance

I am not convinced you have one reason, at this moment
To feel anything other than ecstasy unless you will it so

Meditate on the petals of an orchid, or the spry dandelion
Breath in the salty ocean air.
Thank the heavens for the stars it shares with you, and
Love the ones you're with.

Chakra 5

The fifth chakra is found at the base of the neck extending out from the hollow of the throat in front and extending out from the spine at the top of the torso in back. It provides fueling for all activities related to communication. It is the sibling to the second chakra in the area of communication, with chakra two providing creativity related to the body and chakra five providing creativity related to the mind.

Speech and language is fueled by this chakra. The fifth chakra supports activities such as journaling, book writing, intimate communication and speaking by great orators.

The area it fuels is unique in shape, forming a chalice. The lower part of the goblet is the neck, moving upwards, it then bows outward to include the ears, nose and mouth. The fifth chakra primarily delivers necessary energy for the proper fueling and running of the hormonal system.

The fifth chakra is female in nature: creativity flows from the inside out, providing a way for the manifestation of creativity of the internal landscape to be present and palpable to the outer world. For example, the action of writing these ideas down in book form is fueled by the fifth chakra.

Best to worst on the color scale for chakra five to support the nature of communication:

- **Pink for 100% women and 40% for men:** Communication for a woman at its strongest is delivered from the space of nurturing and love. Pink provides for the amplification of love; it is the divine expression of female love. If a man wants to specifically lead women and match their energy to relay his communications to them, he would choose to have pink in the fifth chakra. A stronger choice for a man is green.

- **Green 100% for men and 90% for women:**For a man, green provides divine male love and healing in his communication chakra. For a man to align with his masculine nature using the direction of green/love is the highest expression of communication for a man. For a woman, green provides balance in her communication. She will experience the yin-yang balance of her female nature with her assertive self.

By now you may notice a pattern emerging in the area of colors best used for men and women. A woman can more easily access the male nature because she is wired with all the male programs in her endocrine system. A woman can implement colors specifically good for a man to use with no real loss in the potency of her chakra energy. A man, however, does not have the same access to the female hormonal body with all the added functions a woman experiences in her symphony of hormones. He will therefore not have such ease and success in using female colors for his chakra journey.

- **Orange 90%:** Communication fueled by happiness resonates as potent and pleasurable to receive.

- **Blue 70%:** Peace and stillness are good attributes for a peacemaker to direct and embody. This aids in effecting change, for example, in a corporation or country.

- **Yellow 30%:** Mental energy loaded with facts and statistics can, on occasion, be useful. However, without love or happiness the information relayed will generally fall on deaf ears.

- **Purple 20%:** In the chakra of communication, purple provides religious fervor. Joel Osteen is a good example of the use of purple in his communication chakra.

- **Red 0.5%:** Red in the chakra of communication is inflammatory. I know a woman born in Ireland who communicates from red. She is often in battle and aggression with her relatives and friends. Real friendship with a person whose communication is fueled by red is virtually impossible.

Chakra 5 spins clockwise in front and spins both clockwise and counter-clockwise in back.

A missing fifth chakra can be caused by cancer, injury and assault.

Great vocalists are a perfect example of the fifth chakra being used to its highest and best expression.

Chakra 6

The sixth chakra is often referred to as the third eye or ajana chakra. It provides the connection and access of human spirit to human body. It also provides energy to the human brain and center of head or golden temple of silence. This is sometimes referred to as the seat of the soul, for the sake of accuracy we will say 'seat of human spirit' or 'control center.'

The sixth chakra projects out from above the bridge of the nose centered between the eyes in front and three inches above where the spine meets the skull in back. It provides access for inner vision. Female in nature, the brow chakra is inward focused.

Best to worst on the color scale for chakra six to support the nature of spirit-body union:

- **Blue 100%:** Blue as eternal peace is the highest expression of the brow center. Blues, especially in the deep rich colors, provide the stillness from which to observe life and choose wisely. In stillness, we come to know our true self as we discover our essential nature and ascend to enlightenment. Meditation amplifies and quickens this spiritual progression. In the Siddha yoga tradition, there is a practice known as the blue pearl meditation.

- **Green 98%:** Green provides vitality in the sixth chakra.

- **Purple 80%:** Purple provides a departure from the physical to a type of regality. An Indian prince I knew well had this purple in his third eye. Purple provided greatness and an outer identification, which is something you might expect from a leader who must make decisions not only for him or her but also for the masses.

- **Yellow 60%:** Yellow provides the developmental energy of wisdom. Keep in mind, yellow found in this space represents a spiritual aspirant developing wisdom. Fully embodied wisdom is royal blue.

- **Pink 60% for women and 50% for men:** Pink provides essential knowledge related to love wisdom. This is also a color that provides a place from which to learn and grow in love wisdom. Pink, love wisdom, is female in nature. (We'll be going deep into love wisdom in the upcoming book *The Seven Stages of Love*.)

- **Orange 20%:** Orange provides a happy mindlessness. It does reflect an unhealthy mind, one out of balance at the very least, and is an indication of dementia.

- **Red 4%:** Red provides an irritable environment. It is rajasic energy in high gear. Mental illness is likely.

Chakra 6 spins counter-clockwise in front and spins both directions in back.

Causes for damaged or missing chakras are injury, brain illness and dementia.

If the sixth chakra is off or missing the person you are looking at is in trouble and needs help immediately. With the sixth chakra off you will not have access to your control center or seat of spirit in the center of the head. Others will choose their life for them, and many times there is a possessions of evil spirits or entities. Dementia and mental illness also fall into this very problematic circumstance.

If on the other hand you have a sixth chakra on and spinning in front and back you will likely meditate and sleep easily as well as feel you are in charge and in the center of your life. You may not always be happy or blissed out but you will be an active creator in your life.

Chakra 7

The seventh chakra provides for direct access to our high self and God - our higher power. The seventh chakra is beautifully positioned over our head and is the only chakra extending upwards. It has both male and female qualities, as it is both receptive and giving.

The seventh chakra appears slightly different then the other six chakras; it appears more pillar-like than cone shaped. Although the seventh chakra does not actually come in contact with the human physical body, it provides energy of the highest essence for human growth in all areas of physical, emotional, mental and spiritual health and vitality. Its energy fuels brain function related to proper body chemistry.

Maria's Story

I worked with a thirty-nine year old woman, Maria, who had a black crown chakra. Knowledge of the Divine could not reach her. In addition all her chakras were grey and black. This was the result of the suicide of her husband eighteen months prior, with whom she was very much in love.

Maria found me through a mutual friend Alice. All of Maria's friends were extremely concerned for her. It seemed she was not present to her life, and was walking around in a trance-like dark haze. The absence of the seventh chakra represented the internal problem Maria was struggling with. In Her mind she had resolved the suicide by thinking; "God was Dead".

Her mother had moved in with Maria, as she could no longer cope with life or with her tiny precious toddler. When we started working together Maria woke up! Just by restoring the chakras and aura to bright colors, she awoke from the dream of death. She literally had been like one of the walking dead, with little memory of life for all those months. A veil lifted, the lights came on and she was able to return to her life.

Best to worst on the color scale for chakra seven to support the nature of divine connection:

173

- **Gold100%:** Gold provides the match of the Divine frequency.

- **Yellow 70%:** Yellow provides a close match to the Divine frequency. Often yellow is the place-holder or stepping stone to the ultimate match of gold. Yellow provides access to spiritual knowledge, where gold is the experience of spiritual wisdom.

- **Green 50%:** I occasionally see light green in the crown chakra. Light green provides connection to the Divine with no experience of the connection.

- **Pink 50%: for women and 30% for men:**For women, pink provides love in the area of connection to the divine with no experience of the connection. For men, pink provides loss of connection without anger. This essentially means being okay about being disconnected from Source.

- **Orange 40%:** Provides the experience of replacing the connection with the Divine with either an attachment to something that is not divine or any addiction.

- **Purple 20%:** Purple provides lost connection. It provides confusion.

- **Red .3%:** Provides rajasic (spiritual irritability) with no experience of connection to high self or the Divine.

- **Blue:** Does not appear here.

Chakra 7 spins in both directions. I have not seen a missing or broken seventh chakra.

The wise elder wisdom you are receiving while absorbing the content of this book will allow you to assist yourself and the ones you love and with whom you work to heal and awaken.

Looping Techniques

I have occasionally used looping techniques to assist in improving a situation. Imagine an energy loop traveling out the front of one chakra and entering a second chakra coming out the back of the body and looping up to the chakra you started with. The energy, once set in motion, would continue to flow in that loop for several minutes as you invite the merging energies of the chakras to support and enhance each other and the area of healing.

Here are a just a few of the hundreds of combinations possible;

- **One and three:** Increase power, strength and physical survival.

- **Two and five:** Increase and amplify creativity.

- **Two and four:** Improve access to love, compassion, tenderness, sensuality and life force.

- **One and two:** Improved connection with life on planet earth.

- **One and four:** Provides a potential for healing a traumatic relationship with a parent in early childhood. Increases sense of love and loving.

- **Five and Six:** Provides an integration of language and higher wisdom. Especially good for foot in mouth disease. I use this when language does not match higher knowing.

- **Six and Seven:** Human and God wisdom, improves the quality of thinking. Improves the awareness of connection with the Divine.

Nadis

According to the Yogic tradition there are many more energy centers in the physical body. There are more then 270 such energy sources, including knees, feet, hands, nipples, ears, which we address in this chapter.

Hand nadis or chakras

Hand chakras are found on the palm of the hand. They extend out about one and three quarter inches and have more of a tubular shape. They are slightly above the skin in the center of the palm quarter inch round and three quarters of an inch round at the outer part.

Hand chakras are vitally important and if you are aware of their function and purpose these chakras are powerful and useful tools. The right hand provides the gift of energy transmission. Energy flows out of this center. The left hand provides the gift of receiving and provides a perfect environment for reading or understanding what is in front of the hand or the information you are receiving while healing someone. With training, you can use both hands for either function.

One of the special qualities of the hand chakras used during healing is that you can join forces with healing energies beyond your own skill and capability. An example of this is a Christ-force healing. By opening your hand chakras, you can allow Christ energy into the back of the palm which then flows through the palm and out. You have now amplified your energy significantly.

If you choose to experiment with this, be sure to clear your hands prior to and after each healing. You must know the energy that you are bringing in and make sure that the energy is completely cleared from your hands each and every time.

You may be wondering how can I effectively clear the hand chakra? Imagine the palm of the hand has a camera lens in it. This lens opens and shuts when there is need. What if however when the lens were open some refuse got stuck in the lens causing it to be permanently partially open, and now collecting gunk longingly as it is stuck open.

- Make a conscious choice to close the two 'lens like' chakras on your right and left hands.
- Now do the Rose Bomb procedure until there is no kinesiology reading that reveals a disruption.

Special note * If this is not done, you run the risk of attracting energies that are foreign to you, confusing your muscle testing/kinesiology readings.

Knee chakras or nadis

Knee chakras are amazing. The metaphoric power of the knees is the ability to honor yourself, to really lovingly presence yourself.

The Christians from olden times knew the honor of self and the connection of the knees for kneeling in prayer. Pray daily on your knees and begin to observe your knee chakras turn into golden crowns. There was a point where I was kneeling in prayer every day and my knees became luminous. The legend is that you begin to wear your heavenly crowns here on earth! How cool is that!

When you create the time to pray you are honoring you own divinity. Making time for connection with God is elevating your energy and feeding you nourishing manna from the heavenly realms. Everyone is invited to pray, but who actually takes the time to really worship and celebrate Divine God connection. It is fine to come with problems for assistance, but the power of prayer is in the celebration of all that is good and right. When you can access in your being the very 'GLORY' then, my friend, you know God.

Feet chakras or nadis

Your feet provide an amazing map for the entire workings of the body. The bottoms of the feet provide the path to your soul understanding. Being disconnected from your feet can cause endless challenges. Just like the hands, where you can open the chakras for energy access, the feet chakras can be opened to access earth energy. This provides connection and grounding. Normally the right side is assertive while the left side is receptive. However, the feet chakras, located in the soft part of the foot towards the heel, are both receptive. They are three inches in length, circular, and do not spin.

All of our meditations have the cues to open the feet chakras to earth energy and bring earth energy up through the feet ankles shins and calves, knees, thighs, through the hips and down the grounding cord.

Just as I described in the hand chakra section, the feet chakras have a 'camera lens' quality to them where they can be opened. Opening to earth energy grounds and reconnects you with this planet.

Nipple nadis

I mention nipple nadis as they are the energy feed for our incoming generation. They continue to fortify the infant with their mother's energy. They are tiny, only three quarters of an inch and are small replicas of the body chakras. They are an eighth of an inch in diameter at the nipple to three eighths of an inch in diameter away from the body. Nursing your newborn is the only way your mother chakra energy is transferred to the baby for up to about eight months.

Ear nadis

Ear nadis are tubular in shape, one and a half inches in length, starting at the opening of the ear and extending out. They help with ear function, such as balance, and hearing.

Table 8-1 Summary of Chakra Colors

Chakra	1	2	3	4	5	6	7
Fuels	Survival	Physical Creativity	Will	Love	Commun-ication	Spirit-Body	Divine Access
	Red 100%	Pink 100% w	Green 100%	Red 100%	Pink 100% w	Blue 100%	Gold 100%
	Green 90%	Pink 60% m	Red 90%	Pink 99% w	Pink 40% m	Green 98%	Yellow 70%
	Pink 80%	Green 100% m	Pink 50%	Pink 40% m	Green 100% m	Purple 80%	Green 50%
	Purple 57%	Green 97% w	Purple 40%	Green 97% m	Green 90% w	Yellow 60%	Pink 50% w
	Orange 30%	Red 80%	Yellow 20%	Green 70% w	Orange 905	Pink 60% w	Pink 30% m
	Yellow 5%	Purple 50%	Orange 4%	Peach 91%	Blue 70%	Pink 50% m	Orange 40%
	Blue 3%	Orange 40%	Blue 0.2%	Orange 95%	Yellow 30%	Orange 20%	Purple 20%
		Yellow 10%		Blue 24%	Purple 20%	Red 4%	Red 0.3%
		Blue 1%		Yellow 20%	Red 0.5%		Blue never
				Purple 10%			

180

Chapter 9: Divine Connection

One
I remember a time
When time was not
When all that was
Was what could not be
When who was All
And I was We.

When I existed as We
We were ablaze
The fire was power
The light was life
And I was not
Alone did not exist

But some part of the We broke off
And throwing us out of balance
No longer a single living cell
We scattered in many directions

The Divine connection is the state of being where you and the Divine, whatever that means to you, exists in a free flowing connection. Your prayers, meditation and positive attitude nurture your connection to the Divine. It is oneness at its best.

In contrast, your Divine connection is weakened by negative conversations and attitudes that resemble an atheist mindset, essentially not believing miracles are possible for you or anyone else.

Your Divine connection occurs naturally; everyone is born

with this connection intact. Only you can break your connection with the Divine. You have to decide to sever the connection to have it unhooked. One of the reasons an individual chooses to disconnect from the Divine is the set of circumstances around their upbringing.

As a child grows, the emotional brain is developing. If their parent or guardian is particularly abusive or harmful, the child can develop a mindset where they believe there is no God and no hope. Ninety-nine percent of the time this detachment occurs prior to age ten. About three percent of humans are currently detached from their Divine connection.

At age twenty-five I disconnected from the Divine and lived as if God were dead for three years. Wow, you might wonder, how could a devout woman who prays all the time disconnect. Sometimes God says no, and in the no there is no 'knowing'.

The years leading up to this point were some of the most difficult in my life. I had married a man committed to drinking, among other things. After seven years of marriage, much of which was unhappy, trying to survive it and provide some happiness for my little ones, I finally broke into pieces. I developed terminal cancer, and was in a relationship most would consider abusive. I was sick, tired, depressed and hopeless. I was in and out of hospitals and had been in a mental health hospital struggling with my emotions and severe depression.

Finally the doctors told me they would not allow me to return home because they feared for my death. I had to find a place to live and learn to live away from my husband and the stressors of an unhealthy relationship. I did this. This was the hardest thing I had ever done up to that point. I was

182

alone in the world. I wanted very much to have my children with me and fought for custody. However, I lost in divorce court.

I had never considered life without my children, and it was unbearable. As I look back, I understand the court's decision. I was so young and so very sick, how could the judge have made any other decision?

I was in unbearable pain. My prayers had fallen on deaf ears and so God must be d-e-a-d?

This was most assuredly my 'dark night of the soul'. I attended college and cried all day long. My solace was Mr. Rogers on the TV at my lunch break. I returned home to have a meal and catch soothing Mr. Rogers. I guess he held the comforting God space until I could return to my direct connection with the Divine.

Life happens. Bad things happen to really good people and we learn and grow and take our spiritual steps out of these challenges. I do believe all the hardship in my life had purpose and formed me into the woman I am today. I am grateful for all the challenges. If I had physically raised my three children, I would not be now doing the work in the world I came to do, so it was a necessary severing of ties.

One day I had had enough, I missed my connection and as if I had awoken from a dream, I was back in the loving arms of Father God. Life for me is a million times better with the connection than without. If you have gone through this experience you will understand what I am talking about.

People whose Divine connection is severed will not see the value of reconnecting the link. Their energy vibration will typically be under a hundred and the way they view the world is from a lower, darker perspective.

If you don't feel your connection, but have a desire to be connected, you can activate the link with some very simple steps.

*"**Know** that it is already there,*
That you are bringing this connection back into the light."

This is easier than you think.

Three Simple Steps to Improving Your Divine Connection

1. Sit quietly and breathe in pink and gold energy deeply, breathe out and use your breath as signal to your body that it is time to relax.
2. Imagine yourself as a spirit, now seated in the center of your head.
3. Send a gold cord up from the center of head to the Divine. Imagine it connecting in with the Divine.

Congratulations you are connected!

Just in case you are struggling with an external block, say, some negative energy source outside you:

- Imagine a new connection cord pops over the old one and causes the older cord to disappear. Do this five times.
- Each time, you replace the old cord with a new golden cord the former cord will disappear.
- Once you have activated the golden cord linking the center of head to the Divine five times, you will be connected.

184

The brightest parts became
The stars and planets
Those parts of the We those were small
Became less brilliant
Because we could not access All
Of the light of the We

We became confused in the spinning off
We became the many
We forgot the we

The self
The sparkle
The glimmer
Became encompassed by a mass
It had weight
It moved, thought and felt

It responded to the temporary
The unreal came to be
The unquestioned truth
Though we all knew it was a lie

What could we do?

Repetition for Clearing Energy

Repetition is one of the most consistent and effective ways to clear unwanted energy. Think about it: the Catholic rosary is the repetition of a prayer fifty-three times and the Yogic mantras are the repetition of a mantra 108 times. The Buddhist, Sikhs, Sufis and virtually all major religious and spiritual groups have their own unique prayers for clearing.

If you would like to experience this process in a prayer

format, I have created *Illumination*, an advanced form of the Christ/Mary-inspired rosary. This rosary will raise your energetic signature, which supports the creation of miracles.

Divine connection can also be restored through reading scripture, especially high and inspiring passages. Such passages include the yogic sutras of Patanjali or the numerous Biblical passages related to love.

> *Beloved let us love one another,*
> *For love is of God and everyone who loveth,*
> *Is born of God and knoweth God*
> *He that loveth not, knoweth not God*
> *For God Is Love.*
> *Beloved let us love one another.*
> **1 John 4:7&8**

If your Divine connection is broken, you have willingly chosen to turn away from it in this life or in a past life. For example, I noticed a large tattoo on a man's forearm in the Las Vegas airport the other day, proclaiming him a 'bad ass.' Choosing to deliberately disconnect and then seal that concept into his cellular body by announcing it to everyone, he is creating a group meme or group mindset. He is broadcasting to all the folks that come in contact with him that he is "tough, doesn't need anyone. He rules his bad ass kingdom, so look out."

He might have thought it was super cool when he had the tattoo imbedded in his skin. However, if the intention is to strengthen the Divine connection, my suggestion is to let that concept go, perhaps even remove the tattoo. Connecting with lower vibration levels and a preoccupation with bad, satanic, and demonic concepts will block a person from the blissful, Divine connection.

In the last chapter we ended with the concept of GLORY. This is what you shared when you are connected and actively accessing your connection. So many people have the connection but never open the door. Which one are you? When was the last time you connected in a deep way to the Divine? When would 'now' be a good time to get connected?

I lacked in spark
My flame grew dangerously small
I longed for the fire of the We
The time of no time
When all that was was not
And nothing was real

I longed for the We
The blaze and the brilliance
The completion.

There is a new
A beingness
A brightness
Found from the we

I in myself
Encompassed by the mass
Lacking in spark
Have glimpsed at the new

It is purest light
Brightest love
The new is the ancient revealed

It is a glimmer of the Omni
It is the remembrance of the We
Truth is that which is unreal

I am and exist truly in the We
Only in my lack of existence
Am I free to be what is not.

Chapter 10: Spiritual Health

I remember a time when there was no
speaking
When sound was outside the realm

The self was still
There was no separation from the great We
We heard the vibrations of brilliance
We heard the voice of love
Our self responded to the beckoning

A time when Real was All
And manifest was illusion

The We knew the self fully
The self knew the We

In this chapter we explore how you can take care of your spiritual body and introduce you to the five intervals of health.

Have you ever wondered why, in the Old Testament, that individuals are said to have lived to seven hundred years or more? When you heard that as a child, what did you think? Is there any evidence in your world that you would live past eighty or ninety years old?

These are questions many have pondered as children, then were told by their teachers it was just a metaphor or time was 'different' then. By being told this it put the wonderful notion of life extension, real authentic longevity to rest never to be considered again.

Why are most human beings not living youthful lives into their fifties, sixties, seventies and beyond?

Longevity blockers

Here are the longevity blockers as well as the path to safety out of the troubled waters that lead to early death.

1. Group Mind

A powerfully strong agreement exists among you and your tribe around early death. Isolationists have attempted to break the pull of group mind by separating themselves from the "virus." Listen how people reference their longevity and their expectations of the future. Notice how you might even reference yourself; "I'm getting old...."

Overcoming a meme (group mind) or a miasm (group virus) is simple enough. It involves intentionally pumping the gold energy towards the group mind or miasm. This clears the program leaving you free to clear your unhealthy references to aging.

There are religious group mind programs that are very strong. For example "My reward is not here on earth, but in heaven." So if you were going through a difficult passage, you might begin to embrace the idea that life on earth is difficult and something to get through. You might think, I will be rewarded in the afterlife and the afterlife is Nirvana. The mind would match up with the hypnotic group mind that is program into the minds of Judo-Christians of death bring your reward and your escape from this hell on earth.

Another approach to understanding challenges is to think of

them as opportunities you set up for yourself prior to coming into this body for personal growth, awareness and even the path to enlightenment and ascension. When a challenge comes to you, embrace the opportunity to learn and grow. Do not resist it, allow it to hone down your ruff edges, as you become your multifaceted diamond self. Every problem is an opportunity to be and become more authentically you. Celebrate your challenges and see the ease in which you traverse your life.

Suicide and Sin

Last year a husband of an acquaintance committed suicide. For some reason, with group mind embedded in his thoughts and essence he decided that death was a better place. He saw the severing of his body from spirit offered him the elusive peace he imagined. This is definitely group mind at play. What if you knew that when you left your body as a spirit the final time, you would be in the exact same place as when you were in your body? So, if you were very happy in love with your life then in your afterlife you would experience something much like that; a wonderful heavenly paradise.

There is this funny misconception of what sin is. Sin is not a wrong you do and something held in an accounting with God or St. Peter at the pearly gates. You answer to no one, except yourself when you do a wrong. Living a good life, a life a of contribution where you learn from your mistakes and adapt and adjust to better more loving ways of being, is a true and proper understanding of growing from sin. The word 'sin' is so charged that you might even have a hard time reading it. You might be thinking, "Why is she addressing this here?" I'm addressing it because a sin is something you do against yourself, not God. It is harm you do to yourself, to your spirit, to your essence.

When a person takes their own life they are doing harm to themselves. They did not give themselves the time or the love, or the connection to God to resolve their problems so they could experience the joy, the paradise that is here on earth. They may have sinned, but not against God. Once you are on the other side you cannot repair what has manifested in this earthly plane. You must come back again and face those challenges yet again.

Coming back to our concept of group mind; James plugged into an idea that life was better out of body. What he discovered on the other side was that he was still in a terrible fix, but no longer had the body to correct the issues. His wife, unable to hear or feel him, retreated into grief and pulled away from her community to bear the shame and loss alone. None of this was better for James.

2. Global depression, lack of self-purpose and mission

Have you ever heard retirement community 'seniors' having the conversation of, "being in God's waiting room"? They go there to hang out and get ready to move out of their bodies. If a husband passes, a few weeks later the wife will pass, and before you know it her best friend has also made her transition. There is no sense of future or vitality or joy, just a certain ending.

Just yesterday Jenny told me of someone who received the diagnosis of pancreatic cancer a few weeks back, and had already passed. Jenny said her friend just gave up, hopeless and without mission or purpose they just let the body die.

I am aware that pancreatic cancer is the worst of the worst when it comes to life threatening diseases. However the apathy and the willingness to let go is a sign of this global depression.

192

When facing death I have firmly called upon my strong will and desire to fulfill my legacy with humanity to survive the many brushes with death. My sense of purpose at first was fueled by the desire to see my children grow up. I had a sense of something more to live for even though I didn't yet have it formulated.

It was in an EST meeting (now called the Landmark Forum) that the concept of living one hundred and fifty years was introduced into my consciousness. We did an exercise where we imagined, with focus and intention, what we could do to create change in the world.

The first ideas we wrote in our journal were in response to the following question:
"In the next year with, focused concentration, what could you do to effect change in the world?"
"What if you had 2 years?"
"5 Years?"
"10 years?"
"25 years?"
"50 years?"
"75 years?"

I saw myself helping blast apart the global depression and shifting the notion that there's not enough time to make a change, so why try? I saw myself creating bigger and bigger legacies to create and live into.

Finally they asked us to imagine, "You now have one hundred and fifty years to leave your legacy. With focus and intention what could you do to create change in the world?"

I knew instantly that for me it was about global depression being completely banished. I saw myself living large with my intentions, creating huge pictures of contribution and global change for good."

This experience was an opening for me to break out of the unconscious trance that had affected me my whole life. What was interesting was, I didn't even know it was there. It just was. Everyone was thinking the same thing. We thought that life was short and we would not have enough time to really make a difference. I too saw that, until I woke up. All of the sudden it was no longer my reality, just a lie into which I had been lulled.

Are you ready to wake up with me? What could you do if you knew you had another hundred and fifty years, with focus and concentration, to make the world a better place?

Here are a few ways you can address this global depression:

- Plan not to retire from life until you are 500 - 600 years old.

This means in essence, continue to be alive and a contributor to life and the world. Retiring is this way of stepping away from activity to rest. To retire from dinner is to leave the meal and go to rest. But with regular retirement there is no returning to life. Have purpose and meaning in every day here on earth.

- Live a life of contribution and gratitude.

When you are busy appreciating all the wonder and magnificence in this life and on this Garden of Eden planet, you are aligning yourself with the highest expression a human can experience. Please don't be fooled into thinking you are there when you are using your problems and dramas over and over again to prove that you can turn lemons into lemonade. Stop the drama wheel now. Step away from relationships and experiences that drop you down to the battles of the lower emotional world.

I know a gal who has endless battles with infinite problems. She keeps them brewing on a back burner, telling people about them over and over again.

Listen to me if you are like her**, this will not raise your energy vibration**. It is more like a gambler shooting craps with a hopeful wish that something good might come from the muddle of life, and hey once in a while it does.

Awaken grateful for your good health and your good home and the people in your life who love you and play with you. Even if you feel like some of this is a stretch, do it anyway. If you are alive, even if you are very sick you have something to be grateful for.

- Learn from the masters and continue to create new dreams to fulfill. Boredom with life is most assuredly inviting the Grim Reaper to take your life and vibrancy.

Create plans that are tangible. Forget the 'pie in the sky' dreams for now. I want you to be able to understand how you will get from here to there, and by working backwards from the future dream fulfilled to the present day, you will uncover your path to greatness.

When I lead my *Accelerate Wealth from the Inside Out* program during the first few days, I often notice that my students are working pie in the sky dreams. With the help of some amazing tools students quickly learn how to get their energetic body vibing with the vision, and also the physical tools and circumstances clarify for fully embodied grounded manifestation.

3. External Toxins

Toxins on the earthy plane run rampant. Do your best to live in a clean space and practice spiritual cleansing through meditation, especially while traveling in places that are less than desirable. Here are a few examples of how you can help clean up your toxic environment:

- **Nutrition:** Purchase organic food as much as possible. I suggest you measure the life force of your food with the technique of kinesiology/muscle testing to see if the food registers beneficial enough to truly nurture your body. Research which food and drink is best for you, and then follow through in order to support your vibrant health. Eat foods that are kind to your body and avoid ingesting things that damage your cells, such as chemicals, additives, prescription and non-prescription drugs, GMO foods, etc. In addition, you can add air and water filters to your healthy lifestyle.

- **Sound:** Harmful sounds, such as alarms and bad frequency music, can damage and degrade the cells. Listen to the sounds in the woods such as a bird song, (especially in Spring) the beauty of a symphony or a children's chorus. Sound can do wonders for maintaining the vibrancy and light of cells.

- **Lighting:** Indoor lighting can be harmful to the skin and brain. Choose natural light where possible and healthy lighting choices that can enrich your experience.

4. DNA and Family Programs

When claiming longevity as your divine path you will need to clear away family illness patterns and life span programs. Our Miraculous Living year-long programs and our three-day healing weekend courses provide the recipe for clearing DNA. On a very simplistic level I will explain this process.

1. Imagine you are able to see a DNA strand stretched out in front of you on a view screen. This is a special DNA strand from one of your stem cells.

2. Imagine you are seeing the programming for dying young. Have it show up as black dots on the DNA.

3. Imagine using a golden vacuum cleaner to vacuum up all the darkness.

4. Once you have cleared the black dots see the Divine Human Blueprint restore positive programs for your long life.

5. Pulse gold through the strand.

6. Imagine it coils back up into the stem cell. Have the healthy, improved DNA strand mirror and reflect its healthy state to all the rest of the DNA in the body by pumping gold energy into the stem cell.

7. Pump gold energy into the family DNA bubble to release yourself from the group programming.

9. Finally, go to the baseline program (to which your body resets every morning) as you wake from rest, and shift the reset to that of longevity by again pumping gold into the DNA.

Healthy Bright Miraculous System

Everyone has heard of the aura and the chakras, and yet there are many less-known aspects of the spiritual body and the miraculous system, which, when tuned brightly and to a hundred percent, allow us to live a miraculous life

Additional spiritual body attunements of longevity include brightening the soul/spirit and keeping a life force vibrant and functioning at a hundred percent. The place where spirit and body connect is at the back of your head, one inch above where the spine meets the skull. This channel often becomes restricted, and opening it can prove very, very valuable. To learn the steps to clearing the human access portal.

1. Light of Cell

The final step for Cellular Neo-Genesis is working with the light of cell. Just as the spirit has a body, the cells also have a light. It is like a mini spirit that animates and allows the cells to regenerate. See Chapter 5.

2. Your Halo

The golden rings over your head provide the space of creating miracles. They support you in accessing your creator God force energy. See Chapter 6.

Miraculous Healing Protocols

This book is the guide to healing in the miraculous system using kinesiology (muscle testing) to hone in on the exact order and locations of healings. As you begin, it will feel foreign to you, but like all things new you will discover

198

over a short time that the process becomes effortless and simple.

I suggest you not attempt healings unless you have gotten yourself in a high vibration first. Another important part of caring for your own body while caring for others is to do specific meditations available for miraculous living. I recommend three meditations for daily practice especially if you are healing others.

1. The Definitive Guide to Meditation
This is the basic guide to running energy, clearing systems. It is a great tune in and tune up for vitality gets you flowing in vibrant health. (You can find this and other meditations at www.JulieRenee.com under the meditations tab.)

2. From Fatigued to Fabulous Meditation
This was created for folks who tend to run a lot of stress through their adrenals and nervous system. It is a wonderful refreshing and healing meditation. If you want to feel good all over this may be your answer, especially if you have anxiety or are over-stimulating your nervous system. This meditation will help you find your way back to joy. (Free at www.miraculouslivingtoday.com)

3. Brilliant Brain Meditation
This is an extraordinary tune up for the brain so that your five brains can run on all cylinders, clear and focused for your day. It's time to re-activate the brilliant brain you came with. Students tell me they love this one! (You can find this and other meditations on JulieRenee.com under the meditations tab.)

When you are ready to start your miraculous healing process you will follow these steps. Your body is very wise and will have the perfect recipe and order of healing processes for you. Unlike Western medicine that makes a diagnosis and simply treats the issue, the miraculous healing process will continue to clear and make ready the body until it has cleared well enough for new cell growth and new DNA patterns.

Spiritual health and wellness can be nourished through both the practice of prayer and silent meditation, devotional singing including hymns, chants and mantras as well as times of meditation in the natural world. Since we are in earthly bodies we are meant to be together and celebrate the divinity of life. Some do that by attending a synagogue, church, temple or spiritual center. For miraculous Healing it is important that you be with your heart and spirit community. A good and loving spiritual community can provide a place in which to both serve and fill up. If you are depleted or frustrated with the politics of your community you are not in the right place. You have complete permission to find a place that resonates with who you are now.

From a spiritual health aspect we will now move into the five intervals of health.

The five intervals of health the journey of human spirit in body

From my research into the Divine Human Blueprint, I have discovered that there are five distinct levels or phases of health that individuals experience during their life's journey. Understanding which of the five levels you are currently experiencing provides tremendous information about you. We can see the patterns for life expectancy. We can see if and how much you whole-heartedly embrace and enjoy your life in present time. If you fall into one of the reduced levels, Miraculous Living programs can show you the path back to a more vibrant interval. In addition, you will learn the way to turn back the hands of time and maintain vibrancy for many decades to come.

If your "interval of health" registers as "Level 1" you are in this elite group of individuals who can reverse aging and extend life. Most folks in his interval are young children.

Mapping out the Terrain of the Five Intervals of Health

What follows are the details for each of the intervals and how they express themselves in the body:

Level 5 details:

In Level 5, aging has occurred, typically the individual is over age fifty, and identified as being currently in poor health. Aging patterns and DNA play a large role in getting to this interval so early on. Keep in mind that our bodies were designed for lifespan of up to seven or even eight hundred years. To degenerate at the very, very young age of fifty or sixty (though it is the current trend and our current belief system) was never meant to be part of the human condition.

Nathan is an elder in his early eighties who is a loving kind man aging at the rate and velocity of his group. He has occasional health scares and is hospitalized about three times a year. He is a big kind man who retired years ago and gets excited about his books and audio trainings, and spends much of his day sitting.

Identifying factors in Level 5:

Systems Functionality

System or Symptom Functionality	
Brain 1 – instinctual	20% or less
Brain 2 – emotional	50% or less
Brain 3 – logical	22% or less
Brain 4 – creative	9% or less
Brain 5 – angelic	2% or less

Poor muscle tone 10% or less.
Systems typically are at 30% or less.

Life is lived primarily from the mental body. In other words your enjoyment of life in this phase is experienced by your thoughts conversations and visual experiences, such as watching a sunset, your grandchildren playing or perhaps a movie.

Unfortunately, if the individual in this interval is suffering from some form of dementia, their life and enjoyment narrows significantly.

Sheryl and Arnold approached me for healings three years ago. Arnold was moving rapidly into advanced stages of dementia. His wife of many years, Shirley (fifteen years younger) was hoping to improve the quality of their life together.

As I worked with Arnold, he never spoke to me or had a conversation with me. I could see he would improve only to a certain level. We did manage to help him regain his ability to remember the day's activities and join in on dinner conversations with friends. But after a time we stopped the tune ups and he returned to the unconscious state he had been in. You see he had chosen the path of 'oblivion' and unawareness. With my energy fueling him he could have something different, but without me assisting him he returned to the sleepy unconscious awareness he had when we first met.

Note Dementia is both from DNA and from agreement. Arnold had cheated on his wife for years and hurt her terribly in retirement. He has chosen not to remember the past pains and so he lives with his caring wife without the emotional or mental abilities to repair or restore the past damage. They will likely come back together in a future life to work this issue out.

The physical body requires eleven hours of rest. Sleeping and napping become an important part of the flow of the day. In Interval 5, the individual is unable to really absorb the nutrients needed from diet. This condition causes the body to become malnourished and often overweight.

Toxicity, radiation, memes and miasms, and poor programs in the DNA are primarily responsible for entering this lowest and most challenging interval, which is the precursor to death.

I myself have been at the fifth level eight times. I dipped into this lowest and least healthy level of life during the many days I spent in bed in a great deal of pain. When an individual is this sick, he or she imagines what death will be like.

Nine years ago, I lay on my bed shaking while very, very ill with a kidney infection. I had what is medically referred to as rigors. In laymen's terms, the infection in my kidney had gotten into my brain and heart and I had, perhaps, moments to live. As I lay there shaking, I saw the angel of death above me. (It was a 'he'.) He said, "Okay, you can come with me now." I looked him in the eye and said, "Get thee behind me, Satan. I know you are not Satan, but I will not be tempted by your offer to leave my pain-filled body to join you. My life is not over yet."

Such a response is a true testament to the courage and will power of human spirit. I have seen this happen with other people that should have died and yet haven't. At that time, I was able to move my body to the side of the bed (by sheer will) to reach the phone and call for help.

Upon reaching the hospital my affect was too strong for a dying woman, so although the medical staff triaged me and put in a room, they did not read me as urgent. As a result I was left to wait for a quite a while before the doctor ordered tests. When the test results came back in, a team with a crash cart and multiple stands for IVs ran into the ER cubicle where I was waiting for help. The doctor explained the severity of the infection and started IV's full blast in both arms, draining the icy antibiotic into me. All the while I lay shaking.

I found the hospital unpleasant and several hours after the antibiotics had run, I requested to be sent home, promising to stay resting for the next few weeks and take the meds prescribed. The doctors were again stumped as the hospital rules and perhaps the rules of physiology say, a person with blood pressure under 90/60 cannot stand or walk. Indeed, I did walk the length of the ER hallway with a blood pressure of 80/40. By proving I could walk I was released from the hospital to do my 'magic' on myself at home. I had not yet discovered the human blueprint, but my positive thoughts and actions helped me return to health.

Level 4 details:

In Level 4, aging has occurred, typically the individual is over age forty, and is identified as currently in 'acceptable health.' DNA aging patterns, group mind or virus (referred to as a miasm) and associated societal rules play a large part in moving from a healthier function to this less healthy interval.

Examples of a societal rules: "People in their forties don't have time to play basketball" or "Once you're past thirty-five, you can forget ballet dancing." You hear such rules all the time. Excellence in physical activity, mental agility, or even creative expression are slowed down with age in steady conversational streams by the 'herd'.

Identifying factors in Level 4:

System or Symptom Functionality	
Brain 1 – instinctual	40% or less
Brain 2 – emotional	70% or less
Brain 3 – logical	40% or less
Brain 4 – creative	20% or less
Brain 5 – angelic	3% or less

Reduced muscle tone 50% or less.
Systems typically are at 52% or less.

Life and its enjoyment in Level 4 are primarily lived from the mental and spiritual body. It is not always this way but this is a good norm from which to understand this interval.
Another distinguishing factor is the appearance of aches and pains in the body. The importance of this is two-fold:

The aches are wearing on the nervous system and will cause fatigue. On top of that, an overtaxed nervous system will cause brain chemistry for the happy chemicals to dip to all time lows. People can have difficulty laughing or finding joy in this level, despite there being nothing apparent or overtly wrong.

The physical body requires nine hours of rest. At Level 4, the individual is able to absorb about thirty percent of the nutrients needed for optimal health from diet. This condition can often cause the body to become overweight.

Tamara is a forty-seven year-old female currently in stage four and is reversing her circumstances as she practices the miraculous healing protocols and returns to a more active life. Her symptomology of back pain and an overall achy body was exacerbated when she lost a corporate job after seven years of service to the company. Downsizing complied with extreme emotional challenges from menopause and deteriorating spinal issues land Tamara in level 4. She is soon to return to level 3 as she is actively using the meditations to restore her emotions, hormonal body and her spinal issues.

Level 3 details:

Those in Level 3 typically include ages twenty-seven and younger. At this stage, the body stops its rapid regeneration and begins following the family aging DNA programs. It is an important time as the mind is now ready to formulate a plan for adult life. Some of the agility of youth and energy wanes. Naturally, life begins to focus around the mental body.

Identifying factors in Level 3:

Systems and symptoms Functionality

Brain Functionality	
Brain 1 – instinctual	70% or less
Brain 2 – emotional	90% or less
Brain 3 – logical	70% or less
Brain 4 – creative	50% or less
Brain 5 – angelic	40% or less

Reduced Muscle tone 80%

Systems typically are at 80% or less .

Human expression and fulfillment come from all areas, physical, emotional, mental and spiritual.

In Level 3, one experiences relatively little difficulty in operating the body or the mind. They are becoming wise, gathering knowledge and owning their authority.

The physical body requires seven hours of rest. In Level 3, the individual is able to absorb about eighty percent of the nutrients needed for optimal health from diet.

If you are generally healthy and in the middle of your life, this is likely the category you are in. Melissa is at level three moving into level 4. She has just turned fifty and in the past two years has had lypo-suction, breast lift and implants and has just completed a neck lift. She is aware that youth and vitality are not as accessible as they used to be and is attempting to surgically hold on to the appearance of youth. She has a natural health quality about her and has not suffered with illness or significant disease. She would dramatically improve her circumstances with meditation and healthy lifestyle choices.

Level 2 details:

Those in Level 2 typically include ages twelve and above. They are in good health, their body is functioning very well, but they have discovered their bodies are fallible. They are in a period of generation, growing and developing while learning and absorbing all the knowledge and information they can.
Identifying factors in Level 2:

Systems Functionality

Brain Functionality	
Brain 1 – instinctual	90% or more
Brain 2 – emotional	95% or more
Brain 3 – logical	82% or more
Brain 4 – creative	98% or more
Brain 5 – angelic	80% more or less

Muscle tone typically 100%
Systems typically are at 90% function or better

At Level 2, they require nine hours of sleep to build new cells in all areas of the body. This is a wonderful and challenging time. The development of the 'ego' can begin to undermine confidence. Programs and patterns for self-criticism develop, such as the constant comparison to others who are stronger, more intelligent, more athletic or more beautiful. These patterns lead a person down the path of envy and coveting, where perfection is sought from outside oneself. From this condition, self-sabotage begins the creation of memes or miasms for degeneration and premature aging.

Level 2 lets you experience joy and competency in operating the body and mind. You are becoming self-actualized, growing your physical body and gathering knowledge.

David is a young healthy level 2. He came to me with some lower functions with emotions and trauma, which we 'happily' corrected and he is resiliently, back in his life as himself.

Each interval has eight levels. You could be on the high or low end of the interval closer to the smaller or larger next interval. Just because you are in interval four or five does not mean you have to stay there. Now that you are aware, you can begin to do something to change your circumstances if you so desire!

Level 1 Details:

Those in Level 1 include those just born and older. They are in great health, their body is functioning very well and they are innocent to the influences of negative programs. They are in a rapid period of generation: growing the body and brain; developing, learning, and absorbing all the knowledge and information they can.

Identifying factors in Level 1:

Systems Functionality

Brain Functionality	
Brain 1 – instinctual	100%
Brain 2 – emotional	100%
Brain 3 – logical	100%
Brain 4 – creative	99% or more
Brain 5 – angelic	82% or more

Muscles 100%
Systems typically are at 100%

Level 1 people require twelve hours of sleep as they build new cells in all areas of the body. This is a wonderful and exciting time.

Human expression and fulfillment come from all areas: physical, emotional, mental and spiritual.

Unique to Level 1 is the innocence, that is, lacking programs and societal pressures that would have them think they are less than perfect. The Waldorf educational programs are keen to this concept: they request no TV and no technology in early years to facilitate the safe and loving development of the creative expressive human.

The concept of regeneration and maintaining a young healthy life for hundreds of years leads us to the unique path of remembering the truth about who we are. We can choose to let go of the negative influences of the media, memes and DNA patterning that has us experience the deterioration of life, making it short-lived.

There is much to learn and understand about the reversal of aging and the complete regeneration of the human body leading to a greater longevity. We stand at the precipice of new knowledge as science and spirituality come together and as the walls that kept us in the dark fall away. We emerge with a new knowledge, that is, that of 'Cellular Quantum Mechanics. '

The Umbrella 1995

Up and Down without a complaint,
Down and Up with no restraint!

Up the shaft my hand slides harder,
Caught by winds, my sails reverse!
Bruised by little hail bombs flight,
Hold me now, hold on tight!

Up and down silently moving,
My rain parasol has lost a spoke.
A triangle terand the sails collapse
Laughing umbrella with a joke

Moral; one can live in a down pour so long
Before they finally give up, as is the way
of all things in life.

Chapter 11: Soul and Prana

One remembered

And it came to pass
And the We cried for the loss of the selves
And the selves knew of separateness
And the selves forgot the vibrations of the
We

The selves became engulfed in illusion
And knew for the first time aloneness

As the selves forgot the We
Desire arose
The selves clung to what was manifest
Attachment to the transient
Became the replacement for the We

Once strong and brilliant
Now only a dim memory
Many parts of the We became dangerously
dark

In our modern American culture we have lost the meaning of soul. We use 'Soul' and 'Spirit' interchangeably in our conversations, on book covers and even in the sermons at church. I would like to clear up the confusion of what exactly your soul is and the purpose and benefit of having a soul.

If for example you sold your soul to the devil as in the movie *Bedazzled*, the Devil (if there is such a thing) would not own you. You, and your essence and information are human spirit. You would have sold the outer protective layer of spirit to Satan.

Now, let's look deeper now into what exactly is soul.

Your soul provides the protection for your spirit and is the outer layer that contains our spirit during human incarnation.

There is a beautiful legend from the Ancient Gnostic tradition about the creation of human spirit and soul.

> Creator God the Father, finding himself lonely, broke off part of himself and created his female half, Creator Goddess the Mother.
>
> God continued to create and in his creation he made the human race.
>
> *"I remember a time when time was not, when all that was, was what could not be, when who was, was what and I was we...."*
>
> Father God had put his attention on his creations and now Mother Goddess was becoming lonely also.
>
> After a while the Mother Goddess noticed the children of Earth were losing their original brightness and light. The nature of a male is to create, as the nature of a female is to hold and nurture. Although Father God could continue to create, he could not bring the brightness back to his creation.
>
> The Mother (Sophia), sensing human anguish, gave her life to the depths of matter and embracing each human spirit she became the sacred chalice that holds

the light for every human. She became the *soul*, the protective womb where our spirit is held and protected, while we live out our physical incarnation.

Human spirit is essential, being in the form of a magnificent light body, vibrating at the frequency of our particular energetic signature. Human spirit animates the physical body, without human spirit our body would not survive.

Spirit is essential to human life

And the mother
The magnificent soul of the We
Encompassed each part
Ensuring each tiny flicker would not extinguish
But would remain enshrined in her great love

She became the holder of the flame
She who's womb is the gateway to all the worlds
Gave with abandon

She became separate
To each flame her womb became a soul
And so it was

As a lamp holds the light
So it is the soul holds the spirit

She held the parts of the We
And though we knew separateness
We could also feel the great mother
Who's memory of the great We

214

Became permanently protected
    In the vibrations of the soul
Though many dangers threatened to extinguish the We
Now clad in its new pelvic armor
It was again safe

And so it was that the great mother
Gave to all, and lost her being to save the We

The We was grateful to the mother
And again remembered the time of no time
When all that was We
And so it was.

Several years back I received a very sad phone call from a lady in Scotland. Her thirty-four year-old son had mysteriously passed away a few weeks prior to the call and her pain was unbearable. She called me with the hope of getting some answers and connecting one last time with her son to say good-bye.

In our research we discovered that he had been working with high tech sound and light show. While setting up for a big event he had an accident with the lasers. He tripped over some equipment and the silver chord, that attached him as spirit to his body, was severed. This left him completely unattached to his body. When he went to bed and fell asleep, he floated out of his body, as he had done many times before. However, without an attachment to his body, he could not find his way back into his body when morning came. After several days, even though he had no physical ailments, he just died.

Without human spirit there is no human life.

Role of soul

Contemplating the role of the soul, we can see that it directly correlates with the life force of an individual. If the life force is at twenty percent the reading of the soul will match it and provide only twenty percent protection. The reason for a drop in the soul reading is a simple one. As an individual's life force wanes, it is a trigger to the spirit to prepare to leave and re-enter to realm of spirit. The soul exists entirely to protect the light of human spirit while in a physical body. If the body is letting go, the spirit will naturally leave with ease as the protective chalice (soul) falls away.

Karen's story

When Karen contacted me, I was alarmed at her life force reading. She was referred to me by her close friend, Darby, a business connection of mine. Her friend wanted to see if I could help in some way. Karen could no longer walk. Her body was filled with lots of extra fluid (edema), and she was afraid for her life. We spoke on the phone for some time and I urged her to see me immediately and not wait. She scheduled the first of many healings the next day.

Karen felt my urgency, but at the time I had not revealed the low reading of her life force. Her two percent life force and soul readings meant she would have passed away that week. I began the complex process of removing death energy and boosting life force at every juncture. Four months of intensive sessions restored her to her happy, playful self, back into life, and enjoying her family more than ever.

Lynn Ann's Story

Lynn Ann also came to me with a life force and soul reading well below five percent. She too was days from her demise. She arrived at my doorstep with husband and an eleven-year-old daughter. Her husband got her to the sofa where she lay, having difficulty breathing. She was clearly in overwhelming pain. Lynn Ann was dying from seven infections in her colon.

Stanford doctors told her she was dying and had advised her to take steps to tie up loose ends.

The first day we worked together I removed eighteen inches of black (death) energy from her body. Over time we rebuilt her systems and the damaged and sick organs. During the four months of her initial treatment, we cleared all of the infections. The true sign that she was well was reflected in a life force reading consistently over ninety percent and soul readings returning to a hundred percent.

Prana

Breathe on me Breath of God,
Fill me with life anew,
That I might love as though has loved,
And do what though wouldst do.
From the Lutheran Hymnal

Breath represents life anew and provides for peak human expression. For where there is breath, there is life. Where there is breath, there is peace. Where there is breath, there is vitality. Where there is breath, there is love.

Prana provides birth for the spirit in the body. The breath of life, the first breath, is the action that seals the deal so to speak, in the absolute connection of spirit to body. The concept of Prana existed long before the Yogic tradition gave it a name. The mechanism of Prana has existed since humans have been incarnating into physical bodies.

As an infant prepares to come into the world, he or she begins to establish a relationship to the mother. During the nine months of gestation, the infant shares in the Prana of the mother's body. Upon entry (birth) breath begins and thus Prana or the breath of life begins. This breath can heal the body. The magic and science of Prana has been deeply studied and developed through the practice of Pranayam, titled many ways from various traditions. A person can use breath to heal the body and restore vitality and health.

Prana is the spiritual aspect of breath while living.

Nowadays, you might find simple Pranayam methods taught by hatha and tantric yoga teachers. The practice of breath is mostly taught from the sadhu's traditions of India. For thousands of years, sadhus have kept the yogic secrets of breath and vitality alive.

Three Pranayam Breathing Techniques

Practice 1
Slow conscious breathing ten count.

- Find yourself in a comfortable seated position, either cross-legged or seated in a chair, spine erect, with feet on the floor.

- Allow your eyes to close.

- Imagine the air you are breathing in is infused with

pink and gold energy (pink representing divine love and gold representing divine vitality).

- Connect with the bottom of your spine and breathe deeply into the base of the spine for four counts.

- Hold the breath for sixteen counts and allow the fullness of the breath to supply a rich supply of oxygenated blood to the entire body.

- As you breathe out slowly for eight counts, breathe out any negativity or darkness.

Continue nine additional rounds

- Completion breath: Breathe in deeply. Hold the breath for sixty counts, and feel the shifts that have taken place during your pranic practice. Feel the new you, refreshed and revitalized.

Ta tas tuo ~ So be it!

Practice 2
Alternate Nostril Breathing

- Find yourself in a comfortable seated position, either cross-legged or seated in a chair, spine erect, with feet on the floor.

- Allow your eyes to close.

- Imagine the air you are breathing in is infused with pink and gold energy (pink representing divine love and gold representing divine vitality).

- With your right hand up to your nose, press the right thumb against the right nostril.
- Bend the index and middle finger in towards the palm.

- Place the ring finger and pinkie against the left nostril.

- Began by pressing the thumb against the right nostril and breathing in four counts through open left nostril.

- Close both nostrils, hold the breath deep in the lungs for sixteen counts.

- Exhale through the right nostril eight counts.

- Breathe in through the right nostril four counts, holding the left nostril closed.

- Close both nostrils holding in breath for sixteen counts, allowing oxygen to flow through the body.

- Release the left nostril and breathe out for eight counts.

Repeat practice for an additional nine cycles.

- Completion breath: Breathe in deeply and feel the shifts that have taken place during your Pranic practice. Feel the new you, refreshed and revitalized.

  The benefit of these practices is that the right and left brains are now beautifully balanced.

Practice 3
Kabala Bhati Breathing

- Find yourself in a comfortable seated position, either cross-legged or seated in a chair, spine erect, with feet on the floor.

- Allow your eyes to close.

- Imagine the air you are breathing in is infused with pink and gold energy (pink representing divine love and gold representing divine vitality).

- Take in a deep cleansing breath through the nose and breathe out through the mouth. Hold and release.

- Breathe in short bursts, pumping the navel.

- Rapidly breathe in and out.

- With each exhalation, physically pump the belly inwards with the muscles in the abdomen.

- The responding inhalation relaxes the belly outwards.

- Continue with sixty consecutive breaths pumping the navel in and outwards.

- As you complete each breath cycle, focus on the seed syllables:

Sat Nam ~ truth is my name

- Completion breath:

> Step 1: Upon the sixtieth exhalation, breathe in deeply and exhale slowly.
>
> Step 2: Breathe in deeply filling the lungs all the way down the diaphram, imagining the breath going into the pelvic cradle. While your body is bathed with a rich supply of oxygenated blood, feel the shifts that have taken place during your Pranic practice.
>
> This supports energy and vitality.

Repeat this process for two additional cycles.

> *Namaste ~ The god in me honors the god in you.*

Soul relates to life force while prana relates to breathe and both are a vital force for the existence of human life. To have the experience of vibrant health and life force of a hundred percent to have the joy of deep breathing into your very core with oxygen and life force feeding and nourishing all of us that is human is amazing.

If your vital energy is waning and life force is low, you can use our miraculous healing technique of pumping gold into your life force and soul. This will give you some relief until you are able to identify the cause of the low reading, which is typically and illness or serious health problem.

As I always say, "It ain't over till it's over, and it ain't over till we say so!" I say it just that way. Death isn't something we should tip toe around, but rather put some silliness into the pictures and start breaking up those death patterns making room for life! Your Miracle Starts Today! Choose life!

Morning Sun 1995

I am the morning sun
I break open the dark egg of night
I shine through the longest day
I die with the end of light.

A faithful friend, I am
Each day I'm born again
I encourage you on and brighten your way
Depend on me every dawn

I am the soul-ar panel of life
I wrap you in a blanket of love
My fires scorch fiercely on high
Down here, I am gentle as a dove.

Chapter 12:   Energetic Signature

Love is the Greatest Teacher 1989

Love is the greatest teacher and healer in our human plan made manifest We should with great intensity search for purest love within ourselves

There is no better between love and light
Love serves the purpose of helping us realize our full standing in light
Love is the great teacher, the great healer

When we finally return to light, love will disappear into the rainbow
As it has always been the hidden factor when light was divided.

After noted researcher David Hawkins PHD came out with his revolutionary book *Power Verses Force*, identifying energy signatures we as a population of spiritual seekers began to comprehend on a deeper level the science of enlightenment. I have had the pleasure of teaching at the Institute of Noetic Science and from the institute's beginnings the taste of this organization founded by astronaut- Edgar D. Mitchell, ScDwas to comprehend spiritual phenomenon through science.

Science and spirituality are no longer diametrically opposed. As a matter of fact, in the area of quantum mechanics or physics you will find many spirit seekers exploring the meaning and relationship of their experience with what the new scientific researchers are now bringing into consciousness.
We finally understand the vibration a person embodies is

the energetic signature that reflects the vibration that they have mastered so far in human body. Vibrational signatures for a human (spirit in body) range from 0-1,000, zero being the low or dark end of human expression and 1,000 being a high, elevated essence of humankind.

In my research into the human energy spectrum I have identified a qualitative description of each energetic vibration and the corresponding juncture of human development.

Table 12-1 Energetic Scale Human Spirit in Body

Vibration signature	Human expression
0-100	Jealousy, Fear
100-200	Neediness, Aggression, Righteous
200-300	Desire, Morality, Competition, Passion
300-400	Neutrality, Compassion
400-500	Hope, Appreciation, Awakening
500-600	Unconditional Love, Joy
600-700	Oneness, Accelerated Awareness, Love Wisdom
700-800	Enlightenment
800-900	Spiritual Emotional Access
900-1000	Christ Consciousness Affected by Humanity *(Sometimes empathy or an unresolved mental body challenge can lower a 1,000 individual slightly)*
1000	Christ Consciousness (Meaning the highest state of enlightenment, such as the Buddha, Rama state of full enlightenment)

The average person moves less than eight points up the energetic signature scale in a lifetime. What they have accomplished prior to coming into this life largely determines the energetic signature they access during their lifetime. For example they start at 180 when born and when they die they have raised to 188 vibrationally.

It is possible for spiritual seekers who have the intention of raising their vibration to experience successful in their quest. However, it is important to remember that moving up the scale cannot happen by force of will, mental maneuvering, or longing. Even the desire to shift up on the energetic scale can lock a person into struggle and failure. When you are in the struggle of not liking where you are and thinking the grass is greener on the other side you are creating a dichotomy and a struggle. A better approach is to love where you are with the knowledge that you will grow and change as your life progresses.

It is good to reflect on where you have come from and all you have accomplished so far. Take time to celebrate your wins. Appreciate the steps you have already taken and know that you have completed that part of the journey. Those steps are now complete.

Imagine the human ascension process as a rose. There is nothing wrong with being a young rose bud. If you are a person who is not appreciating the journey, or honoring your passage you are actually committing violence against your own spirit (which in this case is the developing rose bud). There is no reason to hate the bud, or 'hack' at it or want something entirely new. Just like a fragrant garden rose when given love and nourishment it opens in its own proper time. You will also open and grow as the time is right and you are ready. By loving who you are now, you have fulfilled that energy vibration and the rose bud of life can open its petals to reveal the next level.

Spiritual jealousy

It is important to take a look at this issue as it oddly surfaces at higher levels of energy vibrations. At a level of 360 to about 448 it seems to matter and stimulate this unpleasant envy/emotion. If you have felt envious or jealous of someone who has reached a higher state of awareness, follow these steps to release the emotional dis-ease.

1. Ask yourself; why you want to move up the energetic scale?

2. Are you motivated by either of the following?
   - Spiritual jealousy
   - Competition: "I want what she has," "I should be higher than her because..."etc., etc., etc.

3. Or are you motivated by the pure intention of transformation and enlightenment?

Missy, a grade school science teacher, was a student of mine. She and her husband, Ron, loved attending my courses and subscribed to my monthly program. They measured very high in energetic vibration, at 465 and 490. They readily caught onto the concepts and processes. Clearly, they had enjoyed a life of study and spiritual exploration.

Over a period of months, we had been able to create some cool miracles in health and wealth for both of them.

At some point, the miracles came to a screeching halt. I noticed they weren't able to attend the classes and phone calls and canceled their monthly series so I called her to find out what happened. She told me that she was struggling with jealousy over my spiritual access and she just wanted to focus on her shamanic practice.

I was surprised to hear this. The only thing I could do was wish her well and invite her to come back in at any time, that she was always welcome. What I noticed is, often for women, once they reach this 450-490 vibration they can get hooked up with spiritual jealousy. This can take them down and move them out of the growth experience.

If you hit a spot like this, I suggest you just pray it away. *It's really that simple.*

God,
   I don't know how to let go of this jealousy but I am willing to have you help me. Please, take it away from me. I wish the best for everyone and I know that as I celebrate (so and so's) spiritual essence, I will move into my own fully expressed spiritual life. I love my life!
   Thank you.
   Amen

Through the years, I have found women who have almost reached the state of unconditional love, will get tripped up and take a few steps back with this challenge. I encourage you not to let it take you out. You've got to clear this space, so you are only interested in spiritually opening to your highest and best self in this lifetime. Focus on growing in a healthy vibrant way. Your advancement in this area has to come from a pure place.

* See Chapter 2, Recessive DNA Obliteration, if jealousy is a program running in the cellular body. Check also if jealousy is in the spiritual timeline (past life condition). If this is the case, clear the energy from the spiritual timeline related to the original problem. This might mean checking

back as far as six prior lifetimes. It is not necessary to know what happened, just identify the location of the original problem on the timeline and clear it with a gold pumping process or use a golden vacuum in order to lift off the black energy. Then send a golden pulse into the time line to seal up the change and prevent it from returning.

How to experience temporary higher energetic states

A temporary elevation of your energetic state can be made with conscious actions. Very few humans experience 500-1,000 as their daily energetic signature. Yet many of my students and individuals who are actively involved in spiritual connection cultivation will regularly have minutes or hours in higher states of consciousness.

Did you ever notice when you:
- Are participating in a group meditation, that your energy may really be lifted?
- Experience the mystic version of communion, your energy soars?
- Feel uplifted as a result of practicing repetitive prayer and mantra?

To be clear, I am not, at this point, speaking about the negative/positive ion balancing that happens when in nature at the beach or in the forest. This is actually a real and very wonderful chemical response to an improved physical environment.

You can, with intention and practice, routinely raise your energy to the state of unconditional love and above by matching the truth vibration of an action or activity.

Three Vibration Elevators

Practice One: Holy communion (mystic version)

- While receiving the sacrament, clear your mind of unworthiness.

- You may use this pre-sacrament time to purify your thoughts and send love to those to whom you may have somehow been an impediment.

- Match the energy of the bread and wine to the symbolic essence of the body and blood of Christ.
- As you receive the body and blood of Christ, you are vibrating at 1000, Christ consciousness, know that in this moment you are one essence with the Divine.

- Allow the energized bread and wine to mirror the energy of Christ consciousness to all the cells of the body. Feel the flood of light flash through your body as you are temporarily matching Christ force energy.

This experience can last from a few minutes to several hours.

"The more love and appreciation you are embodying during this time, the longer you will be able to hold this blessed energy vibration."

Energy reads in this elevated state often read from 700-900

Practice Two: Focused love and appreciation for 60 minutes

Write a love letter to your maker include:

- All that you love about your life.

230

- Reveling in this amazing Garden of Eden in which you live.

- Appreciate the physical and the natural world:
  - Flowers
  - Fruits
  - Trees
  - The Blessedness of Creation

- Continue on appreciating the perfection of life and the extraordinary way.

Energy readings in this elevated state often read from 500-800

Practice Three: Illumination Rosary

Over ten years I have refined my understanding of the power of prayers to Mother Mary in the traditional Rosary. Saying the traditional rosary can read around 530. I have continued to work with the vibration of the words used in the prayers. The Illumination Rosary from Miraculous Living now registers at 974. The prayers, when said with great devotion and conviction, take you to 1000, and restore you to your divinity and blissful state as you come to the completion of the prayers. Below I have included the Love- Wisdom Creed and the Lord's Prayer for you to experience the blissful energy of the Illumination Rosary. For the full experience you will want to get your own copy of these beautiful prayers by visiting our website, http://julierenee.com/illumination/.

Love Wisdom Creed

There is one infinite God/Goddess vibration of love that creates everything seen and unseen. This all-prevailing presence is light, love, miraculous creation, and the sacred

231

expression of inclusion. Divine love embraces all humanity, regardless of religious preference or any other human selective difference. Heaven is here on earth.

I am free to live a life of spiritual freedom and full self-expression liberated in love, gratitude and mastery in this body here and now. My spirit is limitless. I am responsible for any limits I experience in this body and have complete access to the Divine through prayer and contemplation to release myself from any human bonds I have worn as spiritual clothing that no longer resonate with my essence.

I enjoy direct mystical access and divine union while practicing spiritual rites. These sacred rites belong to all humanity. In the Christian tradition they are known as Baptism, Rebirth, the Communion of Saints, the Sacrament of Communion and the Mystical Bridal Chamber. I follow the sacred path towards Spiritual Awakening, Enlightenment, Transmutation and Ascension in this life.

I experience the presence of the Christed one known to me as Jesus the Christ. Jesus Christ was Avatar, Teacher, Guide and friend. I revere blessed Mother Mary, who is compassion, love, forgiveness and healing. I trust in the existence of Holy Spirit who is essence living in me as life force.

I trust in the reality of the Holy Ones, the Divine Male and Female Deities who have sprung forth from all the great and lesser-known spiritual paths to teach and guide us on the path of Love Wisdom.

I am ageless and timeless. My life continues in or out of

this human temple I call my body. Whatever I have done willingly or unknowingly to myself or others that does not resonate with pure truth, can be washed from me through the power of forgiveness and the unending limitless power of LOVE.

The Lord's Prayer

Oh Magnificent Source of everything, breath of life, you who are the realm of sound and light, may I experience your glorious nature in my essence. The veil between heaven and earth becomes transparent in this realm. In my great gratitude and love I ask that your divine will become the guiding truth of this wondrous human domain.

I am profoundly grateful for your guidance, moving my thoughts and actions towards embodied wisdom and understanding. I celebrate your generous assistance in manifesting my daily needs. Detach the fetters of faults that bind me karmically and support me in discovering the deeper blessings of challenge and discordance. Point my focused direction to contribution and depth, free from those actions that take me away from my highest expression of self.

You are the source of pure truth, power, grace and beauty. You are constant throughout the ages of humankind. Sealed in trust, faith and truth. Amen

There are many choices to dramatically raise your vibrational energy signature. Part of the ease of this comes when you match the energy of one who has lived on earth and reached the highest vibration for a human spirit in body, which is 1000.

233

Jesus Christ, Buddha, Krishna, and Rama were all at 1000. Chanting or praying the name of one such master will lift your energy. This is your special time. Thoughts of worldly concerns leave your mind and focus on oneness with your own Divine state. After all,

You can experience yourself as a Radiant Being of Light today!

Chapter 13: Life Force

Gentle Night 2004

Gentle night, rain falling softly
Gentle night soft falls the rain
We are One with the raindrops
We are One with the God of rain

Gentle rain cleansing my spirit
Soft falling rain wash away my tears
All is well in the house of the raindrops
All is well in the garden of love

As we discuss in the previous chapter of on Soul and Prana, life force is intimately tied to the percentage of protection you are receiving from the soul.

When you are born your life force can be all over the board. If your mother had a difficult labor and delivery, the little body may be struggling to survive. Their 'Apgar score,' a measure of infant vitality, reflects what's happening with life force. If the Apgar score is at a four, life force will read in the low fortieth percentile. Over the next few days, while you gain strength and momentum, your life force usually rises naturally as the infant gains ownership of their body.

But that's jumping ahead. Let's go back to the beginning. Life force begins at eleven days and two hours past the moment of conception. Life force belongs to the body, which we sometimes referred to human animal. It is the third of the energy-body programs to come online. Light of cell in the stem cells begins at conception and the meridians begin to form at about 3 days past conception.

Life force provides energy to the physical body, that is, the body as human animal. Life force is the energetic twin to spirit and assists in the body's operations. The program for life force comes from the fifth stem cell, that is, early cells that begin their division at conception.

In a normal birth, life force will be around 50%. We are extremely dependent on our parents to provide and care for us as we develop and grow into an individuated, fully energized adult. At age four years and four months, our life force reaches 100%.

As you travel through life, your life force will read as a kind of barometer reflecting on your health or lack thereof. A bad bout of chickenpox may drop your life force to 20%, but in the succeeding weeks, your body and life force will return naturally to 100%.

People begin to lose some of the potency in life force as they age. As DNA programs of degeneration and illness play out, life force moves down in percentage and does not return to the pristine 100% of its former glorious youth on its own. If childhood illness is not a strong factor, an average age of loss of life force begins around age 25.

One of the wonderful properties of the gold healing energy from our miraculous cellular quantum mechanics is that you do not need to have life force of 100% to regenerate and heal the body. If however you are very healthy and are now looking to use this technique to actually reverse aging, your life force will need to stabilize at 100%.

Major surgery requires an anesthesiologist to take a persons life force down to 1%. Many people never return to 100% life force after a surgery. Later in this chapter, we will give you the remedy to return your life force to 100%.

The following chart gives you a range of life force adjustments down related health. The first number is the high range of the adjustment down and the second number is the lower drop a person could experience from the related illness.

Table 13-1 Drop in life force resulting from illness:

Common Cold	90% - 40%
Viruses	93% - 10%
Asthma	80% - 3%
Parkinson's	60% - 1%
Muscular Dystrophy	40% - 4%
Cancers	50% - 1%
Depression/Mental illness	60% - 6%
Fibromyalgia/Autoimmune	50% - 5%
Panic, Anxiety/Stress	50% - 9%

Carrie's Story

Carrie is an art professor at an esteemed university. In her younger years, she explored the music scene and was hanging out in clubs. She was in the fast lane going through quite a number of men, cars and money before she settled into her present life. Along the way, drugs and alcohol left a permanent imprint on her liver and unfortunately she picked up hepatitis 3.

She was holding her own until an extreme disappointment in her personal life toppled her emotional life. Her health rapidly deteriorated. I had known Carrie for years. She is an interesting, colorful person, intelligent and well versed in the language of creativity.

Prior to this event, her life force was up around 60%. This is the norm for her circumstance since she was in her mid-fifties and had asthma. As the emotional crisis amplified, her health tanked. She came in weeping, unraveling a betrayal that looked like it would cause her collapse and perhaps death from a broken heart. Her first session revealed a body in crisis; her life force of 6% told the whole story.

Over a period of fourteen weeks, I helped her rebuild a body in total crisis. During that time, we were able to successfully remove the hepatitis from her physical body. Over these months, we were able to bring her back to a stronger 80% life force and dramatically improve all functions of glands and organs. While I was working with her, I insisted no smoking or drinking and a practice of a balanced life. She was able to comply with my restrictions. Unfortunately, I understand that she chose not to continue a healthy lifestyle and went back to her old habits and now four years later at age sixty reads at 30% life force.

You get to choose. How do you receive a gift? Do you treasure it and acknowledge it is a treasure from above and live the rest of your life with the knowing you have been truly blessed, or do you squander it away and drop back into the amnesia of a lower energy lifestyle.

Marla's Story

Marla, a young thirty-one year-old mother, struggled with anxiety and depression. She was married to a fellow who did not express himself well and, at times, appeared aloof or even verbally abusive. When she began treatment with me, her life force was 50% due to her struggles.

As she found meaning and value in her life, her depression and anxiety lifted some. Her online boutique began to become a real career. However, due to her unresolved issues with an incident of sexual abuse much earlier in her life, and her insistence to live with a man who could not give her love and tenderness, her life force went up only 2%.

Marla shows us the negative results of holding on to that which does not serve us. She actually has a young, healthy, beautiful body. Her outer appearance does not match her inner landscape and energy.

Stacy's Story

Five-year-old Stacy has been receiving miraculous healings for her autism and has been really improving as the weeks go by and life normalizes.

Prior to our sessions, her life force measured typically around 21%. As we have gently paced her into a healthy relationship with her body, emotions, and mind, she has continued to strengthen in life force. Now after four months of sessions spread out to once every three weeks, she is reading as a normal child at 99% life force.

Unlike Stacy, twin teenage boys I know are advancing into maturity and so completely unrelated to their bodies they read at 12% life force. The have a flat affect and move their bodies with human animal controls, no real appearance of animation or vitality.

Barry's Story

Barry came to me as a pancreatic cancer patient at age eighty. As he was helped into my home for sessions, I saw him as frail and ready to die. I asked his family members to leave us for a while. He shared with me that he was really happy with his life. He was an amazing and daring fellow.

In his life, he was an incredible painter. In addition, he was a peer of Jack LaLanne. Barry was a fitness guy keeping his body in beautiful shape. As a result, he starred in adult films among his many erotic exploits.

Barry was a gentle sweet soul who told me he was content. He didn't want to live a long time; he just wanted to feel good in his body until he left. He came to me with a life force of 3%, ready to slip away in fragility and illness. We began to work together; the miraculous healings were amazing for him. The cancer did not disappear, but his life force jumped up to 70%.

He was able to do what he wanted during his last months. His life was filled with parties and workouts in the gym as well as hosting a few last adult swinger parties in his home. The day before he passed his life force was 60%. He went to bed and twelve hours later with no suffering he left.

I have shared a number of stories of how individuals have dramatically can improve in life force and vital energy. You can also choose not to keep life force high.

My story of survival and return to vibrant health is a shining example of enhancing the regeneration and going on to live a vibrant life with my life force routinely between 90% and 100%.

Life force is part of our God make up. You can, by will, force your life force up. Whether or not is stays up is often regulated by how healthy your lifestyle is.

Life force movers

Hearing the stories of peoples' challenges may get you thinking, I wonder if I can improve my life force? The answer is yes. The following are actions both positive and negative that affect the level of life force:

1. Mind and thoughts
What the mind can believe and conceive it will achieve. A great example of this is the example of what we do when someone tells us we are dying. Think about the 'normal' response of the woman who heard she had cancer and slipped away 9 days later. Her mind complied to the Doctors prediction. In contrast a 'dying' healer who said 'no' to the angel of death and recovered against all odds.

2. Connection with God
Disconnection with God from anger or hopelessness lowers life force, while reconnection with God though prayer, including the intersession of prayers from loved ones, can improve life force.

3. Miraculous Healings
This healing is one tiny part of what is possible by activating the human blueprint. By pumping gold into life force you can raise the percentage dramatically.

4. Possession of body by spiritual parasites
Your life force is reduced by the occupation of the body from evil spirits, entities and demons. If this is your situation, please refer to Chapter 29: *All Things of Spirit* to learn more about how spiritual parasites exist in the body and how to remove them successfully.

Life force is your conscious choice
As you can see much of life force is your conscious choice.

Marilyn was hanging on with impossible odds. She had a daughter and daughter in-law pregnant as well as a daughter getting married. She was receiving food from a tube and made it for months. She was very sick with an untreatable stomach cancer. This was years before I had the tools to help this condition. But she had me come daily to give nurturing massages and give her a break from family worries.

One day, while I was there the doctor arrived and we all cleared the room. He proceeded to tell Marilyn she was dying and there was no hope. Eleven days later she died. She was literally told to die. Good grief. And I can tell you that on the other side she was extremely upset she had made that choice. She longed to be physically with her growing family.

You can choose to live and choose to have a life force that reflects a healthy energized body. Use your mind for the good. Focus positivity and gratitude towards the parts of your health that are good. Pray for your loved ones who are sick, and see them returning to great health. Life force responds to prayers, as it is a gift from the Divine.

The Woman in the Mirror 1993

Confusion,
Will soon end
I see myself

I ask questions
I look for correction
Clarity stands at my gate
Ready to open
Anxious to reveal herself to me

242

True Self-Love requires
Unending ease
And unrelenting acceptance
(An impossible quest at this moment)

I will find a way to nurture
Spaces and places hidden
Undiscovered or still worse
Imprisoned by a frightened mind

Love will prevail
With the woman in the mirror

Chapter 14: Auric Field

Goddess wraps her
Loving arms around me
And I am free   2003

Your aura is a beautiful jeweled color field of energy surrounding your physical body. It provides a filter and sensitivity for awareness beyond your cellular body. It also provides a code for your integration of spirit, emotional, mental and physical body. At its best and in its most brilliant phase it will be luscious and multi-hued. At its worst it will be black and grey and appear as a death shroud around you.

An aura filled with refuse can cause vision problems along with a nasty environment preventing healing from all types of dysfunction and illness.

A common belief is that there are seven layers to the aura, each with its own color and meaning. There are typically seven obvious layers and two extraneous layers. On occasion there are less layers under unique circumstances.

When you first meet someone, you have a sense of who they are immediately. You know if you can trust them, if they are a happy person and even if you will be safe with them or they present a danger. Your body has the ability to read the auric field of another person and report those findings through your senses, delivering the information to your survival brain within seconds of coming in contact with a new person.

Ariel, a graphic artist, had heard about the work I was doing through a business client of hers who had been working with me for a number of years. She was hopeful that I could assist her with some significant issues she was experiencing which appeared as mental illness.

As she approached my front door her nerves were frayed and she moved as if in a fog. I answered the door, to observe a troubled woman, with a mental illness and an aura so dirty I had difficulty seeing her face and body well. You likely have met someone like Ariel: it seems like they really have a thick dark cloud surrounding them. I think about the Charlie Brown character, Pigpen. This little guy has a dust cloud moving with him in his wake. Ariel was just the same.

When you are with someone like this, you will notice a pattern of darkness around his or her eyes that is unmistakable. You will also feel that you are not comfortable standing too close to them. The fog doesn't feel dangerous, however it does feel toxic. The aura is full of refuse and they are literally magnetizing a junkyard of energetic debris into the field around them. They seemingly have no ability to clear this debris.

Another aspect of this malady is chemical imbalance and entity occupation. What this means is that spiritual parasites will be attracted to this malady and will hang out around the person. To learn more about spiritual parasites see Chapter 28 *All things of Spirit*

When a person is under siege, which is what this malady feels like, their life is in chaos. They may have wonderful skills and be extremely talented, but with this much muddle, their thinking and choices will have no clarity. They will be unlucky. If something can go wrong, it likely will. They will have a difficult time navigating in the social world and put people off just by their aura being funky.

I sing for those who cannot sing 4-22-96

I sing for those who cannot sing
I cry for those without tears
I ache to soothe the numb, the still
I scream for those without fear

I touch for those who are timid
I stain for those who remain clean
I swim naked in jungle streams
For the shy who linger unseen

I laugh for those in deep sorrow
I learn for the simple of mind
Round sacred fires I dance circles
For the empty, forgotten, Divine

I am a sponge in the ocean
The essence of healing sublime
A conduit of energy flows
Out of my body into thine

I sing because I could not sing
I've recovered my frozen voice
I cry because I did not cry
The tears now fall freely by my choice

I touch
I learn
I dance
I grow
I swim naked
I laugh
I'm Divine

Bad times will come and good times will go

Right now we stand firm alive

I love because I was born to love
Tenderness and compassion combined
I am rage, fury and power
Awakened in a Christed mind

I could not feel your burning pain
If I had not suffered myself
In weakness I found my power
In my darkness I merged with the light

I am you
Feel me now
We are one

The aura of a leader will be very different than the aura of a schoolteacher or a construction worker. The colors we unconsciously choose to surround us support who we are and reflect our recent past. As we take our next steps colors of the aura shift and change.

My experiment with aura color

Back in the day, the local psychic institute had an aura camera. There was an opportunity during the psychic fairs to have an aura photo taken. I had three photos taken, each about two months apart each. Over six months my aura glowed with beautiful primary colors of red, yellow and orange. During one of these events I stood in line with a lady whose auric photo was entirely purple. I thought 'what fun! I think I'll try wearing a purple aura.'

For a few days I focused my meditation on shifting my aura. I could feel the shift. My version of purple was an indigo blue. All seven layers were a single color. I had lost my primary colors and my aura for perhaps the first time was entirely a deep dark rich blue/purple.

It was a fascinating experiment and the results of the aura change were surprising and actually a little frustrating. Once my aura had totally shifted to purple, I had literally become invisible. I would stand in line at Safeway or Walgreens, and when it was my turn to check out and pay for my purchase the teller would not see me. Instead of speaking to me, they would ignore me. The teller would address the next person standing in the line behind me. If I moved around and spoke they would respond, but if I said nothing I was entirely overlooked.

After a month of indigo blue I happily returned to my bright colors and my visibility returned.

Layer colors and meaning

Each of the seven layers of the aura can have one unique color or many colors filling in the stratums. Every color appears in the auric field for a specific purpose. Since the aura is your energetic bubble, the original program for the construction and the development of the aura is sourced from the DNA. Once the auric design is installed around the physical body the brain is largely responsible for how the colors appear.

Aura Layer One

Layer one is closest to the body. It is the layer touching the body and is related to survival of the physical body.

Colors for layer one in order of most optimum to least

Green	Vitality, well being 100%
Blue	Hope, ease, gentleness, calm 92%
Pink	Self-love 88%
Purple	Honor 63%
Red	Passion 46%
Yellow	Misplaced thinking (ruminations) 31%
Orange	Craziness 11%
Brown	Depression 3%
Grey	Illness &disease emotional physical or spiritual -20%
Black	Illness and death ideations -30%
White	Someone else is in control of your survival -80%

As I mentioned anyone may have just one color in their aura, or many colors. When you are testing for colors, also test for the percentage of color. For example layer one could be 70% grey and 30% orange, which equals 100% of the aura.

You may discover that a portion of the aura has been torn off, shredded or damaged in some way. Also an aura ding can remain from a simple everyday incident. For example someone throws energy/anger at you because you cut in front of him or her on the freeway. In this case an actual indentation happens in the aura. But such dings are simple to fix as the aura is very pliable and easy to repair.

Aura Layer Two

Layer two is the second closest to the body. It is the layer that starts five inches out from the body and extends out seven inches from the body. Layer two is related to four senses: taste, smell, touch and sight as well as reproduction. *Please keep in mind that layers shift and move and although I am defining a physical location at any moment these parameters can be different.

249

Colors for layer two in order of most optimum to least

Pink/green	Sense and Sexuality, (pink female green male) 100%
Orange	Happiness, Fulfillment 86%
Green	Vitality 84%
Blue/purple	Peace 52%
Yellow	Worries, Obsessive thoughts 42%
Red	Pain, Anger 14%
Brown	Depression 4%
Grey	Emotional, Physical Failings -5%
Black	Violence, Death -30%
White	Someone else is in control of your senses

Aura Layer Three

Layer three is the third layer from the body. It is the layer ten inches away from the body and is related to physical expression of the body. Layer one and three are strongly related, layer one being survival of the physical and layer three is the strength and movement of the physical body.

Colors for layer three in order of most optimum to least

Red	Strength, Power 100%
Green	Force, Potency 96%
Orange	Optimism 93%
Purple	Regality 73%
Yellow	Misplaced Thinking, Panic 63%
Blue	Frozen, Stuck 46%
Pink	Helplessness 23%
Brown	Disease mental, emotional 3%
Grey	Disease physical -51%
Black	Physical illness and death-83%
White	Someone outside yourself is tempering your power & strength

Aura Layer Four

Layer four is 16 inches from the body in the middle of the auric field. It is the layer that begins to reach into spiritual issues as the previous layers were all related entirely to the physical functioning of the body. Layer four is the connection layer and unites the inner and out worlds as well as the higher and lower realms.

Colors in order of most optimum to least in the fourth layer

Pink	Balance (for women 100%)(for men 42% Emotional Weakness)
Green	Integration (for men 100%) (for women 97% Growth)
Peach	Calm, Soothing 60%
Red	Excitation, Irritation 44%
Yellow	Obsessive behaviors 10%
Purple	Narcissism, Overly self identified 1%
Blue	Sluggish, Stagnant .5%
Brown	Lonely, Isolated 0%
Grey	Disease spiritual lacking moral compass -34%
Black	Illness Love Related -66%
White	Someone else is in control of your ability to connect

Aura Layer Five

Layer five is twenty-two inches outside the body. It is one of the middle layers and is related to communication.

Colors in order of most optimum to least in the fifth layer

Pink	Ease, Communion, Grace 100% women 72% men
Peach	Self Love, Connection 100% women 92% men
Green	Individuation, Calm 60%women 100% men
Yellow	Overusing Mental Body 80%
Red	Rage, Combat, Fighting, Manipulation52%
Orange	Danger, Unpredictable, Unreliable 11%
Blue	Frozen, Stuck 4%
Purple	Invisible, Ineffectual 1%
Brown	Spiritual Illness .3%
Grey	Loss of God Connection -10%
Black	Disease of the Mind -73%
White	Someone else directs your communications & the strength of your connections.

251

Aura Layer Six

Layer six is part of the two layers you show to the outside world. It helps people get a read on who you are, or at least 'who' you will allow them to see. It is about 28 inches from your body and part of your facade. Even if you spruce up this layer, if you are dishonest or untrustworthy, people will feel it.

Colors for layer six in order of most optimum to least

Green	New Fresh, Healing 100% men 98% women
Pink	Love, Safety 100% women 60% men
Peach	Compassion 30% men 40% women
Red	Passion 10% women 8% men

Blue	Calm 6%
Purple	Strong Spiritual Connection 3%
Yellow	Multi-tasker, Doer 1%
Orange	Outrageous, Over the top .3%

Brown	Mental illness, including ADD and Autism -3%
Grey	Disease physical -3%
Black	Death ideations of self and others (i.e. grieving) - 42%
White	Someone else is in control of how you appear in the world

Aura Layer Seven

Layer Seven is your crowning glory and is that jeweled self you show to the world. It is the layer people come in contact with first when they interact with you. It will show you as trustworthy, truthful, loving, thoughtful and other things like weak, cheating, a liar and a thief. It is the outer layer of your aura and in a 36 inch aura (auras range from very close to the body to very expanded) will appear at the 34-inch mark. The best size of aura is anywhere from 23 inches to 64 inches from the body.

Colors for layer seven in order of most optimum to least

Peach	Joy, Love 100% women 72% men
Blue	Peace 91%
Pink	Love 100% women 70% men
Aqua	Creative 30%
Yellow	Intelligent 8%
Emerald Green	Success, Wealth 100%

Red	Passion, Enthusiasm 30%
Green	Wellness 40%
Orange	Happiness 50%
Purple	Playful 20%

Brown	Spiritual illness 2%
Grey	Disease physical -30%
Black	Death ideations, self and others, drug use -62%
White	Someone else is in control of how you appear in the world

Why auras have different sizes

Have you ever thought about your own aura and really felt into it? Did you notice if it was close to your body, or spread so thin and expanded that you couldn't feel it at all?

Here's a little experiment for you to help yourself become more aware of your energy field. Grab a friend and try this out.

Have your friend sit in a chair and have them imagine pulling their aura in to three feet around their body.

Stand a few feet away from them. Rub your hands together until your palms are feeling the heat from friction and your own energy.

Starting at about eight feet away from your friend, walk slowly towards them with your hands held so that your palms face towards them.

When you feel them, stop and notice where you began to pick up their energy transmission (aura).

Using your hands, begin to explore the curves and shape of the aura while your friend continues to sit in the chair. Notice if there are holes in the energy field, places you feel no energy. The discovery of a hole is an opportunity to fill in the missing energy transmission (aura).

People have different size auras based on how they are using their auras in the world.
People who have large, expanded auras operate from a severe deficit. They are using their aura to read many people and to be aware of what is happening in their space.
Having an overly enlarged aura is a habituated 'behavior' carried from lifetime to lifetime.

Reasons for the original over expansion are abuse, fear and violence. An aura extended two blocks is a sign of energetic illness and weakens both the physical body and the energetic system. Where it begins to read as an illness is when it remains over extended beyond forty-seven feet.

Think of it like a womb. It is capable of stretching and enlarging for a specific purpose, so at times it might be useful (temporarily) to have the aura enlarged, however its optimal resting space is twenty-one inches to sixty inches around the body. I encourage students to maintain a thirty-six inch aura, giving them a good awareness of positioning for energetic fortitude.
I suggest when in a large group with dispersed or chaotic energy to pull your aura into eighteen inches around your body. That way you will feel more comfortable and will pick up much less energetic gunk that you would need to clean out later.

254

The case of the missing half

Can twins share energy systems and aura? The answer to that is typically no. Each child has their own unique body, their own unique spirit and will have their own specific formula for how their energetic body lines up.

Marybeth, a fifty year-old woman had trouble with her aura. She was literally trying to fix it and fill it in everyday in meditation. If she forgot to check it, a few days would pass and she would again be missing the back of her aura. You can imagine her frustration about having a gaping hole where supportive protective energy should have been.

When we first spoke she mentioned she had been a twin and her twin had died in the third month of pregnancy. She suspected her problems were related to her brother and his passing.

As we explored further we discovered poor energetic DNA programs were the largest factor in the partially missing aura. To address this issue requires an activation of the human blueprint to establish a healthy energetic system program.

Did her brother have anything to do with this condition? She was naturally curious to know. Yes the emotional loss and grief in the womb caused her to withdraw her support in funding the baby body project. Without her spirit close, loving and nurturing her body she lacked the spark needed for full health. What she might have been able to improve, had she had enthusiasm and excitement for her new life, was not present as her body developed and thus a number of challenges developed.

Coronas on the aura

One of the fun techniques I use regularly is to have my students imagine a golden or blue corona at the outside edge of the aura. The use of coronas can help burn off unwanted energies and thought forms attempting to make an impact on the mind/body.

A cobalt blue corona is known for burning off alien and foreign energy. You can imagine a sun-like corona with blue flames jumping off the edge of your aura. This is a hot, effective flame, like a gas flame, burning any unwanted programs attempting to permeate your aura.

A golden aura is a purification aura. It is beautiful to light up the flame when you are in ceremony or meditation. It likens your energies to that of the Divine.

How to heal and improve colors in the aura

Clearing the aura is multifaceted. Part of the process resembles cleaning the 'air' of the aura. There is the more advanced part of aura clearing which is upgrading the colors of the aura for success, great health and joy.

Clearing Gunk in the Aura

Two favorite techniques I use in my teachings are as follows:

1. Imagine a golden rumba (automated vacuum cleaner) at the top of your head and set it on 'clean'. Have it spiral around your head, neck, shoulders, arms, waist, hips thighs, legs, knee, calves, feet and under the feet, vacuuming out all the muddle and spiritual dust bunnies that have collected in your aura. When complete, throw the golden rumba down the grounding cord.

2. Sitting in meditation, bring cosmic energy (that is energy that is harmony with your highest expression of self) into the back of your head one inch above where the spine meets the skull. Bring cosmic energy down through the neck and shoulders, arms, elbows, forearms, wrists, through the hands and out the fingertips. Bring more of this cosmic energy down through the back channel, looping up through the pelvic cradle and up through the belly, chest, neck and head, fountaining out the top of the head, bathing and cleansing your aura. Excess energy and debris can be sent down the big grounding cord at the base of the spine.

Clearing colors of the aura

As you have read in the descriptions of color and meaning of the seven layers, the colors represent the projects you are currently working on. If you have been in grief for a long time, or if you are really tired of the same old low energy funk or worse, altering the colors of the aura is an effective way of making a big change in your energy. What you do after you have made the change will determine whether you will hold the upgrades or fall back to lower colors.

Test layer one for color. Discover if you have more than one color in the layer. (When I recently tested, layer one had three colors.)

Note the percentage of the color. For example grey is 70% pink is 25% and green is 5%.

Focus on the layer or part of the layer you intend to upgrade and pump gold energy into that area until it has lifted to a higher color.

You can also test for curses in the low energy of the aura. Read more about curses in the chapter about memes miasms and curses.

The mermaid with five layers

I was fascinated by a show on the Mexican discovery channel about the evolution of merpeople. As it turns out there is scientific evidence to support the existence of these human-like beings here in the Earth's oceans, where they are said to live in harmony with whales and dolphins.

Before I ever saw this show I met a woman who was not a normal human. Four lifetimes back she had crossed over from being a 'mermaid' to being a human, and was again in a human body in this life. Every life had a similar issue: she loved the water but in midlife she lost the use of her legs and lived as an invalid in a wheel chair. Intelligent, funny a joy to be with, her favorite haunt was the pool.

Merpeople apparently only need three auric layers. She had, over several lifetimes, managed to create five thinly woven layers to the aura. If you are a realm jumper you may not be fully equipped to manage this human psyche. I mention this not because it is common, it is totally out of the ordinary, but is fun to know.

Aura as a death shroud for miscarriage and abortion

The shroud of death and the grief and pain of loss can be alleviated by lightening up the aura. Miscarriage is so sad, and unfortunately the loss of a child will inevitably send the mother's body into grief. We are wired to feel such loss, the chemistry of pregnancy with all its hormonal rushes is shockingly and abruptly ended with the loss of a fetus. The chemistry of this is painful and the aura responds to the loss of the new life and the grief of the body.

This is true even when a person has decided she does not want to carry the pregnancy through and opts out. The aura will go black/grey following an abortion. She will look

258

older and a level of sadness follows her for five months.

In both cases the aura can be lightened up and will likely hold the upgrades making life more enjoyable and lighter for the woman.

This condition also happens with the loss of a parent, a spouse or a sibling. Clear the aura and lift the grief in the aura, and you will lift the person into a stage of possibility and hope.

The way of glory

Your aura and your essence can hold, share and reveal the Glory of God! How you are seen in the world and how you contribute in the world has much to do with who you are committed to being in the world.

A Glorious Aura is an aura of one who wishes to embody the glories and gifts of the Divine through their presence in their community.

St. Francis saw the Glory of God and then wore it in his aura for the rest of his days.

> *Lord make me an instrument of thy peace!*

Perhaps if you are a healer you could affirm;
> *Lord make me an instrument of thy healing powers.*
> *or*
> *Lord use me, I offer my life for the advancement of humanity.*

When I think about the Glory of God, I am so grateful for the role I play in this glory. Every day, in so many countless ways, I am provided the glories of God to distribute in service to the world. Whenever you are committed whole heartily to a higher purpose, thy will not mine, my Lord, there shall the legions of angles and helpers be to assist you in your work.

The 'Glory' is the miraculous manifestation and power of that which is beyond understanding.

In the Stillness 03
In the stillness
In the quiet
In the open heart
There I am
I am essence
I am breath
I am light of god
I am I am

Chapter 15: Miraculous Healing Protocols

The Miraculous Healing protocols are used to access vital information from the body of the person requesting the healing. This information tells us where the healing starts and how to progress for restoring the most important issues in the body, in the proper order. It is important to take one step at a time, healing first one issue, followed by a new query to discover what to attend to next. It is less effective to go through a whole diagnosis then heal the issues afterwards. This can result in an incomplete healing.

Questions are asked of the body using kinesiology. I use a finger technique. Applying pressure to the ring finger of the right hand. A yes holds strong while a no drops or causes the finger to become weak.

The first question you will ask the body receiving the healing:

Beloved Body, do I start with the:
- **Spiritual**
- **Emotional**
- **Mental**
- **Physical**

While you are asking this question you are muscle testing for a "yes" on one of the four options. For the option you get a yes, proceed to the topic. For example, if you got a "yes" on spiritual, you will progress to the next list of questions found under the heading 'spiritual' and ask the question again, like this:

Spiritual

Ask the question, "Beloved Body, in the spiritual body what is the next step?"

One Spirit Body

If you get a yes here, check is there a

* Spiritual illness
    Or
* Problems in the spiritual timeline?

If you do not get a positive when asking the above question go to the energetic body next.

Two Energetic Body

If you get a yes with energetic body check for the following areas of concern

- **Aura**

  If one or more layers of the aura have black or grey death energy they will require a tune-up to restore vibrancy in the individual's field.

- **Human Spirit Access Portal**

  Its location is one inch above where the spine meets the skull and if you have a "yes" here, there is a blockage. Refer to Chapter 7 on the human spirit access portal for further direction on healing.

- **Soul-Life Force**

  The soul is the protection around the human spirit. It reflects life force and vibrancy or lack thereof. The percentage of function, found by muscle testing, may be waning from prolonged poor health. If this is the case, you may not be able to do a bigger healing without first pumping up the soul and life force to 100% with gold energy through the right hand.

- **Chakras**

The chakras source energy to regions and systems of the body; this energy is required to regenerate. Please refer to Chapter 8 on chakras. Proceed with a tune-up to the chakra or chakras that need improvement.

Three Spiritual Timeline (past life issues in present time)

The past life timeline requires a bit of research. Identify the:

- **Lifetime or lifetimes involved in the problematic issue**
- **Than identify the specific issue**

If you have not yet developed the skill to figure out the issue you can identify the approximate age of the individual in the lifetime where the problem occurred. This can be done by decades.

For example:
  0-10, 10-20, and so forth
  Then if you got a yes you would test.
  0,1,2,3,4,5,6,7,8,9,10.
  Until you get a yes.

Sometimes the age will trigger a knowing either in you or one being healed. If you still aren't clear about the past life event that is currently causing trouble in the present life, simply holding an intention to clear the problem is effective.

Typically, the research and originating problem go back no more than six lifetimes. I have seen an event only twice in two decades that happened nine lives back which affected their present body. It is a rare, but possible occurrence.

Once you have found the original problem, you can see how it is reflecting in the individual's current life. For example, a disease in the colon that caused great suffering or death in a previous life can cause the same illness or a similar one starting in the present lifetime at about the same age.

I call these 'spiritual time bombs.' Imagine that you are going along healthy and one day you realize you have diabetes. The timeline issue may have triggered from a past life where you had a sugar imbalance of a broken heart or abusive relationship since diabetes is an issue of love.

To understand the concept of the illness coming from a past life you must first understand an imprint of trauma has embedded into the spiritual DNA (not to be confused with the physical DNA). Once the trauma embeds it becomes a strong impetus for reoccurrence. The reason it becomes a part the spiritual DNA is that it has to have been a problem the person really had a desire to cure or resolve in the former life. The attachment or desire to resolve the issue will in your current life trigger the generation of a new DNA program, which provides the opportunity for resolution and understanding, perhaps victory in a future life.

It will not surface in every future life, but you might test to find that three or five lives read with the same susceptibility or weakness. The pattern, once in place, will not vanish until a) the individual successfully cures the problem or b) a miraculous healing takes place, and it is removed from the originating lifetime and all other lifetimes that it has recurred.

Miraculous Healing for this issue is extremely effective.

When you have completed the clearing process, using kinesiology you can check to see if it is already a program designated to a future life. This transpires because a person has a **recurring thought** (amplified by trauma and extreme emotion) that imprints the pattern on a future life. If this is the case, remove it from the future also.

The methods to remove spiritual timeline problems consist of two equally effective techniques:

Removal of programming from lifetimes related to date:

- Using kinesiology, identify the first lifetime it occurred, the age to within twelve months, and the specific problem.
- Pump gold energy into the lifetime, event age and problem.

Here are two examples:

- 6 lifetimes ago, 24 years old, thyroid disease.
- 5 lifetimes ago, 55 years old, mental degradation/dementia.

Be clear you are only removing the negative programming information. In fact, you can ask if the person would like to store the information they learned (while ill in their former lifetime) in their Akashic records.

- To send the information to the Akashic records, imagine sending this collection of details to a librarian on the astral in charge of this person's ongoing information.

If you are performing an information transfer, which is slightly different, identify all affected lives including the originating lifetime, remove and transfer information, then proceed to dissolve the program. In this case, it will be related to the desire to break attachment to the ailment.

If you have not done the information transfer to the Akashic records then:

- Proceed up the ladder of lifetimes until all related information from each lifetime (in which it occurred) is vanquished. This means starting with the oldest problem from the lifetime farthest back proceeding up to the present lifetime.

The following example illustrates how an originating problem manifests slightly differently but affects the same area of the body. The originating lifetime was six lives ago and the disease was cancer of the colon. Then four lifetimes ago it manifested as Crohn's disease, two lifetimes ago as polyps and infections, and in the present lifetime as stage-four colon cancer.

Alternative procedure to remove past life related challenges:

Timeline clearing

- Extend a time line out your back as far as you can imagine, and then out the front as far as you can imagine.
- Intend for the problem energy to appear as black dots on the time line.
- Use a golden spiritual vacuum cleaner to suction of all the black dots on the time line, both back through history and out into the future.

- When you muscle-test all dots and related energy/programs are cleared send a golden pulse, like a radio wave, through the future timeline and the past timeline to seal up the transformation.

Spiritual Parasites

The last chapter of this book goes into great detail on the subject of spiritual parasite. This topic includes entities, evil spirits and demons. Just like a parasite in the intestines, they exist and cause problems including causing intense pain and reducing function. The directions for clearing spiritual parasites is found in chapter 29.

This takes you through all the possible concerns for a positive reading on spiritual timelines. The next element in the Miraculous protocols is emotional.

Emotional

The following is the checklist for emotional issues coming up as positive with some helpful guidelines on how to use Miraculous Healing techniques to improve the emotional body, be it a blockage or programs.

Included below are some rapid clearings for moving into healing the physical body. I have also included emotional clearing related to relationships (which supports unlimited love and frees up the body for vibrant health) as well as a guide to living a balanced life.

One Emotional Body

Before I teach you the steps for healing the emotional body, it is important for you to understand what I am referring to.

The *emotional body* is intelligence; it overlays the physical body. This was not part of the original design of "human spirit in body" but came as an added improved element. This detail became available about 10,000 years ago. Prior to that time, human emotion came from body chemistry and hormones. This identified an important step for "human spirit" to evolve from "human animal." Until then, "human animal" exhibited less sophistication.

After the development of the *emotional body*, the first incarnation for the human spirit provided the original spiritual DNA program that is simply set to develop with the chakra system. When human spirit engages a physical body, the emotional body expands for full use. This happens at age twenty-one for female bodies and age twenty-eight to thirty for male bodies.

When a human body dies, it is possible to retain the *emotional body* for years as a layered aspect of *human spirit*. However, the aspect of the expanded *emotional body* must diminish prior to establishing a relationship with the parents for the next incarnation.

- If you have gotten a yes for the emotional body, locate black or grey in the emotional body and remove emotional death energy. Ten percent of humans have this issue.
- Pump gold energy from your right hand into the emotional body until clear.

Two Emotional Timeline

Since the *emotional body* is intelligence, it stores collected developmental steps and impactful events. There is literally not a timeline but a sequence of events we will refer to as the emotional timeline. All records of emotional development are part of this 'timeline'. Typically the ones that impact health are extreme emotional events.

Three the Emotional brain

You will be addressing two distinct parts of the emotional brain. The problem can be stored in the patterns and information from one of these two areas.

- Amygdala this is the part of the emotional brain that develops prior to age three and forms the basis of our emotional responses and interpretations.
- The maturing and adult mammalian brain. This is the social brain and contains all the programs and patterns of the developing and adult emotional/social structure.

In the emotional brain, identifying the pattern specifically will take some skill. Those programs are removable by pumping gold energy into the program until it test positive for clear.

You may discover a larger issue for example assault in the emotional brain. There are much more detailed clearing instructions and processes for something like this, See
- Chapter 27 on healing assault
- Chapter 28 on healing pain
- Chapter 22 on healing autism

Emotional balance and relationships may play a role in a disharmony or illness and are covered in greater detail in the relationships chapter and in my *Balance Your Life Now* book.

After the emotions we look to the mental element which include the mental body and brain as well as memes miasms curses and black magic.

Mental

One Brain

If you get a yes on the brain, discover which of the following five areas are affected?

1- survival or reptilian brain
2- emotional brain, amygdala
3- right neo-cortex: creative brain
4- left neo-cortex: logical brain
5- frontal lobe: out of the box thinking

Once you have identified the location in the brain you will want to go to the section of the brain chapter to assist you in your healings protocols.

Two Mental body

Mental body can include the mental timeline. The mental body is a component of human spirit and carries our mental information forward from lifetime to lifetime. There is rarely an issue here, however I have seen it several times so I include it in the protocols.

Three Memes, Miasm, Curses and Black Magic

This is a major section and is addressed in most healings in some form or fashion.

Meme is a group mind agreement affecting the issue. Similarly the Miasm is a group mind virus causing a problem and preventing a full healing.

Curses can be deliberate as seen by cultures who go to

great lengths with elaborate complex curses. These complex curses are not part of the American culture, so they are not typical. A full on curse will be complex and may have over 15 aspects to clear before the full curse has finally been removed.

Black magic is the final mental body issue. It can be cause from another or by the person who is having the problem. Black magic is the words repeated over and over that cast a spell of illness.

The last of the four elements is Physical. This section includes all the aspects of the physical body are included here.

Physical

Glands
See Chapter 17 on the endocrine system and glands and Chapter 26 on adrenal failure.
> Pineal,
> Pituitary
> Hypothalamus
> Thyroid
> Para-thyroid
> Thymus
> Pancreas
> Adrenals
> Ovaries
> Testicles

Organs
> Lungs/bronchi
> Heart

Stomach
Intestines
Liver
Kidneys
Gallbladder
Spleen
Skin

In addition, see Chapter 21 on vision.

Systems

See Chapter 18 on systems:
Circulatory
Respiratory
Immune
Cardiovascular
Muscular skeleton
Lymphatic
Digestive

DNA

If you discover the challenge is in the DNA you will want to use the DNA Obliteration process. This technique allows you to improve the condition of the DNA and to remove harmful programs.
See Chapter 2 on recessive DNA obliteration.

Once you have identified a physical element, unlike some of the other sections, the healings are deep and often complex. The aspects of healing the physical body are exciting and assessable and can be done with great effectiveness using gold creator god force energy (essentially quantum energy) from the golden rings and the process of Cellular Neo Genesis.

There are many things to consider when approaching this profound healing process. As I mentioned earlier, using the protocols in this way will help you locate the conditions that are most urgent to repair rejuvenate and correct.

Once you have done a thorough job of healing all urgent issues, you may chose to address issues that are of lowest function in the body. There are many parts of the body that are not necessary to live that can function at a very low level. However these areas must also be brought up to 100% to experience full health and rejuvenation.

Chapter 16: Brain

Introduction

Marty, a forty-eight year-old, highly-skilled mechanic, loved motorcycles. To say he loved motorcycles is probably an understatement as he owned sixteen of them and knew everything about the unique qualities of each manufacturer. He had been working for Tenant Company his entire adult life, a company that manufactures street sweepers and Zamboni ice surfacing machines (for hockey and skating rinks). But Marty didn't start loving machines as an adult. I remember him as a child disassembling anything mechanical and building new contraptions. I think his favorite was his go-carts, using motors provided by old lawnmowers.

One sunny day, Marty was riding his Indian (a motorcycle). A reckless teenage driver didn't see him coming and pulled out in front of him. Marty, in all his protective gear and helmet, T-boned the teenager's vehicle. It was a terrible crash with screeching wheels and the strong thud of death.

Marty was dead, floating over his crumpled, mangled body with every bone broken.

The ambulance raced to the scene, sirens screaming. An EMT emerged with board and head/neck brace in hand, running to the mangled biker. Had he been dead long? No pulse, no breathing, no heartbeat.

Pounding on his chest, mouth-to-mouth, and another pound. "Come on man, come back." The EMT used his mind to command Marty's spirit into the vacant body. And then something happened. Marty's heart started beating.

Breathe. He needed help breathing. Finally he was getting much needed oxygen to his brain and body.

Marty, as a spirit, stayed with his unidentified body. His identification had been lost at the scene of the accident. As the team of medical professionals hovered over his comatose body, they began to assess the damage. If he lived, what kind of life would he have?

X-rays revealed that almost every bone in his body was broken, some were just fragments. Legs and wrists needed to be rebuilt first. Marty was given two metal external shells, one for the body and one for the head and neck (called halos) which would hold bones in place as they were mending.

Eight years have now passed. Somehow Marty survived. He lives independently, though unable to hold a 'real job', his life is richly filled with his volunteer work at Methodist Hospital, where he was awarded 'volunteer of the year' helping other traumatic brain injury victims. He is also able to spend loads of time with his children and grandchildren. He is a happy man.

After eight years of pain, he had given up hope that Western medicine could help him control his pain. He had also not been able to walk unaided since that time, and relied on a cane to help him hobble around. His left foot had been without feeling or sensation. That's when Marty, my big brother, decided to explore the Miraculous Healing Program for himself.

This was the first time in eight years he asked for my assistance to provide him with a healing he could not have imagined.

In a three-day weekend we did profound healings on the emotional body and brain. By dramatically improving brain function and by literally growing back new brain cells for eighteen days, Marty has truly experienced a *miraculous healing*.

One of the markers for healing was the dramatic improvement of nerve function: he had both a significant reduction in pain and feeling return to his left foot. Shortly afterwards he walked without pain, without limping, and with no need for a cane. Within two months he was able to hike six miles on steep mountain trail for ten days in a row, with great joy and no assistance from a cane.

The role of your healthy brain

The role of your healthy brain plays an important part in optimizing your entire existence. Through your brain you view and understand your world. Your brain provides much of the content of your personality, character, judgment and ability to make good choices. When your brain is working well, so are you. However, when your brain vitality is in trouble, you will notice a diminished ability in all areas of your life.

Recent studies have revealed a startling fact about brain and obesity. It turns out that as your waistline gets larger your brain is actually shrinking. This is not good news for a country where at least thirty-percent of the population is struggling with weight issues.

A gestating woman's brain will shrink in the third trimester and return to full capacity six months after birth. This is a natural program wired into 'human animal' to ensure the mother will be all about baby and less observant of her surroundings when the baby really needs all her attention. Her brain is naturally wired to return to full function. Similarly, function will improve as fat comes off of a person moving out of obesity back to a healthy weight.

Miraculous healing brain protocols working through the human blueprint are quite possibly the most powerful of all the healings we are able to provide. The brain, with all its amazing complexities, when restored to high functionality, can improve virtually all bodily conditions of malfunction.

The brain controls all the systems of the physical body and even some parts of the energetic body. For people in pain, healing the brain can restore the nerves to ease and equilibrium, resulting in reduced pain sensations or even a total clearing of pain. Digestion is also affected positively by restoring the brain to a healthy state.

My research on the brain began many years ago as I have experienced two traumatic brain injuries, both related to moving vehicles. What I've discovered in this research is that if you heal the brain, even post-traumatic stress disappears as the new brain cells and brain patterns literally erase the PTSD from the field of memory.

We do not heal the brain first unless an unhealed brain is a block to a healing elsewhere. We would normally prepare the body for a brain healing by clearing relationship-love dysfunction and restoring the energetic body, including the chakras and aura, prior to beginning to work on the brain.

I suggest you follow the Miraculous Healing protocols prior to any work on the brain, asking whether the brain is ready to receive a healing and discover what is needed to prepare the brain for a permanent healing.

As we progress through the brain chapter, we will cover the basic brain healing and unique protocols for attention deficit, autism, traumatic brain injury, and dementia.

The first brain (also referred to as survival/reptilian brain)

This is the part of the brain accountable for instinctual responses and survival reactions. When thinking about the "first brain", imagine a little lizard dodging from here to there, finding a rock to hide under, or a clear path to skedaddle down to escape a predator. It is constantly responding to any stimulus as if its life depended on it getting away.

Part of our brain is actually wired that way. Now imagine you have a teenage
son. Let's say his name is Jason. Jason is currently responding to the dings, beeps and alarms from a 'humungous' pile of technology, such as phones, computers, clocks, and electronic games.

Much like the instinctual little lizard, your first brain is trained to respond dynamically as the signal to go to high alert lands from the eardrums to the autonomic response of the first brain.

Okay, back to the image of your teenage son, Jason, sitting on the sofa playing

Nintendo. Intense, heavy metal music screams into the space as his phone alerts him of the arrival of a new text. He's hungry so naturally he grabs the nearest junk food and throws it in the microwave. Five minutes later, "beep, beep, beep," alerts him those nasty pizza roll-ups are fully nuked.

The landline rings, "It's for you, Jason." His friend Marcus rings the doorbell, "ding dong." Before you know it, game on! The Nintendo game belts out another litany of noises.

What happens when the instinctual brain receives an alarm? Just like the little lizard, your brain darts around in response. No matter that this is not a life and death situation, just a game, a microwave and a doorbell. The instinctual brain reacts anyway, adrenal chemistry is injected into your veins and the nervous system is launched into the sympathetic or high alert state.

Your sympathetic system is now on and it will remain on for thirty minutes even with no additional stimulation. However, if you decide to get cozy on the sofa and watch an action/suspense movie such as 'Bourne Identity,' your high alert system will remain activated for hours.

Well, what's so bad about that? In the sympathetic mode, you are ready to run away from a dangerous saber tooth tiger or a grizzly bear. Your body is pumping out the high energy chemicals needed to keep you on high alert and wired to respond quickly to keep you safe, just like the lizard. However, unlike lizards that have no higher brain function and can sometimes grow a new tail, ***we must be in the parasympathetic mode to regenerate and heal.***

The average yogi who is calm and peaceful much of his life will appear ten and sometimes twenty years younger than other folks his age. This system is an ancient one and no longer really suited for the way we use a body now. However, it is the system we have. Less adrenaline-rising activities and more calm will yield an excellent result with the human physique, leading to a healthier more vibrant life.

Best colors for the first brain

100%	Green	Health, Vitality, Full Function
92%	Blue	Stillness, Health, Ease (seen after a stress pattern is healed)
90%	Pink	Mother Energy, Strength, Purpose, Steadfast, Obligation, Duty

60%	Orange	Begins lower or malfunction Overactive, Stimulated, Losing Health
50%	Purple	Spiritual, Showing Age forty Plus, Reduced function
30%	Yellow	Exhaustion, Difficulty Dealing
3%	Red	Agitation, Intense, Overage
	White	Control Energy
	Black, Grey	Serious Malfunction Death Energy

The first brain is fueled by the fifth chakra as well as eight nadis. Nourishment is provided by blood, oxygen and synovial fluid.

First Brain Healing Protocols

1. Using kinesiology, begin by reading the color and percentage of functions of the first brain, which is

your instinctual or reptilian brain. Chart color and function percentage.

2. Pump gold energy into the first brain if it has a reduced function and color.

How to handle specific brain issues while healing:

There are many possible circumstances that arise during a brain healing. Here are a couple of examples:

- You can assist a blue brain at 92% to ascend to green at 100%. After clearing the stress syndrome, a person's first brain will not be able to get higher than blue unless you assist. It is wise to clear the spiritual timeline and DNA programs that caused the stress condition in the first place.

- If a woman is in agreement to move her first brain from pink to green you can assist her in that process. Remember that both blue and pink are not considered malfunction colors, however these colors will influence how the first brain responds.

3. In the first brain, if you have completed a color and function percentage healing, your next step will be a DNA obliteration process. In the DNA process, look for causes of the malfunction for removal. If the brain malfunction was congenital, activate the universal human blueprint. Draw on the code from the blueprint to create a new path for the first brain.
Note: Later in the chapter there are a good number of brain maladies for you to reference for clarification on specific disorders and the steps to healing them.

4. The next step is to ask if Cellular Neo-Genesis is required. If so, proceed with the rebuilding of the master cell and mirroring/building of new cells. See Chapter three.

5. Ask if the healing is complete, check if the first brain will need follow up healings and document the next possible day suited for healing.

Brain 1 Illnesses and related colors

1. Black or Grey	Dementia Attention deficit Bio-toxin contamination, e.g. agent orange, nuclear radiation exposure Psychosis Psychopathy
2. Black	Chemotherapy patient Pain, the state of Recent death of a spouse or child including abortion miscarriage and stillbirth, seen in parents Schizophrenic Sociopath
3. Grey	Depression
4. Red	Mania Agitation condition Violence, state of
5. Yellow	Autism Asperger's Down syndrome

The second brain (also referred to as emotional or mammalian brain)

The second brain, which I refer to as the emotional or mammalian brain gives us all of our human animal emotional programs from which we respond, feel and relate to others. The sixth brain (the heart) gives us access to love. You cannot love from the mind, but it provides the mental programs that allow a sense of safety and relatedness. Actual love comes the ability to access your God-self. The human heart provides the access to the state of love.

The second brain has several unique features, including the amygdala, providing important programs accrued through your early emotional research prior to age three.

Differences In Men And Women

For females, the emotional brain is marinating in estrogen throughout her life, giving her a steady stream of content for understanding socialization and relatedness.
Please let it be known that men are not deficient when compared to women. The testosterone that marinates their brains over a lifetime provides logic, clarity, and focus. What allows a woman to process her feelings and emotions for hours, can wear thin on a male brain.

The condition of unique and different brains exemplifies the edict of function following form. Men as human animal are responsible for providing and protecting. The testosterone in their bran allows for strength and focus. They have the power and strength to naturally provide safety for their partner and offspring. Men function out in the world very well. Their human animal nature makes them good hunters. Their single-mindedness will support

283

them in completing a project, regardless of the number of obstacles.

Their best advice, which they deliver routinely to the females around them, is to focus. This is their solution and one that helps them in many ways to accomplish the great and wonderful feats of providing and protecting.

Unlike the testosterone-driven brain, the estrogen brain provides women with diffuse awareness. We are easily able to multitask and keep track of lost keys and socks. Women's brains are wired to gather and nurture. We can use the aspects of our brain that resembles a male to focus on the task at hand, such as successfully holding executive careers in large corporations. But to really enjoy the balance of being a woman, when leaving work we must allow our female brains to re-emerge.

A perfect example of this is the large group entrepreneurial trainings I participate in with my business coach, James Malinchak. He provides an incredible training for speakers and information product marketers. James, who was featured on NBC's Secret Millionaire, definitely has a mind for business and really knows his stuff. His trainings provide the way to make it BIG in the speaking world.

My friends were surprised when I signed up with James a couple years ago. They felt he did not match my spiritual nature. Yet my logic told me he understood the secrets of a material world that I would never receive in a spiritual training program.

My challenge became, "How do I not crash and burn while sitting in James' boot camps?" My social brain that I've used for painting, playing harp, meditation, and sharing ideas, would become completely overloaded. With the out of balance focus of long twelve-hour training days I would feel overwhelmed. By the second or third day it felt as if someone was hitting my head with a sledgehammer. The men in the trainings had quite the opposite response as their focused testosterone-driven brains were equipped to conquer their domain.

I, like many of the women training with James, have found my balance. Occasionally taking an hour to rest or visiting with a girlfriend in the hallway during the conference helps create more space in my wonderfully diffuse brain for some more goodies!

Healthy Emotional Brain Development

At two years old, Britta Carrie already had an estrogen flood in her early female development. Her behavior illustrated the development of the emotional, mammalian brain so perfectly.

Britta was named for her fifth generation great grandmother, a truly great woman from 150 years ago. Great Grandmother Britta made her arduous pilgrimage from her birthplace, Sweden. She, her husband, and her sons settled in the beautiful prairies of southwest Minnesota, where they homesteaded their land. Grandma Britta, with some medical training and a strong constitution, delivered all the babies born to the immigrant settlers of this wild land.

Her strong constitution and healthy emotional brain made her a perfect midwife. My grown daughter Britta has so many of these amazing pioneers qualities. It is a true joy to behold.

When Britta, was very young, she was a brilliant light. She was smart, engaging, and so funny. She loved connection and couldn't get enough of it. She jumped up in my lap to snuggle and cuddle at every opportune moment, as well as a few inopportune moments.

Her social emotional brain was on overdrive with nurturing and caretaking. She would mimic my behaviors and when little sister came home for the first time, Britta saw her mommy nursing her new little sister. From her birth, she had breastfed but to comprehend it visually was astonishing for her.

From that moment on, she was nursing everything she could hold. The dolls and stuffed animals kind of made sense, but the train, cars, trucks and mini farm equipment were over the top. She was making sure everything in her domain was well cared for and nourished.

She traveled with me wherever I went, never staying with a babysitter. My visit to the doctor's office made a profound impression on her and she began treating her loyal subjects with a play doctor kit.

Her unusual insight made me laugh so much. One day we set off on the long drive to see Great Aunt Bessie who was in a nursing home just over the boarder in Iowa. As we drove we sang happy songs; "This little light of mine, I'm gonna let it shine!" Life was good.

Britta, bounced up excitedly shouting "Mommy, Mommy, guess what?"

Do you remember the 'guess what' game with your two or three year old?

"Mommy, Bessie lives in a home just like us!"

Hmmm, okay. I'm not sure how a state run nursing home is similar to our ancient salt-box farmstead, but lets see where this goes.

"How do you figure that, honey?"

"Well, she lives in a nursing home and so do we!"

Laughter and gleeful silliness ensued as my little mammalian-brained daughter was peaking in her socialization and instinctual nurturing.

Britta became a nurse's aid at sixteen and went on to become an RN. She has truly followed in her Great Granny's footsteps as she has cared for the worst of the injured and sick as a trauma nurse for many years now. Nurses decide to become nurses from their second brain!

Unhealthy Emotional Brain Consequences

If the emotional brain is out of whack it can wreak havoc in your relationships and love life.
Melinda and Joe really struggled in their marriage with constant misunderstandings. I could see the marriage was based on chemistry with Joe being a bad boy in need of rehabilitation. Melinda, like many women, seemed to have married a project rather than a beloved.

She would call me for spiritual/emotional advice and consulting, a role even I found challenging. They had accrued a fortune through their sixteen years together. Assets and children kept them together the last few years of their marriage.

Joe was under 'house arrest' from Melinda at one point. Every step he made was scrutinized under a microscope. At some point he snapped. I believe men genuinely want to please and satisfy the woman they are with. However, for Joe, the constant fights, accusations of disloyalty and '*you are failing miserably to protect us*', sent him off the rails and he became what his wife kept accusing him of being.

Infidelity came first. Then surveillance equipment was installed on Melinda's car phone and computer so he could track her. Then, unbelievably, he attempted to poison and kill her. Fortunately, he failed.

When askew, the emotional brain can prevent people from experiencing love as warnings of unsafe feeling surface. These are related to the early emotional traumas programmed into the amygdala.

Best Colors for Second Brain

100%	Green	Male: Ease, Contentment, Confidence
100%	Pink	Female: Satisfaction, Serenity and Safety
97%	Green	Female: Safe, Contentment
94%	Pink	Male: Contentment, Gentleness (compensation for sins of the father, self, or past life aggression) tempered
86%	Orange	Happiness, Hope (Pollyanna experience - a reaction to difficulty)
84%	Purple	Male leaders: Intelligence (providing additional emotional intelligence beyond normal male programming) (I have not seen this color in a woman in the second brain)
20%	Red	Begins Lower or malfunction Fire, Hostility
4%	Blue	Frozen, Lifeless, Vacant
2%	Yellow	Confused, Chaotic
	White	Control energy
	Black, Grey	Serious Malfunction Death Energy

Malfunction in the Second Brain

The second brain is fueled by the sixth chakra as well as eight nadis. Nourishment is provided by the blood oxygen and synovial fluid. This brain's health is supported by the senses including music, fragrance (olfactory and auditory senses).

Second Brain Protocols

1. Begin by reading the color and percentage of functions of the second brain, which is your emotional or mammalian brain. Chart color and function percentage.

2. Pump gold energy into the brain if it has a reduced function and color.

> Note: There are numerous colors over 86% that are not considered a malfunction of the second brain.

3. In the second brain, if you have completed a color and function percentage healing, your next step will be a spiritual timeline clearing. This process supports clearing harmful events responsible for fear responses in the emotional brain.

4. After the spiritual timeline clearing, the next step is to heal the early emotional memory/response programs found in the amygdala. Our wellness recovery process is not related to psychotherapeutic style, meaning no processing or conversations about the memory/response program, how it got there or how it has played out.

5.   Using kinesiology muscle test the number of these programs available for use. For example, say you discover 42 of these programs.

6.   Picture a magnetic red rose that is grounded to the center of the earth, and from the emotional brain magnetize out all the energy related to the memory/response programs.

Very important; these memory/response programs are much like post-traumatic stress. In order to heal the reactive nature of this, the original memory must become a memory without any punch.

7.   Using kinesiology, again test for the number of memory/response programs available. When you have been successful in removing all the energy through the magnet rose technique, you will read zero.

8. Using kinesiology check to see if cellular neo-genesis is required.
If yes proceed with the steps for regeneration found in Chapter 3.

If no:

9. Test to learn if the DNA obliteration process is required for vibrant health in the emotional brain. In the DNA process look for causes of the malfunction for removal. If the brain malfunction is congenital, activate the universal human blueprint encoding to create a new path for the second brain.
10. DNA programs to look for include emotional malfunction, depression, mental illnesses, neurosis,

as well as self-esteem, self-affinity and social proficiency.

11. When DNA Procedure is complete; ask if the healing is complete. Check if the second brain will need follow up healings and document the next possible day suited for healing.

Brain 2 Illnesses And Related Colors

1. Black or Grey	Depression Psychotic Sociopath Dementia
2. Black	Chemotherapy patient Agitation condition Psychopath Schizophrenic Violence, state of Recent death of a spouse miscarriage and stillbirth, seen in parents
3. Grey	Attention deficit Bio toxin contamination over 40% affected. E.g., agent orange, nuclear radiation exposure Pain, the state of Recent abortion Autism Asperger's
4. Red	Mania
5. Orange	Down syndrome

The third or creative brain (right neo cortex)

The third brain is the right neo-cortex and is known as the creative brain. Creative and imaginative actions, such as art, stem from this brain. You might remember a wonderful guide to accessing this brain came out in 1979 by Author/Artist Betty Edwards, entitled *"Drawing on the Right Side of the Brain."* Creativity stems from five areas; our energetic systems, the second and fifth chakras, our emotional body and senses, and our third brain.

In our Miraculous Living "Balance Your Life Now," program, creativity plays an important role on the balance wheel. This is about being able to completely embody a fully self-expressed human life. Fulfillment on the balance wheel and in a human life, filled with both mastery in the spiritual realm and mastery in the physical realm, requires the fulfillment of creative expression with regularity.

The new "enlightenment" in the Age of Aquarius is mastery in both spiritual and physical realms. I highlight this here as a good number of individuals coming to the coaching and training program have allotted little energy or time for developing and expressing creativity. Absence of creativity, that is, without authentic expression coming from the individual, leaves a person lacking. For example being a bystander occasionally tuning into some music or dance performance, does not fill the creative requirement.

For full self-expression and fulfillment on the balance wheel, a person would need to spend some percentage of time in creative expression. Ideal creative expression ranges from 7% to 42%. The high end would represent a mastery level fine artist or professional musician/dancer.

Best Colors for Third Brain

100%	Green	Conceptual Development, Imaginative, Talent
92%	Pink	Ability, Craftsmanship, Beauty
83%	Red	Leaping (from malfunction to vibrant creative brain)

51%	Yellow	Begins lower or malfunction Calculating
40%	Orange	Affected, Creates out of struggle, Because of something creativity exist rather then the authentic expression. Could show depression, mania, autism.
21%	Purple	Lacking ability to embrace this realm, attention deficient
11%	Blue	Still, Expressionless, much of the time early choice not to express creativity, or mental illness like PTSD
7%	Brown	Contamination
	White	Control energy
	Black, Grey	Serious Malfunction Death Energy

The third brain is fueled by the sixth and seventh chakras as well as thirteen nadis. Nourishment is provided by the blood oxygen and synovial fluid and is supported by expression.

Third Brain Healing Protocols

1. Begin by reading the color and percentage of functions of the third brain, which is your creative

brain and right hemisphere. Chart color and function percentage.

2. Pump gold energy into the brain if it has a reduced function and color.

Note: Red is evidence that by outer action and commitment a brain is improving on its own, it can readily be assisted up to green or pink by pumping gold.

3. In the third brain, if you have completed a color and function percentage healing, your next step will be a to check if Cellular Neo-Genesis is required.
If yes: proceed with the cellular neo genesis process in Chapter 3.

If no:
4.Using kinesiology test to learn if the DNA obliteration process is required for vibrant health in the creative brain. In the DNA process look for causes of the malfunction for removal. If the brain malfunction was congenital, activate the universal human blueprint encoding to create a new path for the third brain.

5. DNA programs to look for include: creative malfunction; conception, ability, over calculating, creativity driven by struggle, contamination

6. When DNA procedure is complete, check to see if a timeline clearing is next. You will remove the impact of events preventing the free flow of expression.

7. Ask if the healing is complete.

8. Check if the third brain will need follow up healings and document the next possible day suited for healing.

Third Brain Illnesses And Related Colors

1. Black or Grey	Depression Agitation condition Schizophrenia Psychosis
2. Black	Chemotherapy patient Psychopathic Violence, state of
3. Grey	Attention deficit Recent abortion Dementia Sociopathic
4. Yellow	Obsessive-compulsive disorder
5. Orange	Autism
6. Purple	Down syndrome
7. Blue	Bio toxin contamination i.e. Agent Orange, Nuclear Radiation exposure Recent death of a spouse miscarriage and stillbirth, seen in parents
8. Brown	Pain, the state of Asperger's Mania

The fourth brain (also referred to as logical brain)

The fourth brain is the left neo cortex, also called the logical brain. This part of the brain provides the efficient analytical interpreter to perform function related to mathematics and science. Sound common sense, focus, and clarity come from its healthy function. Where estrogen provides fertilizer for the emotional second brain, testosterone can serve as enrichment to the soil of the fourth brain. We are approaching the domain of male accomplishment and outer achievement. The ability to focus for prolonged periods and produce commonsense results is instrumental in our survival as humans.

In the section on the second brain above, we discussed the development of little girls, specifically Britta, and how her mammalian brain dictated many of her actions during a time when high levels of estrogen were being released into her system. The way our female bodies are wired helps us develop a strong nurturing capacity early in life. This program embedded into a female psyche prior to age three greatly influenced her actions and responses during the rest of her days.

For a human male, the fourth brain, logical, problem solving and his protective nature begins as his toddler brain is bathed in testosterone and continues to play a strong part in providing clarity for his role throughout life.

Having a son after two daughters was an amazing shock. My toddler daughters were interested in singing, playing, learning, and exploring together socially. When my little man came into the world, everything changed.

When little boys' brains and bodies get their infusion of testosterone, they begin the journey of a hunter and protector. As a child, having no reference or clear understanding of how to channel that energy into activities that are enjoyable or even understandable to the girls around them, they began the "destroy and conquer" phase. Later logic and reason become apparent. You will see the shift as a boy moves into adventure and understanding, where strategy and planning become a part of their 'game'.

To my friends, I would refer to my toddler son as little 'destructo-man'. He had his angelic moments, like when he was fast asleep in his bed, and a glow of angel dust shone around him, magically washing away all the offenses of the day. Just like that, my little man was restored to his princely position.

Two excellent books on the development of men that help to unlock the mysteries of their motivation and behavior are: *"The Amazing Development of Men,"* and *"Keys to the Kingdom"*, both by author Alison Armstrong. I love her exploration and roadmap to helping us understand and appreciate the extraordinary and different qualities in each of the genders.

This discussion around the fourth and logical brain is a great place to interject details of the brain in competition. As I write this chapter, the 2012 Olympics are underway. As an athlete and sports enthusiast myself, I have been posting articles online in response to the wins and challenges of the Olympians.

I was intrigued to learn about the challenges of our national swimming hero Michael Phelps, who has used several obstacles related to brain function to fuel his world record career as the most decorated gold medal winner in Olympic history.

As a child, Michael received the diagnosis of ADHD; Attention-Deficit/Hyperactivity Disorder. His mother used athletics to help channel Michael's energy towards a positive activity. His coach of sixteen years intentionally created additional challenges for Michael, causing Michael to use his brain for accomplishment, preparing him for difficulties that might arise in live competitions.

It has truly been a winning strategy, transforming Michael into a consummate winner with resilience and kindheartedness in his nature. This was possible because of his wise elder guides who helped him make those good choices until he could for himself become the extraordinary man he is now.

For him, there was a shift from the last Olympics, including gold medal wins, to the current games. Michael has seemed to step into a new mature man. Leaving behind the knight slaying dragons, perhaps with a bit less vigor on the win, he has moved into the next phase of level of wise elder love.

As it turns out, after the last wins, Michael hit a wall and began to question the value of his life and the meaning of the wins. And so ensued a depression and weight gain followed by a good amount of self-reflection and 'soul' searching. This relates both to the period of his Saturn return, which is a phase of moving into adulthood and positioning for adult life, starting at age twenty-eight.

It is typical for an individual to examine their way of being, and reframe their life in a more mature way, which then leads to their next steps in life. It is possible to put aside previous life experiences and instead, start an entirely new career with more meaning and a deeper sense of contribution, or reframe their present career by building on the accomplishments of the past.

I see that Michael is actually doing both. He also arrived early into the 'tunnel', which is a phase of manhood described in Alison Armstrong's wonderful book, *"Keys to the Kingdom."* This phase is often thought of as a mid-life crisis and can last anywhere from a few months to, typically, a year and a half. It resembles depression. In this phase, a man may become self- questioning and uncertain of the meaning of his life; he may look at his contributions and how he wants the rest of his life to play out.

Michael has moved from the stage of prince to that of king, where he now is looking at his Kingdom and how he can make a difference in his world. Michael arrived here early because of the intense celebrity spotlight he has been standing under for sixteen years. We now see him looking to his future life and retiring from the Olympic games.

Healing the fourth brain:

Depression is a brain malady as is ADHD. An "energetic" healer would see a brain in depression with all five brains under a black influence. We refer to this blackness as a death energy, which means a dormancy in activity. As anyone who has undergone a period of depression will tell you, they lived under a dark cloud or in a haze. The language descriptions are actually very accurate for what is happening on an energetic level. As the haze lifts, all portions of the magnificent brain - from the instinctual and logical brains to the emotional, creative, and angelic brains - begin to lighten up again.

This is the period where hope or life returns.

Looking back into Michael's challenge with his first brain: ADHD. Individuals who experience this condition are often creative individuals, who have - for the journey of spirit - created situations that will rapidly accelerate the concepts of compassion, empathy, and understanding.

If you are individual of faith and believe the "hand of God" is influencing your incarnation and how your life unfolds, or if you are a person of self actualization, and believe you play a role in the circumstances and programs that you have set to play out in your life, these concepts will make sense to you.

Whether the "Hand of God" or personal spirit choice, challenging life patterns do develop from the individual's desire to grow rapidly on their spirit journey. They will have a life filled with material and circumstances to assist in this rapid acceleration.

On a physical level, Michael and others like him with ADHD typically have more than the standard three pathways of communication between the right and left hemispheres of the brain. For children, learning to harness the rapid fire cross-communication between logic and creativity can be an overwhelming challenge. For loving wise elder guides, such as parents, coaches, and teachers or even therapists, they can help people with ADHD understand the benefits of their obstacle. These specific challenges can strengthen character, deepen compassion, and produce a lifetime of incredible accomplishment.

Looking at the brains of Olympic gold medal winners, we see some common themes in the colors of the champions.

Starting with Michael Phelps at the time of receiving his fifteenth and nineteenth Olympic medals our hero had a range of hues in his different brains: an orange hue in the first or instinctual brain and the second (or emotional) brain; green in the third (or creative) right brain, purple in the fourth (or logical) brain; and gold in the fifth frontal lobe (or angelic brain).

I don't literally mean the brain has changed colors on a physical level. I am referring to the colors an energetic healer can read which represent the health of the brain.

Orange in the first two brains represents bliss or extreme happiness. Green in the creative brain represent vibrant health, purple in the fourth represents a kind of regality and personal acceptance of royal status, and gold in the angelic brain shows divine expression.

McKayla Maroney, a gymnastics elite world champion and gold medal winner at the 2012 Olympics, gives the female version of the champion's brain colors: First brain orange; second brain green; third brain orange; fourth brain orange, and fifth brain gold. For McKayla who is under the youthful influence of both hormones and sheer excitement her youthful female brain reflects a celebratory champion.

Orange again in the instinctual or survival brain is happiness. The green emotional brain represents a healing she went through in her emotional body after her disappointment two days prior, where she lost the opportunity to compete for individual world champion. The second brain was actively restoring its equilibrium. The third brain, the creative brain, as orange shows sheer joy and really reflects her artistry and full creative engagement in her sport, as she gave quite possibly the best performance of her life.

Remember we have identified the fourth brain as the brain of logic and competition, with orange representing so much joy and enthusiasm. The angelic brain gold represents divine expression.

Colors that influence and nurture the activities of the brain change occasionally. What we do in the Miraculous Living healing program is help individuals get to the brain colors that support their vibrant joy and health.

The application and importance of using color to heal can make a huge difference with a vet who suffers from PTSD, restoring him to his condition prior to traumatic event that shut him down. We can lift an accident survivor out of pain and literally get his brain communicating with his legs again. We can open up a world of peace and ease for a depressed world leader.

Although the conversations about Olympic competition and brain function could have easily fit into any of the brain conversations, I choose to add them here in the fourth or logical brain, as this is the brain from which strategy logic and competition are born.

Best Colors for Fourth Brain

100%	Primary Green	Conceptual Focus, Logic
99%	Olive Green	Routine
76%	Blue	Composed

56%	Primary Yellow	Begins lower or malfunction Intense, wounded
12%	Red	Aggression, vicious
4%	Yellowish- Green	Excitable (Mania)
2%	Purple	Dissociated
	White	Control energy
	Black, Grey	Serious Malfunction Death Energy

Colors Of The Malfunctioning Fourth Brain

The fourth brain is fueled by the first and sixth chakras as well as five nadis. Nourishment is provided by the blood oxygen and synovial fluid and is supported by DNA programs.

Healing Protocols for the Fourth Brain

1. Using kinesiology, begin by reading the color and percentage of functions of the fourth brain, which is your creative brain and right hemisphere. Chart color and function percentage.

2. Pump gold energy into the fourth brain if it has a reduced function and color.

Note: Red is a danger sign. It is evidence this individual is participating in violent activity

3. In the fourth brain, if you have completed a color and function percentage healing, your next step will be to check if spirit is well connected with this brain. Both congenital issues and brain trauma can be at fault for the disconnect, regardless of the reason the spirit connection must be fortified to (hopefully) 100% or as high as you can possibly get it, for a lasting improvement. There are two aspects for this healing: one is spiritual the other is to dramatically improve the physical chemistry of the brain.

4. Focus gold energy to the area not occupied by spirit. Your job as healer is to guide the spirit into this part of the brain.

5. Focus gold energy towards the overall brain with the intention of improving brain chemistry.

6. Once you have a clear reading that spirit connection with the brain has been restored and the chemistry is now supporting the spirit occupation of the brain, test if Cellular Neo-Genesis is required.

If yes, proceed with the cellular neo genesis process on page 51

If no

7. Using kinesiology test to learn if the DNA obliteration process is required for vibrant health in the logical brain. In the DNA process look for causes of the malfunction for removal. If the brain malfunction was congenital, activate the universal human blueprint encoding to create a new path for the fourth brain.

8. DNA programs to look for include: violence/victim, mania, lack of composure, dissociative issues, lack of permission to use logic (found in females) servitude, even reading math and science skills can be improved from DNA shifts.

9. When DNA procedure is complete; check to see if a timeline clearing is next. You will remove the impact of events preventing the logic, strategy, clarity and focus.

10. Ask if the healing is complete.

11. Check if the fourth brain will need follow up healings and document the next possible day suited for healing.

Fourth Brain Illnesses And Related Colors

1. Black or Grey	Depression Agitation condition Schizophrenia Psychosis
2. Black	Chemotherapy patient Psychopath Violence state of Recent abortion Pain, the state of
3. Grey	Sociopath Mania Down syndrome Nuclear Radiation exposure Recent death of a spouse miscarriage and stillbirth, seen in parents
4. Yellow	Bio toxin contamination i.e. Agent Orange
5. Orange	Attention deficit Asperger's
6. Green	Autism
7. Brown	Dementia

The fifth or angelic brain

The fifth brain is the frontal lobe, found behind the forehead and provides access to out of the box thinking. Its function is to provide the launch pad for magic, genius innovation and invention. It provides a gateway with admittance to the entirety of earthly existence.

My ability to write this manuscript is largely dependent on my traversing the natural corridor into the realm of "All."

There was a time in my life when I lived between two realms. By the time I reached my early thirties I had survived so much illness and surgery and, because of this, I was unable to get a hold of my body and enjoy the journey of life. Up to that point, my waking time had been spent as a realtor. Then I had had two significant bouts of allergic reactions that had forced my doctors to insist I discontinue working. Obviously, these were very serious life-threatening episodes. At that point, I retreated from the world.

Life in a bubble

Though I wasn't literally in a bubble, I lived my days in my Minnetonka home, spending most of my life in the 2200 square foot spilt level house. I had the environment sparsely furnished so it was easy to keep it orderly and free of allergens.

Having the need to retreat and a home to nest in, I spent much of the day in prayer, contemplation, meditation, and study. My health issues were extremely unpleasant. The upside of this situation was the time and safety to spend hours on end in and out of body, exploring the heavenly realms.

Days and nights often became indistinguishable, as both realms were very real to me. You will understand how this feels if you have experienced lucid dreaming: this is a dream where you are yourself and are not drifting in a fantastical dream. Instead, you are interacting, speaking, and connecting with others.

I was becoming a visionary. My inner eyes were awakening: access to the miracles of earthly existence and maturity as a human spirit in body were accelerated. Truly, this was an initiation and, as if in my own private ashram in

308

reverie, I joined the saints and sages of several spiritual traditions to receive my preparation and direction.

It also felt like a time when I was being guided to awaken from the dream of my human life and see myself for who I have always been. I made some extremely difficult decisions to remove myself completely from the familiar patterns with family that would have prevented me from awakening.

Jesus said you must die to the self to be born again, born into the heavenly understanding. He pointed out the difficulty of knowing yourself while living in the shared dream of sleepwalking loved ones.

I engaged my time in learning and studies, not sure if I would survive or if I even wanted to survive another year. At thirty-two, it became imperative to me that my life should have some meaning, that my existence on earth would make a positive and loving impact, and that I would not die in vain. What I mean by that is that I didn't want to just go through a difficult life and then die, having neither experiencing the "Garden of Eden" or the satisfaction of leaving a personal legacy.

About midway through my year in the bubble, my trance state became elevated and I begin writing content flowing through fifth brain access. This manuscript felt like scripture, precious and enlightening.

One

I remember a time when time was not,
When all that was, was what could not be,
When who was, was what and I was We.

When I existed as We, we were ablaze.

The fire was power, the light was life,
And I was not, alone did not exist.

But some part of the We broke off, throwing us out of
balance,
No longer a single living cell, We scattered in many
directions,
The brightest parts became the stars and planets.

Those parts of the We that were small became less brilliant,
Because we could not access all of the light of the We,
We became confused in the spinning off.

We became the many.

We forgot the We.

The Self,
     The Sparkle,
The Glimmer.

Became encompassed by a mass,
It had weight, it moved, thought and felt.
It responded to the temporary, the unreal became the
unquestioned truth,
Though we all knew it was a lie.
What could we do?

I lacked in spark, my flame grew dangerously small.
I longed for the fire of the We, the time of no time,
When all was what was not and nothing was real.

I longed for the We, the blaze, the brilliance, and the
completion.

There is a new, a beingness, a brightness found from the
We,
I in myself, encompassed by the mass, Lacking in spark
have glimpsed at the new.

It is purest light,
Brightest love.
The new is the ancient revealed, it is a glimmer of the
Omni,
 The remembrance of the We, It is the We.

I am not, it is not, truth is that which is unreal.
I am and exist truly in the We.
Only in my lack of existence I am free to be what is not.

While in this state of focus and access, I wrote much philosophical and profoundly spiritual poetry.

The fifth brain, the angelic brain is the brain of geniuses. There is IQ and there is "I Am." Knowing requires use of the physical brain and access to the storage lockers where accumulated information is stored, compared, integrated, implemented and placed for future use.

"I Am" is the experience of the awareness of existence. It is authentically complete on its own and is often the revelations shared with the world, as the experience of full access of the "I am" is brought to the realm of translation, comprehension, and understanding.

I have described the genius access through this fifth brain, but what about the normal people who are not geniuses and don't have revelations? How do "normal" folks use this magical/angelic brain?

Mathematics, calculation, scientific exploration, music, fine art and many additional expressive actions and engagements are a beautiful way to use a healthy fifth brain.

Best Colors for Fifth Brain

100%	Pink	Brilliance, Calculation
96%	Yellow	Association, Connection
73%	Blue	Inspiration

40%	Purple	Begins lower or malfunction Vision, ESP
37%	Green	Dissociation
32%	Orange	Bombastic, Verbose
9%	Red	Obsession, Hysteria
	White	Control energy
	Black, Grey	Serious Malfunction Death Energy

The fifth brain is fueled by the seventh chakra as well as five nadis. Nourishment is provided by the blood, oxygen and synovial fluid and is supported by spiritual development.

Healing Protocols For The Fifth Brain

1. Using kinesiology, begin by reading the color and percentage of functions of the fifth brain, which is your angelic out of the box and frontal lobe. Chart color and function percentage.

2. Pump gold energy into the fifth brain with a reduced function and color.

Note: ESP and vision are on the lower end at 40% and purple. This reflects an individual not relating well to their body. (Clairaudience, clairvoyance, clairsentience do not come from the fifth brain.)

3. In the fifth brain, if you have completed a color and function percentage healing, check to see if the Cellular Neo-Genesis is needed. If yes, proceed using the information in Chapter 3.

If no:

4. Test to learn if the DNA obliteration process is required for vibrant health in the fifth brain. In the DNA process look for causes of the malfunction for removal. If the brain malfunction was congenital, activate the universal human blueprint encoding to create a new path for the fifth brain.
5. Ask if the healing is complete.

6. Check if the fifth brain will need follow up healings and document the next possible day suited for healing.

Fifth Brain Illnesses and Related Colors

1. Black or Grey	Psychotic Psychopath Pain, the state of
2. Black	Chemotherapy patient Depression Schizophrenic Recent death of a spouse miscarriage and stillbirth, seen in parents
3. Grey	Nuclear Radiation exposure Sociopath Agitation condition Bio toxin contamination i.e. Agent Orange
4. Yellow	Down syndrome
5. Orange	Violence, state of
6. Green	Autism Mania
7. Blue	Asperger's
8. Purple	Obsessive-compulsive disorder Attention deficit
9. Brown	Dementia Recent abortion

While we are a blastocyst, 180 dividing cells, the same embryonic material that forms the brain also forms the skin and nervous system.

Depression

I am often asked to assist an individual in healing the mental challenge of depression. Depression is a mental illness, that is an illness of the mind, and when prolonged, it can shorten life by up to ten years. It is an intense condition of hopelessness and despondency. A person who is depressed knows life can feel better because depression is not a constant state: mood is in constant flux. However, once in the depressed state, they do not see the possibility of getting better, but rather seek to survive.

Depression is a spiritual malady. It means the survival (first) and the emotional (second) brains are black, while the other three brains can be black or grey. The energy is that of death. When you are depressed, you feel somehow that the lights have been turned off and all the joy in your life has gone. You feel you'll never experience that light and joy again. You also feel you have lost your connection with God and life becomes empty, with little value or meaning.

Curing depression for the Miraculous Living Healer can mean pacing someone back into a happy life, but it is necessary to discover where the source of the depression began and what is needed to restore vibrancy.

About four years ago I assisted a woman, Maya, in restoring joy to her life after a severe bout of grief and depression. Her trigger was her husband's suicide after their daughter was born. Both her brain and aura went black.

It was as if she had died herself. The death of her husband, who had been struggling with sleeplessness and depression, had triggered for her the end of her life as she knew it. This ending of Maya's joy was actually a death experience of everything she knew and loved.

She didn't find me for several months. When we met, her husband had been gone nine months and her daughter was now a toddler at eighteen months. Since Maya was not able to function or care for herself or her child, Maya's mother had moved in with her to care for both of them.

We began by clearing her husband's residual energy from her and returning her energy from him and the past. The awakening was dramatic and swift. Over just a few weeks we brightened the aura and the brain and restored the organs, systems, and glands from a death pattern. She literally came back to life.

Within four weeks Maya was awake and she realized she had missed nine months of her daughter's life. She had been out of her body in a sort of waking coma. But she came back strong and fast: after just a couple months she was out having a social life, working on an art show and thoroughly enjoying her active little girl.

If depression is grief related, in some ways, it is easier to assign blame and work towards restoration. In a person's mind, they can anchor the depression to a specific event and know that they, like many others who have grieved, can return to a normal life.

When depression is without an event, either chemical or a response to ongoing abuse or intolerable conditions, it is more difficult to use logic to pull oneself out of it.

I struggled with a deep, all consuming depression for many years. At times, the doctors label it 'severe depression', and at other times, it was 'major depression with an anxiety disorder.' Much of the cause of my depression ascribed by the medical practitioners (who were treating me) was the chemical disparity from the cancer, hormone imbalances, and the abuse I suffered from early life.

Since depression is a mental illness, an illness of the brain, you must use your thoughts to assist yourself at every turn. I learned to be a loving mother to myself in crisis. I would praise my image when I look in the mirror and speak to myself lovingly, reassuring myself I was all right. Honestly, sometimes I thought I had gone off the deep end; I wondered if I would ever rise to the surface to enjoy the light of day, but I persevered. What I did not have access to back then, and can now share with you, is how to restore the brain, aura and other affected areas of your being in order to move back into a joyous, fulfilled life.

When I was leaving my abusive husband long ago, I read some Bible quotes that said it was a sin to live without joy every day, that God had intended us to experience the wonder and majesty of this realm. This thought helped me take my first steps to a life free from daily abuse. Many years later, I was completely restored to the joy of human essence.

When you are experiencing depression, your energy vibration is low. You are in a tunnel and self-focused. Everything is weighed and measured by what you are feeling and whether you have enough emotional or mental energy to deal with a situation.

Although you may be a wonderful individual with a high-energy vibration, the frequency of depression comes in around 120-180. This frequency does not support the miraculous; nor does it support a sense of love or connection with the Divine.

Protocols For Restoring The Mind To Balance After Depression:

Healing low mental vibration

Step number one involves the process of clearing the seven layers of the aura one by one. When depressed, it is likely they are all black, grey, brown or white.

Clear The Aura

1. Using kinesiology, identify the seven layers of the aura starting with layer one closet to the body, with its color.
2. Clear the colors of the aura starting with layer one, pumping gold energy from the right hand into the aura.

3. Then proceed to layer two and identify its color and so forth until you reach the outer edge which is layer seven, thus, identifying all layers of the aura and the current color of each layer.

   Once you have cleared each layer and are able to identify a primary color now as the signature color for the layer you are ready to move to the next step.

4. Access the emotional timeline. Using kinesiology with the timeline extending back up to nine lives, have all episodes and causes of depression appear on the time line as black dots.

5. Use a golden shop vacuum to clean of all dark areas related to these two issues. Using kinesiology test clear.

6. Pulse a golden wave, like a radio wave, back through the timeline, sealing up the healing.

Execute DNA Obliteration Procedure

Depression and mental illness run in families. It is very likely the decks are stacked against you and you are wired for depression in your DNA. Now is your opportunity to clear all related circumstances to depression and mental illness from the DNA. *Use the DNA obliteration process in Chapter 2.*

Clear The Five Brains

Clear the five brains using the brain healing protocols found in this chapter.

Clear The Respiratory System.
Remember the process of breathing is linked to having right to take up space. "I have a right to take up space."

Clear The Stomach

Execute DNA family bubble procedure

Complete DNA resets

Seal Up With Gold Energy

Once you have successfully cleared the energy and frequency of depression, practice once or twice daily a miraculous living meditation. These meditations are designed to keep you clear focused and upbeat. *The Brilliant Brain* is a lovely healing mediation you might ad to your practice once weekly until you are firmly established in your joyous mental health.

If you have been depressed for a while, you may want to also improve your relationship with wealth and abundance as that frequently suffers. There is a free 7-day introduction to the 21-day course, (www.miraculouslivingwealth.com)

which is designed to lift the spirits and restore a positive joyful abundance energy field and mindset.

So many of my students have raved about the sense of well being and connectedness while they are in their 21-day cycle. Many choose to continue for two or three 21-day cycles, enjoying a return to joyful anticipation and active manifestation. This is a perfect course for you after these healings as you are working on significantly shifting your frequency and energy field.

I believe in you. You can and will heal. Believe in yourself. Putting life into balance and removing the roadblocks to joy, and the downers in life will make a great difference in how blissfully you return to life.

As a side note, if you have been depressed a while, you may have gathered some unwanted spiritual parasites. Go to chapter 29, All Things Spiritual, test for unwanted energies, and clear. Do this after you have done all of the above clearings. Restoring yourself to rightness is much more important than a few spiritual cockroaches. When you are restored, you will want to move forward and move them out.

Successful Healing Results

In a recent Miraculous Healing Weekend, we saw how three men with traumatic brain injury experienced a profound and miraculous healing as a result of restoring the first and second brains.

I have occasionally opened the Miraculous Living Training up for interested participants to attend. Among those participants are noted authors, physicists, psychiatrists, biblical scholars along with medical doctors and professionals. A second type of guest also attends these open weekends, those with profound injury and illness.

Bill flew in from Phoenix, not really sure what he was getting into, but willing and ready to have his life get better. He was curious about this process I had described to him of healing with no pills, surgery or other therapeutic methodology. He is the CEO of company promoting a wonderful stem-cell-inspired skin product.

Donald was a brutal accident survivor. He had 38 years of reduced brain function and unhappiness prior to attending the healing weekend.

You have already been introduced to the third man, my brother Marty, who flew into the Bay area for the first time, not knowing what to expect but ready to receive any healing his body would accept.

For Bill, a Vietnam vet, who is kind, interesting and was somewhat expressionless. The miracle happened in his first brain restoration. Post-traumatic stress had robbed Bill of his joy and appreciation of life. The trauma found in the first brain was removed in the healings. Bill received the antidote for his post-traumatic stress, which up until the weekend, had caused him a life without joy.

I received an excited and joyous call from Bill a week later as he had just experienced Disneyland with his grandchildren and, for the first time, could feel happiness and excitement. He was literally not just providing the experience for the kids to enjoy, he was sharing in the elated feelings of a much younger time. Now in his late sixties, having lived nearly fifty years on emotional flatline, he declared, "I'm back!"

Donald's story is an incredible story of pain and survival. A terrible accident thirty-six years ago left an extensive brain injury. He was often in pain, unable to move his head from side to side. His days were filled with a constant reminder of this long ago event.

For Donald, the fourth Brain restoration (right neo cortex/creative brain) did the trick as it lifted him out of pain into a life of ease and movement.

Marty had an equally severe brain trauma. His release, however, came from the healing of the third left neo cortex/logical brain.

All three men have an incredible story to tell of post event brain cell growth. As we tested their days of cell growth in the entire brain, we got eighteen and nineteen days. The men were sleeping the first couple days as cells grew rapidly. Lights started coming on and pathways, long shut down, were now open and giving them access to movement, peace, ease joy, that is, a life renewed.

It has been a thrill to experience conversations with my brother, as he sounds younger by the day. He keeps telling me life is very, very good!

Table 16-1 Summary: Colors Of The Brains And Their Percentage Function.

Brain	1	2	3	4	5
Function:	Survival	Emotional	Creative	Logical	Angelic
	Green 100%	Green 100% m	Green 100%	Green 100%	Pink 100%
	Blue 92%	Pink 100% w	Pink 92%	Emerald Green 99% w	Yellow 96%
	Pink 90%	Green 97% w	Red 83%	Olive Green 40% m	Blue 73%
	Orange 60%	Pink 94% m	Yellow 51%	Blue 97% m	Purple 40%
	Purple 50%	Orange 86%	Orange 40%	Orange 56%	Green 37%
	Yellow 30%	Purple 84%	Purple 21%	Red 12%	Orange 32%
	Red 3%	Red 20%	Blue 11%	Yellow 4%	Red 9%
For All:	White Control	Blue 4%	Brown 7%	Purple 2%	
	Black, Gray Malfunction, Death	Yellow 2%			

Chapter 17: Endocrine System

Our endocrine system is the physical sibling to our spirit. The functions of the endocrine system in the physical body resemble functions of the spirit in the body. Men and women share the joys of owning a human body and many similar endocrine functions however they experience their hormonal bodies in unique ways.

The endocrine system is a particularly important area of research and discovery for me. It is instrumental in rebuilding and restoring the human body. For example, when I was exposed to nuclear radiation as a child, my body began to lose healthy thyroid function. As a result, when I was twenty-four, my thyroid experienced the ravages of a toxic world. The diagnosis of follicular thyroid cancer with papillary tendencies indicated 'trouble in River City'. This very sick thyroid demanded my attention. I had to wake up to the fact my compromised endocrine system was at best struggling to adequately function.

Just prior to this, I had wrestled with the unpredictable condition of pancreas distress, hypoglycemia. Years later I faced complete adrenal failure. The grand finale to my long and arduous life of toil came with the removal of my ovaries and entire 'baby making equipment'. My poisoned-diseased female gear shocked my gynecologist. He reported his frightening findings to me after the difficult surgery. He told me that my uterus appeared as a grey brain exposing ten large tumors with angry red spots.

I stopped seeking treatment with western medicine at that point. I believe the work western medical professionals do a good service and offer solutions to very real and challenging illnesses. However, the three doctors I was seeing post surgery all were sending me death pictures.

What that means is others and myself would pick up on telepathic images. Here is what those images were saying: "If your uterus is in that bad of a condition the rest of your organs must be that bad or worse. You are going to die, there is no way you can survive this."

Having western medicine as your health plan can be a little like wearing a hospital gown. You think you are covered. Vibrant health I've discovered is so much more than the treatment of illness. The over all human blueprint includes spiritual, emotional, mental and physical aspects of life. Treating illness is antidotal, and will largely missed the deeper causes and even the life meanings of the challenges occurring in the body.

After both the first and the last surgery the surgeons were traumatized by the appearance of the tumors. Both times they appeared to be in shock when they spoke to me.

At one point during my treatment I remember the endocrinologist offering to put me on antidepressants. I had come in with a list of twelve significant health concerns. Her solution (one I refused) was to treat me with serotonin uptake inhibitors. She thought I would have more resilience to deal with the advancing and destructive break down of my body if I were on an anti-depressant.

I removed myself from the medical health care system. It was around that point I understood a project I had unconsciously been working on over a lifetime. I was attempting to use the illness and overcoming against all odds as a shining example to western medical professionals that there is in deed more to us then we know. I was attempting instinctively to have documented; my survival and recovery. Though the old patriarchal system of western medicine was recording my survival I realized this was not the path to changing the way we think about illness and health globally.

As I pulled out of the HMO, I let myself off the hook to show, through my own recovery, the concepts I teach now without illness taking me down just next to death's door. I committed to a new course of action, a conscious plan to transform how I think about my wellness and eventually a way of teaching what I have learned through the years. I can now show how every single person can access their unique miraculous system and enjoy a long and very happy, healthy life. Not long after I made this shift, I began receiving 'the downloads' I share with you now.

When entering into the healing sanctuary of restoring the endocrine system, unless there is an urgent problem in one specific gland, begin with the glands of the brain. Then proceed down to the glands and organs in the neck and torso having hormonal function.

Hypothalamus

In the center of the brain, though not a gland itself, it plays the role of producer/director to the entire body. This director is releasing chemical communications into the body to instruct the system players when to activate and when to release the hormones and chemistry necessary for a healthy vibrant existence.

When observing the hypothalamus, using kinesiology, you can evaluate the percentage of function and color of the gland director.

Best Colors for the Hypothalamus:

Yellow	100%
Light green	80%
Pink	6%
Orange	3%
Red	1%
Black	Indicates a serious malfunction, this signals a death energy
White	Represents control energy
Pink	and below represent a malfunction of the Director/Hypothalamus.

Fuel for the Hypothalamus is energy provided from the seventh and sixth chakra.

Protocols for healing the hypothalamus

- Bring gold energy coming through the back of your head, down your right arm and out your right finger tips. Pump gold towards the hypothalamus, bringing the percentage up to 100%. Clear colors, again by simply by pumping the gold energy.

- Once you have completed the color and percentage healing, using kinesiology, ask if the healing is complete or if Cellular Neo-Genesis (the restoring of the healthy cell) is the next step.

- If yes: do all the steps laid out for Cellular Neo-Genesis process

If the Master cell in the hypothalamus is black, do Cellular Neo Genesis. Check the condition of the DNA strand while doing the Cellular Neo-Genesis protocol, as it is likely broken. The DNA is part of the intelligence of the cell, as is the membrane and nucleus. They must all be repaired and restored at the same time to get a great result.

- Upon completion of Cellular Neo-Genesis, flood the area with gold and mirror the master cell to the entirety of cells in the hypothalamus.

- Using kinesiology test the cell improvement, and also the percentage of cells that received the new information.

- Test the number of future days of new cell growth.

- Test if the healing is complete at the end of the designated healing day or if there will be steps ahead for more healings.

- If the answer is no, or if the answer is that the hypothalamus/director will still be at a reduced level, check for when the body would be ready for its next healing.

Note: With the hypothalamus gland functioning poorly a person generally experiences poor health and erratic unpredictable problems. They tend to struggle in life. Their friends and family have a difficult time relating to them, as it seems unbelievable the amount of challenges they are experiencing.

Doctors often miss diagnosing the role the hypothalamus plays in a larger health problem. They may look to one of the low functioning glands in the main part of the body and treat that area rather than the original source of the problem, which is often in the hypothalamus.

Take heart, if this is one of your challenges, you can, over time, get much better. By doing a full healing of the endocrine system you are able to restore healthy communication inside your body. With intention and the beautiful design of the human blueprint activation, function and chemistry get better and you return to a normal healthy life.

Pituitary gland

The pituitary gland is our fountain of youth gland. Its function is to provide the body human growth hormone. A healthy child will grow and mature thanks to the assistance of this wonderful gland. There are children who do not have a pituitary gland at full function. Born at a normal birth weight they will be slow to grow once outside the womb.

Several years ago I sat in on a lecture on infant/childhood low growth rate and the treatments option of injectable HGH. The boosters of the hormone helped get the two twelve year-old children in this test group into a normal height and weight range. The doctor reporting his study was happy with the results and spoke to some of the complications and issues of maturing. At a certain point, boys in this category may also need testosterone injections to reach full male maturity.

I found it a fascinating conversation, one I have pondered. The common 'slow down' of the function of the pituitary gland happens at about age twenty-seven. This gland sluggishness corresponds with a young adult advancing into the first major Saturn-return that is a cycle of their astrological chart. The Saturn return phenomenon happens at age twenty-eight and signals the step into adulthood.

This sluggishness of the pituitary gland has not always occurred at this early age throughout human development.

The last fifteen hundred years of progressive human health history have yielded a quickening of life. Not involved with the brutal aspects of existence from the more primitive era, some of our body mechanics have become obsolete.

With life spans of fifty to eighty years, the gland bearing the fountain of youth label is not required to produce hormones at the same level as in youth. Think about supply and demand here and it will make sense.

As a young wife on a family farm, I had some organic knowledge about nature. My in-laws somehow did not have this information. At the time of our marriage the farm had been in my in-law's family for one hundred and thirty-seven years. The homestead we lived on was considered a heritage farm.

My former husband's ancestors had been among the first to settle in the area. They had brought their love of the land, hard work and pioneer spirit with them from Sweden. Britta was the fifth generation great grandmother to my own daughter Britta, and was the midwife of the area. She was a small stout woman who could haul a hundred pound sack of dry goods all the way home from town (a ten mile hike) carrying it on her back. She is a legend in the family. Likely she was the one in her senior years to have adorned the farm homestead area with the now ancient fragrant lilac trees, persistent lilies and tulips, and an old apple tree.

The apple tree had been ignored for so many years it was considered a nuisance. After a spring and summer season of not being watered or cared for it would drop almost a hundred wormy apples on the ground, and then in alternate years no apples would come at all.

I had this strong 'knowing' that the reason the tree did not produce was because it knew on some level that it was not needed. No-one was eating the apples. My in-laws and husband discouraged my notion that we could get usable apples from this rotten hundred year-old tree. As a matter of fact, they told me, we should cut it down. We were not going to do that, however, because of the stump and root system that would require days of work to remove. With a hundred and sixty acres there were already too many undone tasks to think of adding to the list. This tree removal was not going to happen.

I decided that I could make a difference, but I needed to perform my apple tree resurrection project with stealth. I watered it with the garden hose several times weekly during the heat of summer and spoke to it lovingly when I was around it. For some unknown reason the tree that was on its barren year produced a big harvest of 'wormy fruit'.

Actually hundreds of apples adorned the tree that year. When they were ripe they started to fall to the ground. I would go out to the back yard where the tree stood and pick up every single fallen apple. Whether they were wormy, rotten or usable they were all removed from under the tree.

Into the old farmhouse kitchen I brought my treasures for cleaning. As a newlywed I painted the kitchen a lime green. There were sizeable radiators (heaters) and ancient century-old glass paned windows. The kitchen had high ceilings and an antique linoleum floor that routinely required me to go to hands and knees for scrubbing and waxing.

The dining room displayed colorful textured glass in smaller windowpanes, similar to stained glass. The colorful windows were a lovely reminder of the home in Sweden the family had left behind for this new life. There was a simplistic elegance to the rustic saltbox farmstead. Each

Sunday the entire family (all wearing smart, clean clothes) would gather for dinner, sitting at a beautifully dressed oak table, with silver and fine china.

It is at that same old, round table that I sat with my bucket of apples. This very table had provided the level plan for thousands of meals to be both prepared and served to hungry field hands and hard-working family members.

Apple in hand I cut around the worms, core, seeds and stem. Buckets of the cut away produce went to the pigs; who enjoyed a heyday in 'hog heaven' when the pail arrived. From what was left I cooked up some super yummy applesauce. I used a First Lutheran Church cookbook recipe for a cinnamon enhanced apple butter to spread on home-baked bread for my babies. There were beautiful apple slices deposited in my grandmother Grace's incredible piecrust recipe producing the best ever award-winning apple pies! (I won a blue ribbon at the Nobles County Fair for my baked goods, the pie among my entries.) There were ample pies for the farm hands and for church functions.

As the apples were cut, the Johnny Appleseed song had to be sung!

Apples, Apples, Apples are fun to eat
Apples, Apples, Apples a real good treat
Harlems and Jonathons and by gosh
Golden Delicious Applesauce
UMMM Ummm Ummm
Apples, Apples, Apples are fun to EAT!

By the end of the season I had so many apples I had made-up many bags of pie apples for the freezer and umpteen jars of applesauce, enough to carry us through the winter and have some to give away.

As the weather turned chilly, I went out to the ageless apple tree to clean her up. As I removed the last of the hanging wormy apples I sang to her. My baby girl, Britta Carrie played under the tree laughing and singing with mommy, as I filled the final bucket. I used a ladder to get every last one.

Mother tree was cleaned properly. I new if there were no apple left on the tree or on the ground she would have a reason to produce more.

When I first started cleaning apples my relatives said 'oh just throw them away, they're no good.' But I could see there were small parts of the apple that were actually delicious and unaffected by worms so heck no, I cleaned those apples up and used them.

Did the tree know her apples were being used to feed children and farm workers?

Definitely, yes.

Years later I read the brilliant book by author Cleve Backster who is best known for his experiments with bio-communication in plant and animal cells using a polygraph machine back in the sixties. He began his careers as an interrogation specialist with the CIA. Plants are amazingly tuned in and connected. The truth is they stay connected with their parts.

Fruit itself is an offering or the giving back of the tree. For our beloved tree the apples become the blessing, the gift of the tree. It is what she has to offer and nurture those with whom she shares mother earth.

At that time I was about nineteen years old and I was a

terrible housekeeper. I had moved into a large four-bedroom farmhouse filled with my in-law's stuff, and we basically lived in a nest. But it was truly a mess. I hardly ever washed the dishes; there just was way too much living that needed to happen. I can understand why my in-laws might not have thought they should discourage me from spending hours cleaning wormy apples.

After this amazing result, however, I was told, "Well that's that, because the tree produced fruit this year, there will be no apples next year." I am sure they believed it. However I did not. I felt like ancient apple tree now knew she was needed and would respond appropriately.

I asked my husband to prune her and he was sweet enough to comply. He dutifully butchered the branches, which freaked me out a bit. But you know, mother tree didn't mind at all. She was happy to provide new limbs and in the Spring we had a wondrous surprise!

The tree produced a bloom like it had not produced for eighty years. Honestly there were thousands of blossoms the following spring, and many healthy apples grew from the renewed tree to the chagrin and total surprise of the meme (group mind) dominating the homestead. I continued to care for her and other living beings on the farm in the same way.

This was a profound lesson in supply and demand. If you understand current human lifestyle does not demand and appreciate the regeneration abilities provided by this amazing pituitary gland, it will slow down and eventually produce minimal results.

As I scan back over the centuries this gland at one point used to function at full strength for many more years.

Imagine having full access to the regeneration of human growth hormone for seventy-five years!

There has been much experimentation of the use of fetal stem cells and HGH (Human Growth Hormone). I have only observed from a distance as an acquaintance was following this course working with a doctor (under the radar) many years ago. She reported feeling euphoric and blissful for days after the embryonic stem cells were implanted in to her inner thigh.

What I am excited about is the ability we now have to apply what the medical researchers were exploring years ago; a natural non-harmful (in other words no aborted fetuses involved) way of renewing vibrant health and youthful bliss to the human body.

When observing the pituitary gland, in addition to color and function percentage, please look at the gland to see if it has been encapsulated with calcium. This is problematic for this particular gland. If calcium entombment is the case, the person may be getting no benefits from the gland, or have no delivery of the good chemistry throughout the body from the pituitary gland.

Healing the pituitary gland follows the same protocol as above, with the exception of a calcium encapsulation healing if needed.

When observing the pituitary gland, using kinesiology, you can evaluate the percentage of function and color of the gland.

Best Colors for Pituitary Gland:

Pink	100%
Deep blue	98%
Dark Green	96%
Light Green	90%
Purple	20% serious malfunction
Yellow	3%
White	Represents control energy
Black, Grey or Brown	Indicates a serious malfunction signaling a death energy

- With the gold energy coming through the back of your head down through your right arm and out your right finger tips, pump the percentage up to 100% and clear colors simply by pumping the gold energy.

- Complete the color and percentage healing.

- Use kinesiology, check for the calcium encapsulation.

- If yes, do the following healing, if no, go to the next step.

Calcium encapsulation clearing process

- The technique requires using both hands in a kind of chopping motion. In this case there is **no color**, rather it is like a sculptor chipping away at marble.

- Check every few minutes, making sure the percentage of calcium is going down. Do this procedure for 10 minutes.

337

- Even if you haven't achieved a 100% clear, stop at the 10-minute point.

- Document what you were able to do and move on to the next step.

- Ask if the healing is complete.

- If yes, stop here fill with gold.

- Next step, proceed to the recessive DNA Obliterations process followed by a family DNA clearing and reset.

- If no, ask if Cellular Neo-Genesis (the restoring of the healthy cell) is the next step.

- If yes, do all steps laid out for Cellular Neo-Genesis process. If the pituitary gland was black grey or brown you must regenerate the master cell by doing Cellular Neo-Genesis on the DNA strand as it is likely broken.

- Upon completion, flood the area with gold and mirror the master cell to all the cells in the pituitary gland. This is vital.

- Read the cell improvement, and percentage of cells that received the new information.

- Test for the number of days new cells will be growing.

- Test if the healing is complete at the end of the designated healing day.

- If the answer is no, or you test that the fountain of youth gland will still be at a reduced level, check on when the body would be ready for the next healing.

It is possible once you have completed Cellular Neo-Genesis that you will be directed to the recessive DNA obliteration process or some additional next step. Continue to ask the body:

- What's next?

- Has the body received enough healing for the day?

It's conceivable that after forty minutes or an hour of healing the body will need time (hours, days, or even weeks) to integrate the shifts produced from the healing. Do not over tax the body and put it into a healing crisis just because you can do more. Listen to the body, it will tell you how much and when to stop, and it will tell you how many days to wait till the next healing.

Without good function from the pituitary gland people generally experience a very slow healing process and a rapid aging. From a poor functioning pituitary gland and also poor DNA programs for cellular body, we see the answer to why some folks look older than others in the same age group.

Mae's Story

I was totally blown away by my client Mae. She was a coaching client in her mid forties. She was a stay at home mom and brilliant attorney. Married to a medical doctor, she was looking to find more balance and happiness for her and her family. As we worked together, she was learning about life in balance and relationship healings.

At one point in her coaching she felt it would add to her life to do a physical tune-up and cleanse. I was able to rapidly tune up her systems, glands and organs, as well as her energetic body. She loved the refreshed energy and vitality that was coming from our work together.

As I read her physical body I discovered that Mae had a pituitary gland reading of a hundred percent. Honestly at that point in my practice I had never seen that. A forty-six year-old woman with a perfect pituitary gland! WOW! I hadn't even seen a thirty year-old at a hundred percent!

She obviously was not doing sessions with me for health, because as you can imagine her health was stellar.

Looking further, she mentioned her father's pituitary function had followed a similar path. In his mid seventies, he was still an active marathon runner and a big thinker. When I looked his pituitary function it was still up over sixty percent.

What made this wonderful situation was a strong pattern in the DNA. Other than toxicity or illness, the DNA is in charge of the programs of function in glands through the years. Once you have tuned up the pituitary, or any other gland, it is an excellent idea to clear the DNA through the recessive DNA Obliteration process. Then reset the DNA to the new higher percentage.

Pineal gland

Sleeping Beauty had a pineal gland that worked way to well! The Pineal gland is the gland that provides deep and restful sleep and calm serene meditation. How it accomplishes this is through the chemical melatonin. The pineal gland looks a little like a coffee bean.

How many people do you know who have the issue of restless or no sleep, or they say they have an inability to meditate? I have always been a good sleeper; this would indicate my pineal gland functions at a very high level.

Best Colors for the Pineal Gland:

Medium Brown	100%
Deep Brown	90%
Green	30% Serious Malfunction
Orange	5%
Red	3%
White	Represents control energy
Black, Grey or Brown	Indicates a serious malfunction signaling a death energy

Healing the Pineal Gland

- With the gold energy coming through the back of your head down through your right arm and out your right finger tips, pump the percentage up to 100% and clear colors simply by pumping in gold energy.

- Once you have completed the color and percentage healing, ask if the healing is complete.
- If yes, stop here fill with gold. Go to DNA obliteration process and then reset.

- If no, is Cellular Neo-Genesis (the restoring of the healthy cell) the next step?

- If yes, do all steps laid out for Cellular Neo-

Genesis process starting on page xxx.

- If the pineal gland was black or grey you must regenerate the master cell by doing Cellular Neo-Genesis.

- Check on the DNA strand as it is likely broken. This is a specialized healing taught in the Miraculous Living Apprentice program. To find out more go to www.julierenee.com/mlapprentice

- A good temporary solution for bonding broken DNA is to pump gold energy into the broken strand, visualizing the pieces coming back together. This will give you a partial result.

- Upon completion, flood the area with gold and mirror the master cell to all the cell in the pineal gland.

- Test the cell improvement, and percentage of cells that received the new information.

- Test how many days new cells will be growing.

- Test if the healing is complete at the end of the designated healing day.

- If the answer is no, or that the Pineal gland will still be at a reduced level, check when the body would be ready for the next healing.

Without good function in the pineal gland people generally experience difficulty sleeping and meditating. Once you've tuned up this gland, if the individual still has difficulty sleeping, it is likely a problem in the nervous system and or the adrenal glands.

It is amazing how this simple tune-up for a woman in peri-menopause will help so much.

Lana was a busy Medical professional with a lot on her plate. She always seemed to be burning the candle at three ends – bottom, top and middle. She was jumpstarting a reinvented career as well as taking care of her two (children) dogs and her elderly parents. She had virtually no free time.

I was able to provide a fabulous healing for Lana working diligently on the pineal gland and getting the adrenal function up to a much higher number. Her restful sleep returned and for many weeks Lana was a happy camper. She practiced her from fatigue to fabulous meditation daily and returned to sleeping like a baby.

★ for your free meditation download go to www.miraculouslivingtoday.com

I provided her with the tools for living life in balance, and the *'Balance Your Life Now Book'* and *'Balance Your Life Action Guide.'*

To be successful in maintaining this healing you need to take personal responsibility for how you design your life. Lana stopped doing her practice, moved, lost one of her dogs to old age and hired a couple of new employees.
When you have a lot of chaos in your life, you need to step back and look at what you are creating. This is a real lesson in self-love and planning for life.

In Lana's case, I could see the chaos coming and gently reminded her to stay on track. She was coached and agreed to meditate, eat well and as much as possible, get out in nature for quiet rejuvenation time.

Four months after the initial healing Lana was back to not sleeping, feeling irritable and wanting her next fix. Since I am not a 'dealer' for healing junkies, I did not provide her with the next healing. It would have been a waste of my time and hers as she was unable to make the shifts she needed to maintain it.

Over the past twenty years I've discovered that not everyone treasures and values miraculous healing. Some people get it. They understand that this process provides results well beyond what traditional medical models are able to accomplish. Things that appear to have no solution are possible to heal completely. The people who treasure miraculous healings are the people who can incorporate the changes in lifestyle and attitude to maintain good health. Others, however, disrespect themselves and the preciousness of the miracle. They squander away the treasured health results. Which one are you?

Do you love yourself enough to embrace a new healthy lifestyle? If you are not there yet, what would it take to get there? Towards the end of this book I have included a wonderful chapter on letting go of pain. Please review this chapter a few times until you understand what you get out of the unhealthy life and habits. Look at what thoughts you need to adjust to take a step up in self-care and self-nurturing.
You don't have to unplug from your current life. You might however, temporarily need to adjust and slow life down to get back to vibrant health. It's all about finding the balance, and living into authentic joy. If you are so

massively busy and stressed where is the joy in that?

What I have come to understand is that sometimes your cells are 'running you'. This phenomenon happens when your strong family programs override your own wishes and desires. This is a perfect situation to make use of the recessive DNA Obliteration process. You will discover the programs that are causing the challenges. For example family DNA programs that have you not loved or protected yourself. You can get better, everyone can. It is important to keep the vibrant health picture in mind, and choose your lifestyle consciously.

Thyroid

The thyroid gland provides many wonderful happenings for the body, including producing and releasing the powerful hormones T3 and T4: which support healthy metabolism, temperature and weight.

On the front line, this gland is most susceptible to contaminants. It will be first to go when exposed to radiation poisoning from nuclear waste, Agent Orange, and other bio-warfare toxins.

In the endocrine system the second top dog is the thyroid. Without it or the chemical equivalent (replacement) your body will not live.

Best Colors for the Thyroid:

Blue	100%
Green	70%
Purple	60%
Pink	40% serious malfunction
Yellow	3%
White	Represents control energy
Black, Grey or Brown	Indicates a serious malfunction signaling a death energy

Energy is provided for the thyroid from the fifth chakra

Healing the Thyroid Gland

- Pump Gold energy into the thyroid till it reads as 100%. Clear colors simply by pumping gold energy.

- Once you have completed the color and percentage healing, test, using kinesiology, if the healing is complete or if Cellular Neo-Genesis (the restoring of the healthy cell) is the next step.

- If yes, do all steps laid out for Cellular Neo-Genesis process

Note: If the master cell in the thyroid is black, or grey you will need to do Cellular

Neo-Genesis.

- If it continues to appear white, pump gold energy to remove medical control energy.

- Check the condition of the DNA strand while doing Cellular Neo-Genesis, as it is likely broken. The DNA is susceptible to breaking or even totally disappearing especially when biological weapons and nuclear radiation have damaged the gland.

- The DNA strand is necessary in the master cell and all thyroid cells. DNA must be repaired and restored to get a great result.

346

- At the completion of Cellular Neo-Genesis, flood the area with gold and mirror the healthy master cell to the entirety of cells in the thyroid.

- Test for cell improvement, and percentage of cells that received the new information.

- Test for the number of days of new cell growth.

- Test if the healing is complete at the end of the designated healing day or if there will be steps ahead for more healings.

- If the answer is no, or that the thyroid will still be functioning at a reduced level, check on when the body would be ready for the next healing.

Because of exposure to underground nuclear testing as a child my thyroid became ill. The appearance of the illness started around twenty-one, when I was not able to keep my weight up. While pregnant I would eat five plates of food at a time and weigh in at a hundred and ten pounds. As the pregnancy progressed the baby and baby fluids would help my weight go up twenty-three or twenty-five pounds, but as soon as the baby was born I was back to super skinny.

At twenty-four and pregnant with baby number three, I got the news I had a very serious cancer affecting more than half of the anvil shaped gland. For my life to be saved I would be required to undergo a four-hour surgical procedure during my son's fourth month of gestation. I was in bad shape emotionally and in a loveless marriage. I had no physical energy to care for my daughters. And now this.

However, the shock of the news served to focus me. I needed to rally. I needed to survive for the life growing in my womb. Had I not been pregnant I seriously wonder if I would have used so much of my will to keep myself alive.

Whenever one definitely commits to a course of action, nothing can stop them from their goal. Know this to be true, because I am here, alive writing these words. Born to live. Even when doctors told family and friends it was unlikely I would survive, I did!

It was a truly wretched surgery. I was left with a frightening external scar on my neck and my vocal chords (so precious for singing) were paralyzed. Not only that, but several of my para-thyroids were nicked and permanently damaged.

I had descended to a living hell on earth. I returned home unable to care for my home or children well. I had no help. Dishes mounded to stacks upon stacks all over the kitchen. Neighbors didn't realize I was pregnant till the seventh month. I was gaunt, frail and in a depression you can't imagine. But I pulled through for my son and daughters. Children will inspire heroic acts and my sweet little angels did just that.

Two months later I had a third surgery. I had a tumor removed from my back while I was six months pregnant. They removed the second half of the thyroid Four and a half months later when Peter was six weeks old. For the next ten years additional thyroid cells appeared on cancer scans and I was given massive doses of radiation to kill off all of them.

I have been experimenting with Cellular Neo-Genesis and have produced some healthy thyroid cell growth. However, at the time of writing this book, I have yet to entirely re-grow and use a healthy thyroid of my own.

Last year I was able to go for nine months with no thyroid medication or supplements, however it was a challenge for my body. I decided that when I could fully dedicate myself to re-growth, that would be the best time to stop taking thyroid medication. At that point I decided I would focus my efforts on research and development for the entire Divine Human Blueprint. It is my intention in a future book to report to you a success story on the re-growth of my thyroid gland.

Parathyroid

Responsible for calcium levels in the body touching the thyroid. There are four little ball-shaped glands in two stacks of two, one on top of the other. This is the only gland or organ that appears white or light blue when healthy. White is generally considered a control energy, however in this case the color is related to the function of the gland, which is to produce calcium.

The function of this gland is often at a hundred percent. However women who are prone to osteoporosis and seniors with fragile bones are likely candidates for this upgrade/healing. This parathyroid gland typically stays at full functions until around age forty-three. It will often stay over ninety percent until age eighty.

Best Colors for the Parathyroid:

White	100%
Light blue	96%
Pale White Brown	80% Malfunction
Pale Grey	40% serious malfunction
Pink	30%
Red	3%
Layer White	Can represent control you will know if the gland reads white but has low function, test to see if it is multilayered and clear the control energy.
Grey	Serious malfunction represents death energy.

Energy is provided by the fifth chakra.

Healing the Parathyroid Gland

- Pump gold energy into the parathyroid until it tests at 100% and clear colors simply by pumping up gold energy.

- Once you have completed the color and percentage healing fill with gold.

- If necessary, proceed to DNA Obliteration process and reset.

- This gland receives Cellular Neo-Genesis in the case of injury or disease. Look for a missing nucleus if you are guided to do cell regeneration.

It's rare to have a problem in this gland as it is sturdy, resilient and has but one function. I did however have damage in the parathyroid from a surgical mishap. Plenty of folks have thyroid surgery and this is one possible complication. DNA programming is a second possible cause for poor function in the gland.

While in hospital for my first surgery I felt miserable all the time. However many special measures were taken in the hospital to support my nutritional and cellular needs. In the second thyroid surgery performed at the Mayo clinic I had a different experience and learned how bad you can feel when those innocent little glands aren't kicking into gear.

I remember so clearly my surgeon, Dr. Michael Brennan (from Ireland) who was the hotshot doc who specialized in three kinds of thyroid cancer. He was young for this expertise - I would place him in his mid-late thirties at the time of my procedure. Yet he was confident and very caring. He explained the procedure to me carefully. We spoke of my concerns. Seeing the damage to my neck he brought in experts to repair the scar tissue to make sure I had a much better result from this surgery. It was then I met the team of plastic surgeons they had brought in to repair the frightening Frankenstein scar at the base of my neck. Dr. Brennan was rapid fire with his message. He made me feel I was in good hands.

I was in Rochester with my husband, my best friend, Darcy and my six-week old son (who coincidentally now works at that very Mayo Clinic with his wife, who is also employed there.) If all went well the doctors wanted to send me home in two days. This included a surgical day and a day to make sure I had recovered.

It had been explained to me there was a chance I would not survive. I took this very seriously and waited six weeks so that my blonde-haired, pink-skinned, long-lashed little boy could have some bonding time with his mommy.

It was my intention to breast feed for at least six months with Peter, so I had my girlfriend who had a two year-old still nursing accompany me to the hospital. That way she could nurse him while I was in surgery and recovery. I attempted to make it as easy as possible for my little man.

Again, the surgery took longer than expected, only his time it wasn't from an inept surgeon but was the result of multiple procedures and some very fine handiwork being performed.

I awoke in the recovery room dazed happy to be alive.

Doc Brennan popped his head in to say, "It went well." He spent time describing what he found and gave a good prognosis for recovery from the surgery.

The plastic surgery team also came in and explained how they had removed the damaged skin and done a multi layered under stitch resulting in no surface stitches. They explained that over time the scar would become virtually undetectable, looking like a thin line at the base of my neck.

I was wheeled on a gurney from the recovery room to my shared room. There I settled in with family, baby in arms. I thought to myself; "Okay, I can do this."

After a while an odd thing started to happen. My hands were going numb and my eyes and upper cheeks were twitching. A press of the button and a nurse appeared, followed quickly by the doctor.

My body was going into shock, apparently from the parathyroid being damaged or removed altogether. He actually didn't know. His surgery did not remove any tissue other than the thyroid, but he said it could have stimulated problems from the previous surgery. He actually didn't know if there were any of the four balls of parathyroid left.

He was resting on the idea that there must have been at least one left because I had gotten to him functioning.

The surgery and the removal of all thyroid tissue meant I would need thyroid medication for the rest of my life. If the parathyroid were gone I would also be on a medicinal dose of calcium forever. (Of course none of us knew about a miraculous system back then). Now, if I am called in on this kind of a case I clear the medical control energy and regenerate the damaged or traumatized/injured cells.

The treatment for this development was to feed me dairy, as much as I could get down me, for the next few hours and see if the remaining pieces of the parathyroid would awaken.

Victory! After several helpings of ice cream, cottage cheese, pudding, milk, American cheese slices and yogurt, the twitching and numbness stopped and we were back in business. I was given another day for observation and went home to the farm as thin a rail with an extremely low life force. However, at least one ball of parathyroid was operational.

Thymus

The thymus provides the immune system instructions and can be considered the director of the immune system.

I respectfully refer to this gland as the Harvard law school of the body as it is the educational center for the T cells. In this gland the T cells learn how to protect the body. If this gland is strong and healthy you will have a great professor. If the gland is weak you may end up with T cells that act like they were preschoolers attending a community college. These less-educated cells may gobble up healthy cells and let damaging invaders run rampant because they don't have the training and discernment to know the difference.

Best Colors for the Thymus:

Light Green	100%
All shades of Green	90%
Yellow	90%
Orange	20% serious malfunction
Red	3%
White	Represents control energy.
Black	Indicates a serious malfunction, signals a death energy

Energy is provided for the thymus gland from the fourth and fifth chakra

Healing the Thymus Gland

- With gold energy pump the percentage up to 100%. Clear colors simply by pumping gold energy.

- Once you have completed the color and percentage healing, using kinesiology, ask if the healing is complete or if Cellular Neo-Genesis is the next step.

- If yes, do all steps laid out for Cellular Neo-Genesis process

- Special note, since the thymus is an education center, the DNA strand which provides a great deal of program and process information, is particularly important in the master cell and all thymus cells. DNA must all be repaired, replaced and restored to get a great result.

- At the completion of Cellular Neo-Genesis, flood the area with gold and mirror the healthy master cell to the entirety of cells in the thymus.

- Test the cell improvement, and percentage of cells that received the new information.

- Test for how many future days of new cells growth.

- Test if the healing is complete at the end of the designated healing day or if there will be steps ahead for more healings.

- If the answer is no, or that the thymus will still be at a reduced level, check for when the body would be ready for the next healing.

Heart

The heart assists many structures in a human body including the cardio vascular, circulatory and respiratory systems. One of the lesser functions for the heart is the process of providing an anti-cramp hormone to the muscles.

Best Colors for the Heart:

Pink	100%
Red	99%
Green	96%
Peach	70%
Purple	50% Malfunction
Orange	30% Serious malfunction
Blue	10%
Yellow	3%
White	Represents control energy
Black or Grey	Indicates a serious malfunction, signals a death energy

Energy is provided for the heart from the fourth chakra

Healing the Hormonal Heart Function

- With gold energy pump the percentage up to 100%. Clear colors simply by pumping gold energy.

- Once you have completed the color and percentage healing, using kinesiology, ask if the healing is complete or if Cellular Neo-Genesis is the next step.

- If yes: do all steps laid out for Cellular Neo-Genesis process found on page 51

- If the master cell in the heart is black or grey you will need to do the Cellular Neo-Genesis

Note: Since the early nineties we have known that the heart has brain function. The neurons of the heart assist in many important choices. There is good reason for the heart to be associated with love. This is because the intelligence of the heart is uniquely related to understanding and responding to all relationships. The DNA strand provides tremendous input into this arena. All DNA must be repaired and restored to get a great result.

- At the completion of Cellular Neo-Genesis, flood the area with gold and mirror the healthy master cell to the entirety of cells in the heart.

- Test the cell improvement, and percentage of

cells that received the new information.

- Test the improvement of heart chemistry. If the percentage of heart chemistry did not energy go up, pump gold energy into the heart to improve heart chemistry.

- Test for how many future days of new cell growth.

- Test if the healing is complete at the end of the designated healing day or if there will be steps ahead for more healings.

- If the answer is no, or that the heart will still be at a reduced level, check on when the body would be ready for the next healing.

Pancreas

A healthy pancreas is a joy to behold! The pancreas provides insulin, supporting healthy energy and blood sugar. Illnesses from an unhealthy pancreas include diabetes, hypoglycemia, pancreatitis and pancreatic cancer.

Almost as sensitive as the thyroid, the pancreas can be poisoned by toxins and too much sugar.

In terms of shape of this potent gland looks like a cross between a hotdog and an ear of corn. This is also an enormously intelligent gland both in chemistry, physical power and in support of an individual's wisdom for self-love.

Best Colors for the Pancreas:

Light Pink	100%
Light Blue	97%
Light Green	88%
Yellow	10% Serious malfunction
Red	1%
White	Represents control energy
Grey	Indicates a serious malfunction, signals a death energy

Energy is provided for the Pancreas from the third chakra

Healing the Pancreas

- With gold energy pump the percentage up to 100%. Clear colors simply by pumping gold energy.

- Once you have completed the color and percentage healing, using kinesiology, ask if the healing is complete or if Cellular Neo-Genesis is the next step.
- If yes: do all steps laid out for Cellular Neo-Genesis process

- If the master cell in the pancreas is grey you will need to do the Cellular Neo-Genesis.

- At the completion of Cellular Neo-Genesis, flood the area with gold. Mirror the healthy master cell to the entirety of cells in the pancreas.

- Test the cell improvement, and percentage of cells that received the new information.

- Test chemistry function of pancreas. If

chemistry is not 100% you can pump additional gold into the pancreas, and return to the pancreas for additional healings in the future.

- Test for the number of future days of new cell growth.

- Test if the healing is complete at the end of the designated healing day or if there will be steps ahead for more healings.

- If the answer is no, or that the pancreas will still be at a reduced level, check for when the body would be ready for the next healing.

Adrenals

The adrenals provide adrenaline and cortisol, testosterone and many other hormones and chemicals for the body. They are a veritable chemical factory for the body. These two small, acorn-shaped glands have their work cut out for them. They are responsible for survival energy.

You can think of these glands as the power plant of the body, providing fast energy to run away from the saber tooth tiger. They also will help you keep running, pumping cortisol into the body so you can store fat for extra reserves. If these glands malfunction they will make it virtually impossible or you to lose weight.

Best Colors for the Adrenals:

Caramel	100%
Brown	85%
Green	82%
Yellow	60% Malfunction
Red	50% Serious malfunction
Blue	14%
Orange	11%
Purple	6%
White	Represents control energy
Black or Grey	Indicates a serious malfunction, signals a death energy

Energy is provided for the adrenals from the third chakra.

Healing the Adrenal Glands

- With gold energy pump the percentage up to 100%. Clear colors simply by pumping the gold energy.

- Once you have completed the color and percentage healing, using kinesiology, asks if the healing is complete or if Cellular Neo-Genesis is the next step.

- If yes, do all steps laid out for Cellular Neo-Genesis process

- If the master cell in the adrenals is black, or grey you will need to do Cellular Neo-Genesis.

- At the completion of Cellular Neo-Genesis, flood the area with gold. Mirroring the healthy master cell to the entirety of cells in the thyroid is vital.

- Test for the cell improvement, and

percentage of cells that received the new information.

- Test for the number of future days of new cell growth.

- Test if the healing is complete at the end of the designated healing day or if there will be steps ahead for more healings.

- If the answer is no, or that the adrenals will still be at a reduced level, check for when the body will be ready for the next healing.

- When at low function from stress, the adrenals will take time to re establish health. We have provided a free daily meditation for you called, *"From Fatigued to Fabulous"* at www.miraculous-livingtoday.com

Do this every day for twelve weeks and you will notice that your adrenals and nervous system are completely refreshed and revitalized.

Ovaries

Healthy ovaries provide estrogen, progesterone, testosterone and other chemicals for the body as well as healthy eggs for reproduction. The ovaries are egg-shaped glands connected by a flower-like stem (the fallopian tubes) to the uterus.

The ovaries sit surprisingly low in the pelvic cradle.

Best Colors for the Ovaries:

Pink	100%
Green	98%
Yellow	96%
Orange	60% Malfunction
Purple	42%
Red	5%
Blue	4%
White	Represents control energy
Black or Grey	Indicates a serious malfunction, signals a death energy

Energy is provided for the ovaries from the second chakra

Healing the Ovaries

- With the gold energy pump the percentage up to 100%. Clear colors simply by pumping the gold energy.

- Once you have completed the color and percentage healing, using kinesiology, ask if the healing is complete or if Cellular Neo-Genesis is the next step.

- If yes: do all steps laid out for Cellular Neo-Genesis process

- If the master cell in the ovary is black, or grey, brown you will need to do Cellular Neo-Genesis.

- At the completion of Cellular Neo-Genesis, flood the area with gold. Mirror the healthy master cell to the entirety of cells in the ovary.

- Test the cell improvement, and percentage of cells that received the new information.

- Test for the number of future days of new cell growth.

- Test if the healing is complete at the end of the designated healing day or if there will be steps ahead for more healings.

- If the answer is no, or that the ovaries will still be at a reduced level, check for when the body would be ready for the next healing.

Note: I use one master cell for both ovaries and improve them both. From time to time you will see one much worse than the other. Use the master cell in the Cellular Neo-Genesis process from the worst one.

All our Miraculous Living meditations include an ovary clear out. If this is a significant challenge for you, I recommend you use the Happy Hormone program which features a full length healing on the female baby-making parts. Add this meditation to your regular practice once a week till a healthy balance has been restored.

The energetic function of the ovaries is to assist a woman with her healing projects. Consider their location in the woman's body. New life and babies are nurtured from this area. What happens when there is no new life growing? A woman still has this potent healing power to love and care for her family and friends. Without realizing where the energy is coming from, all women are using their ovaries for healing others.

Even when the physical ovaries have been removed surgically, the imprint (or spiritual ovaries) continue to exist. Women continue to do healings from this area.

Ovaries lose their physical potency around age thirty-eight.

In human development this was not always the situation. There was a time when ovaries were providing healthy hormones to women in their eighties. The eggs stopped becoming viable in the sixties.

The medicine woman

I love the tropics I've vacationed in rural Mexico off and on for fifteen years. Early in my travels I came in contact with the little round artisans who native to Mexico, the Huichol Indians. The artwork and traditions are amazingly detailed and beautiful.

While in Puerto Vallarta in 1996 I met a Mexican woman, Ana, who admired the native people very much. We met on the streets of PV and decided to head over to a little café for a glass of ice tea and a chat. Ana relayed a story to me of a Huichol Medicine woman in the mountain region of Jalisco:

"She was an extraordinary woman keeping to the diet and traditions of the tribe, delivering the babies for her community. Through the years she moved farther into the wilds as the modern world, with its pollution and unnatural ways, began to overtake her home. For her it was a natural occurrence for life to expand as the times were right and food was ample. The body would naturally know it was safe to give birth again, and happily conceive to bring in a healthy baby to join the world."

As Ana spoke I thought of the problems of the west, women out of sync with their bodies, struggling in male designed careers. They lose their fertility as early as thirty-one and out of touch with their own natural rhythms. I too began to admire this medicine woman's ways.

Ana continued to reveal the final chapter of the medicine

woman's story to me:

"At age sixty-seven this woman gave birth to her ninth child. After the birth she told her community, 'That is enough now! No more babies for me!' And as simple as that she decided she had fulfilled her birthing and tribal responsibility for contributing children to the tribe."
I thanked Ana for sharing this amazing story with me. It opened my eyes to the naturalness of healthy hormones and healthy, prolonged, natural fertility.

Factors and reasons in the Western fertility crisis and how to turn it all around
I have assisted a hundred and forty classified 'high risk' gestation and births as well as assisting numerous medically infertile couples conceive and joyfully birth children of their own.

How did we get to the point of having such a large portion of our female population in childbearing years with reduced fertility or complete infertility?

There are some who blame the problem on our cultural mores; when the process of fertility and birth was institutionalized and put in the hands of largely male doctors. Birth and conception became a regulated, unnatural experience. There is of course truth in this idea, but it is a small part of a much larger problem. Humanity is moving away from a natural life style. They no longer well in their bodies and they have forgotten their natural rhythms, such as rising with the sun and drifting into sleep as the sun sets.

Unless you are one of those observing a Paleolithic diet (considered fringe) you are likely eating a lot of non-food, foods containing harmful chemicals and toxic amounts of refined sugars, saturated fats and salt. The common diet of a westerner is a diet lacking life force energy or vitality, and it will poison the body causing an early demise, dementia, cancer, and every other disease you can imagine.

Earlier in this section we saw how toxicity can cause glands to fail. Fertility, which requires a tremendous amount of life force, is unsupported by the western diet. I estimate forty percent of infants born are born malnourished. The mother's diet of fast and manufactured food does not convert to high enough nutrition to give the fetus the best possible nourishment. Taking one vitamin a day to make up for a poor diet is not enough.

Child obesity also represents malnourishment.

Another big factor in infertility is a stressful lifestyle. When the woman's body is under stress and duress she stays in the sympathetic nervous system.

The sympathetic system is designed to pull all the energy from the main part of the body and send it out to the limbs in order to help a person escape from a charging bear. The sympathetic adrenal function pour adrenaline and cortisol into the mix, so you can hold onto your fat reserves. That means that if you are in danger for a few days, unable to get to food, your fat reserves will fuel you to keep you your feet and running.

Our stress system was never upgraded to handle the kinds of stress we are now encountering. Our design is an ancient design that worked well thousands of years ago and which hasn't completely adapted to our current situation.
In ancient times, perhaps two or three times monthly your alarms would trigger you into the sympathetic system. These triggers would respond to imminent danger and

366

stimulate action so you could get to safety by being fully supported in your body, even if it took hours or days, because your body was wired for this.

Your body was not wired for the lifestyle you are likely living today. Here are ten sympathetic triggers you could change:

Blasting Alarm Clock
Many folks wake up with loud sounds which trigger the sympathetic system. To rectify this you could go to bed at a reasonable hour and awaken naturally, or have chimes or bells gently signaling morning.

Time Pressures in morning
This can be experienced as an internal stress whether you live alone or with others: "We've got to get going," "Get in the car!" "Finish your breakfast." These stress or trigger high alert. The solution. Create a new pattern. Get up early enough, enjoy a naturally healthy meal and be out the door in a happy joyous mood.

Car: Late or Gotta Get There Now
Just getting in the car will, for many, trigger high alert. Think about it. Your life is in danger from other cars on the road. The added element of pushing to get somewhere will get you into the sympathetic system and get your adrenals pumping.

Horns honking, sirens, work alarms
These trigger reptilian brain responses and send you off into stress. When I became conscious of this I made an effort to avoid places that had this going on. However I live in a populated area, so if I hear a siren or horn, I notice it and breathe deeply, assuring my body we are safe and all is well. Instead of matching the alarm energy I immediately

go into self-love and self-soothing if needed.

Phones ringing, computer sounds, technology sounds

You have a choice about the technology sounds that come out of your equipment. I have harp arpeggio announcing an incoming call and soft chimes to announce a text. My landline phones are set to a sweet, soft and easy frequency, and I have turned off a majority of computer sounds. What can you make easier on the nerves?

Pain

If you are in pain, you are on high alert in the sympathetic system. That's a fact. Why are you in pain? Are you not getting enough rest? Do you need sleep? Are you letting stress at work or in your relationship get to you? Stop and smell the roses. Rest if you need to and get into a balanced lifestyle. If your pain is from illness or injury you might consider natural healings at the Miraculous Living weekends. A large majority of our participants leave much improved in both health and ease in their bodies.

Violent Films

When watching violent films, your body doesn't know the violence is not for real and thinks you are really in danger. Think about it: you are getting the adrenaline rush as if you were in the car chase or dodging bullets. Give yourself a break - stop watching violent or frightening films.

Fast Food on the Run

In high school there was a popular quote: "Run for fun!" This does not mean you should to be on the run, shoving food down your throat while you rush to the next thing. Stop the madness. I recommend not eating in your car. I recommend not eating highly fatty and sugary unnatural foods. Preplanning works so well for me. I always have a

wild rice and seaweed combo prepared for a quick meal. Seeds, nuts, chopped raw veggies, a ripe apple, these are excellent choices. Chew your food well so you get the benefit of the digestive enzymes in your saliva. You miss thirty percent of the food processing enzymes
if you gobble your food.

Screaming children

If your child is screaming he or she is likely expressing your overwhelm. However if you let them scream, this is impacting your nervous system and making matters worse. You might need a time out. Calm and soothe yourself for a few minutes with the child in their room, then rock and soothe your child. You need to calm yourself, understanding your child's emotions play off of you, especially if you are the mommy.

Financial Pressures

I add this topic as it is something that never allows your body to calm down. You will stay in high alert with financial pressure. Notice how everything is some shade of grey, that life isn't really enjoyable. Make it a priority to resolve the financial situation and get back into a happy, balanced life. Many students have enjoyed real significant breakthroughs in wealth with our free seven-day wealth jumpstart. To receive your free wealth program visit www.miraculouslivingwealth.com/jumpstart

Stressors and diet as major culprits to infertility

We will now consider the effects of lifestyle. Career women often use their brain in a similar fashion to their male counter parts. Rather than working towards creating environments that nurture a woman's gifts of multitasking and diffuse awareness, she seeks to match her male equals. If a woman doesn't shift out of male brain activity when she returns home, she begins to lose parts of her female nature. She will appear to others more male-like in her affect and behavior. Her brain operations will begin to alter the priority of chemical distribution and will signal to the ovaries and pituitary gland a significantly reduced need for baby making hormones. On the supply and demand scale she will then have less female hormones available to her.

The culprit is not work, nor the solution to stop working. Rather the question is, how can I honor my female nature while in the career I love?

Another challenge I see is the thin standard. Without enough fat the body will choose not to conceive, feeling there is not enough nutrition at this time to support life. We have an odd trend of overly-thin young women and many overweight and obese women in our culture. Natural health means having some fat on your body.

Spiritual imbalances can cause the baby not to be able to implant despite a promising conception. Here is an example.

Miraculous Balance brings long awaited conception
Cindy and Ken really wanted a baby and a lifestyle that included of family and community. Cindy was a midwife and specialized in home birth. Ken worked with the EPA, and was a big mountain man with shoulder-length hair. This couple fit in with the 'Granola' crowd. When they found me they had been attempting conception for three years and were at each other's throats in frustration. Cindy knew all the natural remedies and felt the pain of disappointment with the onset of each cycle.

I suggested she bring her husband in for her session feeling what was in the way had to do with what they were co-creating. As we progressed through the session I found

their aura and chakras were literally short circuiting the others energy body. I was able to restore both of their energy bodies, and then align them with the others.
All their chakras and aura were now in harmony and flowing joyously in harmony.

Six hours after the session they successfully conceived their daughter. The power of alignment produces a miraculous conception!

Testicles

The male body is quite remarkable. Because too much heat destroys the potency of sperm the testicles are the only endocrine gland to hang outside the body. This provides a cooler resting place for the impregnating sperm to flourish. Essential oils from the Jasmine flower are a wonderful male enhancement for love making. Think of the jasmine flower with hundreds of tiny fragrant white flowers and know that this aphrodisiac oil supports the semen/sperm. The testacies provide testosterone.

Best Colors for the Testicles:

Green	100%
Red	80%
Orange	60%
Yellow	26% Serious malfunction
Blue	2%
White	Represents control energy (experienced as extremely unpleasant)
Black or Grey	Indicates a serious malfunction, signals a death energy

Energy provided for the testacies from the first chakra

Healing the Testicles

- With the gold energy pump the percentage up to 100%. Clear colors simply by pumping the gold energy.

- Once you have completed the color and percentage healing, using kinesiology, ask if the healing is complete or if Cellular Neo-Genesis is the next step.

- If yes, do all steps laid out for Cellular Neo-Genesis

- If the master cell in the testicles is black you will need to do the Cellular Neo-Genesis.

- If it continues to appear white, pump gold energy to remove control energy (which, in this case is often female control energy).

- Test the cell improvement, and percentage of cells that received the new information.

- Test for the number of days of new cell growth.

- Test if the healing is complete at the end of the designated healing day or if there will be steps ahead for more healings.

- If the answer is no, or that the testicles will still be at a reduced level, check on when the body would be ready for the next healing.

Note: You can also check on chemistry function related to the testicles. Sometimes men will have to much testosterone in the system making them prone to rage, or too little, causing lethargy, reduction of musculature and motivation.

If you get a high reading on the chemistry, meaning too much testosterone, check if the direction for too much testosterone is being sent from the brain or the gland itself.

Program alteration for overage of testosterone

Three nadis (small energy centers similar to chakras) contain the endocrine system program information. Two of these nadis are located slightly to the left of the hypothalamus, while one sits under the hypothalamus slightly forward and up from the center of the head.

You will likely notice an orange color to the hypothalamus, indicating this failure. Focus gold energy into the area of nadis and hypothalamus and return the hypothalamus and nadis to yellow. The program that was set at the incorrect balance is now ready to shift to the proper hormone distribution for the testicles.

Focus gold energy on the three nadis with the intention of returning to the correct balance. This may require a number of healings; high blood pressure, emotional timeline, relationship and karma clearing, depression and anxiety. Too much testosterone is too much fire, look for where the body is on fire.

Concluding thoughts about the endocrine system

Having a happy hormonal system can make life a sheer joy. On the other hand, having challenges in this complex system can make the body fragile and even threaten life.

There are many illnesses and related to this magical chemistry that makes life possible. The hormones of a woman are like a fully orchestrated symphony creating a rich diversity and beauty beyond imagination. The steadfastness of a healthy man's hormones supports his power and focus.

Chapter 18: Systems

We have looked at the minutest details that cause a miraculous healing and observed how beautifully our four bodies (mental, spiritual, emotional, and physical) synchronize to create the environment for life. You likely replace your computer every three or four years, as technology advances and the older computer slows down and develops problems. I know of no one who is holding onto a thirty year-old computer babying it along. Yet as fabulous as a computer is, it doesn't come close to the amazing design of the whole human system.

Using the protocols successfully will lead you on an adventure in the body you had no idea existed. The following pages will help you understand how each of the systems rely on the other systems as well as components outside that system in order to thrive and function.

My endocrine system began crashing at age nineteen. The toxic exposure to the nuclear radiation was slowly destroying my thyroid and, in the process, as the thyroid was straining to function, other glands became compromised. I became hypoglycemic, with fainting episodes, shaking and headaches.

My pituitary gland was working poorly, and, as the thyroid tanked, so did the thymus and my ability to ward off illness. Eventually, I would lose my ovaries and thyroid as well as experience adrenal failure.

If you are going through this kind of life, you understand how challenging it can be. It feels like just as you get one raging forest fire under control, an entirely new fire breaks out somewhere else. It seems that no matter what you do, things just keep getting progressively worse.

The surgical removal of an ill gland or organ may possibly stop the advancement of an illness, but it creates an entirely new set of difficult circumstances to sort out and live with.

If you can hold onto a gland or organ by a miraculous healing rather than having it surgically removed, this is by far a better option than attempting to grow a new gland or organ from nothing. The difficulty scale of replacing the gland or organ goes way up when you are starting from scratch.

Digestive, absorption and elimination

The director of the digestive system is located in the front area of the emotional brain. Western medicine discovered that if both the brain and the digestive system were treated together, results were phenomenally better than treating digestive system alone. When you think about the connection between digestion and emotions, you will discover there are many clues leading to comprehending the role of the emotional brain, and feelings and emotions experienced in the digestive system

> *I can't stomach this*
> *I find this information difficult to digest*
> *I feel like sh***t*
> *I feel it in my guts*
> *So and so is a pain in the butt (hemorrhoid)*
> *It's tough to swallow*

The administrator of digestion is the nervous system connected to the digestive system. Surprisingly, about sixty percent of the total nerves in the nervous system are involved in the successful function of the digestion system. Without the nerves functioning well, the digestive system would stop.

If you have had difficulties with your nerves, for example, a pain condition for a long time, your nerves end up staying on at high alert in the sympathetic nervous system. The nerves will get hot, inflamed, and angry, as they are never allowed to rest. All the energy within the sympathetic nervous system gets pumped out into the limbs, abandoning the function of digestion.

In the hierarchy of survival, running away from the saber tooth tiger is more important than eliminating your supper. Even if there are no saber tooth tigers chasing you, being on high alert in a similar fashion, a stressful life or a life full of pain, is a reason for the sympathetic nervous system to be on all the time. Digestion works properly when you are relaxed, that is, while the nervous system is functioning in the parasympathetic mode.

Our DNA contains all the information required for the digestive process. As I gaze into the DNA, I see what seems like millions of digestive information details.

The entire digestive system is the cleanup system for not only digestion, but the rest of the body. In other words, it is the janitorial service for the entire body, the digestive system itself included.

Each system will have one or more reliance partners. The role of the reliance partner is to support parts of the system, without actually being a part of the system itself. It is like being a relative of that system, such as a grandchild. In the case of the digestive system, the spleen takes the role of the reliance partner. The spleen supports digestion energetically and is a smaller processing structure.

An excellent digestive system will mean your nutrients are being absorbed and your bowels are moving waste out of your body one to four times daily. There are little finger-like structures with nerves called villi that are inside the intestines. They move the matter down and out as the digestive enzymes provide the chemistry to draw out the nutrients from the food and deliver them to the body.

Chemical support for digestive enzymes is found in the brain, the mouth (saliva), and the stomach. Energetic support for the digestive system is provided by the fourth and sixth chakras, and sixty nadis.

The digestive system protocols

One by one: test color of system components;
>Mouth
>Throat
>Stomach
>Small intestines
>Large intestines

1. One by one test color and percentage of function for the system components.

2. Clear the color and improve the percentage of function of the low functioning system components by pumping gold energy into that part and then continue pumping gold energy raising function to100%.

If you are unable to bring it up fully to 100% this is a clue that you will need to do Cellular Neo-Genesis.

Table 18-1 Components of the digestive systems and their colors

Component	Mouth	Throat	Stomach	Small Intestines	Large Intestines
Function by Color	Red 100%	Green 100%	Pink 100%	Green 100%	Orange 100%
	Green 99%	Pink 98%	Orange 98%	Red 92%	Pink 90%
	Yellow 80%	Orange 80%	Red 92%	Pink 87%	Brown 34%
	Orange 60%	Red 70%	Blue 80%	Orange 60%	Gray 10%
	Blue 40%	Purple 40%	Green 73%	Blue 42%	Black -1%
	Pink 10%	Yellow 20%	Purple 50%	Purple 40%	
	Purple 4%	Brown 4%	Yellow 20%	Brown 30%	
	Gray -40%	Gray -70%	Brown 10%	Yellow 10%	
	Black -90%	Black -100%	Gray -60%	Gray -30%	
			Black -90%	Black – 70%	
	White= Control	White = Control	White= Control	White= Control	White= Control

3. Individually ask if the component that has had any reduction of function, starting with the mouth:

    a. Is a meme or miasm is affecting the component?

    b. If so identify how many years back, starting with 10 and so forth in increments of 10 up to 100, then in increments of 100. (I have never seen a miasm or meme reaching farther back than 300 years)

    c. Clear the meme or miasm.

4. Is Cellular Neo-Genesis next? If so, do the full Cellular Neo-Genesis process found in Chapter 3 or Appendix xx.

Make sure you check each individual component to see if Cellular Neo-Genesis is required in that component.

5. Test to see if the 'DNA Obliteration' process is needed for the following?

    a. Check first on the specific component, for example, the stomach.

    b. Check then on aging DNA

    c. Check for any problems that would occur for that component in the future.

    d. Completely clear DNA by pumping gold energy into the DNA, the future problems, family DNA bubble, and then do your reset.

6. Ask if there is anything else and use the protocols if you get a yes. For example, a spiritual problem could be a timeline issue or a chakra problem, etc.

Gold ribbon healing

Correction of each element of the system continues until the entire system is restored. Once it is all reading at one hundred percent, you can do a gold ribbon healing to connect all the elements with a new golden path, as follows:

After a grounding-and-clearing meditation, imagine yourself sitting at the top of your head as a spirit peacefully like a yogi or yogini, cross-legged and upright. You are sitting in a globe of gold. Imagine grasping a piece of gold, like a thick, silky golden ribbon, then diving down as a spirit into the system you have just restored. Start closest to the head then travel down through each part in the torso. When you have brought the golden ribbon through the element furthest from the head, loop back up through until you have reached the top of the head.

This is less technical than many of the procedures we use and more expressive. It is more like a dance through the body, which supports the creative nature of healing and playfulness of connection.

When a gland or organ has undergone an illness or injury, it changes and becomes both lowering functioning as well as unrelated to the other system components. Connection is vital to reestablish full operations for the overall structure.

Digestion And Elimination Beyond The Digestive System

Our digestive system processes the majority of physical nutrition and waste elimination, yet there are many other aspects in the body that support the process of elimination. For example, the skin is equipped to sweat out toxins and is considered the largest elimination organ.

The carrier fluid surrounds the cells, glands, organs and vessels of the body; it is instrumental in moving out the toxic waste from cells and other sources. If your carrier fluid becomes overloaded with toxic materials, your glands and organs will be marinating in toxic fluid, hindering any progress in healing. For this reason, it is important to keep an eye on the percentage of clarity in the carrier fluid. In addition, a toxic carrier fluid could cause a backslide having the problem resurface after a successful healing, even when every step was done correctly.

The toxins found in carrier fluid have several pathways out of the body: the circulatory and lymphatic systems, the kidneys, and liver are instrumental in clearing this toxic load.

Every cell of our bodies has both an absorption organelle and an elimination organelle. These organelles provide a means to supply the cell with nutrients and dispose of cell waste products, respectively. Sinuses filter impurities attempting access to the respiratory system. There is an amazing set of processes in the body create a vibrant symphony of clearing and cleansing, restoring purity and health.

I have seen the digestive system shut down because the little finger-like nerves, called villi, that move the nourishment through the system had become coated with poisons from the environment. To bring the digestive system back to life, we used a combination of homeopathics and miraculous healings.

The miraculous protocols are strong enough to heal completely. However, when working with nerves, you will need experience and skill to restore them. As I have mentioned, nerve restoration requires more skill than most other processes. You can think about this as a process of paced restoration of your nerves over time.

I am often asked about cleanses. The more natural you can cleanse, the better for you. If you have a build-up along the lining of your digestive system or in your liver, sometimes the fastest solution is using an herbal cleanse. But keep in mind, you can stimulate bowel function without cleanses and laxatives. It is important in any case to stay well hydrated.

The great thing about miraculous healing in digestion is that we are removing the problems so you never have to deal with another digestive issue, especially when you provide the proper care and nourishment, exercise and rest that your body needs in order to function well.

The immune system

To remain safe and healthy, unaffected by the latest virus or bacterial infection, you will want to keep your immune system in tip top shape and running very well. People experiencing an autoimmune illness will be prone to infection, fatigue, and disease (not a fun way to live). After I was treated for cancer, I began to lose my defenses and became more and more susceptible to illness.

At age twenty-six, two years after the first cancer diagnosis, I contracted a devastating disease, one that had no cure according to Western medicine. What I am speaking of is mycoplasms. These tiny organisms, neither bacterial nor virus, get inside the cell and eat away the nucleus of the cell, rendering the cell unintelligent and unable to defend itself. Imagine a master cell having no nucleus. Now the common thought is that there are multiple intelligence processors in the cell, including the DNA strand and the outer membrane. But still, without the nucleus, your cells, at best, yield a D performance.

My immune system, no longer able to fight its own battles, left me open to many challenges such as infections that I was unable to recover from without a full on, prolonged confrontation. I continued to have significant difficulties, even being diagnosed with an autoimmune illness. First they thought it was Chronic Fatigue. However later they labeled the condition as Fibromyalgia. (Note: the average time for diagnosis of Fibromyalgia is about seven years because the symptoms can resemble other problems).

Recovering from an autoimmune illness is not a medical reality. Despite the general consensus that my experience of Fibromyalgia was not a disease, and was therefore untreatable, through miraculous means I did indeed recover. I no longer have the symptoms of Fibromyalgia.

The last I had heard from my pain-treatment physician, as well as the therapists who helped me manage pain, was that I would not die of the autoimmune illness but from related problems. These came from the damage caused by horrendous side effects of medications they were used to control pain and inflammation. One of my medical team informed me I might expect to live another ten to fourteen years. I believe that this Doctor felt he was being helpful. This is an example of a curse, black magic and a miasm.

To tell a person they are doomed to die, and not honor their innate ability to heal is a curse, not one that a spell caster does, but a curse all the same. Black magic is the unconscious insidiousness of this prognosis. It was repeated to others and began to become a reality in the mental plan. With a group of people 'knowing' together this false reality a miasm was then created.

Between the horrible prognosis of autoimmune disease, the extreme pain and the recent bout of cancer, my medical practitioners sent death images to my mind so often (and I was sensitive enough to receive them loud and clear) that I had to stop seeing doctors all together. I quit my HMO seven years ago, and along with it, I left behind the hope that Western medicine could heal me.

Soon after this, I wrote my will and instructed my children about my health care directive. If another awful thing happened to me, I wanted them to pull the plug. I explained; "I have been in too much pain for too long, you are all grown and doing well, I need to be free of pain". My oldest daughter said, "I understand Mom but we want you to stay."

One morning about a week later, I awoke as if I had been in a sleep all these years. I knew what to do; it was simple. Go to the garden, pray and meditate. Simply claim my divine right to health or peace, preferably both.

And I did. The first day after prayer and meditation I requested, "God, take me or make me well. I will not leave the garden without an answer." Each subsequent day I awoke and returned to the garden for a day of prayer, chanting and meditation.

The revelations came soon and I began to receive downloads for the "Divine Human Blueprint." The door was open to the encyclopedia of our elegant design, and specifically how my body could be restored and free from the unrelenting pain and illness I had suffered from for many years.

We can only receive what we are willing to. We can only heal to the extent that we allow ourselves to heal. Many years ago I had pleaded with God to survive, now I would learn to heal and to thrive and to live each day in the 'Garden of Eden.'

Restoring the immune system

The role of director for the immune system is shared by two organs, a specific part of the logical brain and the *thymus*, the gland under the sternum just above the heart chakra. The thymus serves as a professor for the immune system, providing the education necessary to identify harmful or helpful cells and how to remove the unwanted cells rapidly from the system. The students who are trained to administrate the actions in the thymus gland are the T-cells. The emotional body provides significant enhancement of immune function with high emotions and, likewise, low emotions often follow low immune function.

The robustness of the immune system is recorded in our blood: blood reveals how effective the immune system is functioning by measurement of various components, such as, antibodies, cytokines, lymphocytes, etc.

As the immune system works to kill the foreign bodies and unwanted elements, it produces energetic waste. The clean up of this waste is provided by the energetic janitorial staff: the third chakra, which is provide the energy for personal power and will, and the seventh chakra, direct connection with the Divine. Keep in mind, if you don't have the feeling that you have a right to health, or if you can't see that the relationship you have with the illness is a 'gift God has given you,' you will find it hard to accepting the higher option of complete healing.

Reliance partners playing a role in the immune system are the appendix, gallbladder, tonsils and stomach. Success starts with a healthy mindset, which also supports a healthy immune system. In other words, your healthy thoughts and good feelings (or unhealthy and negative thoughts) reveal your relationship with your immune function.

Protocols for the circulatory system

My great grandmother was a most remarkable woman. Her formal name was Elisabeth, but she was not formal. Instead, she was affectionately called Lucy by all those

386

who knew and loved her. Lucy had a wisdom that was straight from God. She loved her simple life and was a compassionate listener to anyone in need. She had cultivated a life of gratitude for the simple pleasures in life. She had come to America as an immigrant in order to provide a better life for her children and she appreciated everything she had available to her.

I was with her when she passed. She was ninety-seven years young, and was committed to living life on Earth until it was time to leave. She was still gardening and walking a mile every day. When her eyesight got so bad, seeing only light and shadows, she took to walking the driveway of her home for a half hour or more every day. On her deathbed, sheets off her legs, she still had the beautiful smooth legs of a teenager. Who knew? She was an old woman everywhere else, but her legs were gorgeous.

Somehow I tie this bible verse from Isaiah with her, 'blessed are the feet of those who preach the gospel' meaning (preach the language of compassion and love) and she was so blessed.

When I was young there was a popular song: *"These boots are made for walking, and that's just what they'll do!"* Walking and loving go hand in hand with good circulation. Many other physical activities support great circulation. The system of blood moving through the body delivering nourishment to the cells of the body requires movement.

The circulatory system is directed first by instructions from the DNA and then, listed in order of importance, by the: lungs, nerves and lymph. The heart, brain and skin administer and direct the circulatory system and its fluid/flow process.

Your healthy emotions enhance your circulation. In contrast, unhealthy and low vibration emotions will serve to degrade circulation. DNA related to the flow and ease of healthy, happy emotions serves to improve the circulation. The resilient emotional body that operates from the position of "everything is pretty good or better" supports the circulation in doing a great job. You can improve your DNA programs around flow and ease of emotions by following the DNA obliteration protocols.

Circulation relies on white blood cells to clean up the blood stream. The body component that partners with circulation to strengthen the process is the muscular system. By engaging your muscles with regular activity and exercise, optimum circulation is stimulated, and vice versa. Years ago, when I was struggling with fibromyalgia, I discovered that my muscles were in a state of starvation and were atrophying from the illness. I learned that regular exercise forced blood and oxygen into the muscles helping them to feel and function better.

Actually that was such a great learning for me. Now, with no autoimmune illness to struggle with, I am delighted to be working out daily to get the blood and oxygen pumping into my healthy, happy muscles.

You can really tell when circulation is in peak performance from optimal mental function with all five areas of the brain receiving the nourishment it needs. Look for clarity and a healthy emotional brain.

Cardio-Vascular System

The cardio-vascular system is highly responsive to the nerves and your emotional state of health. It is easily stimulated when the nature of an individual is to move swiftly into an emotional state of upset or anger.

I worked with a mature Irish immigrant, a woman in her sixties who had struggled most of her life with high blood pressure. The fiery bloodline of the Irish can leave this entire group prone to high blood pressure. The DNA aging programs of the Irish as a group will manifest the high blood pressure once they reach about the age forty-four (or higher).

Katrina was prone to both bouts of anger and panic attacks. Her behavior, in many ways, was an attempt to free herself from the strong cultural patterns for an aggressive lifestyle. However, she would often rationalize her poor behavior and miss the opportunity to move past them and lose the need for them. I found her difficult to work with. However, she was a good study for me in the challenging life of an individual with these very difficult patterns.

To help Katrina, we needed her to alter the diet that inflamed her situation. We needed to do many clearings on the nervous system until she was no longer having panic attacks. Once the panic ended, we could dramatically improve her blood pressure and ease her off the high blood pressure medicines she had been taking for years.

When you have a miraculous healing and you become well, you need to alter your lifestyle to fully hold the healing. For Katrina, a year of meditation and attending healing classes supported this healthy new system. Unfortunately, negative emotions stimulated her negative health patterns. She was jealous of her ex-husband's dating and other agitations; she constantly battled with neighbors over property lines; she fought the homeowner's association with lawyers, etc. This resulted in her former problems returning with a vengeance to dominate her life.

In the chapter about pain, Chapter 28, I discuss attitudes that need to shift in order for illness and pain to leave. People become accustomed to or even enjoy the high they get from the blood pumping and adrenaline rising. They return to their old patterns to get their fix. And they literally are hooked to the chemistry of their addiction.

Anger, jealousy, and even panic produced a chemistry Katrina was used to; she felt normal or even excited about them. For example, she could rush to the emergency room and have attention from the male physicians and garner their concern and attention regarding her illness. When she used lawyers to fight the association, she could have someone say to her she was justified, and she needed to defend herself.

On numerous occasions, I attempted to show her what she was doing, but was unsuccessful. She called recently with all symptoms flaring, and I referred her to an audio program for stress.

A miraculous healing is truly a gift. Just like the parable of the king dispersing talents; if you take your talent and bury it or worse discard it, you will be given no more, until you realize what you have been given and give it it's proper due. I can't give you what you can't receive.

I believe in Katrina's capacity to heal. It may take her some time but I believe she will contact me in the future knowing what is possible and at that time ready to alter her lifestyle for good. I will welcome her with open arms and rejoice!

The cardio-vascular system is directed by forty percent of the muscles; including the heart, and inner chest cavity musculature. These are the muscles that direct circulation, and of course all muscles benefit from the healthy operations of this system When I am observing which muscles are involved, they start about three inches below the waist line going up to three inches below where shoulders and neck meet, in other words the upper three-quarters of the torso.

Employing your muscles in healthy ways gives the cardio-vascular system a good basis from which to function. The heart administrates the activity of the system by providing the muscular strength and stamina to operate the human organism. Neurons enhance embodiment where cardio-vascular function is eighty percent human body and twenty percent human spirit. The veins and the vascular wall serve to maintain health of the cardio-vascular system and provide purity.

The emotional brain and part of the left brain provide partnership and alliance to the body's successful balancing for the strength of the system. Emotional temperament indicates harmony or disharmony in the system of strength.

Low blood pressure generally does not cause the life threatening circumstances that the condition of high blood pressure does. However, low blood pressure can be troublesome and can cause fainting or a sense of weakness for the sufferer.

Restoring blood pressure to optimal function

1. Using kinesiology test to see if this is the healing the body needs.

2. If yes, begin by clearing the cardio-vascular system. Chart both the color and percentage of functionality. With both high and low blood pressure, you will see a black or grey energy over shadowing the system.

Colors of the system and their functionality:

Red	100%
Orange	97%
Burgundy	94%
Pink	80%
Purple	40%
Blue	10%
Yellow	7%
Grey	-2%
Brown	-6%
White	Someone else is in control

3. Using kinesiology test to see if miasms (group virus) are a factor. If yes, clear the miasms and related to frustration, anger and high blood pressure issues.

4. Test to see if there are problematic energies or colors in the aura (specifically layer two) related to the miasm you just cleared. If yes, clear the problematic energy by pumping gold into those layers.

Excessive mental energy: related to the mental body

The energy of high blood pressure is mental, meaning there will be too much energy in the mental body. For example, if I were to look at Katrina in a high blood pressure phase she would have a read of 400% of her energy in her mental body, leaving none to balance the emotional physical and spiritual body. Mental energy like this will balloon out above the head.

5. Test to see the percentage of energy in the mental body. Pumping gold with the intention of returning the mental energy to balance (and 100%) will restore the mental energy to its proper location and percentage.

Vessel

6. Look for the number three vessel (your body will understand this) it will be black, clear this vessel and any other vessel reading dark by pumping gold energy into the area. Muscle test until you read a bright color.

7. Chakras 3 and 7 will not be functioning at their norm, either off or missing altogether. Restore chakra 3 and chakra 7, both front and back.

8. DNA obliteration process- Clear high blood pressure programs and all future problem blood pressure programs all the way to the end of the body and do resets.

There are many reasons for high blood pressure. Follow protocols to discover other areas that may need improvement.

Respiratory system

The respiratory system provides freedom for the healthy individual able to breathe deeply and enjoy life. For the sufferer of lung illness, a life of restriction and adapting to less becomes the norm. They struggle to exist. They lack the sense of self-value and a place honor in their own life. People with lung illness and low function are convinced they do not have a right to take up space or to be fully who they are. Just as they adapt to the reduced lung function and lower their activities, they also lower their expectations on what kind of life they can anticipate.

Regardless of the source of the illness: whether it originated in the DNA, a response to outer toxins, or a mental response to a dominating family member or friend, the story is the same. Life can simply be snuffed out if they aren't careful: this is the reality they live with daily.

I contracted silent pneumonia over the holidays last year. I hadn't been breathing well for a few weeks. One day I awoke and it was too much effort to speak or get out of bed and walk to the kitchen. I had experienced the regular variety of pneumonia for the two previous winters and thought I had gotten all the programs out through my healings. However, there was some residual program running that needed me to see it and clear it (which I did).

Think about the folks you know who have asthma or another lung condition. How big do they play? Can you see the struggle pattern? I think about a business friend, Lidia who suffers from asthma. She is constantly facing the struggle of having a right to exist. Literally, her grown children are attempting to take her home away from her and clear out what little she has managed to save. I see her puffing away on her inhaler as her challenging life attempts to snuff her out.

There is hope for lung illness sufferers. The solution takes courage, healing and letting go of the past to step into the new and happy reality that has only been dreamed of.

The respiratory system includes the sinuses, air passages, bronchi, lungs and carotid artery.

The real director of the respiratory system is self-esteem. A healthy ego will override some negative DNA; a fragile ego will succumb much more rapidly to the lung illness.

The healthy lungs administrate function and a good understanding of life. Healthy respiration is nerve enhanced. Creative brain is in service to purify respiration function with wholesome self-loving thoughts and expression of a new reality.

The respiratory system becomes ill from consciously ingested toxins from smoking whether cigarettes or dope. This 'addiction' speaks to the right to take up space and the need to contaminate the body for the chemical high and confidence that comes from nicotine, or the non-stress that comes from marijuana.

My grandfather Herb was a kind and quiet man. He struggled to make a life for his wife and children. By almost anyone's standards, Grampa never made it. He had been a navy man in the World War I, serving as a cook on a battle ship. Ironically Herb could not swim.

He married the girl of his dreams, Adelia. She was from a family that was more well-to-do, but her eye was on her beloved. They married and began having children, some who died and some who lived.

They were very poor. Grampa just had no luck, no right to take up space. He thought he would buy some baby chicks and raise chickens, but the money wasn't there to feed them and no one would lend him the feed so he and his boys had to kill the baby chicks. Then life got even more difficult. At one point, having no money and no food the family ate ketchup soup for a week, But not the ketchup you buy in the store, but some homemade concoction to flavor the water.

When I think of my grandparents, they loved and were devoted to each other. Grampa with his thick German accent had a funny saying, "And that's the truth so there!" that he used all the time. He was a sweet man.

Herbert Doering finally died of a broken heart, when the gas company needed his home and land for a power plant. They condemned the land and gave Grampa pennies on the dollar for his home. This happened the year he was set to retire. He developed lung cancer immediately following this atrocity, and passed within a year.

Follow the Miraculous Healing protocols and you will be able to heal lung and respiratory challenges.

Lymphatic system

Yahoo, you've gotta love the system that tidies the body and removes toxic waste from the carrier fluid. The lymph system can be temperamental especially related to pregnancy and aging issues.

I cared for many, many high-risk pregnancy clients during a four-year period when I specialized in this field. While developing my miraculous healing skills, I had the incredible opportunity to support the birthing community and specialists working with women and babies who were categorized as high risk. This meant they were possibly an older first time mom, a mom who had serious health issues and still choose to carry a baby, and babies who were identified during gestation to have worrisome abnormalities.

This category came with a high level of anxiety and need for physical and emotional/spiritual support during the term of pregnancy. I really loved this work, and the only reason I moved away from it was the intense, long hours as I would often stay with the new mothers to support the process of birth and bringing their babies in the world.

Mothers found me because I specialized in pregnancy and birthing massage as well as infant massage. I assisted moms in getting through the pregnancy and often followed them for the first six months to one year postpartum.

In this category, eighty percent of the women I saw and supported had lymphatic issues. Some of them gained so much water weight they referred to themselves as beached whales while others very specifically had lymphatic back up in the limbs.

Massage is awesome way to get the lymph moving as is thirty or more minutes of swimming. However, when your lymph system is presenting a problem and you're not pregnant, you won't be able to have relief when the baby is born. It's time for a solution that can really restore you.

The director of this purifying system is found in the first (survival) brain. Carrier fluid moves unwanted chemicals into the lymphatic system. The DNA provides the vital diagram for implementing flow and amount of collecting fluid responding to injury.

The lymphatic system takes unwanted chemicals and drains them into the liver. The circulatory system does some of the lymphatic system's job if it's compromised or in a reduced function mode. The parasympathetic nervous system needs to be 'on' for the lymphatic system to function.

Lymph nodes in neck are not technically part of the purification system we are discussing, however these and the saliva glands play a role in informing us of the healthy chemistry of the area.

Protocols for restoring the lymphatic system

Best colors for the lymphatic system and functionality

Peach	100%
Orange	90%
Light Green	82%
Blue	80%
Pink	54%
Lavender	50%
Yellow	40%
Dark Green	20%
Brown	5%
Grey	-20%
White	-70%
Black	-100%

If you are deliberately tuning up this system, I encourage you to attempt to restore it to 100%. Anything less will not provide the best results.

1. Using kinesiology, test the level and percentage and color of the lymph system.

2. Pump gold energy into the system until it comes to peach and 100%.

3. Restore the mental body to 100%. Pump gold with right hand into the mental body until it tests at a normal 100% read.

Lymphatic imbalances and malfunctions go hand in hand with extra energy going into the mental body. This excess energy balloons up over the head. The result of this excess energy in the mental body is that it draws important energy away from the lymphatic system.

4. Test carrier fluid for level of toxicity.

5. Pump gold until you have a read of 0% toxicity.

With this process, I would like you to think of this as a time-lapse process and do this clearing five separate times with ten days between each clearing. Even though you will pump to a clearing of 100%, the spiritual body will be clear, however he physically body will still be working towards clarity. The miraculous purification will require five unique clearings.

6. Using kinesiology, observe the skin, color and function. If the lymph is malfunctioning the skin is showing spiritually as black.

7. Clear the skin by pumping gold till it goes up to 100% green.

8. Clear the spiritual timeline of impediments from past lives in relation to the lymphatic system.

  8a. Identify the number of each life affecting the lymph and pump gold to clear each event. This is like clearing the post-traumatic information that never allows the situation to regenerate.

9. Perform the Cellular Neo-Genesis process next for the entire system.

10. Regenerate the director of lymphatic function in the first brain. You will again use Cellular Neo-Genesis this time in a master cell in the upper left area of the first brain. Intend the regeneration focus on restoration.

11. Follow with DNA obliteration process to remove present time and future problematic lymph patterns. Be sure to include family bubble and resets.

If you have experienced problems in the lymphatic system, you will understand the significance of this healing. To have feet or ankles swollen means you will experience difficultly walking, which ultimately means you will lose muscle tone/strength and the ability to enjoy movement. Lymph patterns show up with the aging DNA patterns for many humans, and in an odd way, convinces you that you are old, feeble, and are ready to go when your time comes. When life presents too many challenges, the mind goes to the miasm of "this is what it is to get old", or "I'm falling apart", or "that's just part of getting older."

There are so many messages in the language to excuse and not correct issues like this that we come to expect the issue and accept it without giving it a second thought.

The importance of language

I would love for you to think about how you use language. Do you include little acronyms for aging, cute little metaphors for explaining away imbalance, pain, or some new illness?

I recently heard Dr Daniel Amen speak. He said people who are just happy-go-lucky and don't challenge the status quo die much earlier than those who don't readily accept everything that comes their way as true for themselves.

A great example of this is my brother Marty. I love and respect my brother. He is a cool dude. After his terrible accident and recovery, he decided he must comply with medical policies and procedures to assist him in surviving.

He eventually found a place for himself in a brain injury clinic at a hospital, serving as a volunteer. He felt his pain and poor brain function was just "the way it was." He felt his lot in life was to help others deal with the confusion of a brain injury and unrelenting pain. And so his life, in the conventional medical model, progressed as he won an award for "volunteer of the year" in a competition with two thousand others. Marty was well-loved but also in a lot of pain and with many areas of the brain not functioning.

I was anxious to work with my brother because I knew he would get better. However he wasn't ready. His reality had to shift to the point where he could say, "I have done everything Western medicine has to offer and there are no other options: it is time for me to move on." He got to that point just a few months back and is rapidly regenerating inside and out.

The chapter on pain was very helpful for him in turning around his somewhat cemented position; "This is why I came back (survived horrendous situations) in order to help others survive through their painful confusing lives."

You can't wish someone to change: they have to move into a readiness and a desire to take personal responsibility in the process.

Muscular skeletal system

You've got the power!

Muscles and bones make the human life we live possible. People who do not have use of muscles and joints are thoughtlessly called (vegetables) and none of us wants to be in a vegetative state. We take precautions even to the point of having legal documents drawn up: "in case of coma, do not resuscitate."

On the other hand, in the recent Olympics we enjoyed the beauty and artistry of pure strength as the athletes with gleaming muscle and strong healthy bones, leapt, swam, ran, and cycled across our screen in absolute wonder and majesty!

I would love for you to remember when you were in your peak body. Were you an athlete? How did you use your God-given gift of strength and power? Did you comprehend how absolutely amazing your body was?

Likely not, as you have never known anything different.

I loved being an athlete. I really didn't think about athletics, I thought about training, the skill, the camaraderie, and the sheer joy of running, skiing, skating, and playing ball.

In high school, before I got so sick, I was a powerhouse. I competed routinely in the 440-yard race in track and field, cross-country running and skiing, and was a red-cross-certified swimmer. I could even do back flips off the high diving board.

I was fearless in my body and ran for the joy of running. I enjoyed skating on ice for the aesthetic beauty of the dance and the thrill of the twirl. I was "all in" when it came to enjoying the body I had been gifted.

Lately, I have been hanging around young people who use their body this way and I realized I had lost the 'bar' from which to measure the joy of a youthful, healthy body. With this in mind, I am back into my youthful activities, pacing back into a much more vibrant lifestyle.

I'm loving my workouts. But after repelling down a sheer rock face a couple of months back where I got pretty bruised up and broke my toe, I decided it was time to return to the youthful muscle strength I enjoyed in my teens. Each day is an adventure in training and, of course, shooting gold light into my muscles for help is getting there faster. I am in dance aerobics, lifting small weights, practicing yoga, and, now something super fun I had forgotten I loved; swimming and ice-skating.

In my morning swim I do forty laps, followed by some underwater spins and summersaults, a backwards dolphin move, and maybe swimming under water. I even started diving. It might seem absolutely ridiculous to have it be such a big deal, but many years ago while being treated for cancer, I had doctors tell me I should never swim again. The water wasn't clean enough and I could not fight off any infections. Their reasoning was that having treated me for three years on antibiotics, and everything else they could think of to help me, I had been put in a weakened immune state.

Years later, now healthy, but still having those (PTSD) conversations running: I was thinking, it's natural to swim and could it help me recover the knees I tweaked running. Can it? I wonder, I wonder if I can?

Did someone tell you not to use your body in some way? That it's not ladylike or you should act your age? Did you begin to have an achy joint or an injury and take it as a sign you should back down on your activities?

If so, I challenge you to do a big clearing of your timeline and all the slow downs that got you to where you are now. Next pace back into your blissful youthful body with vim, vigor and enthusiasm. Because my friend, "it ain't over till it's over."

These are actually personal miasms, however you might also be experiencing group mind and memes on what you should or shouldn't do.

Clue: To be successful, be sure to remove muscular skeletal system aging programs in the DNA.

I was visiting my folks a few years back. I was in good shape and was wearing a gorgeous designer blouse from Germany. It was see through with a camisole beneath. It was not a particularly racy blouse; it wasn't low cut and had long flowing sleeves. My mom, so freaked out by the blouse, threw her size fourteen sweater on top of me, and said, "Cover up, my friends will think you're a prostitute!"

She was sending me the message: you are not being appropriate for your age and she was sending strong control pictures to me. Have you similar communications about you health and wellbeing? Recently my mother pulled me aside and said, "My friends and I have been talking. You do know you don't look your age?" "Yes. Mom I know. I like it and I am doing this on purpose."

"Ohhh."

Did you put on weight when a lover hurt you? Did someone tell you that you were too attractive or something was your fault because of your looks? That's the "garbage" we need to look out for when it comes to re-owning your body in a youthful and powerful way.

Healing injury in bones and muscles

Bones and muscles are relatively easy to repair. They appear very different than the cellular body, the nerves, and brain. Think of this as the easy system. It is ready to regenerate and return to good shape.

Bone Protocols

1. When healing bones that are broken, proceed by clearing dark colors from the broken bone by pumping gold energy into the break.

As you pump gold into the broken area as the bone will mend. It will appear as tree roots bonding together, from both sides until the mend is complete. This process has been done in as little as twenty minutes. The rapidity of the healing largely depends on the force and power of the gold energy you are administering to the break.

Christine, seventy-five, came into our Miraculous Apprentice weekend feeling pretty miserable. She had taken a fall and was nursing two broken ribs as she struggled to stay focused and in the process of learning.

It was a perfect segue, even though it wasn't included in the lesson plan to teach bone regeneration. We, as a group, read her and proceeded to pump gold energy. Christine reported feeling a warm, water-like experience where the bones where growing back. Within twenty minutes, we got a read that the healing was compete and a surprised

Christine was without discomfort, filled with energy and more ready to learn than ever.

Ligaments and tendons

It's pretty much the same only faster for ligaments and tendons. If you have the misfortune of having a severed ligament, meaning there is no attachment, it is still possible to mend by using the "human blueprint" entirely as you pump gold and watch the ligament or tendon grow back.

I met Mark at a business-networking event. He was there with his business partner, Amy, promoting their joint venture and networking. My friend, Caral, is a super awesome connecter and she brought Mark into my room for the healing demonstration I was doing.

He raised his hand when I was done speaking and said he had a torn ligament behind his knee. In a matter of seven minutes, we had gotten him out of pain and largely restored the ligament. He was happily surprised to discover he had full flexibility in the joint and could stand on the leg without pain.

When re-growing any component of the muscular skeletal system, I encourage you to do at least one follow-up healing. You will get a 100% read, however it's been set at 100%. Being set at 100% means that there will be days involved in healing to have the physical ligament go to 100%. Negative thoughts can prevent the full healing from finishing. Restoration may take days depending on the damage to the area and the strength of the healer. As you complete the protocols, you can get a read, on how long to anticipate new growth. For example you may get bone growth for another eleven days.

The muscular skeletal system is directed by part of the second brain, which is the emotional brain. Administrative programs for repair and regeneration are provided by the DNA. The fifth brain formats how far you can access the power provided by this system. (The fifth brain is the angelic out-of-the-box thinking brain.) Chakras move unwanted energies out efficiently and bring in the right nourishment for this system to thrive.

To be the captain of the skeletal system, you could imagine the advantage of having a calcium-producing gland on your team to provide you with the necessary repair ingredient. This is exactly why the para-thyriod is a reliance partner.

The mental body keeps tally of the 'wins' of the physical body. This is not the brain, but rather the mental body that stores information and brings it forward into future incarnations.

Nervous system

Nancy is a well-loved girl's coach who'd formally worked in the Pentagon in brain-based learning. She is an amazing woman with a heart of gold and lived a life truly in service contribution on a grand scale of love, love, love. Nancy sought me out for assistance with an anxiety problem that would not leave her in peace. Anxiety is a malfunctioning of the nervous system. Sometimes it comes from a condition of mental health, but usually I see it as stemming from emotions and the nervous system.

Imagine playing this big in the world, having your own MTV show, and appearing on large stages all over the country while struggling with panic and anxiety. It's just no fun.

Marty, my brother, had been in a terrible accident. His nerves were malfunctioning in every way you can imagine from being in high alert all the time due to pain. Despite his inability to feel his foot or even leg, his back was on fire with nerve pain. This level of malfunction was truly making his life a living hell.

Kathy came from a family of amputees. As we spoke about her numb feet and legs, she recounted that all the grandparents and great grandparents on both sides who had had legs and feet amputated. Now, at the same age, her DNA time bomb had blasted into the scene. Nerve pain and numbness were out of control.

These people were all cured from their maladies with the help of Miraculous Healing protocols.

The brain directs the nervous system, including part of the right cortex, the frontal lobe and heart. The adrenal glands administer chemistry for dictating how the nerves will function at any given time. The aura provides energetic information to the nerves on sympathetic high alert moments. The mental body gathers and stores nervous system information in intelligence.

Emotions can rapidly purify and restore frayed nerves to a relaxed state. The spine provides tremendous support to give structure to the lacy network of nerves living in the spine. The neurons of the heart reflect a successful happy system or a strained compromised system.

Nervous system restoration protocols

1. Using kinesiology, read the energy and color of the system.

Colors for the nervous system and their energies:

Dark blue	100%
Great	96%
Purple	66%
Yellow	20%
Orange	5%
Brown	3%
Red	1%
Grey	-50%
White	Someone else is controlling your nerves

2. Pump gold to clear color and raise energy to 100%.

3. Clear areas in the third and fifth brain, directing the function of the nervous system. These areas will likely be grey if the nervous system in at a reduced level.

4. Clear mental imbalance. Using kinesiology read the percentage of energy in the mental body. It will be over 100% and will be expanded and up around the head. Pump gold energy to bring it back down to 100%

5. Check for spiritual timeline issues up to nine lives back and clear using the spiritual timeline technique.

6. Using the DNA Obliteration process, clear all difficulties and challenges from the nervous system, including future, family bubble and resets.

7. Do Cellular Neo-Genesis for twenty master cells in the nervous system. Don't worry about counting. Instead, intend it and it will happen.

8. Clear muscles related to the nervous system (they will likely be grey).

9. Do a gold ribbon healing of the whole nervous system.)

409

Curing anxiety and chronic distress

This clearing is a combination of past life issues, dominant DNA, family patterns, nerves, adrenals, and emotional temperament.

1. Using kinesiology, test the nervous system for function.

2. Pump gold energy into the nervous system bringing it up to 100%

3. Clear the DNA issues of anxiety, stress, and worry with DNA Obliteration process.

4. Proceed to Cellular Neo-Genesis of the nervous system.

5. Clear the third and sixth chakras. Make sure they're on and spinning in front and back.

6. Using kinesiology read the cardio-vascular system for function and color.

7. If it's less than 100%, pump gold energy into it until it reads 100%.

8. Using kinesiology ready the color and function of the intestines. When there are problems in the nervous system the intestines will be black.

9. Pump gold energy to clear the color and function of the intestines to bring them up to 100%.

10. Using kinesiology test mental body function. You will find it expanded over the head and the number will range from 200 – 400%.

11. Pump gold energy to restore it to 100%.

410

12. Clear the emotional brain (second brain) and amygdala of anxiety, worry, and stress by pumping gold energy into the second brain.

13. Clear survival brain (first brain).

14. Using kinesiology test to see if the first and second brain need Cellular Neo-Genesis. If yes, perform Cellular Neo-Genesis for cleared brains

15. Clear emotional timeline of any anxiety, worry or stress, especially as it pertains to this life.

16. Using kinesiology test for fifth brain function. It is typically shut down, so pump gold energy to restore to 100%.

17. Clear the lungs and respiratory system. If it doesn't completely clear, use kinesiology to check the following items: past lives, DNA and personal affirmations: "I have a right to take up space. I have a right to exist." Clear the items that tests as positive.

18. Clear endocrine system; follow endocrine protocols

19. With a nervous system problem the skin with be grey or black. Pump gold energy to bring to a healthy color.

20. Using kinesiology test for memes around anxiety and worry, and clear them by pumping gold energy

21. Using kinesiology, test for emotional timeline issues, especially around fear and death. Proceed to clear emotional timeline issues.

22. With nervous systems issues the stomach will often be black of grey. Using kinesiology test for color and function of stomach, and restore to full function by pumping gold energy. At the completion of the restoration test to see if Cellular Neo-Genesis is needed, If yes, proceed to Cellular Neo-Genesis

23. We have already cleared the endocrine system, however we've just gone through a whole sequence of further clearings so it's possible that the thyroid has addition issues that have surfaced to clear. Using kinesiology test the thyroid for color and function again. If needed, pump gold energy to restore color and function to 100%. Test to see if Cellular Neo-Genesis is needed. If yes, proceed to Cellular Neo-Genesis

24. Using kinesiology, test for color and function of the knees, which represent the ability to honor yourself. Clear knees to 100% as well as restoring the chakras to 100%.

25. Using kinesiology, test for emotional miasms: small, frightened, helpless, stuck in a child's body or emotions. Pumping gold energy proceed to clear.

26. Using kinesiology, test immune system. Since the system requires self-love and nourishment, it is important to create a new foundation. Restore immune system to 100%.

27. Although we have already cleared the adrenals in the endocrine healing, since we've done additional healing we may find the adrenals need a deeper healing. Test for function and color. If less than restore to 100% and proceed to test if CNG is required. If yes, Perform Cellular Neo-Genesis.

28. Test adrenals for adrenal obliteration looking for strain on adrenals or low function. Then proceed to DNA obliteration process restoring adrenals, clearing problem energy.

29. Pump gold energy into the brain and body.

Lifestyle changes for stress reduction

Stress, panic, anxiety, and worry are a chosen lifestyle. You can make a new choice.
Start by removing the alarms and high stress sounds in your environment: every time an alarm goes off, the adrenals set the nervous system on high alert, and you are in the sympathetic mode. Nothing regenerates or heals when your nervous system is in sympathetic mode: energy abandons your body and, instead, fuels limbs so you can run quickly from danger.

Your lifestyle may be confusing your automatic responses to danger. Stress for the body is danger. You are not safe when you are experiencing danger.

You can consciously choose to be around loving supportive people. Change your music to classical or easy listening, uplifting sounds. Relax in a bubble bath, light a candle and meditate, walk in the woods, and take time to stop and smell the roses. This is your life. How good it becomes, how wonderful it is, is entirely up to you and no one else.

Once you have cleared anxiety and panic, you may want to review the karma clearing and love clearing processes. What a perfect time to remove old difficult, connections and start with a new emotional and relationship environment.

Table 18-2 Systems And Their Colors – Functionality

System	Cardio Vascular	Lymphatic	Nervous
	Red 100%	Peach 100%	Dark Blue 100%
	Orange 97%	Orange 90%	Green 96%
	Burgundy 94%	Light green 82%	Purple 66%
	Pink 80%	Blue 80%	Yellow 20%
	Purple 40%	Pink 54%	Orange 5%
	Blue 10%	Lavender 50%	Brown 3%
	Yellow 7%	Yellow 40%	Red 1%
	Gray -2%	Dark green 20%	Gray -50%
	Brown -6%	Brown 5%	Black -90%
	Black -70%	Gray -20%	
		White -70%	White=
		Black-100%	Control

Chapter 19: Dynamism

We hear a lot of talk about '*energy*'. Whether a fuel source that can deliver energy or something of spirit, energy surrounds us. As a commodity, it is the most sought after which means that controlling, enhancing, and manufacturing energy is a very well-compensated business. Mobil Oil and the 5-Hour-Energy-Drink manufacturers are just two examples of how lucrative this market is.

What is energy?

Energy is the dynamic aspect of life that has no form or weight; it is light and movement. *When you are filled with energy you are capable of turning your thoughts into physical reality.*

Our DNA is encoded with the programs for the Divine Human Blueprint and the miraculous system of energy support. It becomes activated as life begins. Our energy support system consists of the chakras, aura, life force, spirit, and Golden Rings as well as the mental body and light of cell. The chakras develop over the first seven years of life, receiving their directions from the DNA programs, as well as the aura, life force, spirit and Golden Rings!

The physical energy systems of our bodies consist of the thyroid, heart, pancreas, mitochondria, neurons, brain, and adrenals.

How does proper distribution of energy support the body? A healthy life lived in balance emotionally, physically, and spiritually provides abundant energy, yielding a symphony of energy reserves that can be accessed throughout the journey of existence.

Golden rings

Starting with your halo and moving upwards, the Golden Rings provide you with the energy to literally transform yourself, as well as others, to vibrant health. This Golden Ring energy is the transformative cellular quantum mechanical energy we have explored throughout the pages of this book. When you have mastered the ability to access and direct the use of this energy, it is virtually without limits. It is your creator god power.

You can use this source of golden light to restore energy centers in any failing physical, energetic systems and generally juice up all your entire body. You can even reverse the process of aging. The dynamic energy of the Golden Rings is your "Ticket to Ride!"

Human spirit

Human Spirit must be present in a human animal for life to begin at birth. Ideally, for the best mental and physical health, the spirit should be well-ensconced in the body, extending out to our extremities. Surprisingly, large numbers of individuals do not get well-established in their bodies and live only partially connected to their spirits, usually just through the head and part of the torso.

How can this be? Without a spiritual midwife present during birth, for example, spirit is left to its own devices to sort out how it relates to the body it occupies.

My estimate is that upwards of seventy percent of individuals never get their spirits into their limbs, hands or feet, and approximately forty percent have little to no relationship with their torso.

Connecting spirit into body, or rather a failure to connect, has been a unique development in our spiritual societal evolution. Is our condition of disconnectedness a failure of human spirit? I think not.

We must consider our journey as one of experimentation and discovery. The process of learning and growing is one of the unique features of humanity's individuation process.

As more spiritual researchers like myself are able to identify and refine how we function, advance, and, finally, how we perfect our relationship of the human spirit to human physique, our evolutionary process, just like the exploration into space, will experience a time of rapid internal growth.

As I write this Neil Armstrong has just passed at the age of eighty-two. "One small step for man, one giant leap for mankind!" Mr. Armstrong, a shy, very talented pilot, holds the distinction of being the first man to walk on the moon. From that time to the present, our technological advances have been off the charts.

Similarly, there will be a skyrocketing in human evolution over the coming fifty years. Medicine has given us pieces of the puzzle, the understanding of the physical body. Seeing ourselves as purely physical actually only gives us part of the story. As in an original Star Trek episode, Doctor Leonard McCoy ('Bones') observes a person treated for cancer in his past and declares the treatment 'barbaric.'

As we advance in our understanding of the human spirit our understanding of the physical body connection, of how imbalances affect the dis-ease process, and our ability to heal the 'whole' human essence will advance rapidly. For example, if you know that you are less connected than you could be for optimum health, wellbeing, and vibrancy, you will begin to take actions to correct that situation.

A pessimistic response to this is: "Oh no, another thing that's got to be fixed." This could actually be the first response of many. However, once we establish a group consciousness around full connection of spirit to body, future generations will be blessed with an effortless connection.

An optimistic response to this situation is: "Fantastic, I can make things even better than they already are! How cool is that!"

How you respond will support or detract from your next step. I often ask my students, "Are You Ready for a Miracle? Say yes!" Be the "yes" and the enthusiastic response to this news.

Does a fully embodied human spirit in its physical body provide more energy? In this case, the word is "strength": *you have more strength.* Super-human feats have been attributed to a full human-spirit embodiment. When your human spirit fully fills out your entire human/animal body, as you might imagine, it fortifies your muscles and bones.

Neurons

Brain, nerves and skin are fortified by healthy neurons. Neurons provide the current or electricity of the body. The neurons support movement as well as provide energy to the five senses. Your ability to feel a feather across your skin comes from neuron responsiveness. Neurons transmit the signal needed for taste buds to receive and understand the information.

As I test myself, I have sixty percent of the neurons active for optimal vibrancy and enjoyment of the human life. I will begin my gold pumping with the right hand to increase the percentage of responsive neurons in my body. I test that three fifteen minute restorations will get me to my hundred percent.

When you don't have the optimum number of neurons responding, no other system can pick up the slack, you are just depleted. For example, cancer treatments and radiation significantly reduce the percentage of responsive neurons, leaving you tired and worn out.

Eighty percent of the body uses the electric fuel neurons provide.

Chakras and aura

The chakras and the aura provide a great deal of support to specific areas in and around the body. The chakras, appearing like vortexes, provide an influx of energetic fuel to the system, gland, or organ it is providing for.

The colors of the aura have a direct bearing on how you appear energetically to others. The dark colors will drag you down physically as well as spiritually, mentally and emotionally. Tuning up the auric field and seven layers to bright colors can significantly assist you in feeling better, stronger more vibrant and vital.

Light of cell

The light of cell is found primarily in the master or stem cells and in all cells that are in the process of healing or regenerating. I have used this blessed system to literally alter and reverse the damage of illness and radiation and restore my body to a significantly younger state.

419

Light of cell provides the miracle energy on a cellular level to grow new cells, and literally grow back glands and organs as well as restore damaged tissue to a healthy state.

Mitochondria

Mitochondria are the cell generators, the individualized fuel source for the cells. They resemble a funny sort of caterpillar in appearance. The mitochondria will lose functionality significantly if the fluid surrounding your cells is contaminated. I call this *'carrier fluid'* (interseitlum) the fluid that surrounds the cell.

The mitochondria are directly affected by the health and purity of the carrier fluid. This discovery was made after I restored the cellular body, working specifically on restoring glands and organs. After the healing, I was often surprised when function and percentage activation would mysteriously go down. After some research, I learned just how important clean carrier fluid is for maintaining full restoration. If your body's glands and organs are marinating in toxic fluid they can't possibly hold the upgrades permanently.

My mitochondria had grown dangerously low giving me only fifteen percent of the energy I required to operate my physical body. When the mitochondria read low, you are overcome by a feeling of weakness and a fatigue that rest does not restore.

I used to wonder and worry about this odd situation: I seemed to be more fatigued and ill when I took a whole day to rest. I did better being up and moving around.

In order to restore your energy you need to first clear carrier fluid, then pump up the mitochondria, in that order.

Mitochondria provide the energy for naturally occurring light of cell.

Life force

Reading your life force reveals how strong you are in your body. Many people are able to maintain a hundred percent reading even without a healthy lifestyle. The major determinant in strength of your life force is found in your DNA. If your family is known for having a strong constitution, this goes hand in hand with a strong life force.

If on the other hand your family is known for illness, breakdown and disease, such as a delicate constitution, your life force, even with a very healthy lifestyle, may read as low or weak.

When life force drops, the protection afforded your spirit from soul also drops.

The program for constitution is derived from the spiritual body and it's initial connections with your new fetus/body. Your spirit essentially gives your DNA the program for this life in relationship to how much illness and fragility you are planning to experience in order to get the spiritual growth for which you aspire.

Adrenals

The adrenals are the emergency backup that provides a life saving burst of energy when you are under extreme duress. The adrenals accomplish this task by rapidly and intensely dispersing chemicals that provide thirty times the regular energy to muscles, including the entire cardio-vascular system and extremities. Adrenalin and Cortisol are only the tip of the iceberg as forty-eight other chemicals boost energy for enduring danger and attack.

A major challenge we face, however, in our modern day world is that adrenal function is not hard wired for technology. The adrenals are ancient glands whose function has not evolved rapidly enough for the conditions humans now find themselves in. In a matter of just a few centuries, we have gotten away from dangers found in the wild but instead routinely have alarms, whistles, and jackhammers triggering our adrenals to react.

Where adrenals used to respond to dangerous situations once every few days or so, they are now firing off one hundred or more times a day. This has led to a new and alarming trend of strained and failing adrenals, especially in the young.

If a child is computer savvy, which most are, they might be on the computer and on some kind of technology for hours each day. In these hours, they are barraged with adrenal-stimulating alarms. Consider a computer game with all its noises, beeps, and bells, which trigger a fast response. These stimulate the reptilian brain and the adrenals (adrenalin rush). Now for the first time in human history, children as young as age fourteen are suffering from debilitating adrenal fatigue.

Entrepreneurs and business people alike are overworking and under-managing healthy balanced living. Adrenal fatigue and adrenal failure is rampant in the self-employed and self-starters.

The popularity of drinks like Red Bull and 5-Hour-Energy directly relate to a culture that clearly does not yet understand how to care for the emergency system. Rather than understand their situation and shift to a new lifestyle supporting healthy adrenal function, so many individuals chug down an energy drink and, like a slave driver, push their unstable human body by pumping in new and foreign stimulating chemicals.

The free meditation program "From Fatigued to Fabulous" on our website (miraculouslivingtoday.com) offers a great deal of support to restoring the adrenals to their healthy state.

Heart

The heart is part of the electric system and provides strength and endurance. It is the most important muscle in the body. When your heart is strong and vibrant so are you. You have the power to move your way through life energetically. When your heart is weak or compromised, you become fragile and your strength wanes.

Thyroid

The thyroid provides both heat and metabolism. If you have good metabolism, and heat, your body is self-sufficient and self-regulating. You experience a freedom to come and go as you please, and in many ways are 'low maintenance'. For example, you are at a friend's house watching a movie. As your body relaxes, it has adjusted to the room temperature. You are warm enough and need no extra blanket. Although you notice when you're in hot weather, your body's natural cooling system kicks in, you begin sweating, and your core temperature drops.

If however your thyroid is not up to par, you will not have the dynamic energy to burn fat or maintain the constant desirable body weight.

Muscles

Determined by DNA and enhanced by exercise and nutrition, the muscles in your body support power and perseverance. Think about someone who is called a weakling: they are small and underdeveloped and bring little to the table that is energetic. Think of someone called muscle-bound, or a muscle head. They are going to provide a ton of energy to a situation, perhaps moving mountains.

To use and keep muscles strong is much of what keeps us young and juiced up. There is a strong correlation between muscle mass and healthy brain function as well.

Nine years ago, when I moved house shortly after the accident, I had to be super careful with the funds I had and I wasn't capable of much lifting. I invited some of my he-man friends to assist me in the moving process. When you've got three or four big guys on your team to do something physical, you are in luck. They are fast, efficient, and magically they seem have the pulley and ropes in the truck to get the oversized sofa and chair up from ground level, over the balcony and safely into the living room with no damage or scratches. They can muscle their way up over the fence or railing because they have the brute strength to get-'er-done!

Muscles can turn black energetically from illness or lack of use. They can also lose potency and power in DNA aging programs. These circumstances are all correctable. You must first clear the dark color, remove the DNA patterns or illness, and possibly regenerate cells.

Make sure you use your muscles. I work out an hour or two every day. Since writing is very sedentary, I am doing an hour of aerobic dance and an hour of swimming with some gentle weight training and stretching. I am improving my muscle tone while writing a book.

424

Pancreas

Everybody knows sugar creates a burst of energy. The pancreas is your sugar regulator. If your blood sugar is too high, the pancreas distributes insulin to the body to bring it back to normal levels. When it is too low, it secretes glucagon to release energy stored as fat in your body.

When you think about an individual who has a pancreatic issue, perhaps a friend of yours who is diabetic, do they embody strength, or stamina?

Without stable blood sugar, inner confidence disappears and folks look outside themselves and their body for praise, approval and validation to fortify the weakened energy aspect.

Mental Body

One of my favorite workout trainers from Beach body is Chalene Johnson. I use her turbo fire workouts to sculpt and tone my body. She is always saying during her workouts, "Your energy comes from your mind. If you tell yourself you're tired, then guess what? You're tired. But if you tell yourself, I have lots of energy, then that's what you get, more energy."

Well, as we have discovered, energy comes from a lot of places. However, she is right: if you tell yourself "I am tired," you will accomplish that result. You mind believes what you are saying. It does its best to deliver those results. If you tell yourself, "I am energized," even if it isn't a hundred percent true, your body will give you more energy. This is because you are giving your mental body that program to work with.

Creative brain

The creative brain enhances energy. Creativity is an antidote for depletion. Engaging the creative brain will bring in creative energy. Creative energy is the same energy as creator God energy, in other words the power of creation.

Feeling low? Pick up an instrument or your paintbrush and enjoying the gentle flow of creation energy begin to fill your limbs, your body and your being. This is directly juxtaposed to the slave 'picture' of guzzling down a 5-hour-energy drink to force the body to work more and deplete it further. I invite you back to your divine creator self, and experience union, even reunion with the god/goddess energy of creation.

What is your energy enhancer? How do you return to vibrancy? Are you willing to live a lifestyle that is in harmony with your energy centers and supports a natural fully embodied life?

Likely one of the biggest moneymakers in America is the production of energy, and when you think about what you pay and require daily (such as coffee, sodas, sugars, carbs and pills) to keep your energy up and at peak, you'll be surprised.
I will suggest you are not wrong in wanting peak energy. Energy is good; feeling strong and vibrant is awesome. Ask yourself in what areas you might begin to return yourself to the natural production of energy. Use the healings described throughout the book to improve these key energy promoters and thrive. After all you are reading this book, which means: **it's your time to shine!**

Chapter 20: Memes and Miasms and Curses

As you do clearings; memes, miasms and curses come under either the mental or the spiritual category.

A *meme* is a group agreement; it is group mind's phenomenon. It is restricted to the group mind influences of the individual's lifetime and involves all the people thinking the same way about something. It is not truth. It is infectious, controlling and often a blind spot. It is insidious.

I am unaware of a positive meme, as it overrides your own reasoning and controls your thoughts and conclusions.

An example of a meme can be found in moralistic religious groups. The attitude of the group, which is the group meme, has been that homosexuality is a sin and therefore wrong and should not be tolerated. Everyone in the group will match up, and there will be tremendous peer pressure to hold the line, even if a beloved family member is gay.

To illustrate the difference between a meme and a miasm I have included the following example.

A *miasm* is a group virus. It was discovered by Dr. Samuel Hahnemann, the founder of homeopathy and defined as a 'sickness' or group virus mindset. Like a meme it is contagious, but it also expands in its reach back up to three-hundred years, affecting the individual or the ancestors of the individual.

While visiting the Mayan historical site, Chichen-Itza, I discovered the Mayans were masters at group mind control. The unique pyramid structures were architecturally designed to affect sound and impact individuals on group ceremony. The amplification of the noises the priests made and the gruesome human sacrifices performed in a strategic way (so as to convince the chosen individual they must comply) convinced them it was the only choice.

Raphael, the tour guide, an older gentleman of Mayan descent, shared with us his insights about the ancient Mayan culture. He relayed a scene from the movie, Avatar, of the group sitting chanting around the tree of life as a scene that could have been taken from the Mayan historical archives. The only difference was that instead of a tree, they sat around their pyramid with a temple at the top. Chanting together opened the worshippers to the group virus, controlled by what they all saw and then felt together. The murderous slayings were said to secure an immortal life with the Gods.

When I asked our guide, Raphael, "did they like it?" He said, "they were convinced, and so it was." The followers could have moved out of the metropolis, but instead they stayed until it grew, at one point, to 400,000 people.

Although you don't have to remember which is which, your kinesiology testing will be able to identify if the situation is a meme or a miasm.

When I am testing, I look for the nature of the group mind issue and with muscle testing confirm that I am on the right track.

To clear a meme or miasm simply requires identifying it, and for the miasm, the time it got implanted. Then pump gold energy into it to clear the issue.

Even though they are relatively simple to clear, they should not be overlooked as they can prevent a healing from being permanent.

The miasm of healers; can't help self

I hear this so often: An individual healer does great work with others and struggles with health or emotional issues, even mental illness and yet they cannot help themselves.

This is a combination of a miasm and a curse.

Four hundred years ago the cultural and political climate was threatening to anything health-related, which was not directly proclaimed by the patriarchal church and medical professionals. Healers had gone through witch burnings and unimagined atrocities, and had gone underground to survive the active group mind which encouraged compliance with the powers that controlled religion, government and medicine.

This group mind miasm/curse could not control the healing gifts of natural healers, but would invalidate healers' work. This meant that a healer would struggle with her own issues, and her own cures would remain hidden to her.

Another part of this curse was to keep healers underground. They would work alone, one on one out of homes or small offices, never joining forces like our large HMO's and health conglomerates do today. This part of the curse also prevents any consistent data and proof.

The mental body would continue to hold this information from lifetime to lifetime. When the healer would pick up momentum with skill and power, an overwhelming fear would surface - that death was possible if she continued on this path.

For each healer the curse and the cure will be unique. In some, it affects their chakras, glands and organs. It will remain hidden and obscure to the healer as a veil of

429

unconsciousness while control beings (spirits on the other side) will both hide and enforce this sense of eminent threat.

Breaking free is not a battle, but rather a moving into freedom. The pieces of the curse are removed and future timeline issues are also cleared. Freedom and a sense of being able to breathe more deeply and express more fully, permeates the healer who is no longer under any aspects of this miasm/curse.

To learn about the techniques for clearing miasms and curses and well as curing illness with miraculous healing, you are invited to join the year-long Miraculous Healing Apprentice program. If you need healing now, a one-on-one session is your answer!

A life is destroyed by a miasm

The release of Leo Tolstoy's book-made-screenplay "Anna Karenina" has sent me into realms I could not have expected. On first blush there plays out a difficult love triangle that turns sour as Anna falls in "love" (chemistry) with a younger man, Vronsky. This presents a significant relationship problem because unlike the men's rule, to get married and then have your affairs, women were not held to the same standard. It looks like Anna, due to the love affair and birth of her daughter (fathered by the lover) is naturally on a downward spiral she cannot survive. She begins to lose balance in life, to drink and use morphine to help her manage her emotions, till she can handle no more, and then kills herself.

So it looks like dear Anna, naïve of the ways of the world, thinks that she has the right to love and be loved, the same as a man who might find this infidelity as the solution to an unsatisfying marriage. But sadly, she finds she has "broken

430

the rules" and finds herself with unhealthy relationships, abandoned by all her friends and loved ones.

The pain of miasm

The shock of such an extreme group mind agreement, which cut her off from her friends and society, caused Anna to become depressed, even delusional. This painful illness caused by a group "Miasm," is the cause of her drug addiction and ultimate madness and death.

Miasms and out of control chemistry are worthy topics of the Miraculous Lifestyle conversation.

Out of control chemistry is the theme of the novel. A beautiful, slightly ignored aristocrat leaves home for the first time since her thirteen-year marriage discovers she is the object of affection of a handsome younger military man. He makes her breathless and careless as she first resists the affections, then dives wholeheartedly into out of control passion. With her relationship problems, Anna, starved for attention and overly attracted to her young paramour, acts foolishly as she can no longer think.

Relationships are best formed first from friendship and then from passion. When chemistry is too strong, both men and women lose logic and reason and make many mistakes along the way. It is rare to have both lovers in the same level of "chemistry" so one will inevitably have more power than the other. Leading to unhealthy relationships. The person having the highest attraction will not really have the freedom to be themselves in the relationship because there is too much at stake; so they will withhold their authentic self and ultimately experience an unsatisfying relationship.

What I am more interested in with this film is the glaring

example of a real miasm, which is a group agreement, not of love or support or caring and not based in truth. To see this on the big screen is exciting and helps me see with transparency the affects upon women from the societal shunning miasm, and how this form of miasm still happens in today's era.

My client Mary's story begins when she leaves her husband. His father was running for State Representative. His family had founded the town and the church and were completely connected and part of the elite community in southern Minnesota. Now the family did not have great wealth, but they did have five generations of land ownership and a vast number of members in the farming community.

Breaking the rules

Although Anna's Karenina's "sin" was having an affair, her actual break with society is when se left her husband in favor of living with her paramour Count Vronsky.

But Mary's rule breaking had nothing to do with infidelity. She was simply not allowed to leave the family. Once accepted into the family culture she was expected to stay. All of her ex-husband's family attended Divorce court during and would not allow the children leave the clan.

A miasm like this makes a woman feel that life — her life — is worth nothing. Mary shared how her constant thinking in those early days after the divorced were constantly looping on the rumination, "Life without my children is unbearable." Thank God she broke the spell of this group mind and went on to live and love and laugh once again with the help of miraculous relationship and miasm healings.

A miasm like these extreme relationship problems, can cause thoughts of suicide. This was the case with our Heroine Anna. Imagine having many people all thinking you are unworthy. Much like a broadcast from radiation, these thoughts act like a deadly virus and enter an individual's psyche and create a cloud of hopelessness.

Anna could have lived with love. She could have survived the divorce and a new group of friends, but the hateful group mind was more than she could overcome.

In the 100% You Immersion program, we remove miasms with little effort. In many cases, miasm is much like a curse, and will prevent a person from experiencing health and vitality as well as emotional, mental and spiritual health.

Chapter 21: Vision

It's very exciting to realize that you can improve your vision without surgical procedures or vision enhancements, such as glasses, contacts or laser surgery. At Miraculous Living, we have discovered how discovered to restore lost vision using several innovative and efficient procedures.

Vision and how you see the world can make a huge difference in your comprehension and understanding of the world. Improving vision was my first experiment nine years ago having worn glasses for reading since I was eighteen. With the evolution of my healing skills, I decided to access my regeneration abilities and strengthen my vision. This was prior to my understanding of the divine human blueprint, and yet, despite my lack of full understanding of the visual system, I was successful in reversing a vision condition that had been declining for twenty-six years.

I created a strong intention, amplified by meditation and prayer and over a period of six months, my vision improved.

I was also struggling with a weakened immune system. I started thinking that growing back my adenoids and tonsils might make a significant difference to my health and vitality, so I intended to grow them back in meditation.

When I went in for my annual vision test, my ophthalmologist declared, "Your vision has improved! That never happens in your age group. The results from the last exam must have been wrong." I assured him, no, it was correct. I intended to improve my vision. He responded, "It's not possible." He checked to see who had done the last eye exam. "Puzzling," he said, scratching his head, "I did the exam."

Maybe one restoration is a fluke, but at my next medical visit, my endocrinologist noticed I not only had tonsils, but full-grown tonsils. He said, "They must have been there all along." I assured him that he had examined me six months earlier and there were none. They were surgically removed at age three.

I shifted my health pictures around that time. I realized on some level I wanted the western medicine professionals to acknowledge that miracles are possible, that we have more power than we know. But, clearly, in the way I was going about it, that was not going to happen.

I love that I currently have representatives from the scientific and medical professions training with me. I realized I had to step into my own authority and let go of attempting to 'prove' anything to non-believers.

If you begin with the understanding that vision challenges are correctable and that clearing *miasms* (group thought virus) and poor DNA programs, many of the vision issues can be permanently corrected.

If your career requires looking at a computer screen for many hours a day, imagining an orange disc between you and the screen can serve to protect your vision. With technology the eyes begin to match machine energy, which is grey. When your vision centers (eyeballs, optic nerve and visual cortex) go grey, vision dramatically reduces.

Healing the eyes

- Test for color of the right and left eyeballs. I estimate 90% of adults are living with a diminished eye color such as grey or black. Clearing the color by pumping gold from the right hand to the eyes will improve many people's vision right away. The eyes should come up to pink or green.

- Test if Cellular Neo-Genesis is the next step and, if yes, proceed to Chapter 3.

- Test for color of the optic nerve and connection from eyeball to the visual cortex. If a person has the need for glasses or has had laser surgery on the eyes, this area will be grey or black. Clear the grey and black colors by pumping gold from the right hand towards the optic nerve. We are looking for the optic nerve to become green.

- Test if Cellular Neo-Genesis is the next step and, if yes, proceed to Chapter 3.

- Test for color of the visual cortex. If grey or black, clear the color by pumping gold from the right hand to the visual cortex, bringing this part of the brain to green or pink.

- Test if Cellular Neo-Genesis is the next step and, if yes, proceed to Chapter 3.

Now that we have done a basic tune-up, it is time to discover why the eyes lost their full function and correct these issues. The first natural area we will look to is the DNA programming.

436

Everyone knows we get our eye patterns from our family. That's a no-brainer. Thus if family history gives you poor vision or near-sightedness (myopia) let's clear that program once and for all and set you on a path of clearing and restoring your sight.

Use the DNA obliteration process found in Chapter 2 to clear:

> a. All low-function eye programs
> b. All illnesses-in-eyes programs
> c. All old-age eye-degeneration programs

- Once the negative programs have been cleared, pump gold into the DNA to activate the healthy eye program in the human blueprint. Make sure that you clear all future issues through till the end of the body.

- Pump gold energy into the DNA resets for the new healthy setting.

- Using kinesiology ask the body if clearing a miasm is next.

- If yes, pump gold energy into the group mind belief that is affecting poor vision until you have entirely cleared the miasm.

- Test if a spiritual timeline issue is affecting vision. Look for things that happened prior to the beginning of the body that are affecting vision. Spiritual timeline clearings are super easy.

Sometimes a prior-to-birth a decision is made and the person at birth is unable to connect with their eyes as a spirit. If this happens, vision will be dependent on the physical body (human animal) for vision health and information. To correct this condition:

- Pulse lavender energy from the left hand into the eyes for about 6 minutes. The lavender energy comes from your golden rings. If you have not yet mastered the art of using your golden rings, use universal lavender.

- Test to see if the healing is complete for human spirit connection to eyes. If you test no:

- A Spiritual timeline clearing removes painful episodes from previous lives that provide reasons to not want to see or see clearly.
- An aging pattern in the eye that diminishes vision is a hardening lens. Soften lenses of the eyes with pink energy. You can access pink energy from the golden rings.

A physicist presented this question. "How do I soften my lenses? As the human body matures the lenses become hard and as a result, close-up vision is lost. I love having folks from the scientific community in the program, because as a scientist she will know a question that I will not have considered based on my vantage point.

When she presented this question in class at a recent 100% Healthy

Weekend, I tested that a pink healing would soften the lenses. The entire class proceeded to work on their lenses restoring the soft flexibility of youth, and the clarity of vision that comes with it.

For myself, I had done all the eye clearings but had not yet gone to 20/20. As a result of the pink lens healing, my vision has been excellent ever since. I can work on the computer for hours without eyestrain. I had started writing this book twelve weeks ago using size fourteen font with reading glasses (strength 1.0). I am now using size twelve font and can very comfortably read and type away for hours without glasses.

A faulty immune system can be another cause of some eye and vision issues. Seventy-eight year old Pierre, a longtime client, and now student in 100% You Immersion program, has suffered from the insidious illness referred to as macular degeneration. Once a brilliant French baker, Pierre used to make treats for the high-end clientele of the San Francisco's elite hotels. He speaks with a lovely, thick French intonation and is a joy to be around. We have been able to make some headway in his challenges with eyes, and during events he experiences greater vision and clarity as well as new-found relief from a previously uncomfortable sandy feeling in his eyes.

You can start your miraculous healing process, at any age. The healings and gifts are for everyone, no one is too old or too sick to receive them. However there can be some additional challenges that come with starting the process after seventy, so the earlier people address their health challenges, the better.

Something I highly recommend is using the daily meditations to hold the new health you are experiencing with the healings. A second recommendation is that you take on personal responsibility for your health, even if you are in collaboration with a more skilled healer. When you say, "These are my eyes, I need them to work well the rest of my days," is a very different affirmation than, "They are always this way."

It is one thing to experience the miracles provided for you by a healer, and an entirely different one to say, "I claim health for myself and will not stop until every stone is overturned," and, "I am experiencing the vision I know is mine by my divine birth right order."

With cases such as Pierre's experience of macular degeneration, there are family matters in this lifetime that need clearing each time we do an eye healing. Think about what you may not want to see, or hear, if hearing is your challenge. I recommend the love and karma clearings for vision issues, and also illnesses related to family and relationship pains. You can find the karma clearing and love meditations at www.julierenee.com.

Adrenal fatigue can also affect focus and vision. The chemistry of adrenal fatigue can cause a problem with dilation. The obvious fix, if you test positive on this issue, is do a full healing on adrenals and stress. Healing the adrenals can be hugely supported by the free "From Fatigued to Fabulous" meditation program, which includes daily meditations to help reverse the condition. You can find this program at: www.miraculouslivingtoday.com

I occasionally meet people who have auras as thick as pea soup. Fatima, a gen-y coaching client and medical professional of Middle-Eastern descent came to me with a number of challenges. The first thing we needed to do was a big clearing from the inside out. She had many control issues, and was often distrustful of people, thinking they were plotting against her or betraying her, and as a result she was not at peace.

440

Her emotions were constantly on high alert; I found her extremely challenging to assist, as we routinely had to lay a whole new safety groundwork for her. The first big leap she made was when, in a deep inner clearing, I removed all the debris that had gathered in her aura, and suddenly she could see much more clearly.

Magda a Tasmanian immigrant, had a similar issue. Her vision also improved greatly with the clearing.

Is a cloudy aura more common in first generation immigrants? Probably not. It's more likely to be a cellular issue, with fear pictures steeped in the DNA and cellular body. Fear, like a magnet, holds everything you are afraid of close to you.

In both cases it was not difficult to clear the aura. However, each of these gen-y gals, would return the following week, with their auras muddled up again, because their DNA and cellular body had not been cleared.

In addition to the DNA, spiritual time line programs may provide more cause for the reduced vision circumstances. However, the main vision problems will most assuredly start in the DNA and cellular body.

For the two gen-y gals and people like them, pacing the healing process is essential with this condition. Nothing too fast, no big leaps. A slow and steady pace heals the fear pictures and the neuroses that they produce.

If your vision has improved in a healing process, and reverts back to the previous condition, there are three culprits you can clear to restore the improvement:

a. Miasm
b. Empathetic response (see below)
c. DNA program

Miasms

Even with this careful reprogramming, a body will want to make the human group ideas of others right. The body will mirror degeneration and eye failure just by being around people who believe that eyes are programmed to get worse. This actual process is a ***miasm***. Basically it is a group virus (false belief) that, when matched, makes the experience real. What the mind can believe it will achieve and this holds true for the cellular body, so when the cellular body receives this information and believes it, it will match it. You body wants to make the people you love right. It will try to match up with their programs to make them right. This is how a miasm takes root in your body.

To clear a miasm for the failing eye group mind virus, again pump gold into the miasm until it is clear.

Empathic response

If someone tells you after your eye's have healed, "Well ya know I'm getting old and
my eye's aren't as good as they used to be. It's just a fact of life." Now your body has
just heard what most people believe. If your personality is that of a peacemaker or

an empath, you will naturally want to validate and make the other's ideas right. When your cells cooperate with the other person ideas, the healing crashes. Good news: as quickly as it goes away, it can be restored.

442

How to avoid an empathetic response

There are some people who are more susceptible to this. If you are one of them *don't make yourself wrong*. Empathetic and peacemaking people are amazing healers because they seek to understand others in a profound way. An excellent approach to take is is to become like a scientific researcher gathering data. Your entire life has been set to certain parameters and now you are gathering information so you can bring about change.

Do not throw the baby out with the bath water. In other words, you can still empathize but that does not mean you need to absorb other people's mistaken ideas. Just observe where in your being the match with other's erroneous beliefs about eyes happens. Very likely it will be in the first brain, the instinctual/survival brain. Cobalt blue directed at the program for "matching" will help, especially if you imagine that the information is coming in there. Either way, later or on the spot, cobalt blue will deprogram this.

As you progress, you may discover that you are matching and empathizing less, as you are able to protect yourself and practice love wisdom. With love wisdom, it is more important to know who you are and what you are committed to than what others are thinking or feeling. Empathy and peacemaking are younger versions of love wisdom.

DNA programming

The second reason for degeneration in the eyes after healing is found in the DNA:

> d. Were you successful in clearing aging and future eye degeneration and illness from the DNA encoding? If not, do that now.

443

Have you been around your family and has the family DNA bubble reset your DNA to the family degeneration programs? If so, clear the family DNA bubble's influence towards eye illness and reduction of function.

Illness can affect vision, both eye and body illnesses.

I am speaking here of things like pink eye, allergies in the eye even a virus like the herpes virus. Once you have cleared the illness, you may need to redo the eye protocols in their entirety.

Follow the basic Miraculous Living protocols to clear illness in the eyes, as each illness will present unique circumstances. You will want to address the need of each person's illness exactly as it is being presented to you for the most complete healing.

Once the protocols are completed, a common occurrence is that people don't need their glasses. Expect a good result the first time. It may represent an inconvenience if you have to wean yourself off glasses, as your eyes get stronger.

Seventy-six year old Sarah, a pediatric nurse in the Miraculous Living Apprentice program, had just purchased a new pair of glasses prior to attending an apprentice weekend. During the program we covered the eye protocols and she was left with much improved vision and useless glasses. I am sure if you are wearing glasses you would not mind having this issue. It's a good problem to have.

There is a Bengali song I learned from Ali Akbar Khan that sums up the privilege of living on earth with eyes to see:
Suddhi Bisa Ragahi Bisa Ragahi ajah

"My God when I look around and see all that you have given me, I am overwhelmed.
My heart is overflowing and my eyes are filled with tears."

You will find this recording and five other amazing compositions are recorded on my Gratitude CD.

Chapter 22: Autism

My Autistic Core

"Who am I?" she asked herself.
"Why am I in this place?"
I don't know what I'm doing here,
What problems must I face?

I think I'm not this body.
It feels too heavy to me.
I can't understand the sounds.
Are these people reaching out to me?

Am I a sex, a color?
Am I my intelligence?
Do I want to reach out of myself,
To these people who beat and hurt me?

They say behind me,
"She's retarded and slow."
I am confused, should I answer their questions?
What value is the interaction, I want to know?

Excerpt from the self published book of poems *Breaking Through* published in 1996
by Julie Renee Doering.

The number of children diagnosed with some form of autism grows every year and parents and family members are wondering why. Many rise to the occasion, doing everything possible to help their child participate in mainstream education and have an enjoyable life. Others distance themselves from the problem, sending the "deficient" child to a boarding home/school where they receive what money and the latest information can provide. Yet, to date there have been no good answers for parents of autistic children as to the cause of autism.

This chapter is dedicated to curing the condition known as autism, and all its lesser versions. It is a highly complex condition. I recommend you participate in the Miraculous Living Apprentice year-long program to heal effectively at mastery level. The program is dedicated to helping you accomplish your goals and gain mastery in the routine creation of miracles, otherwise referred to as cellular quantum mechanics.

I am currently working with a number of autistic children and have been able to identify important common factors in the challenge of autism. I will provide you with guidelines and suggestions for healing, and of course, as always, each case will be unique so you must go through the Miraculous Protocols for a full healing.

Katy's Story

Katy has experienced Asperger's and is now seventeen. In so many ways she is a normal teenager. She is adorable, loves fashion and Facebook, and focuses on outer accomplishment, appearance, and being her best.

Katy, like many autistic youngsters, is super intelligent. She excitedly told me "I got a twenty-eight without studying on my SATs, Julie Renee. What do you think? Should I take the test again only this time prepare? I bet I could get a really high score!" She is honor roll all the way. Her extracurricular activities include being an enthusiastic member of the debate team and editor of the high school yearbook. And yet, with all this going for her, she lacks social skill and real friends.

Looking specifically at Katy, the origins of her disconnect may be partially attributed to her speech center in her mental processor. While she understands language and how to use language skillfully, she does not receive communication in its multifaceted levels. She comprehends the literal words.

She does not have the broad and narrow band telepathy available to use for comprehension. Broad and narrow band telepathy add deeper meaning and comprehension to communication. Broadband telepathy is the broadcast of pictures and images along with speech from a person communicating to a group. For Katy, it appears this mechanism is missing. To compete in debate and win (which she does) she needs to be extremely skilled at the value and measure of the words she uses to compel listeners to her viewpoint.

Katy, like most high-functioning autistic youth, has some similar spiritual markers that serve as a common thread to identify the group of spirits experimenting with this unique set of circumstances. Keep in mind that each person creates unique challenges to learn and grow in each lifetime, and although it may look from the outside as an unfortunate accident, each child chooses this challenge.

Katy's human spirit animates her two legs, left arm, torso, first brain (the instinctual brain) and fifth brain (the frontal lobe).

Identifying common circumstances for Individuals with autism

Typically, human spirit does not occupy their physical limbs, arms and legs. This is a condition of all persons with Autism. How the condition appears is that the relationship with arms and legs is controlled and supported only by human animal, meaning, the body and brain control the limbs. Without the spirit animating the limbs, autistic children appear listless and somewhat unrelated to the physical world and nature.

The advanced autistic individual will have no relationship as a spirit to their torso. Individuals with Asperger's will get into their body and animate their torso with spirit, unlike children with full autism who will not.

Because of this circumstance, human spirit, when animating a human body is stimulating many of the operating systems of the physical body.

In the condition of autism things are very, very different.

Autistic individuals experience support only from "human animal" in many aspects of running the human. Therefore, "human spirit" does not provide systems support for the following systems:

Healing protocols for unsupported systems in an autistic person

System	Missing Functionality	Protocol For Protection
Cardio Vascular	Stimulation	Pump lavender 50 times from your left hand to the cardio vascular system. This action supports human spirit in correcting this challenge. Take special note this is not done with the left hand and does not involve pumping gold.
Respiratory	Activation	Pump gold from the right hand towards the respiratory system. About 40 pumps will set human spirit to activate pranic breath.
Digestive	Operation	Proceed to Cellular Neo-Genesis protocols, using the original master cell for digestion to rebuild the cellular structure. Using either hand pump pink into the digestive system 5 times to assist in the human spirit connection or bond.
Nervous	Stimulation	Go to the procedure of Cellular Neo Genesis. Pay close attention to ensuring the nucleus is at 100%. Once you have completed the cellular upgrade pump lavender with the left hand 15 times.
Sense	Perception	Pump gold into all the sensory benefactors (eyes, ears, mouth nose and skin) in the physical body. To have a full clearing in sense perception you must next proceed to restoring and clearing the human access portal. Next from your golden rings pump lavender into the senses. Finally, use Cellular Neo Genesis in a master cell for the skin. This will shift the sensory experiences to that of more integration.

When the physical body has no access to the integrating and enriching contributions of spirit, the senses go into overload. One of the biggest challenges for autistic toddlers is getting their hair cut. Because the relationship of their physical body is so minimal they occupy their mental body is a highly expanded way. To add to that complication they have no maturity to comprehend the buzzing of the electric razor around their head. The sound and the actual vibration will cause them to go "crazy." Could you imagine all your sensory information being channeled through your mental body? That's a tough picture to live with.

It's quiet here, I don't hear their sounds.
Singularly I stand alone.
I made a fine pillow and feather bed,
In this brain I call my home.

If you call me forth, emerge I will.
But this body's world is a dive.
Don't presume I'd want to stay.
I do not.

Lead me from one place to another.
Like an empty shell I follow.
Though I might vomit, feed me food,
The only nourishment you offer.

Who is at home, with no lights on?
The eyes show an empty host
Yet somewhere buried deep inside,
Are pieces of me still alive.

James and Elan's Story

As children, James and Élan had a terrible time of it when it came to participating in activities that would have been considered easy for "normal children." James would run to his mother in a panic with a small amount of food residue on his hands: "Get it off, get it off!" he'd yell as if the sticky food was literally causing him pain.

The real challenge, however, was getting their hair cut. Their mother Rosita hired help when the haircuts could wait no longer. An occupational therapist would meet them at the Barbershop and literally hold them tight, like a human straight jacket as the boys freaked out, screaming and shaking while their hair was rapidly cut. The occupational therapists attempted to acclimate the boys. They tried buzzers in the boys' hands to help pull the stimulation down from the head to the hands. It was suggested to Rosita to drug them and literally knock them out for a hair cut, but she knew her boys would not have a normal life unless they adjusted and learned how to handle the massive stimulation.

To correct autism early for a child can mean a tremendous difference in their contentment and over all sense of wellbeing and connection in the world.

System	Missing Functionality	Protocol For Protection
Lymphatic and Circulation	Stimulation	Pump lavender up to 100 times towards the circulatory and lymphatic system simultaneously. Human spirit will now properly stimulate the lymphatic system. Note: You must include the circulatory system in the process to shift the balance between the two. Without Lymphatic stimulation from human spirit, circulation bears the burden of both systems.
DNA programs related to body function	Activation	Connect spirit with the intelligence of the DNA, fast feels big and expansive. Spirit and DNA intelligence are now in partnership. This is corrected in the process of the entire completion of protocols for healing autism.
Chakra	Operations	Refer to the chapter on Chakras found on Page xxx. One by one, starting at the root chakra, you will develop a healthy, functioning chakra.

Case by case: Some individuals with autism have chakras that exist and function, while others have virtually no energy support from active chakras.

It is vital to cover all chakras covered in the chapter, the 7 main chakras, and feet, knees, hands and elbows.

System	Missing Functionality	Protocol For Protection
Nadis	Development /Operations	Pump orange with your right hand into the energetic body. The human blue print contains knowledge of the nadis, their function and development. Patience is the key here. You will do this process once every 14 days, over a period of 6 months for 20 minutes at a time.
Mental body & brain including Pituitary & hypothalamus	Stimulation	Read the color and function percentage of the pituitary and pineal glands. Most autistics will read black in these glands. Pump gold energy into the pituitary and pineal glands to raise color and function percentage.
Golden Rings	Pattern	The Golden Rings did not form with the typical development of the energetic body. The human blueprint provides the pattern. Pump gold energy once every three days for a period of 90 days, for 3 minutes at a time.

Because each of these procedures happens over a period of weeks, I encourage you to be patient and persevere.

Other aspects of human body and human incarnation influenced or affected by human spirit:

The thymus provides operation information for this director of the immune system only to the physical body (human animal) not the spirit.

Pump gold energy into the immune system including thymus, T cells, appendix and gall bladder for four minutes.

The pancreas is a vital part of stabilizing human spirit in relation to the physical body. Autistic children lack this stabilizing connection and so experience a discord between body and spirit. The pancreas is addressed later in this chapter.

Another circumstance I have observed in autistic individuals is an interesting tie in to intelligence and formation of comprehending their environment. The skin of the autistic children I have worked with appears energetically as grey. The nervous system appears as black.

The significance of this is extremely important in intelligence and how completely they will be able to take in information.

I'm only hiding, can't you see me?
Someone has forced me in.
You might be the unlocking key,
From my prisoners exile within.

If I emerge, please promise me
With care you will respond.
Emergence is the hardest time,
To trust another and bond.

I cannot trust when I'm afraid.
Don't let harmful folks around.
I'd rather stay in my quiet shell
Then to arise only to be knocked back
down.

I have special gifts, you could not know.
I can read your energy.
I feel you enter in the room,
And see you without my eyes

Spirit access to body

Many years ago I taught infant massage. While training for the certification I learned some interesting facts about the information receiving systems. When a newly forming human is less then a week old, the same embryonic material that forms the skin and nervous system is forming the brain. The nerves and the skin are meant to serve as information gathering tools in service along with the brain. Without these tools the stream of information coming in will be very one-dimensional. For a young autistic child the sense of touch may be overwhelming as there is no way to judge it or understand it.

A typical individual with autism will have access to their head, including brain, but will never actually animate it, meaning the spirit lives mostly outside the body. In other words they will use it, just like they will use a computer, but they will never "own" it, *i.e.*, this is "me."

Élan and James are twins. Born premature they both suffer from autism. Élan has done somewhat better with managing his body, though both boys are challenged with difficult relationships to the physical world.

456

When the boys were infants, progressing into preschool, their wonderful mother did everything she possibly could to help them live normal lives. They had play and physical therapy as well as occupational therapy. They were encouraged to live in their bodies as much as they could.

Élan found his way into his torso as a spirit as a result of all his therapies. To the outside world he appears stronger and more stable. James, on the other hand, appears fragile, and weak - thinner and smaller than his brother. Neither of the boys experience much energy, appearing somewhat lethargic. They would be content to sit and stare or play a video game for the entire day, having no real desire to eat or be active like normal teenage boys.

Élan inhabits his right leg, right arm, torso and James does not own any parts of his body.

Why would human spirit take on this kind of life? What would they hope to gain or learn from these circumstances?

If we are moving away from a life related to nature, it is possible these children are doing research to find out whether some version of the current model of humans will be suited for life related to technology and mental body activities.

The Divine Human Blueprint we currently live with is meant to be supported in the physical environment and out in nature. Our cellular body is nourished in God's good earth. The trees balance our ions, as do the ocean waves. The vibrant healthy nature surrounding us uplifts and restores us, evoking emotions of peace, joy and elation. We as human spirit animating human animal, find the perfect balance of the mental, emotional, spiritual and physical bodies here on mother earth.

457

The experiment of autism

The new trend, which involves people spending hours on technology, was not part of the original blueprint. There used to be plenty of room for our minds to expand, to access our genius in art, music, science and the advancement of our spiritual depth. We were not designed to live in a world of machines and technology, absent from the very nature that provides our landscape for our success.

Children experimenting with autism are trying out a new blueprint for a technological age. If this age gets out of the testing phase and moves into a pilot program, we will see many more individuals exhibiting similar traits.

Can children and their families choose to come out of the experiment of autism?

I can block out a world of pain.
I can cancel all sight and sound,
Slow my heart, refuse your food,
create a symphony,
In my undisturbed realm where I am
found

Touch me please, it soothes my soul,
And encourages me to explore.
Avoid your language of nouns and
verbs,
Mime, and touch opens my door.

Take steps towards me, but don't
come too fast
Or you'll frighten me back in my
burrow
For I am not the dumb child you
might think I am.

458

I need your touch to grow.

*Caress my cheeks when I trust you
well.
Hold me long in your tender arms.
Lay still and silent at my side
Put away your psychiatric charms.*

Everything I have described about the lack of relationship of spirit to body can be brought up to today's high standards. This is a group experiment; it is a spiritual body experiment on "how little can they live in their body and still use it?"

Getting the musculature to decrease more rapidly for a technological age where the physical body is used much less, the human animal body is forced to live out of the brain rather than the animating spirit.

Autism and the agreement for autism appear to run in families. It is a spiritual illness when looked at from a healthy human experience. The spiritual illness gene is encoded in the DNA and is sometimes (though not always) triggered by a mental illness program.

I discovered with an eight year-old, David, that an injury at birth on his frontal lobe actually helped him own that one part of his brain. All the other four sections of the brain were grey. His frontal lobe was like a garden with fresh green growth. David's spirit animates his torso, left arm and fifth brain (frontal lobe).

As previously mentioned, a common thread among these children is a lack of connection with their body. Aaron, now seventeen, has amazingly diligent parents. He has been encouraged to be a boy all the way, although his instincts

459

were to retreat inside, like Élan and James, and not to participate in external activities that were usual for other boys his age. Aaron's parents were constantly involved with him, coaxing him out of his retreating preference. He attended sporting events and his dad stayed and coached. Aaron was in the Boy Scouts, and continues to do well in the physical world. Like other autistics, he is not animating limbs, but he is occupying his torso and neck very well. He accesses well his first brain (the instinctual brain) and the left side of his frontal lobe (advanced thinking).

Autism appears to be a failed experiment.

Protocols for improving the quality of life

Keep in mind the individual has to see the value of the improvement and approve of the help.

1. Begin by asking the body which healing is required first, using the Miraculous Living protocols. For this particular circumstance, more than 80% of the time you will be led to clear the physical body of grey.

Special Note: If the individual is an adult and has done a lot of healing on themselves, a lavender healing on the entire human organism, cellular body, and everything that comprises the human organism should be done. Pump lavender from your right hand to the whole physical body for 5 minutes.

All colors can be obtained from the Golden Rings or if you have not yet mastered the golden ring healings use color from the universe.

2. Pump gold into the person's skin first; continue until the skin reads green.

3. Clear the grey from the five brains one by one starting with the instinctual brain and advancing to the frontal lobe or fifth brain by pumping gold.

4. Clear the nervous system, read color and function. (It is largely black in this circumstance.) Continue till you read the system as electric blue.

5. Read the dominance of the mental body in relation to its normal human blueprint program. This next process will turn the dial down. For example David is at 170% in his mental body reading and Aaron is at 150%. My most recent read on overactive mental body logged in at 240% (belonging to an adult autistic with genus IQ). The goal is to keep the mental body at 100%. Pump lavender energy into the mental body, this will tone it down to a 100% read. Once you have changed this you must do the DNA shifts related to this or it will return rapidly to the old program.

6. Look into the DNA for programs related to spiritual illness (remember autism is a spiritual illness, so you must shift this). Then check for mental illness and over-functioning mental body.

Proceed to the DNA Obliteration process.

While in the DNA remove the program for black skin and grey brains. Clear family patterns and remember to change the reset for all the new programs in the DNA.

7. Proceed to brain healing. Using a gold pumping process bring each brain up to pink and proceed with Cellular Neo-Genesis found on page xxx.

Note: You will likely not get a read to do Cellular Neo-Genesis on brain one; brains 2-4 are a definite yes; and 5 may or may not require the procedure, based on if the individual had already been inhabiting the fifth brain. You can look at this as a rehab process. Imagine an apartment building, sitting vacant for years has become dingy and grey. You are making the brains habitable. The difference here from the example of the apartment building is that the brain never had been inhabited.

8. Using kinesiology, read the muscles and the muscle command centers in the brain.

Muscles will be at a reduced level, likely in the brown color zone even if they have gotten a lot of stimulus from activities provided for them by parents. You don't need to know where the control centers for muscle are in the brain, just intend that you get to all the 11 points that direct muscular activity. Any bright color will be a good shift for both the muscles and the individual.

9. The pancreas is the next tune up. It is typically white with this condition. Pump gold energy into the pancreas to return it to a frosty pink, blue or green.

30% of the time you will also need to proceed to the Cellular Neo-Genesis process on the pancreas for a full correction. Using kinesiology, test to discover if Cellular Neo-Genesis is your next step.

By showing the pancreas to the individual's spirit, you can assist the person in making a connection to the pancreas. Pumping yellow around the pancreas 15 times will show the human spirit where to connect into the body. This connection of human spirit to the pancreas also stabilizes blood sugar.

Multi-layered and complex, when this circumstance happens, you will be successful if you do these steps.

Once you have completed all of the healings for autism, recommend using the *Definitive Guide To Meditation*. This is a beautiful guided meditation that helps you keep the connection between spirit and body strong and keeps energy centers clear. Using this meditation two times daily is an excellent way to continue to firm up the relationship of human spirit in the body.

My Story

Had I been born in this era, I would have received the diagnosis of Autism. I remember that I did not speak until age three and the reason I spoke then was because a doctor told my parents I needed my tonsils and adenoids removed and this would cause me to speak.

Though, as a toddler, I did not struggle like the young men James and Élan, I cried at every haircut. When I spoke, I spoke in full sentences, however no one understood what I was saying and in my first few years in school I received special training in diction and hearing sounds. After several years I spoke with perfect enunciation and my fantastic comprehension was now balanced by my ability to communicate clearly in the outer world.

During my early childhood I became invisible in groups and cocooned into myself, especially during play activities. I loved aspects of learning; creativity and envisioning came easily while mathematics and science, in the way it was taught to me, was gibberish.

I was tender and compassionate, and loved babies so I excelled in caring for them. I understood this in a formulaic process.

My single-minded focus (despite my diffuse female brain) caused me to excel both in school and as a baby sitter. By the time I was eleven years old, I was literally booked six nights a week. It would have been seven nights, but my mother insisted I have one night off. Rules, in some ways, were extraordinarily helpful for me. Once I had the formula or rules down, I could repeat and improve the processes for better and better results.

In some of my promotional materials, there is a line we use, "Life doesn't come with an instructional manual so Julie Renee created one for you!" This is what I did for myself in order to understand my world and have life be more palatable.

The person experiencing autism will not experience the full realm of emotions. The emotions they do experience will mostly come from the survival or instinctual brain.
After all healings in this chapter have been completed (which will take approximately six months to a year) you can improve the emotional landscape also.

The average person has access to 70% of the emotional body, the person growing up with autism has access to 10%. Just by setting the emotional access up using a gold pumping energy into the emotional body, an individual can more fully experience their emotions. Do *not* do this all at once — 25% increments are plenty good. If you move a person up too quickly and they will be basking in emotions they are unfamiliar with and have no understanding of how to manage.

Again, proceed with a slow and steady healing pace. We much prefer a paced result that doesn't overwhelm the person and send them back to comfortable isolation. Helping them come out a little at a time is the way to progress and permanently shift them to spiritual and mental wellness.

At a low point, one of my students stated, "This is an overwhelming, really bad world. We are so screwed up, no one has it good, I wonder why anyone would ever choose to be born."

Our realm is a realm of learning and growth. It is important to comprehend, with wise-elder wisdom, that we have chosen — conscious or not — challenges that will help us grow and mature as a human spirit. We are scientists, we are researchers, and we are on an amazing journey.

If you identify with the illness or challenge, you have become it, you have made it your own and now you are in the struggle of overcoming an obstacle. This could be the perfect choice for you. It can give you lots of material for growth and development. I want to remind you that you can choose not to identify with any illness or challenge. This gives you an entirely different experience.

Do you remember the lady with breast cancer in the movie *The Secret*? She set her mind to prayer and laughter, believing she was already healed. Her results were phenomenal. Through laughter, prayer and a disciplined mind, she completely cleared the cancer from her body in three months.

Faith and prayer give rise to the unstoppable power of truth. For Christians, the miracles of Jesus Christ and the rich stories of physical healing bring hope; they do for me, too. All spiritual paths speak of miracles.

Our minds are so powerful they can take us out of the game, or they can lead us to victory. I encourage you to practice making wise decisions, and challenging your mental capacities. Learn a new language, a new dance step, a new way home. Keep your mind, like a muscle: strong, agile and flexible. I would like you to imagine you are training your mind for the Olympics. Do that for a lifetime. With you in the driver's seat of your mind, you truly are the creator of your reality.

I am giving you the direct formula for correcting the challenge. It could also be used to measure the improvements as they occur based on faith or prayer.

This actually is the Garden of Eden, and you are already in God's Great Paradise. Do your eyes see and your emotions feel this magnificence?

Chapter 23: Guidelines for Success

When I began implementing what I'd learned about Cellular Quantum Mechanics by working on myself to powerfully healing clients I made an important decision. To this point I had always worked with the Supreme Being. Now I made a choice to make God my business partner. If your path is one of a healer I recommend this path for you also. Especially as you are working with others.

Remember that a perfect healing for you for example your idea of what would be good for the person based on your mind and what you think may be quite different than what is actually the perfect healing for the recipient. It may be great emotional fuel for you to prime your enthusiasm with the desire to do good works and assist people in getting well. This is a great place to start but it is not the place to heal from.

The Spiderman movie had a great quote from uncle Ben 'with great power comes great responsibility'. Your newfound ability to regenerate cells and rewrite DNA is a remarkable gift. This gift is not to be taken lightly. You must understand the impact of removing an illness. This condition may be serving a purpose you could not imagine. Regenerating cells just because you can may actually alter a person's journey dramatically and is not what this is about.

The impact to you for healing when it is not asked for can mean you will take on part of their Karma. You may later develop and illness of another adversity as a result of 'budding in' when you were not asked to.

Here are a few sacred rules to follow when healing others:

1. It is important to ask them what it is they really want for their health picture. If a person has already made their agreement to leave the body, working to bring vibrancy to the cells of the body till passing is the best approach. Once they have verbally told you what they want, muscle test if this is true. If there are family members in the room, they should wait elsewhere. This is a sacred calling, it is important for you to get it right.

2. DNA changes can only be made if you have looked the person in the eye and gotten a verbal go ahead. When you are altering the DNA, change only the item that does not support vibrant health. I heard about a clairvoyant student in a spiritual wellness program that, without supervision, attempted to remove all of her healies maternal DNA. In other words, she tried to remove half that person's DNA. That is very bad because it would mean massive body failure. A large part of our DNA provides the wonderful programming that makes life work so very well. So new rule:

   A tiny shift in DNA can affect big changes!

3. It is helpful to identify what you 'think' should be done and what the other person is wanting or needing. Practice not 'thinking.' Be a great listener, both with spoken communication and muscle testing. Be willing to let their body surprise and amaze you, which it will, if you are in the celebration of who they are.

468

4. Unplug from their drama and stories. It is best to simply validate that they are suffering and that there is hope. My philosophy is to tell them it is better not to talk too much, and to talk about neutral of happy subjects. This keeps the energy off worry and so they do not accidently block the healing.

Of course, there are always exceptions. If they are having a bad day and talking will discharge the negativity, I let them talk. I do say to them, when they are able to hear,
that the negative conversations lower the energy in the room and can possibly slow down or inhibit their healing for the day. If you have let them vent a little and then lovingly said this to them, they will self-edit in the future and you need not take the role of enforcer.

One of the common mistakes when beginning to learn the healing protocols is to focus on resolving a specific problem. For example, you know someone has a lung issue and you say, I can help you with that. Then you start testing the lungs on where to begin.

Healing this way is significantly less effective than using the protocols. Someone you know is having health issues. They have asked for help. Start by asking the body, what is needed first? Then test with kinesiology spiritual emotional mental of=r physical. By asking the body what needs to clear first, you have set up the best possible solution for creating lasting change.

Another common mistake is to write out a script of what you are going to do in the healing. Making a list of 10 or 12 items prior to stating the healing yields a very different result then clearing one by one and discovering the next step once the first clearing has been completed.

This is so important to understand. Each healing changes the body, and the sequence will change. You will have a significantly reduced result if you follow the big list first and clear after the list is built. Again this is reinforcing being a good listener. You will make the most impact by being in constant communication with the cells and the entirety of the human being you are working with.

Healing in this way is an improvisational dance. As you take a step the other person's body shifts and you must respond to the new position. Healing this way can be exhilarating and extremely gratifying.

I have also noticed a real challenge with getting it right and over thinking. You must learn and studying this is important. Understanding what the colors mean is vital for example what the impact of a black liver (bouts of anger) or a grey bladder (urge for frequent urination). As you gain this awareness you can speak with a knowingness and an awareness of a trained healer. You must not however think your way through a healing. Healings are done entirely by asking the body what it needs and responding to what it has asked for.

Quantum cellular mechanics cannot be developed by reading and thinking. I have seen students fascinated with reading the materials I provide, which of course is important but then not practice for weeks and wonder why they lost the wind in their sails and cannot access the golden ring power they once had.

It may also be a temptation if you are an MD or Scientist to think you know something based on knowledge you gained in your career or education. More than 90% of the time you will be wrong with your theory of what you think the problem or situation might be. I urge you to use your muscle testing to confirm your answers and let the people and their bodies you are healing surprise and inform you correctly.

In the Bible Jesus says; 'you cannot serve two masters'. This is true here also. You must believe that the healing and regeneration are possible. If you are negative or harbor an atheistic attitude you will produce a weak or ineffectual result. By speaking out that you do not believe in a person's ability to heal them self, you have actually said, I do not believe in their divinity, or their light. To be a powerful healer you must see the Divine and the light in each and every person you serve.

Be patient. I know sometimes you just want so badly to make things better and the situation isn't shifting. Trust the process. When facing a difficultly with improving a condition here are some additional things to check and clear

1. spiritual parasites
2. curses
3. black magic
4. can't heal meme or curse
5. cell regeneration
6. DNA problem or reset not holding
7. Family programming and group mind

Now we have addressed what to look for and how to approach the path of healing others. I would like you to consider the inner path towards an awakened and enlightened path as part of the formula for being an extraordinary healer. To be truly wise requires a life lived with self-examination and reflection as a key component of your daily routine.

Seven Fundamentals for Living an Extraordinary Life

I am often asked how I am able to live such a rich and full life. Through the intense illness and the ups and downs mentally and emotionally from having multiple cancers and 17 surgeries. Along the way of 100% health I've discovered the secret path to living an extraordinary life. Your existence is not defined by the complicated set of circumstances life brings you. Rather, living an extraordinary life is a conscious choice to be and become your greatness.

I have discovered seven fundamental elements of life that when engaged to the fullest expression will result in 100% human fulfillment. This is your guide to life well lived.

1. Vitality- having a great cellular constitution

Your vitality and energetic presence gives you the winning edge. When you are healthy, people around you feel safe and confident. More than that, you feel unstoppable. You are able to make plans and follow through with great velocity and intention. Enjoying a healthy body is the most important element, as it creates the ground from which you can soar. Without good health you live a life pieced together, built on a shaky foundation.

2. Alignment and purpose

Alignment with your spiritual journey and connection with source is the second element of living an extraordinary life. To be in alignment will require you to take time away from the hustle and bustle of life and the pressures of group mind and family agreements The greatest quest you can engage in is to discover who you are and what you are up to in this life. To live authentically, you must know who you are and why you are here. Making your best guess or operating on autopilot is not good enough. Make time for you to know you.

3. Discipline to strength

A person who knows disciple is able to fulfill their mission and gains the respect of all those who they come in contact with. Discipline is the path to fulfillment of everything made manifest. To be healthy, wealthy and wise you must engage in a strategic discipline. Personal power comes from the ability to follow through. You can only experience discipline when you have cleared the entire muddle and 'squirrels'/ distractions from your path. You must first fuel yourself, meaning you must fill yourself up to emotional fulfillment. When you are filled up you have a greater capacity to be emotionally generous with yourself and all others.

4. Enthusiasm for truth

When you blend enthusiasm with truth you open to your greatest expression of self. As you enthusiastically call truth to you, you continue your journey towards awakening to your divine nature and powerful access to miraculous energies. Enthusiasm lights the way to higher wisdom. The one caveat to this conversation is to not get caught up with your version of truth. When truth has an opinion it is actually a belief rather than an absolute. Truth has no other version. It just is.

5. Ascension the progress of your awakening

The journey of ascension does not require you to consciously drive towards spiritual awakening. In this case your balanced loving life will move you towards your ascension. I now see the opportunity for full enlightenment, which includes mastery in the spiritual realm as well as the emotional, mental and physical realms is a deeper richer type of enlightenment then just a spiritual awakening. The old awakening model was to throw all your intention into a spiritual journey and remove yourself from the world so as to gain enlightenment. This is still a valid journey, but a higher enlightenment of the human experience is the mastery of all aspects of your life leaving nothing behind.

6. Mindset - Love-magic- Love-wisdom

To have your mind in the right place makes all the difference in living an extraordinary life. Having the brain working well with all the neurotransmitters and chemistry supporting your joyous bliss filled life is a vital part of your successful experience. When you are in love with your life and with all those who you interact with you have mastered your mindset and your life. Remember a healthy brain gives you the ground for healthy emotions. The awareness of the oneness of all things is the mystery and the doorway to glory.

7. Connection - love appreciation

This leads us into the final element and the bookend that holds this magnificent formula together. Appreciation for everything and everyone is the greatest lesson and expression of human kind. Love is always the answer. If your days are filled with gratitude and appreciation for the wonderful life you are now living, even if some days are not so wonderful, staying with the grace of appreciation will install the deepest connection to the Divine and to the greatness majesty and wonder of humankind.

Living into your 100% life means living an exemplary life. You will become the guiding light to your friends and followers as you show the well-lit path towards the ever-unfolding magnificent existence. You choose. Know that you have always had the opportunity to choose. Now I invite you to consciously make a choice for greatness. Join me in living an extraordinary life, and be filled with the peace and bliss that surpasses thought or mental understanding. Be.

Chapter 24: Life or Death

Why some people live and others die

This afternoon I was speaking with one of my Miraculous Living apprentices about a person she has been working with who has ALS. She was disappointed that he had had a huge set back and was in the hospital on life support, ready to die. He had made peace with the idea of dying.

Have you ever wondered why some individuals pull through impossible odds while others just slip away?

Carolyn's Story

In earlier chapters you've heard me talk about Carolyn who was terminally ill. What I'm going to share now is a little more detail about how I worked with her.

Carolyn found her way to me through a mutual connection. I met a business associate of her husband's at a party. He was concerned about Carolyn's rapidly declining health. I actually met this fellow on the dance floor of the Presidio Yacht club. He sensed there was something about me, picked up that I was a powerful healer of some kind, and literally begged me to call his friend. I told him that was not how I worked; they had to call me, and that this step was important. However, he was convinced they would not call me and that it was a matter of life and death. So after some additional urging, I did make the first call.

I did not speak to Carolyn on that first call. Instead her husband Charles answered, and in response to a series of questions I found that he wanted me to convince him;

- That the healing work I did was real

- That it was worth it to pay for a healing

I am not in the habit of doing either. People who are referred to me typically have had a friend who has had a miraculous healing. Rather than speak to the lack of belief, I said I would do a small healing on the phone. They could then make a decision based on a five- minute gift.

Carolyn was alarmingly close to death. I did do a quick healing boost for her, but I knew she would need a lot of my attention, and very quickly, if I was to help her return to her life. Fortunately, she did respond nicely to the short session. When Charles arrived home, she had gotten out of bed on her own, something she had not done for a while. He called and reported the news and booked a session the next morning to see what I could do to help.

Carolyn arrived the next day, too weak to walk on her own, disoriented and distressed, and yet with a sense of hope. I began to work on her energetically as she told me all of her medical diagnoses. I was half listening to her, because I was also observing the family. Charles was preparing and calculating how he would live without Carolyn. Chrissy, their eleven-year-old daughter, sat slumped in her chair away from the adults, massively upset. The concept of growing up without a mom was horrifying for her.

I decided, after looking at Chrissy, that Carolyn would not die. Over my lifetime I have had this opportunity a handful of times to make a strong decision that the person who appeared to have no choice in a serious health crisis would live. My feeling was 'They were not going to die on my watch'. Without this choice I was aware their life force would soon extinguish and physical life would end. At this juncture my personal will is involved and fueling my intention. Having will involved is not a typical part of the cellular quantum mechanics process. Having will involved means is that I've applied my entire physical force and commitment to help someone pull through. I can list these individuals on one hand. They are all still alive today and living happy lives.

Carolyn not only survived, she is now thriving with her family. The difference between her and the ALS patient we spoke of in the beginning of this chapter is that Carolyn chose life instead of making peace with her upcoming death.

Here are the handful of times I prevented death with both force of will and healing power

1. During a difficult delivery Lucia's uterus burst. Her doctor was able to perform emergency surgery but without anesthesia. Since I was present, I gave Lucia my life force and pulled the pain from her body so the doctor was miraculously able to stitch the womb up sufficiently. Dr. Lee followed me out in the hallway when all was said and done and thanked me. She said, "I don't know who you are, but thank you. That would not have gone that way if you had not been there. You can be in my delivery room any time."

2. Two classmates at the herbal medicine school had their car broadsided and dragged down the freeway by a semi-truck. I ran to them and held both their lives in the balance until they were cut free from the mangled vehicle with the Jaws of Life and reached the hospital safely. The attending ER Doc said, "We rarely see cases like this make it in alive, thank you." One of the gals walked out on her own three hours later. Both recovered.

3. Dr. Suzy's heart failed during a difficult delivery. Her

478

husband, a pediatric cardiologist, knew that the chances of his wife making it through the first year alive were very slim. He also remembered that I had helped Suzy get far enough through the pregnancy for infant survival. He called from the hospital to help his wife live. I intervened and she is now raising two healthy boys.

4. Kathy called at the end of her life, desperate. "You've got to help me. Please help me," she begged. She was suffering from a mix of extreme medical issues that were amplified by massive entities (see Chapter 29). It was a phenomenal encounter of the worst kind. It took four months of relentless sessions to conquer death and get her back into her healthy life.

5. And of course, there's my own story with numerous occasions of my body slipping away. Each time, I was able to pull a rabbit out of a hat and survive against all odds.

I have helped many, many others to live healthy lives and come back from illness and these weren't all at death's door.

The people mentioned above are all people who were going to die and didn't. The following group of people are people who came in for a session or two then stopped their healing and passed away.

I think of two individuals that exemplify this category of not making it:

1. Tessa, a beautiful woman, was diagnosed with stage four cancer affecting multiple organs including the pancreas, liver, and lungs. I had booked her for twice weekly sessions, which she never made. She slipped away in her sleep.

2.   Tam had overcome stage four bouts of breast cancer through diet and a healthy lifestyle. Then a difficult family interaction caused the cancer to reappear. She gave up her home and possessions and went to live in a nursing home. It was there, thinking about death all the time, that she thought herself to her end.

Finally, there's the old age category of folks who come in with a wish to feel great till they pass:

3.   Barry, an artist and former porn star was super fit in his youth and still had good health habits. He was diagnosed with stage four pancreatic cancer. He was dropped off for an appointment with me by his loving ex-wife and confided, "I've lived a good life I just want to feel good until I die." This is what he got to experience. He did feel great right up to the end, recovering his vibrancy and vivacity, enjoying workouts, parties and time with friends. Then one night, in no pain, he passed in his sleep.

So why do some people heal and others, given all the same expert attention, pass?

Carolyn had lots of reasons to live. She had been a Dominican sister who had left the convent and married later in life to be blessed with a daughter. Her faith gave her the concept of miracles, so when the obvious health shift began occurring, she could understand that she would get better. Carolyn and her husband went on camera to share her experience

The path was natural. Our first step was to remove all the dark - death energy found throughout the mid region of the body. The first day we removed eighteen inches of black death energy from her belly area. I next needed to clear white medical control energy from her surgeons and the doctors who were predicting her death. Then we removed seven infections from her body and regenerated enough cells in her colon and intestine for the colostomy bag to be removed so she could resume her life.

It was a wonderful experience to work with a woman of faith. I encouraged her to do the rosary and other prayers for health as often as she possibly could. When you have been thinking about death, and even meeting the angel of death in visions, you must return to your life and the thoughts of a healthy person. As her health and the colon function dramatically improved, her thoughts also began to get into focus and she could use her mind to help create her vibrant health.

The illness of the colon and intestines will dramatically affect the clarity of the mind in the person who is ill. You must look to who they are as a spirit, and if some of the thoughts and words are not lining up with good health, gentleness and love will show them the path back. It's not about you having the last word or about them having to understand what you are up to. It's about loving them where they are, knowing they are on the path to vibrant health both in the body and mind.

Tessa's illnesses were also in the colon and digestive organs. In her case she was not able to activate her will to survive. She was an amazing and loving woman who I enjoyed knowing. When she passed, she was surprised and disappointed.

I believe she was experimenting with health (perhaps not intentionally). I observed her borrowing other people's skills. She would have a nutritionist prepare her healing food but would not learn about nutrition herself. She commented several times, "I just want to touch you." The image of the Bible story of the woman touching Jesus' cloak in a crowd and her being healed was the image in her mind when she said this.

Without will engaged while in serious illness, you cannot recover. You must feel it in your bones and be more powerful than the illness itself. The actual feat of overcoming death needs a reason to fuel the shift towards life. Any reason will do. But you need to know why you want to live. Then hold onto your hat and enjoy the ride!

Coming back from death to life is no picnic

I can think of two women that were terminally ill and whose respective husbands were already resigned to life without their wives. These men had imagined it many times and were ready to stop having a sick partner and get on with their life. In the case of one of them, we were able to work together and help him imagine a future with a loving healthy wife and companion. He did make the transition back to seeing his wife healthy and they are enjoying a beautiful bond as they step into a new chapter in their life.

The other husband was resistant to working with me and blamed his wife for spending money to get well. She was at death's door and he was ready for her to die. He was not ready for her to live.

Tam's story was such a sad one. She had survived against all odds with stage four breast cancer. She took treatments down in Mexico and ate a special diet to cure her cancer. Later, after she had been well for a year, she had a painful interaction with her grown kids. Apparently, she was slighted for a Christmas gift she had given them. This one event broke her will. She decided she was not cherished or valued. Eleven weeks later the cancer had returned, but she was no longer the same woman. She did not change her diet or go to Mexico for treatments.

I met her because she was a friend of one of my students. I did five sessions with her. However I could see that, with no will involved, she would not pull through. She lost her ability to walk and not being mobile meant moving into a care facility. No insurance meant a poor care facility. Although it was clean, the food did not have the higher vibration to uplift and heal the cellular body. I would visit her and bags of junk food surrounded her bed. It was as if she thought her body was junk.

I showed her how to access will. I spoke to her about getting up and walking again, of getting out of the bed and down to the exercise room daily. But she never reclaimed her body. She divided up her belongings to her children before death, said good-bye and moved on. It was a sad passing: at fifty years old, her life was over. No will. No reason. No life.

I have had many brushes with death.

The first one was when I was nineteen, birthing my daughter. The doctor and nurses were talking about me dying. I watched in the birthing mirror a red river of blood leave my body. But I had a will to live for my baby girl and after three months of fatigue and low life force I reemerged as a healthy young mother.

Next at twenty-four, I collapsed on the living room floor. I was alone in a little duplex into which I had just moved. I had separated from the father of my children after five surgeries for cancer and the birth of my son, all in one year.

I felt a strong wave of emotion surge through my cellular

body. It was absolute will. I was clear I was not ready to go. I likely didn't need to negotiate with God for 'His' sake but I needed to hold on and say, "I have to stay. I am not going and this is why."

Another time with a fiancé Andrew, doctors had said to him I would not live. I knew things were bad. My organs were shutting down and I was filling with fluid. The crazy thing was he started to want me to die. I think men are so interested in resolving problems that at some point, if there is no solution, their mind jumps to the possibility that maybe death will end the challenge. I moved out of our shared home and survived but not without a great deal of struggle. I experienced a difficult couple of years following our break up as I was maxing out with massive death programs, from my cellular body and spiritual time line. I definitely wanted life.

I sought out a school called Ascelpion and people who knew how to clear death programs. I had over forty such programs, which they helped me remove. I later developed a far more comprehensive system for clearings so that any death programs, once removed, would not reappear.

I was also in a car accident and I had an out of body death experience after my last surgery. Oh and then there was the time I had pneumonia and my life force dropped to two-percent life. When I look at it all, I do fit the nine lives cat picture very well!

It's not over until we say, "It's over". If people around you are thinking, "It's over," as three of my medical doctors were thinking and acting after the last surgery, run. I got out of the medical system and the destructive group mind pictures they were telepathically sending me. And have gone on to live a full and vibrant life.

When you need to recover, surround yourself with positive people who believe in your capacity to heal. Actively take part in your healing. No acquiescing allowed. Bring a strong will to live and you've got an unbeatable combination.

After all you are a radiant being of light with an innate ability to heal. You come with a miraculous system that can help you live hundreds of years. God promised you the Garden of Eden, have you been there lately?

Chapter 25: Adrenal Failure and Fatigue

In 2007 my life was a constant challenge. My days were filled with wedding plans, new home arrangements, fertility doctors, clients in my healing practice and an unhappy fiancé. To top that off, since I had previously been a realtor, I was handling the purchase of our new home, having to learn new contracts and disclosure forms as well as handling all the transaction preparation for the title and mortgage companies.

I am known for superhuman feats, but this combination of stressors put me over the edge with adrenal fatigue and finally adrenal failure.

With the design of our society today, where both men and women need to work to afford a home, people, especially women, are doing a huge amount of multi-tasking to the point of completely overloading the sturdy but not unbreakable adrenal/nervous system.

The fellow I was engaged to was a pediatrician. After we got my 'diagnosis,' we discovered how prevalent adrenal fatigue was amongst teenagers. He was blown away by this statistic. Here's what can lead to adult and childhood adrenal fatigue:

- Parental pressure for academic success. Parents are essentially running control energy in the child, not in harmony with the nature of the child.

  The solution is to have the parent pull out the energy, or if you are working with the child, removing the parental control energy will significantly improve the present and future health of the child and their adrenals.

- For adults, adrenal failure and fatigue is stimulated by driving the body beyond a healthy state and neglecting the actions and activities that add balance and joy. The result of competition and coveting is physical failure and a body drained of energy.

Technology: a removal from the natural world

When a person is plugged into a screen all day, such as a computer, mobile phone, iPad or techno-game, they are plugged into machine energy. They then are separating themselves from biological and natural energy and its soothing effects. In the Divine Human Blueprint, our bodies were designed to move back into a healthy state just by being in nature and receiving the healthy mirroring vibrations. That is, nature sends us healthy signals and we pick up on them. The natural world provides the programs to return our biorhythms back towards wellness.

As a person moves away from the natural world and aligns their energy field with technology, they take on a gray hue in their auric field and begin to lose healthy cell information. We can't really match technology energy but our bodies are constantly reading the consistent flow of information in our space and learning from it. The gray field of the machines, coupled with the persistent alarms sounding from technology, continues to draw a person into their instinctual (reptilian) brain and into survival mode.

This exposure to technology directs the brain to function in the sympathetic nervous system: essentially on high alert. The nerves are never at rest in the sympathetic state. The parasympathetic system is needed for relaxation, rejuvenation, and regeneration. A prolonged overload to the nervous system causes energetic fatigue and adrenal depletion.

For this condition, it is best to clear technology energy from the body and especially from the nervous system and adrenals. You might embark upon a journey of awakening to the natural world through the activation of your senses. Develop new habits of slowing down and enjoying nature. Listen to the sounds of baby birds in the nest, the wind rustling through leaves, water flowing down a babbling brook, and you will reignite your natural health essence.

Restoring adrenals takes time. Working with a Miraculous Healer can help with the process. You will have rapid healthy cell growth restoring the adrenals to their healthy state along with, a tangible clearing of black and gray energy. Remember, it took you time to get to this point; it may take you a period of time to return back to your vibrant energetic self.

Poor health, high pain, autoimmune conditions

In this case, the body does not heal. Here, it remains in a state of constant inflammation. This is quite simply the nervous system always on full blast in the sympathetic system. In this state, rejuvenation from the parasympathetic system never ignites or functions. If you've been in pain or have been chronically ill for several years, you've got adrenal fatigue.

One of the exciting things to come out of our 100% Healthy Weekends is the discovery that a full brain healing turns off pain all over the body. With the mechanism of pain switched off, the body starts healing.

Adrenal fatigue stimulated by abuse and the need to be loved

The circumstance of physical or sexual abuse causes a tremendous stress on a child's body and is out of harmony with authentic love. The child innately understands there is something very wrong here. Stress rises, grades go down, an inner branding of "I am not good enough" permeates all activities, and negativity is often directed towards the child. The solution is to protect the child and remove the negative information from their spiritual time line once they are in a safe environment.

In my scan of the situation, adrenal fatigue and adrenal failure appears to affect aver thirty percent of the US population, including individuals as young as eight years old to seniors in their seventies and eighties. This is a sign of an age out of balance. The American populace is missing some key elements in their comprehension and understanding of how to thrive. We are in a culture run by the mind and often don't have a clue how to truly enjoy the life we were meant to live. Think about the popularity of 5-hour energy and super-caffeinated drinks. I glanced at a lady in her sixties last week slamming down a Red Bull. (WOW what's wrong with this picture???) Many of us are far from our personal Garden of Eden like she is, living in the stressful, high alert, sympathetic system for a majority of the time.

Healing the Adrenals

Step 1: Clear the dark or low energy vibration of the right and left adrenal

The normal healthy color of the adrenals, when viewing clairvoyantly, is a caramel brown. It should read at a hundred percent.

489

While presenting my workshop *The Body Electric--Healing the Endocrine System* in St. Louis, Missouri, I was shocked to discover that this entire group of twenty people had less than fifty percent function in their adrenals. Is it possible that whole regions of the country are matching each other with a really low adrenal energy? YES.

- Pump gold energy into the adrenals until the percentage gets up to 100% and the color returns to some form of brown, hopefully caramel or butterscotch.

If it does not pump up, it means there are factors that are preventing improvement of the function of the adrenals. These issues are usually not in the actual glands. Advanced training for these challenges are taught in the Miraculous Living Apprentice program.

Step 2: Clear the Nervous System

- If you are working on yourself this is most easily done in meditation. All of the meditations from 100% Healthy 100% You include adrenal and nervous system clearings.
- If you are assisting another, imagine the lacy network of nerves in them and clear with gold pumping energy.

Step 3: Clear DNA Patterns

Observe DNA patterns both on mother and father's side related to:
- Overtaxed nerves
- Overused adrenals
- Mental and emotional family patterns related to fatigue

- Self-abuse in the form of over-pushing

Please refer to the DNA Obliteration process for the correct procedures for permanently altering and improving the DNA (Chapter 2).

Step 4: Cellular Neo-Genesis

- Ask if the adrenals need Cellular Neo-Genesis. If so, proceed following the steps laid out for this process in Chapter 3. Afterwards, steadily pulse small golden suns on the adrenals as you move throughout your day.

Remember your adrenals

If you are tired all the time, or bouncing between exhaustion and hyped-up energy, it's time to get back to the basics. Balance your life, take a few steps back and breathe deeply into your life. The body has no joy in this type of exhaustion. It is unpleasant and takes you out of the fun of daily activities.

I have heard Western medical doctors say, "Once the adrenals have failed, you cannot bring them back." I am here to say you can. However you need to really look at how you got here in the first place. Then after a full assessment of all contributing factors, make a choice to love and cherish "you," the physical you. Love the 'you' in this magnificent body.

You are a radiant being of light and you can change. There is no one way you have to be. You will change and grow and become more fully self-expressed as you travel the wondrous human path of life incarnate.

Chapter 26: Healing Assault

Healing from assault steps back to ease and joy

My female body has experienced one of the lowest expressions of man's animal nature in the form of three sexual assaults. I refer to my body undergoing the experience because human spirit leaves the body when trauma is inflicted and may not return fully if the impact has been severe enough.

Many years ago, I was much in need of a vacation after a difficult breakup but had no reserves to actually implement a real holiday. Then a phone call from my friend, Sara, gave me the answer. She had a friend with Crohn's disease and wondered if I would be available to treat him daily with massage in exchange for a trip to Hawaii. I met with him twice prior to the trip and though the feelings were strange, I did decide to go. Little did I know that traveling with this man would turn into a nightmare.

On Thanksgiving Day, two days after arriving in Hawaii, the man I was traveling with disease dropped into his beast. He drugged and brutally raped me. Unable to control my body or for that matter feel my body, I could hear him and the pounding sound on my body, but was unable to stop the event.

This incident was a violent sexual assault. I was torn open to the point of hemorrhaging, bruised to dark purple up and down the inside of my legs, and my skin was torn from the forced entry.

As a result, I was unable, as a spirit to live in my body for a long time after this. When you hear of someone who has been the victim of assault or a violent accident, the process of healing is called 'coming back' for a reason. It took me months to return fully to my battered and abused body.

What kicks a spirit out first is the on rush of violent, human animal. This is entirely to preserve spirit and is a mechanism wired into spiritual DNA. It basically gives the instruction to get out of the body when under violence or duress. What remains is about ten percent of you left intact to ensure that your basic systems stay on.

And the experience is one of shock, incredulity, bewilderment and darkness. No sense of connection or light remains.

During the hours after the occurrence, your angelic helpers assist you. They helped me run my body and have the strength to call a friend. He drove to my location and found a private condo to keep me hidden and safe until could sort myself out.

I felt like death. There was dark, grey, and even black energy inside me. The lights were out in my human home as my spirit (which brings light and joy to me) was absent.

As a point of information, I do believe that we are all researching and discovering the entire realm of humanity. I think this information, catalogued and stored in our Akashic records, documents our experiences for all future lifetimes. Here, safely stored, are my experiences with the darkness of human animal.

Later, I realized that I needed to remove the magnetic pull of the image of assault or I would continue to call it to me. I will share how in the following pages.

In the initial aftermath of this assault, I sat unaware of

myself for hours, with my hair uncombed. I did not know if I had showered or changed my clothes that day.

I then started to bathe obsessively, every couple of hours. However, no matter how much I washed myself, I never felt clean. These odd feelings and behaviors are typical when the spirit does not live in the body, leaving it exposed and unprotected to dark energies passing through.

Ideally, the thing you want to do is get back in your body, restore your connection with your spirit and body, and then clear the episode from body, mind, spiritual timeline and affected cells.

Phase One: physical healing from sexual assault

Remove the assault signature from your body. If done immediately following the assault or months later, this will produce profound healing results.

Personal will provides the power for the re-embodiment of spirit.

- Sit upright in your chair, feet firmly on the ground 10 inches apart from heel to heel.

- Drive a 22 inch wide, grounding cord, hollow in the center, from your vagina/uterus through to the center of the earth. Set a whirling vortex spiraling down the grounding cord to release congestion, violence and darkness left inside you from the assault.

- Imagine the wrongdoer 20 feet in front of you, far enough away that you feel sheltered but can see him clearly. Ground his body to the center of the earth.

Karma ring clearing.

- See a half gold ring in the air space between the two of you.

- Fill the gold ring in completely so it is now a full ring.

- Place a white rose under the Karma ring and ground it to the center of the earth

- Drop the gold karma ring into the white rose and toss a cartoon bomb onto the rose. Blow up this rose containing the complete karma ring! The white rose represents both purity and finality or death to the karmic connection.

- See wrongdoer disappear.

Phase Two: Removing cords. Ending the karmic bond supports a complete healing

- Allow your eyes to close and scan your body. You are searching for cords connecting you.

- Pull the cords out of your body, just like removing an electric cord from the wall. I do not recommend cutting cords, as is the practice of some systems. It is important not to leave any remnants of any cord in your body.

- Proper cord clearing procedure includes:
  1. Removing the cord to the outside edge of the aura.
  2. With your own gold God energy, fill in the place where the cord was originally plugged in.
  3. Seal up and fill in the outer edge of the aura to eliminate holes in the aura so that a cord cannot return.

Why me God?

When I was thirty-three, a Vedic numerologist, Prince Hirindra Singh, read my numbers in relation to the stars and my life. What he discovered is that I had intended to experience in one incarnation what, for many, would take many, many life times. At thirty-three, according to his charts, I had already lived seven of those lifetimes during this incarnation. What that means is in this one lifetime, every few years I experienced the growth and activity and learning of an entire lifetime. I have met others who have also taken on big learning lives: I would not recommend it.

In other lives I had lived as a spiritual teacher and would not have had the opportunity to fully experience all of these physical aberrations and the acts of human animal. Clearly, I wanted a rich variety of the full human experience to add to my research of humankind.

If you have experienced assault or an incredibly difficult life, then you have for some reason prior to incarnating, created this life and the lessons you are experiencing.

Good news! If this is the case, you can, while you are in a body, change your script and alter your future for a happier healthier life!

Here's how:

Phase Three: Obliterate agreements to experience violence

Program: removal from God strand DNA.

- Allow your eyes to close. Imagine yourself in the center of your head, seated on your golden throne looking out

496

onto your view screen.

- Imagine a beautiful blue DNA strand opened up and in the center are your two God strands that are unique to you and unrelated to your family. Have all violence patterns and programs show up as black dots on the DNA strand.

- Pump gold into these programs to obliterate them, and while you are in the DNA, add happy loving images.

- When the DNA shows no additional programs of violence and you muscle test clear, pulse a gold energy, resembling a radio pulse, through the DNA to seal in the new information.

- Prior to completing, make sure to reset the DNA Reset to your new setting without violence, shooting gold into the reset for a few seconds to establish the new pattern.

Phase Four: Physical healing for the injured body

Includes: Vagina, cervix, and womb. Anus, legs, breasts, neck, mouth, scalp and any other parts of the body injured during the assault.

- Send pink and gold energy from your right hand out intending it to heal affected body parts for about 3 minutes.
- Clear dark energy from the affected body parts by shooting gold energy from the right hand out with the intention of it entering the affected areas.

- With kinesiology, test the level of function of each part. Keep pumping gold into each separate area until function reads at 100%. This will take more than one healing to accomplish. Be patient and loving with yourself and, at the same time, be persistent in order to have your will engaged as well.

- If the assault was recent, you may need to do Cellular Neo-Genesis, which will support the new growth of cells. Start this on the first day of healing regardless of the percentage of function you read. If your body is asking for new cells, this is a very, very good sign, meaning that you are coming back!

  Refer to Chapter 2 for Cellular Neo-Genesis procedure. Once you have completed Cellular Neo-Genesis, return to the next step for a compete healing.

Phase Five: Emotional healing

- Imagine again sitting with spine erect, feet on the floor 10 inches apart from heel to heel.

- Breathe in pink and green energy. Breathe out any negativity worry or concern.

Level 1

- Emotions can be stored in the body if not released. Ask your body for help. Have all areas of the body affected by the assault or holding painful emotions become apparent as either a physical feeling or by seeing, with your mind's eye, a dark area. If you do not get a read this way, or you haven't mastered kinesiology (muscle testing) make your best guess. Then create a list until the muscle testing says there are no more affected parts.

- Set a large red magnet rose three feet in front of you and ground the rose to the center of the earth. Turn the magnet on and have all dark and painful emotions magnetized out of the physical body into the rose.

- When you've gotten as much as you possibly can out of your body, blow up the magnet rose.

Level 2

- Place a rose out in front of you and throw a little bomb on it to blow it up. Repeat this 50 times, placing the rose in different locations all around you and blow them up. This will clear blocked and frozen energy providing the next level for healing.

Level 3

- Create the image of a magnetic encyclopedia three feet in front of you, grounded to the center of the Earth.

- Magnetize all harmful information you have gleaned from this experience out of your body. What you're looking to accomplish is removing any information that would get stuck in your physical body and prevent you from returning to grace and ease once again.

- Allow those memories to be stored in your magnetic encyclopedia.

- See the streams of memory flow from you to the encyclopedia.

- When your book is full and you are accessing only the memories that support your vibrant full life, hand the encyclopedia to the Akashic records keeper, who is essentially your personal librarian and is very helpful and readily available.

- Continue to breathe in pink and green energy.

Phase Six: Spiritual timeline assault clearing

- See yourself in a bubble. Imagine a timeline going out the middle of your body extending as far as you can see, both out the back (your history) and out the front (your future).

- Have any assault or violence recorded on your timeline appear as black dots, both back into your history and forward into your future.

Often there are future violent events wired into your timeline. I call these future episodes time bombs. These time bombs produce the problem energy that will cause another violent event. They are set to go off at a particular age or be triggered by a particular experience. This is why we clear both back into the past and forward into the future.

- Clear the timeline with a golden shop vacuum. Suction all black dots containing the information and programs for violence off the future and past timelines. Be sure you have both of them totally cleared. The best diagnostic test is kinesiology. Check your future timeline and past timeline separately.
- When you get a yes that front and back are completely clear, pulse gold energy like a radio wave, through the timeline, sealing up the new program.

30% of the time the significant cause of a violent pattern is hidden in your cellular body. WE find these in your genetic programs. What that means is that you may have past relatives that were:

> criminals
> murderers
> thieves
> perpetrators

or your relatives may have had a history of being slaves that were abused by their masters.

- Use Kinesiology to discover if this is true for you. If it is, go to Phase 7. If it is not an issue, proceed to Phase 8.

Phase Seven: Clearing violent family DNA patterns

- In a comfortable seated position, spine erect, and feet on the floor, allow your eyes to drift shut.

- Imagine sitting in the center of your head on your throne, observing your view screen in front of you. Then imagine your DNA strand open and extended across the view screen.

- Have all programs related to violence (from the above possibility list) show up as black dots on your DNA strand.

- With a golden shop vacuum, suction off all the black dots from both your mother's and father's side.

- When all black dots have been suctioned off pulse gold energy, resembling a radio wave, through the DNA to seal up the shifts. Use kinesiology to ensure you have completed removing problematic programs.

501

- Reset the DNA to the new program by pulsing gold energy.

- Mirror the new DNA program to all the cells of the body and all the DNA. Amplify this process by flooding gold throughout the body.

Phase Eight: Restore the aura, second chakra, life force, spirit in body

- Assault will cause the aura to become a black shroud of death. Pump gold energy through the right hand into the aura until color is restored to the aura. Colors that are really great for healing in the aura are pink and green.

- Identify if the second chakra is damaged or missing. Follow protocols for replacing the chakra found in Chapter 8.

- Identify life force frequency and vibration through muscle testing. Then with a gold pumping technique restore life force to 100%.

- Spirit in body restoration: It is important to return spirit entirely into the body.

- After completing a Miraculous Living meditation, imagine a golden sun at the top of your head.

- Fill your body with this golden sun.

- Create a second golden sun at the top of your head and fill this sun with loving validation:

    ★I love myself

502

★I have a beautiful healthy body

★I am a creative person

★I am loving and lovable

★I have great relationships

★I am strong and powerful

★I am an awesome dancer

★I am a fabulous driver

★I am a great mother

★I am a master of wealth

★ Continue on with your own validations...

- Once you have filled in the golden sun with every possible loving validation you can think of, bring the golden sun of validation into all the cells of your body.

- Take a moment to feel this wonderful feeling of self-love and self-appreciation.

- Place yourself as a spirit, seated on your crown chakra, in a giant golden sun.

- Slip yourself into your body, filling out all your fingers and toes, legs and arms, torso, neck and head.

- Stretch your spirit to the outer edge of your skin.

Phase Nine: Create a happy future

The best technique for creating a happy future is magnetizing all good to you. You will find the Miraculous Living 21-day Accelerate Wealth Program I an excellent choice. This program gives you the opportunity to follow specific meditations in which you create a mock-up bubble then fill the bubble with four to eight future manifestations.

For a free 7-day program with a powerful 'abundance' guided meditation: www.miraculouslivingwealth.com.

Chapter 27: Pain

Ten things doctors don't know about chronic pain and what you can do to feel better right now

You were born a happy, healthy little person, ready to bring on your biggest, best ever life. You progressed through your life and at some time the glow and happy enthusiasm faded and your health began to deteriorate. Over the past twenty years, we at Miraculous Healing have assisted our clients in feeling better in their body regardless of the cause of the pain. We have helped reduce and eliminate pain from illness, injury, nerve damage, and broken bones. In the following paragraphs, we explore where pain comes from, even when it seems mysterious. I will show you how to rapidly shift your circumstances so you can feel vibrant and healthy again.

Working with clients for twenty years I have identified nine causes of persistent pain (or other ailing conditions) and possible solutions. At the end of this article I have included an action plan so you can get started instantly.

I have had a great deal of experience with overcoming pain as you might imagine having gone through many surgeries, several bad car accidents and to top off the list I suffered from fibromyalgia. Personally I found keeping a positive attitude and getting daily exercise both inside and out was incredibly helpful.

In my most difficult times I was treated with a combination of nine Morphine tablets, 2000mlgm time-release anti-inflammatory, three benzodiazepine, as well as specific pills for digestive cramps and migraine medications. It all got to be too much and one day I said enough. I went cold turkey off all the narcotics and tranquilizers at the same time. I locked myself in my home and road out the rough ride alone. I took five baths a day to calm down the 'freak-out' and saw the gremlins, everyone who goes through drug withdrawals sees. I had shakes and sweats and when I had gotten to the other side of it, I was exhausted and relieved.

I had never wanted to take the medications, so withdrawals though rough, Were not the same as someone who had chosen the medicate there emotions with narcotics. I could be with my body, lovingly and patiently as I midwife myself back to a clean body.

I felt it was better to live in pain then to not have use of my brain. Being on that pain 'cocktail' left me a blithering idiot…a side affect I could not live with. Back then I don't think any of my Doctors thought I could pull through. They told me that I would not die of fibromyalgia, but my life expectancy was ten to twelve years if I didn't have another recurrence of cancer (which I did eighteen months later).

Pain is miserable. I was on the right track with wanting my brain back. I felt I could learn grown and heal if I was straight in my mind. Have you ever felt that way? In the Miraculous Healing program we are working on emotions and the brain constantly. So much of our body and how it feels is directed and supported by the miraculous brain.

When we do the five-hour brain healing pain decreases and vitality improves. Having your brain working well means your brain cells are pristine and brain chemistry with neurotransmitters up and functioning well. These improvements improve your feel good experience.

There are many things your medical practitioner will know and share with you about pain. This chapter is dedicated to

506

helping you understand the more hidden aspects of pain, and give you a pathway to understand heal and leave pain in the past.

1. No Nucleus (brain) in the cells affected by pain

How can there be no nucleus, you ask? Without a nucleus, the cell has no brain, no direction. Medical treatment is responsible for sixty percent of the missing nuclei. Toxicity and pollution ingested through air, water and food are responsible for twenty-three percent. Medical illnesses, including a nasty bug called a mycoplasma, are responsible for fifteen percent, and a small percentage is actually congenital.

In the process of Cellular Neo Genesis I explain in great detail how to improve the inner workings of the cell. When I discovered the nucleus was missing in about ninety percent of my cells, it was shocking. My former partner, a medical doctor had assisted (upon my pleading) to help me with the pain. He did some research on fibromyalgia and as he read about it, some of my symptomology was not typical of the usual variety of fibromyalgia. He wrote a note to my doctor at my HMO to request a couple unusual test. The doctor was not thrilled to order the test, however I was able to persuade him. The results came back and my former partner was correct.

In medical science, there is no cure of correction for this condition. They will do up to two years of high potency broad-spectrum antibiotics to kill the mycoplasims, however the damage done cannot be medically corrected. To top that off the Doctor informed me that the treatment would kill me and he would not authorize it. (Thank God!) That sounded awful.

507

So now we knew why the pain was out of control, it would take a few years for me to discover the Divine Human Blueprint in my garden and put an end to pain as I was able to restore the nucleus in a majority of my cells.

Solution to no nucleus (brain) in the cells

Replacing the nucleus in the master cell and then to all the surrounding cells is definitely doable, but not through mainstream Western medicine. In our Miraculous Living Apprentice program, we learn to harness our creator god force. This is the way we replace the nucleus.

Pumping gold energy into the place where the nucleus used to be, over a few minutes and the nucleus will again reappear. At first it will be only a glimmer of what it was but as you continue to revisit the master cell over a series of healings into the nucleus, it will ultimately appear again at a hundred percent.

2. Spiritual body failure

During injuries and illness, the 264 chakras and mini chakras called nadis can fail, stop, be chopped off, and go all together missing. Your body is meant to have energy moving through these channels, in and out of the glands, organs and systems. That energy is an important part of the nourishment of the physical body.

Spiritual body failure can be responsible for both physical pain and emotional, mental pain, which appears as a flat depressed affect. Kevin, a Viet Nam vet, suffered from posttraumatic stress. He had been unable to access his happy emotions for so many years, that when the joy returned to his emotional palette, his elation was beyond words. This result was produced from restoring the energetic body and chakras and restoring the brain.

I also think about Maria whose aura went black after the death of her husband. In the cloud of death Maria could only live in an icy painful fog. For her, days of unbearable emotions, crippled with grief did not allow her to see the light of day. In this fog, she could not hear the birds singing, children laughing or the preciousness of her life.

Restoring the aura as well as chakras, and returning bright colors to the physical body that had become shrouded with death helped Maria step back into her life once again. With the emotional pain turned down from a thousand percent to fifteen percent she was able to return to her life and six weeks later enter her technology art in a competition and begin selling her works.

Solution to spiritual body failure

The seven main body chakras are the priority.

- Chakra one is found at the perineum. It is your base or survival chakra. The best colors here are deep green and red.

- Chakra two is out the front of the body just above the public bone and out the back two inches up from the base of the spine (coccyx). This is the chakra of physical creativity and sensuality. The best colors in this chakra are peach, pink, orange and green.

- Chakra is three about two inches up from the belly button and directly out the back. This chakra is related to will and power/energy. The best colors are green and red.

509

- Chakra four is the heart chakra, two inches up from the base of the sternum and out the back. For women you can find it around your bra line. The best colors are red, pink, peach and all shades green.

- Chakra five is at the base of the neck in front and in back of the neck. It is the chakra of communication. The best colors are pink, green and yellow.

- Chakra six is the center of head chakra or the brow center, often referred to as the third eye. It is out the front of the head between the eyebrows and out the back of the head three inches above where the spine meets the skull. The best color is a deep blue, followed closely by emerald green.

- Chakra seven is your crown chakra and is your direct communication with the divine. The color is gold or yellow and should only be these colors.

Another clearing could include clearing each of the seven layers of the aura. You will find the details of this in chapter14.

We address many more of the spiritual body elements in the Miraculous Living Apprentice program. Having these seven chakras tuned and running well can really help feed the body energy and reduce pain. For a very complete look at the chakras be sure to revisit the chakra chapter found on page 150

3. Emotional body atrophy.

Painful emotions embed in the cells of your body and turn the light off in the cells. These painful emotions in the cells are a death energy that prevents the cells from returning to vibrancy and health.

Amy had an obsession with finding everything wrong and calling a great deal of attention to it. She talked constantly and wanted everyone to agree with how terrible her life and her health was. If you skirted around the issue she would stop talking point her finger at me and say "Julie Renee don't you agree?" Now that was no a question, she demanded agreement.

When I think of a muscle that has atrophied, it is like shoe leather. When I was a masseuse occasionally I would find an occipital ridge muscles, the muscles in the upper neck and back of skull, had dried out and flattened. With the use of regular massage, and palpating the area, it would again plump up and become the spongy. The palpation and stretching would allow a supply of richly oxygenated blood to return to the area.

Use this idea as you think about healing emotionally atrophy. How can you resupply the much-needed vibrancy to the stuck places? Think of breaking down by palpation the emotions that have hardened and nourishing with oxygen and blood possibly getting a whole new fresh perspective on the situation and then fortifying it with gratitude and lots of happy events.

Solution to emotional body atrophy.

Painful emotions become embedded in the cells of your body and turn the light off in the cells. These painful emotions in the cells are a death energy that prevents the cell's return to vibrancy and health. You will find instructions for clearing emotional pain and love entanglements in the chapter on relationships and love found on page 68.

Sit and breathe into the location where the pain is and allow it to move. This takes patience. Love doesn't have to hurt. You may find emotional atrophy is sourced from a meme or miasm as you are stuck with a pattern that does not resonate with truth.

The common places for this kind of atrophy are liver, kidney, spleen, heart and intestines. If you are finding it difficult to get to the bottom of this, as sometimes what may be more oblivious to others remains somewhat invisible to the individual experiencing it a private session with me or one of my certified miraculous healers will be instrumental in clearing these hidden culprits. Emotional atrophy can leave you confused, and stuck on a loop. It will seem like you are constantly circling back and never get a chance to move forward.

Know that you are loved and not alone. This is a common and often very painful situation and there is hope of relief and a future free from this pain. Self love and permission to be spacious and imperfect will help tremendously in shifting this pattern.

4. Brain patterns (conscious)

Holding pain as a familiar feeling. Pain can become a companion and a quiet friend. When asking a pain client, "Would you like the pain taken from your body now, at no cost?" I was told, "No thanks, my life is designed around my pain, everything I do and how I do it is paced around this condition and things would change too much for me."

If you want to see this big time, go to a pain support group. Many lonely people build a lifestyle out of endless doctor visits and treatments and create a family and friend circle entirely around their pain. Just like the AA groups the lifestyle is set up to be the pain, talk about the pain, talk about the treatments of the pain, and set up meetings to support the exhaustion that comes from the pain.

If you are a healthy person without pain, this will seem ludicrous. If you are in pain you want to get back to feeling great a.s.a.p. This reminds me of my dear client Lucia who had a very traumatic birth. She had a normal labor, six hours of breathing and contracting which I had been with her and helped move it along a little more quickly. The arrival of the Dr Lee who was a beautiful Asian woman who had come to the delivery room with a lovely string of pearls clutching her neck and a white doctors coat covering a lovely dinner dress signaled a time to get down to business.

Baby Nicky emerged beautifully and then it was time for the placenta to appear. As the placenta came through Lucia's uterus exploded and she was in grave peril. With a concerned expression Dr Lee looked at me than at Lucia and Jim and said we have to do surgery, no time for medication.

Within seconds surgical tools materialized and she was ready to begin. I took Lucia's face in my hands and said:

Bring your spirit up into the center of your head.

Breathe shallow.
I will pull the pain out of your body.

**You must keep your eyes in my eyes.
Use a panting breath.'**

We three women worked together. Doctor Lee stitching up the many tares as quickly as possible, I became the human anesthesia for Lucia, and Lucia obediently surrendered to my instructions and never let her gaze drift or her fear rise.

And then, it was over, Lucia was holding her baby and I was slipping out quietly as the new family settled into hugs and cuddles. I kissed Lucia on the forehead, told she had done an amazing job and I vanished.

Walking down the hallway I was thanking God for the lives saved and the gratitude to have the gifts to assist. There was a shout from down the hall, the Doctor was running after me. She thanked me for what I had done. "That would not have gone down that way had you not been there, it could have been so much worse. Thank you. You can be in my birthing or operating room any time. Thank you."

Lucia could have gone in to a pain episode and started the process of embedded pain on that day. Her womb could have gone to death energy and she could have lost her sex drive and associated the pain of the birth with the baby. Instead, a surprised mom and dad called me two years later, now in their mid forties they had conceived a little boy! The pregnancy and delivery was a breeze!

What is so remarkable about this couple is that they had tried for twenty-seven years to conceive a child and for seven years they had used fertility medications. Lucia Miscarried at sixteen weeks and that was that, however a month later they discovered there was a second baby in her tummy growing strong. The little baby spirit found me a week before the Doctor recommended she come see me.

514

Little Nicky new here mom was going to have difficulties so she search me out on the astral and made sure her mom had regular sessions with me, and helped her through the birth. Lucia would not give birth she said unless I was there helping her.

I think about Elena who had a difficult birth, and how her emotions got the best of her. She began blaming the midwife and Doctor for her week of labor. She would cry often and speak about the pain and incompetence of her birth. She couldn't let it go. As she progressed with her little man she developed a strange foot malady and then a back injury all related to her embedded emotions. The foot represent your spirit understanding and ability to take your next step and your low back feeling supported and allowing support in your life.

Elena was shown how this was harming herself with the ongoing anger and constant talk about how bad things were, but she was getting a lot of mileage out of listening to her story.

What do you do when you have a painful episode? When I broke my back skiing, I moved on as quickly as possible. I used my thoughts to heal myself and after four months in a Xena warrior princess body brace, I emerge and returned to my exercise routine. I gave no reference or credence to the mending bones just felt into my returning health. I experience no pain in my spine where the injury had been. Like water off a ducks back we can choice how we interpret events in your life.

What is you could just believe that all is well, everything works for the good of your growth and understanding and life is working perfectly no matter how things may temporarily seem to appear?

515

5. Brain patterns (unconscious)

These are programs of influential people and related to how you are loved and given emotional encouragement and support. For example, if your busy husband who is often emotionally absent goes in to protect mode and brings the good stuff when you are in pain, you may hold onto the pain to have the protection and support of your man.

There's a fellow I know whose family had gifted him a series of deep healings with me. I attempted to work at helping him shift his mindset to understand that he was the author of his life. He had awoken slowly from a coma years ago after a terrible accident and had interpreted his painful condition as what was meant to be. He followed the system of pain doctors and narcotics and support groups.

Once we had cleared much of his pain and restored the use of his legs he could see that life was going to change. Since his life was designed around his former disabilities, he continued his volunteer work in a medical office and returned to his support group to commiserate with his other 'disabled' friends. I checked in with him and suggested he keep going with the healing work. He told me he had had enough change in his life and he was good with what he had. 'I'm good.'

I spoke to him several months later and he had returned to the mindset of a disabled person. I was interested in observing the strong group mind program he had willingly returned too. Clearly he was experiencing much less discomfort and his legs were now working, but his mindset was of a weak 'poor happy me I am a making my life work even though I am disabled'. He deliberately chooses not to move back into his life with an income earning job and a social life outside support group and family.

516

This example is both conscious and unconscious. Where can you see in your relationship with pain a pull towards a behavior or mindset that would not see you in great vibrant health?

6. Emotional manipulation (unconscious).

What this means is that the individual experiencing pain, is receiving some sort of benefit by having that condition. They may hold others hostage, giving them a level of control and dominance. The condition gets them attention from others. Shame is often experienced along with this unconscious emotional manipulation. In this situation, your body is trained not to improve.

DNA patterns create a predisposition to having pain patterns similar to your family members.

Have you ever noticed that one person will get an illness and pull in. They get focused, meditate, juice, and exercise their way out of a problem. Then you have a person with the same condition and they fall apart.

I have an acquaintance who I had encouraged to come up for healing weekends since the start of the program. She was always saying maybe someday. She lived forty-five miles away. Then one day Tammy found out she had breast cancer. She gave her girlfriend a list of her thirty friends and acquaintances and had everybody waiting on her had and foot. I found it a little ironic that I was being asked to drive her to chemo appointments and provide her with daily meals (living forty-five miles away) and having had offered her healings for years that she could not attend.

Are you using your pain to gain sympathy and attention? If you are you will likely never release it. Tammy's emotional pain and subsequent community effort around her was giving her outer evidence that she was loved and cared for.

7. Emotional family bubble.

The "what you are supposed to feel at a certain age" syndrome. For example, "I am old, achy, tired, in pain and experiencing headaches all the time". This is sourced from the constant conversation that is subtle. When you hear it, your cells start matching the aches to make the person speaking correct, knowing it has to be fulfilled.

When do you stop knowing you can heal? When do you believe the Doctors prognosis that you can never recover from a problem and you should just get used to it? What is the routine conversation of the elder generation in your family? Is it largely around health problems?

I find this particular issue hypnotic in nature. As you allow yourself to match the energy of the family you begin to wire into your brain, that this is all you have to look forward to. It is a hopeless miasm, that begins the steady movement towards imagining death and how dying will give you relief of your aches and pains. The Heavenly paradise without the pain filled body encourages the ultimate resolution.

In our era, people are dying at an incredibly young age. And the illnesses and treatments to these illnesses are horrendous. There is an invisible age, when unless you are a celebrity, you no longer contribute or ad value. This invisible age is by your choice. It is also supported by group mind.

You can heal at any age. You can become sick at any age and fall into pain, and then check out. Most people are so connected with the group mind and Doctor prognosis that they forget to go inside and ask for what is needed now to heal and bring health back to the body.

8. Nerve pain.

Nerve pain is miserable. Shifting this means getting your body into the parasympathetic mode as much as possible and speaking to the nerves with love, appreciation and gratitude. Great headway can be made by receiving Miraculous Living brain healings in order to create an entirely new direction for the nerves and the body to respond to.

To heal nerve pain is multifaceted. The first thing to check after clearing black off the nerves is, is this pattern in the DNA? Often a program for nerve health or nerve malfunction can be found in the wisdom and programming of the DNA.

The condition of Fibromyalgia is the condition of widespread nerve pain and reversing the autoimmune disease can be accomplished with a multifaceted approach.

People with this condition tend to be outer focused and find the pain inside too great to deal with so deep inner reflection is not the first or fortieth choice they will make unless they know the answers to healing the pain are there. Then it will take considerable courage to address the internal workings that allowed the pain to arise in the first place. I have heard of studies linking the fibromyalgia syndrome to sexual assault/abuse. The numbers of men with the illness are minimal to the large numbers of women suffering.

I have heard women say to me in their session; 'I know that I am doing this to myself. I get myself so stress out that I hardly have a minute to relax and when I do I am so stressed I feel miserable. As a matter of fact, my pain forces me to rest and give my body a break."

Does this sound familiar? Do you wait for your pain or exhaustion to take you out of the game and rest? Is this the R and R you really want to experience? A life out of balance will inevitably be a life filled with pain, physical and emotional.

See the end of this chapter for fibromyalgia protocols.

The guided meditation found in the "From Fatigued to Fabulous" free gift (www.julierenee.com) is designed to help move you away from the sympathetic to the parasympathetic mode of the nervous system. In the parasympathetic system regeneration and healing take place.

9. Mental body shadow pain.

This is a phantom floating pain that lives in the physical body shifts through the mental body, which is similar to the spiritual imprint on the cellular body. Shadow pain can be extremely frustrating, as it seems to have no source in the physical body. A pain Doctor will validate that you are experiencing the pain, but can attach no particular meaning or source to the pain. It to many will appear that you are a bit nutty. Shadow pain can come under the malady of hypochondria, but shadow pain is real pain, it is in the mental body.

Have you ever heard of an amputee who's missing limb continues to throb, ache and cause them pain? This is the pain of the mental body. For an amputee, clearing the mental body of the pain by pumping gold energy into the area will eliminate the pain altogether.

10. Brain patterns (conscious)

This means holding pain as a familiar 'feeling.' If I hold onto this pain life will not change. I know what to expect, and how I respond to the challenges of my life,

If you notice that this is your challenge, the first thing you need to do is make a list of all the things you get, or benefit from, by having ongoing pain. For example, "I get attention from people," "I have friendships bonded through pain," and so on. Be really honest with yourself and write as many "wins" as possible from this condition.

I worked with a lawyer for a short time, Candy. She had fibromyalgia and was dealing with some tough issues in her life. She had everything in her life worked out to the minutest detail. Here's how she managed pain: a half cigarette, a half piece of gum, a Percocet at the exact time.

She had this pattern down to a science. She was seeing me to help with the active grief she was struggling with as her beloved (elderly) husband was passing from gum cancer. We never got to the healing of her pain as she was nursing it along.

When her husband did pass, she was mad at the world, and she blamed everyone. This is a pain pattern that locks the pain in deeper. The narcotics are the relief of the emotional as well as the physical pain, but are the suppressant of real healing. The longer you 'shove pills down your throat and put a gag order on your feelings' the worse the pain monster gets.

521

Love, self-love, needs expression. Do you love yourself enough to come out and heal? If you do, and I am encouraging you to make this choice then it will take every ounce of courage, and when you heal you will live an enlightened, alivened life in a body you love honor and cherish.

Action plan

1. Write all the things you might have to deal with, or face, or create as you heal.

2. Write down what you will experience once the pain has shifted. How will life be? Include all the things you could do, be, have and accomplish if pain were not an issue in your life.

Great now that you are started lets go deeper into discovery

3. Create a list of how I benefit from this condition You will need to completely let go of each item, one by one, in order to move to move on.

4. List all the new challenges I have to face if I no longer have this condition.

5. Use the challenge list and turn it into a strategy list. The two things you will need to address in this list are

How do I find a solution to this problem?

How do I get help from others to find a solution for these circumstances?

6. List all the things you could do, be, or accomplish if this condition were not part of your life.

522

This final list is the catalyst to dynamically move you into freedom. It will help you create a life of grace and ease. You will live your dream life and be able to realize your full potential.

We have loved at many causes of pain and the reasons for pain not leaving; now we will address pain caused from things of spirit and curses.

Pain can be intense and unrelenting and it can appear to be based in some physically reality, but when pain does not clear we must then look to things of spirit for our answer.

I find that the worst culprit for a biting, gripping or stabbing pain is the unpleasant spiritual parasite referred to as a demon.

Demons actually once came from the angelic realm, and have fallen away from the light. The painful gripe of this kind of demon want a fight. In the battle the demon can get stronger and have purpose (albeit harmful). I teach how to clear demons in the year-long apprentice program, and takes some amount of training to do this particular procedure properly, I suggest you not try this until you have been trained.

I have a student in the apprentice program, who thought she was clearing demons and evil spirits, when what she was actually doing was gathering them to her, getting them off of other people. In her first weekend I cleared from her literally hundreds of this nasty things off of her. She was eager to learn how to do this properly, but it takes time. I tell my students, I don't want any of you to become 'ghost busters'. But to do a great job of healing means learning to remove these unwanted parasite.

I do no battle with these beings, but rather remove all their intelligence and return them as an 'empty vessel to the angelic realm'. They will do no harm ever again.

Two of my participants were wracked with pain, one mid spine and the other low back. By removing the demons that were globed onto them they sat up, looked surprised and had no pain.

I worked with an assault survivor who had been drugged and brutally raped, left for dead. So much was better in her life after years of therapy and meditation. Yet she could not have sex without pain medication. Sex hurt. Okay, now that makes sense right? Not really. If we had successfully cleared the trauma, why was she still in pain, in what should be a joyful experience.

What I discovered with her is that two demons during the assault attached to two separate areas of her uterus and vagina, so the repetitive motion of intercourse and the contractions of the uterus during orgasm caused extreme pain as the demons clapped down. Removing the demons for her meant returning to a happy partnership.

Evil spirits can also cause pain in the body. I don't see this as prevalent as Demons, however it happens. An evil spirit is a human spirit who has become bad and is no longer able to take a physical incarnation so they spend their time bothering people in bodies.

Entities, generally they have to be in a swarm (a whole bunch of them) to cause any significant pain. These things really are like cockroaches, they are not from the human or angelic realm, they are parasitical from other planets, and have infested thirty percent of earth, all in populated areas.

To understand about clearings you will find a step by step in *All Things of Spirit* chapter 28.

Curses

Curses are bad intentions and thoughts thrown your direction. Don Ruiz Miguel talks about a black magic we do when we speak unkindly of another. He is so very right. It certainly does not have to be a conscious curse to wreak havoc on a person's health or emotion. Thoughts are things. We you really get that you will have taken a big step up in awareness and realized that you have likely put some bad juju in a few people's spaces that you now wish you hadn't.

Curses can be cleared by using gold energy and pumping into the body or area where the curse has taken root. Sometimes curse can be multifaceted and may involve many layers. This is the conscious curse created by someone practicing actively a form of black magic. Every curse is removable, complex curses require a master to remove them so that nothing is left once the entire curse is removed.

Fibromyalgia

I am often asked about this condition, and having entirely healed from debilitating fibromyalgia. It has many components, nerve pain, atrophying muscles and joint pain as well as headaches difficult digestion and emotional challenges including anxiety.

1. Using kinesiology read the color of the body in relationship to pain. Get a percentage and color. Pump gold energy into the body until you have cleared the color and percentage.

2.   Clear all five brains using the protocols found I the brain chapter.
3.   Clear the nervous system. (Find details in the systems chapter)
4.   Reopen the human access portal
5.   Return the mental body which will be way to high to 100% restoring energy and balance to the emotional physical and spiritual body
6.   Clear the emotional body and emotions related to the condition. It is likely you will need to clear trauma and abuse
7.   Clear the respiratory system remember this system is representing by the statement I have a right to take up space. Clear the physical lungs, bronchi and sinuses/nasal passages and also clear the mental and emotional issue around having a right to exist.
8.   Clear the spiritual time line of any past life's that would cause unrelenting pain an suffering in the body.
9.   If you find a curse related to fibromyalgia clear this now.
10. Restore the energetic system chakras and aura to pristine colors. Double check on chakra function as they may be there and functioning, however only working at 20%. Be sure to increase energy function to 100%

This ten-step procedure will get you a long way into the complete healing of the condition fibromyalgia. Recovery takes time and a positive mental attitude. Stay grateful, exercise and know that you are getting well. Even if you are not prone to illness if you have fibromyalgia you are in a weakened and reduced life and lifestyle. You can entirely and completely heal.

Chapter 28: All Things of Spirit

The realm of spirit activity: unwanted or negative spirits

Although this does not relate to the blueprint of restoration, this knowledge is vital for some people's complete healing as not all breakdown or malfunction in the body is related in injury, illness and/or malfunction. More times than you would expect, an aggravating factor for disorder in the human body is some sort of spirit activity not related to the human-spirit-to-human-body connection.

Case Study: Kathy's Experience

Kathy W. is an amazing woman with a wealth of talents; one of her greatest talents is that of connection. She is fun loving and truly a joy to be around, however when we first met, little of that fun-loving nature showed through.

I was in the mastermind group of Michael Port's "Book Yourself Solid" group, sharing ideas and cheering my team members on. After the conference call ended, I received and urgent email message from Darlene, one of my peers in the group, asking for help. She had been with her friend, Kathy, the night before and she believed Kathy might die.

I responded to Darlene and urged her to have her friend contact me as soon as she could. Within three hours, the call came in. Rinnnnngggg. 'Hello, Julie Renee', 'Hi this is Kathy I am a friend of Darlene's, and I really need your help.' That was the being of a relatively short intake call. What I discovered rapidly that her life force was at 2% and Kathy was not going to be able to hold on to her body much longer. She had made a valiant effort, but the odds were stacked against her from a dark mysterious *attack*, apparently from inside her body.

Her symptoms included crazy, severe high blood pressure; feet feeling like stones; numbness in legs and feet; swelling, bloating and malfunction of the lymphatic system, digestive issues and overall helplessness.

I urged her that she could not wait. If she were wanted to stay alive, we would need to begin our healings that day. And like that, healing Kathy became my vocation for 4 months, multiple times a week, removing from her body the impediments to her health vitality and longevity.

What surprised me was the sheer number of entities, spirits, demons, evil spirits, trans-mortals, and spiders/snakes that occupied a body she no longer had much access to. She responded well to the healings and cellular neo-genesis, but every single time we worked together I removed spirits and entities from her systems, glands, and organs. We were definitely seeing real improvement as her body was beginning to rebuild itself from the inside out, and the attack began to subside.

Having an infestation of entities can be considered a spiritual illness of the physical body. The entities are actually attacking the physical body, not the human spirit. Typically some types of non-human spirits can cause problems for the human spirit.

We cleared an average of 7 'things' weekly, sometimes more, for a grand total of 79 entities, evil spirits, demons, trans -mortals and spider/snakes.

The day came when we addressed the ongoing misery in her belly. Kathy said; "I'm not crazy, I literally can see my stomach move and hear voices coming from my belly."

This idea is generally not accepted: I had recently seen Sylvia Brown speak to a TV audience. A woman stood up and said that she felt like her dead husband was occasionally moaning from her stomach, and Sylvia, dismissed her saying 'don't be ridiculous sprits don't inhabit the body like that so put it out of your mind.' This is paraphrasing but that was the essence of her communication to this unfortunate woman.

In my research I have found quite the opposite. That as much as 20% of the time when illness and physical malfunction are present, there is some negative spirit activity making the situation worse.

I said to Kathy; "let me take a look and see what is going on." We first did a physical healing on the lower abdomen and intestines, than yes there were indeed negative spirits in her belly as she suspected.

What we discovered was a nest of three demonic spirits in her belly. I had seen them on several occasions, but this would be the first time I was going to remove them from a person's body.

I was fearless. I grounded each of the demons, which appeared black and were attempting to frighten me with a variety of scary apparitions. However, I shut down my view screen internally to a great degree, so I was just focusing on the black blob I had grounded to the center of the earth.

Since I could not be easily frightened with my inner vision, the demonic beings pulled another magic trick out of the hat.

One of the ways I created the sanctuary space of healing in my home is to surround myself with bouquets of fresh flowers, which I love. Fresh cut roses have been known to last up to 7 weeks in my living room due to a kind of flower magic I learned during my time in India.

The day I cleared 3 demons from Kathy's belly, I had 3 large vases filled with fresh cut flowers. As I was removing the last of the demons' essence from Kathy, having locked down the other two in a similar way, I noticed a putrid smell.

The flower water in the vases was being transformed into a kind of swamp water, and for special effect they (the demons) had actually managed to get the swampy water to bubble. The air was becoming permeated with putrefied rotten odors. For the next 30 minutes, I continued with my unwavering mission of assisting Kathy in returning to vibrant health, which, in this case, meant removing those three demonic spirits, which was completely successful at the end of the healing that day. Kathy was freed of demonic possession.

Afterward hanging up the phone with Kathy, my flowers were handled with care. I brought the vases into the kitchen, pouring the putrefied water down the drain and carefully rinsed the stems of all the flowers, made a fresh cut an inch up on the stem , and returned them to drink in the new, fresh, crystal-clear water..

No flowers were casualties to the demons magic show. However, if I had believed in the fear and horror that the demons were projecting towards me, my belief would have imagined that the flowers being attacked were going to die. The flowers would have picked up on my thoughts and been compelled to die.

Understand that the demonic reach is largely predicated on how much fear they can get rolling in the environment. Since most humans do not comprehend the power of their thoughts, especially negative ones, they are less then diligent about maintaining a clean healthy environment in their metal patterns and images.

Love is a good place to start.

One premise I have operated with all my life is that I am the stronger one. If it is I versus a thing that has no body, I will prevail. This is my realm, not theirs. To incarnate, I must have surpassed at least 100 other human spirits who do not have a body. Further, I am managing to hold onto this body regardless of the illness and toxic exposure I experienced at an earlier age. I am "wonder woman" to their insignificant bug status.

Allow me to introduce you to my cockroach philosophy. Entities, evil spirits, spiders and snakes, obnoxious aliens all fall under the "cockroach category". Essentially they are, for me, no more than a troublesome bug that has little power because I give them none. I don't fight with them, argue with them, or engage with. I create no battle, nothing to push against or tap into to access my energy.

The secret to experiencing power beyond anything out of your body is you knowing that, "I've got the power!"

Later in this chapter, I will spell out for you exactly what you can do, step by step, to clear away beings that are interfering with your health or the health of clients or loved ones.

Kathy's second big clearing happened two months later. We had done phenomenal work together over the previous

531

three months and there was now a real future for Kathy and her beloved husband, Arthur. Without a doubt, she was getting much better by leaps and bounds: her life and life force coming back rapidly.

It was a Tuesday, as I remember, and we had been working on reversing the nerve diminishment in her leg. And there it was, the first of five huge beings using part of Kathy's body as a portal to the human realm. I have only ever encountered these beings twice in the thousands of healings I have done for people throughout the years. So understand, this is a rare occurrence.

I was working on the nerves in the leg, when Kathy's body gave the direction the next healing would be in the lower right area of the intestines just above the pelvic cradle.

I identified a being quite large being rooted into Kathy. A kind of spirit I had never seen before. I was able to identify it as a trans-mortal being, who was using Kathy's body to leap between its own realm to the human realm. These spirits did give rise to a moment of anxiety for me as they were like an 8 foot brick wall able to resist my clearing techniques, and jump between realms in an instant. But I was there in service to assist a fellow human out of trouble. Then I understood, this is a new hybrid cockroach and I would have to move a little faster come up with a new approach. And I would in the end, because I am wonder woman (in my own mind, of course). I would surpass the obstacles related to Kathy's full restoration and healing.

They did want to talk; get me involved with their shenanigans. In response, I shut off my auditory reception while I continued to work on one after another, til none remained.

Be clear, no being, entity or spirit has a right to invade, inhabit, become a squatter, haunt, or possess a human being. Period. Any conversation that might ensue about why they need to be there is moot, because the human who owns the body does not want them there. You can invite them to leave permanently, and they will turn you down because no human has ever called them on it and they have gotten cozy in these new digs, but if they don't leave, the next step is to in neutrality begin the spirit obliteration process.

The trans-mortals, 5 in all, gave me some valuable information about spirits jumping between realms using a human body as a portal. They had developed a way to leave an anchor to enable a future leap into that body. It was a marker of a kind, and I realized they were not governed by our phenomenon of time passing. To fully remove the impact of these creatures troubling Kathy, I needed to successfully locate and remove all the anchors in her body that they had established.

It took a number of healings for me to find all the anchors, as it was like finding a needle in a haystack, and until I comprehended what it was I was searching for. The search just continued as a valuable research project.

Their ability to break free from my grounding technique, which would hold a being in stasis unable to move while I removed it, was also an important lesson.

What I was able to accomplish with these beings was to remove a lot of their information and permanently prevent them from returning to Kathy's body. I am certain these five trans-mortals have never ventured back into this human realm, though perhaps a few others have.

Where did they come from? How does a different dimension sound? Well if you enjoy science fiction, then this sounds plausible. If not, receive what your mind will let you take in and let go of the rest.

A Real Haunting

The occupation of trans-mortals reminds me of an entirely different spirit occupation, one of a house in San Anselmo, owned by a family in real estate for generations. The house had a couple rooms that were basically unusable.

I will never forget the day I was called into this home: I was running a fever, not feeling too well. However, I had said I would help these folks and I am a woman of my word. The house was only 18 blocks from the home I was residing in, so it was easy enough to pop in on them. I thought no problem, I'll do a quick ghost busting, spend 20 or 30 minutes and be on my way back home to rest.

I was welcomed at the door by Alice, who in proper fashion showed me into a wonderful historic Victorian home, giving me a room by room tour of the house. I was crashing quickly as the spirit activity was off the charts. This was a strain on my physical body; just being in the house exhausted me.

She pointed out two specific rooms where there had been a lot of spirit activity and haunting events. The home had been in the family for three generations. Those two rooms were virtually unused as they were unpleasant to be in.

In my initial research, I discovered a portal from the underworld in two locations in the home that matched up with the locations of the families haunting experiences. While there, I estimated the number of spirits of numerous varieties coming in and out of the house on a daily basis reached up to 300 per day.

When I started sharing my findings with Alice, she was neither shocked nor surprised, even if the underworld portals were new news to her. The current owners had a strong desire to take back the house; they wanted to use those rooms that sat decorated with furniture but never occupied by people. Two generations of family had allowed the squatters, but now as Alice and her fiancé were setting up this house as their home, they looked forward to raising a family here. The spirits and entities had to go.

I dealt with this in a different way than you might expect. Taking on a clearing of hundreds of spirits was not going to work for my ailing physical body, so I devised a way to move the two portals, well away from the home and the local community which is away from human activity.

After successfully moving the portals and the filling in and sealing off any identifying features of the old, well-used portals, I then went room to room and cleared out all remaining spirits and entities. By the time I was in the last room, which was vacant, I was sitting on the berber carpeted floor, exhausted beyond belief. Two hours and fifteen minutes after arriving, I wrapped up.

This house was under siege, and the humans who lived in it were unable to use rooms in their own home because of this circumstance. Think of it, possibly 110 years ago some unfortunate builder built a home on a portal to the underworld. Because of this circumstance, it is likely this family secret meant the house would never be sold to someone outside of the family.

A Second Haunting

A similar, but lesser circumstance was found in a San Rafael family home: the house that Robbie inherited. Robbie and Christy were newlyweds fixing up their home, excited about the future when Christy started noticing some very real movement in the home. Literally items were being moved, doors and windows opened, and her cat 'spooked' routinely.

I was invited to visit Christy in her home. She was an enthusiastic client, who loved the healings and the 'Life in Joy and Balance' coaching program I had for women of ages 26-42 years. She, having grown up in a difficult family with a confusing Mormon background and both her mother and fathered being married multiple times, was wanting to make sense of who she was as a young newlywed and looking for answers to the questions of where true happiness comes from.

In more than one of our sessions, she had mentioned the spirit activities of her home. So it was a natural request, when she was feeling strong in herself, to have her home environment support the shifts she was experiencing in her inner world.

As I walked into her home, I noticed the decorating projects going on in every room. She was definitely doing nesting. I immediately felt the presence of two spirits both female and a very strong attraction they had to a particular window.

These spirits were ghosts. Unlike entities, demons, or trans-mortals, these spirits had at one time lived in a human body. At the end of their lives, they (their spirits) had decided not to move on. Becoming trapped in the physical realm, they didn't realize that they no longer had bodies

536

and continued to live in a house in the neighborhood they had lived in while alive.

These were not malefic ghosts, they were just trying to live their life the best they could with their limited understanding. As I communicated to them, I explained that they were "dead", that they no longer had bodies. This was somewhat unbelievable to them, but with some patience and understanding, I revealed to them evidence that indeed their bodies were gone, and that they were living in a house they no longer (actually never had a right to live in). This is another example of a squatter but here an understandable one.

As they began to comprehend their demise and current circumstances, I explained to them that I could now help them move on.

This is the one exception I make interacting with possessions or hauntings. Human spirits can be confused and not malevolent, but you need to help them understand their circumstances before you take your next step in either assisting them or moving them out.

I was translating to Christy as I was communicating mind to mind with these two stranded spirits. She was so curious about them and also committed to not harming them.

I offered to assist them in moving to a higher realm, a realm shift that is typically done around the passing of the body (time of death) to a few months proceeding death.

In this case, the two ghosts were surprised and delighted to know that this option was available to them. They would willingly move to a higher plane. And so the process, taking only about ten minutes changed the lives of both Christy and Robbie and the fate of two human ghosts.

Distinction Between Ghost and Human Spirit

A human spirit who does not transition out of the physical realm will hang on to about 40% of the soul that protected the spirit while in a physical body. *This human spirit living on the earthly plane past death of the body is a **ghost***. Because they have some material matter, they will have weight and a very thin physical façade. The ghostly movies showing a shadowy presence are fairly accurate at least in the representation of a ghost. The 40% soul gives them a translucent visibility.

Normally, a human spirit leaving his/her body will naturally let go of the soul, allowing them to enter higher realms. A person of faith will have no difficulty with this as they have a firmly preprogrammed concept of the heavenly realms. Any faith, meaning any religious or spiritual path, will give an individual this ability.

The "Kingdom of Heaven" Jesus Christ speaks of is both an attitude, so that heaven can be experienced here on Earth, and a realm. When helping Christians move to a heavenly realm, I naturally call on the assistance of Jesus and Mary and the angels to assist their relocation to the paradise promised in the Bible.

And having helped Buddhists and Hindus in their passage, an equally beautiful healing temple/paradise awaits.

The individual leaving their human body will carry with them all that they have learned in this lifetime. Once they have rested and worked out their next lifetime, they will need to leave behind much of their information to become a baby spirit and begin anew. Some children hold onto many of their memories from other lives, accessing them clearly in their early childhood. This is because they have developed a super brain, one outside spirit that they are able to draw on. However, access to that brain fades to a large extent by age 5 so that set in a firm understanding of their journey and work in this new life they are now able to grow and develop without the confusing ebb and flow of past life and body memories. Once they have reached a certain stage of development, they will again have full access to this super brain and memories.

Reasons for Spirits to Remain as Ghosts

Confusion is a main reason. An abrupt death, like one experienced from an accident can toss a spirit out of body. They do not realize they are not in their body and attempt to live the life or pieces of a life they have access to, getting stuck for up to 600 years.

Another reason would be that the spirit is extremely attached to human life, specifically theirs. Sometimes people with mental disorders, like narcissism, will be so involved with themselves and what they have, they 'see' no possibility for the next step or even something new.

Ghosts can also be victims of violent rape, murder and drug overdose. The spirit having endured what it should not have gone through can actually become ill and deformed. I have seen a human choose to drop into the existence of a dog's body for a couple lifetimes to heal atrocities, then return to the human body form in a future life. I am not saying human spirits animate dog bodies. Dogs are another creature, unique and different from humans. What I am saying is sometimes when a human spirit is so injured, this is one choice they may make. A much better choice is for their loved ones to pray for them daily or get a miraculous healer involved in assisting them to move into a healing temple.

A traumatized human spirit will be placed in a sarcophagus-looking resting place in a healing temple, safe, quiet, and protected, where it can heal and be restored with the light and truth (purity) of life.

Occupation of the Brain by Spirits

Many years ago, shortly after I moved into San Francisco, a friend had recommended I see her psychic friend, to give me some insights into my present situation. Although I rarely advise with other psychics, for some reason I thought it was okay to speak to good ol' Bob. What a bad decision that was.

Bob had somehow been the victim of an alien spirit attack. Every one of the folks who consulted with Bob got, for at least nine-week period afterward, a head full of obnoxious, difficult-to-clear aliens in their head. Now, I would have been Johnny-on-the-spot with my clearing techniques but back then I was tortured with aliens screaming in my brain for three years.

During that "occupation", I sought out the assistance of four of spiritual paths:

> 1. I first went to the Catholics, thinking an exorcism would be the ticket to clearing the beings shouting in my head. They suggested prayer as a way to the restoration of mental health. This may have, over time, been the solution. But at that moment. prayers while connecting me with God were not producing the results I was seeking.

2.   The second spiritual organization I contacted was a Buddhist teacher. I remember him: he taught out of a office in Noe Valley a section of San Francisco.

"How can I help you?" the American born monk asked. I had already told my story to him on the phone, so I said: "I have been struggling with 3 loud voices in my head, talking to each other, shouting like there is a mega phone in my head. I'd like you to help me get them out." His answer: "Lets meditate on this problem together" so I sat by his side and chanted with him, "Nam yo ho ren gae ho," as the aliens laughed and screamed and it felt like they were riding through my brain like the flying trapeze with the greatest of ease.

When we had completed the full round of chanting he asked me, "How are you now?" "It was a lovely chant except for the loud ruckus in my head." "That's all I have to offer you, come prayer and chant with us any time you are always welcome".

3. I left discouraged, but determined not to give up on the situation.   My third venture was a trip to the Vedanta Center, center of yogic practice. I luckily got the opportunity for a private appointment with the Swami. He asked me of my time in India and my understandings and said to use my mantras to heal myself. There were no techniques in these three organizations to extract unwanted spirits.

4. My last resort was The Berkley Psychic Institute. They had an answer for me, but it wasn't what I wanted to hear. However, despite this, I listened and did what they advised.

What ensued was a 6-week training program followed by another and another and finally an 18-month clairvoyant program in which subject of removing unwanted spirits was included during weekend retreats. People mainly came to expand their clairvoyance. Then there are folks like me who have reached the end of the road with traditional methods and are "desperate". Here I learned to heal myself and, in that process, I restored my sanity.

I, at the time, wanted someone to help me, I wanted to be freed of these horrendous alien entities, but the struggle and knowledge I gained from the years of working on removing them have made me one of the most effective "ghost busters" on the planet.

"Who Ya Gonna Call?!!!!"

Schizophrenia

When a person is experiencing schizophrenia, they are under siege from entities and occupying forces. Usually, it is a willing agreement between the person with the body and the entities that share the lifetime with them.

One example, Sean, is the son of one of my long time friends. He is now in his late twenties; he experienced the voices for the first time at age 17. Through the years, I had heard the stories of the crazy behaviors of this Irish immigrant family and the struggles they endured. [who is this Irish immigrant family?, Seans?] I didn't clear him.

You might be curious to know why I wouldn't clear his entities or beings even though I knew how. The answer is one of choice. His choice. Most individuals with this challenge will report to you that they like the entities, they have become like their friends. To clear them of these entities without permission causes a change in their spiritual growth and development. It takes away an opportunity to experience a life of research around mental illness and shared physical body with others. This is a valid life and can give the human spirit a great deal of information.

Such a situation may, for a healer, be distressing to leave unaddressed. Especially if you've developed the skill to move entities and beings out, you may be tempted to resolve the occupation. I advise you not to. This may bring his problems and even his spiritual growth agreements onto your head to fulfill. Some people say this is taking on someone else's karma. You have no right to do this and should not proceed.

Spiders and Snakes

During the 1980's in the Arizona desert, a strange phenomenon dropped down on planet Earth. There was a 11-week period when the sky was lit up similarly to the aurora borealis. This actually was the descent of some visitors, much less that of an entity, but rather in the shapes of spiders and snakes. They have a ghostly appearance and hide out often. I find them in peoples spines and necks. These are pretty simple to remove; they are similar to an insect, without much intelligence and somewhat parasitical in nature.

I mentioned my cockroach philosophy: these are definitely in the category of a cockroach and can be removed without worry. These creatures are not from our realm and like locusts dropped in on us to feed off our energy. If you need to use a lot of energy drinks to keep you going, these spiders and snakes may be a cause for your fatigue.

I have mentioned many unwanted creatures of other realms and have given some stories to help you understand how they affect folks. Keep in mind there are many beings, for example angelic beings, spirit helpers, and legions of holy beings that only want good for humanity.

Since we are in a discussion about health, these negative spirits who can have a tremendously adverse effect to the point of spiritual parasitical death. Western medicine has no answers or comprehension of these beings and so there are no treatments to remove this cause of illness. In the next section, you will get the step-by-step protocols for removing spiritual parasites from the body and from your home.

The Processes for Removal of Unwanted Spirit Activity

Demons

It is my sincere wish that you never encounter these either in yourself or in someone you love or care for. There are numerous stories of Jesus clearing demons from people. As he was clearing them, they may have even forced the person they were occupying to speak blasphemy to Jesus. I, like Jesus, can identify who is doing the speaking.

In Biblical stories, we hear of demons being transferred into the bodies of a heard of pigs, who run over the cliff and die. This is not a solution in our age, as the demons would be free again to harm other people once they were released from the pigs after death.

The technique I teach you will remove their intelligence permanently. This is a complete 'brain' wipe; the demon then becomes just a 'thing'. Once you have completed the process, it is now just a kind of floating energy with no information able to harm any being.

I do not recommend you take this on as a vocation, do just what you need to clear and keep yourself, loved ones, and clients clear. To take on being a spiritual warrior with battling evil and entities, will get you bus loads of these creatures swarming you. So, do not battle. Just follow the procedures below in neutrality with the intention and focus of a brain surgeon.

If you have a choice to get additional help removing a demonic spirit, I recommend you welcome it.

Demonic Obliteration Process

- Ground the person who is being harmed by the demon to the center of the earth and from the crown chakra hook them up to the Supreme Being.

- Identify the demon. It will be black in color, and will have a significant amount of power. It is important that once you identify the demon, that you move into action quickly as they will not expect it and this gives you a great advantage, the element of surprise.

- Tie the demon down to the center of the earth and with the same cable attach the cord to the Supreme Being.

The demon will now be locked in place and unable to move.

I use the rose as the symbol of purity and I use this symbol for step one of the process, however it is not about the rose, you could use the image of an athletic shoe or a large bolder, it doesn't matter what you use, just once you start be consistent and use the same thing.

- Throw the rose on top the image of the locked down demon. I use my right hand, and I may even as I project my hand forward thrusting the rose onto the demon say out loud 'rose'.

- With my left hand I project a cartoonish bomb onto the rose and blow up the rose, saying out loud "bomb'.

- You will do this process for possibly 30 minutes or more. I suggest you stop to check on your progress.

How to check your progress

- Momentarily stop the rose bomb momentum and using your muscle testing as what percentage of the demon has been removed.

- Start the muscle testing at 10% going up to 20% on so forth. If it is more than ten and less than 20%, then start from that point and count up, 11, 12, 13, etc., until you discover where you are in the removal process. It helps to see that you are making progress in order to gain courage and fortitude to continue.

Very Important

You can't stop in the middle, so forge ahead until the demon is testing as completely gone. A few minutes to run to the bathroom or get a drink of water is okay, but you can't take a real break. This is serious stuff and you are doing a delicate procedure, one that will dramatically improve the life of the one being helped.

Take this seriously, just like a brain surgeon, they would not take a supper break while in the middle of an important surgery, they will stay with it until the procedure is done.

- Check to see if the DNA has a program for spiritual parasites or mental illness. If yes, go to the DNA obliteration process to remove these harmful programs. Find the DNA obliteration process in Chapter 2

- All demonic clearings must include a spiritual timeline clearing. This will clear off the past timeline, but more importantly will clear off all the time bombs set to go off in the person's future that would allow for a return of different demonic beings. Find the spiritual time line process on page 81

Follow up After Demonic Obliteration

Spiritual therapy to insure a new pattern is established.

Following the removal, I recommend the person does the

Clearing meditation for 40 days

Our free meditation "From Fatigued to Fabulous" is an excellent clear out. It will, over the next 40 days, set a new energetic pattern for health without parasitical demons.

Clearing on page 81

In the case of multiple demons

Sometimes when there is one there are two or three. I suggest you lock them all down with the same cable to the center of the earth. You can imagine you have thrown a fishing net over them and then send a cable up to the Supreme Being, tying them into position.

What I have found with multiple demons is each takes the same amount of time sequentially rather than simultaneously. For example, for three removals, it will take three times longer. However, since you have safely locked them in position, they are not attacking you or causing pain to the person they are being removed from.

When you are checking progress you will also ask how many are left and what percentage has cleared away. What I have observed with demons is that you clear one completely before the next one starts clearing. They don't clear away simultaneously, only one by one. Your quiet mantra is 'slow and steady wins the race.'

Evil Spirits Obliteration Process

- Ground the person who is being harmed by the evil spirit to the center of the earth and from the crown chakra hook them up to the Supreme Being.

- Identify the evil spirits. They come in bunches and will appear black in color, and will have a significantly less power than a demon yet the force of evil has drive. It is important that once you identify the evil spirits and number them, that you move into action quickly as they will not expect it and this gives you a great advantage, the element of surprise.

548

- Fasten the group of evil spirits down to the center of the earth and with the same shackle attach the lead to the Supreme Being. The evil spirits will now be locked in place and unable to move.

- Throw a rose on top the image of the locked down evil spirits. I use my right hand, and I may even as I project my hand forward thrusting the rose onto the evil spirits say out loud 'rose'.

- With my left hand I project a cartoonish bomb onto the rose and blow up the rose, say out loud "bomb'.

- Do this process for possibly 5 minutes or more. I suggest you stop to check on your progress.

How to check your progress

- Momentarily stop the rose bomb momentum and using your muscle testing as what percentage of the evil spirits have been removed.

- Start the muscle testing at 10% going up to 20% on so forth. If it is more than ten and less than 20% then start from ten and count up, 11, 12, 13, etc., until you discover where you are in the removal process. It helps to see that you are making progress to help have courage and fortitude to continue.

Very Important: complete the process

- Check to see if the DNA has a program for spiritual parasites or mental illness. If yes, go to the DNA obliteration process and remove these harmful programs. Find the DNA obliteration process in Chapter 2.

- All evil spirit clearings must include a spiritual timeline clearing. This will clear off the past timeline, but more importantly will clear off all the time bombs set to go off in the person's future that would allow for a return of different evil beings. Find the spiritual time line process on page 81

Follow up After Evil Spirit Obliteration Process

Spiritual therapy to insure a new pattern is established.

- Following the removal, I recommend the person does the **clearing meditation for 40 days**

- Our free meditation "From Fatigued to Fabulous" is an excellent clear out. It will, over the next 21 days, set a new energetic pattern for health without parasitical demons. clearing on page 81

Trans-mortals Obliteration Process

- Ground the person who is being harmed by the trans-mortal spirits to the center of the earth and from the crown chakra, hook them up to the Supreme Being.

- Identify the trans-mortals. The few times I encountered them, there were 3 or 4 together. Assume they have come with others and look carefully for them. They will feel gigantic, appear grey in color, and will have a significantly more power than anything else on the astral plane. This is not a job for the easily frightened. It is important that once you identify the trans-mortals and number them, that you move into action quickly as they will not expect it and this gives you a great advantage: the element of surprise.

- Fasten each trans-mortal down individually immediately upon identifying them until they are all locked down to the center of the earth and with binding attach the lead to the Supreme Being. The trans-mortals will now be locked in place and unable to move.

- Throw a rose on top the image of the locked down trans-mortal. I use my right hand, and I may even as I project my hand forward thrusting the rose onto the evil spirits say out loud 'rose'.

- With my left hand I project a cartoonish bomb onto the rose and blow up the rose, say out loud "bomb'.
- Repeat the last two steps until each of them is removed entirely, again one by one

- Do this process for possibly 2 hours or more. I suggest you stop to check on your progress.

How to check your progress

- Momentarily stop the rose bomb momentum and using your muscle testing as what percentage of the trans mortal has been removed.

- Start the muscle testing at 10% going up to 20% on so forth. If it is more than ten and less than 20% then start from ten and count up, 11, 12, 13, etc., until you discover where you are in the removal process. It helps to see that you are making progress to give you courage and fortitude to continue.

Very Important: to complete the process

- With trans-mortals you are thrusting them back into their realm permanently. They are a type of alien. I look at their behavior as resembling teenage drunken mischief. They have jumped realms and are hanging out causing problems for another type of being (a human) and they think it's funny. They are neither collecting data/research nor being a parasite; they are jokesters. Move them out to restore peace to the poor unfortunate person who got in the way of their landing strip.

- All trans-mortal clearings must include a spiritual timeline clearing. This will clear off the past timeline but more importantly will clear off all the time bombs set to go off in the person's future that would allow for a return of different evil beings. Find the spiritual time line process on page 81

- All trans-mortal clearings must also include a search of the physical body for any anchors: you might read them as eggs that the trans-mortals can jump into in the future. They can leave behind identification, a sort of GPS navigation inside the human. After these are entirely cleared, clear in the same way you did in the above obliteration process. Repeat the steps for each egg/anchor you find till it is entirely gone.

Follow–Up: after trans-mortal obliteration process

Spiritual therapy to insure a new pattern is established.

Following the removal, I recommend the person does the **Clearing meditation for 6 months**

Best choice for this circumstance is to enroll in the 12-month Miraculous Elite Healing Program. Details on our website julierenee.com

Entity Obliteration Process

- Ground the person who is being infested by the entities to the center of the earth, and from the crown chakra, connect them to the Supreme Being.

- Identify the circumstances of the infestation, how many entities and what colors. They come in bunches and will appear in all primary colors and do not appear black. The power they process is much like an ant crawling up the inside of your pant leg. Significantly annoying at times but, on their own, they aren't going to do much. They are definitely parasitical in nature. They have virtually no power and are easily removed if you follow the steps exactly. Just like an ant if you don't lock them down right away, they can move all over and be extremely annoying. Move into action quickly as they will not expect it. This gives you a great advantage, the element of surprise.

- Fasten the group of entities down to the center of the earth and with the same shackle attach the lead to the Supreme Being. The entities will now be locked in place and unable to move.

- Throw a rose on top the image of the locked down entities. I use my right hand, and I may even as I project my hand forward thrusting the rose onto the evil spirits say out loud 'rose'.

- With my left hand I project a cartoonish bomb onto the rose and blow up the rose, say out loud "bomb'.

- Do this process for possibly 3 minutes or more. I suggest you stop to check on your progress after 3 minutes.

How to check your progress

- Momentarily stop the rose-bomb momentum and using your muscle testing to determine what percentage of the evil spirits have been removed.

- Start the muscle testing at 10% going up to 20% on so forth. If it is more than ten and less than 20% then start from ten and count up, 11, 12, 13,etc., until you discover where you are in the removal process. It helps to see that you are making progress which will give you courage and fortitude to continue.

Very Important: complete the process

- Check if the DNA has a program for spiritual parasites or mental illness. If yes. go to the DNA obliteration process (see Chapter 2) and remove these harmful programs.

Follow up After Entity Obliteration Process

Spiritual therapy to insure a new pattern is established.

Following the removal, I recommend the person does the :
Clearing meditation for 21 days

Our free meditation "From Fatigued to Fabulous" is an excellent clear out. It will set a new energetic pattern for health without parasitical demons over the next 21 days. Clearing on page 81

Spiders and Snakes: Obliteration Process

- Ground the person who is being infested by the spider or snake to the center of the earth and from the crown chakra hook them up to the Supreme Being.

- Identify the circumstances of the infestation and how many of either spiders or snakes. They are typically grey. They are often alone but there can be a couple. They are definitely parasitical in nature. They have virtually no power and are easily removed if you follow the steps exactly. I have found them to be evasive and sneaky so get them locked in right away. Move into action quickly as they will not expect it. This gives you a great advantage, the element of surprise.

- Fasten the spider or snake down to the center of the earth and with the same shackle attach the lead to the Supreme Being. The spider or snake will now be locked in place and unable to move.

- Throw a rose on top the image of the locked down spider or snake. I use my right hand, and I may even as I project my hand forward thrusting the rose onto the evil spirits say out loud 'rose'.

- With my left hand I project a cartoonish bomb onto the rose and blow up the rose, say out loud "bomb'.

- Do this process for 5 or more repetitions. I suggest you stop to check on your progress after 5 repetitions of rose/bomb.

Follow up After Spider or Snake Obliteration Process

Spiritual therapy to insure a new pattern is established. Following the removal, I recommend the person does the **clearing meditation for 2 days**

Our free meditation "From Fatigued to Fabulous" is an excellent clear out. It will set a new energetic pattern for health without parasitical spiders and snakes over the next 2 days. Clearing on page 81

Ghost Removal

When we look at removing ghosts we are not looking at an inhabitation of the ghost in a person, but rather a ghost squatting in a home or other physical location.

Special Ghost Transition

Sometimes these human spirits stuck on the earthly plan without a body. They are unaware of this circumstance: with a gentle conversation letting them know they are no longer alive and that they can move to a healing temple will be enough to move them on their way. These are not malevolent beings, you speak to them as a confused or troubled spirit; there is no aggression or assertive 'posturing'. The idea is to have them feel safe so they can make a good choice to leave.

I recommend you speak to them for a short time, say a couple minutes, as an authority to convince them they are no longer alive. You can help them move on to a healing temple. Ask, "Would you like that?"

Do not, however, get into a long conversation with them. Do not think their stories are interesting and/or get tricked into buying into their world and reasons for being stuck. Just tell them who you are, that they are 'dead', don't have a physical body any longer, and you can help them move into a physical healing temple.

If the answer is, "Yes," find out what their faith at birth was, if possible. If you aren't real adept at clairaudience, use muscle testing. And finally make your best guess. They will ultimately get to the right place, even if you start them somewhere at a starter healing temple.

If they are Christian, identify who you will call in to assist you, Christ or Mary.

Ask for Mary, for example, to come and help you with the process

"Mary, this is so-and-so. They would like to join you in a healing temple and need assistance."

Typically Mary will have her initiates, they look like nuns in black robes, help her. She may or may not hug the person/ghost. Typically she will not. She hugs the faithful who have just passed over and are moving into her tutelage.

The two initiates will take the person/ghost by the upper arms and lift it up.

In this process, the "soul matter" is left behind and the spirit is now more ready to take its place in the lower heavenly realms.

Mary will tell you if they are in bad shape, but the prognosis is to go to a resting state for a prolonged period, to restore the spirit to a cleaner, purer state. I think this might have been the idea of purgatory. However, I know this is not a place of suffering and penance; instead, it is a place of restoration.

You may actually feel them lifted up and out and in moments they will be gone from the physical plane.

After I had done many of these healings, Mary, Mother of Jesus, began to thank me at the end of the healings. I was so touched when this started. I have always been willing to help a lost spirit find their way back to the 'Kingdom of Heaven' whatever that is for them.

For Buddhists, I call in Kuan Yin or Buddha; for Jews, I call in Abraham and Sara. You can look to a guide or Avatar of the spiritual system they belonged to and get them moved up and on.

If, on the other hand, the ghost is malevolent you must now prepare to do an "obliteration process" without hesitation.

Malevolent Ghost Obliteration Process

- Ground yourself to the center of the earth

- Ground the ghost to the center of the earth and hook the top of their head with a cord to the Supreme Being. The ghost will now be locked into place and unable to move.

- Throw the rose on top of the locked down ghost. I use my right hand and I may even as I project my hand forward thrusting the rose onto the ghost say out loud 'rose'.

- With my left hand I project a cartoonish bomb onto the rose and blow up the rose, saying out loud "bomb'.

- You will do this process for possibly 7 minutes or more. I suggest you stop to check on your progress.

How to check your progress

- Momentarily stop the rose-bomb momentum then using muscle testing, determine what percentage of the ghost has been removed. Keep in mind you cannot "kill" this human spirit, what you are doing is making all of their intelligence vanish so they will no longer be harmful or a nuisance to people who are living in a body on earth. They will be starting at ground zero, without any information. They are beginning the long journey of spiritual development again: hopefully this time they will do better. You are essentially wiping their slate clean.

- Start the muscle testing at 10% going up to 20% on so forth. If it is more than ten and less than twenty percent then start from ten and count up, 11, 12, 13, etc., until you discover where you are in the removal process. It helps to see that you are making progress to give you courage and fortitude to continue.

Very Important

Do not stop in the middle. Forge ahead until the ghost is tested as completely gone.

When I was new at this and clearing myself, I once ended up with an evil spirit hanging out the right neo-cortex. It had positioned itself literally in my brain, and try as I may, it had gotten a jump on me and locked itself in there. I did not like the idea of a spirit hanging out the top of my head, so I did rose-bombs in my head for a good 5 minutes, and I totally cleared it...and some of my own intelligence. It was a good experiment it took about a week for my intelligence to completely returned, so I recommend locking these spirits and demons down if at all possible away from your brain and body.

As I mentioned earlier in this chapter, this is not part of the human blueprint, yet without addressing how to remove and clear these unwanted visitors, it is possible that the individual would not ever fully heal.

The experience of having demons evil spirits entities spiders and snakes in your body is a spiritual illness. When going through the protocols asking if is this a spiritual illness and then you find them, you now have a way to address this unfortunate and all-too-common situation.

I am aware that entitles will get into technology such as your computer, printer or cell phone or even your Wi-Fi connection and mess things up. You can follow the exact same procedures laid out above to remove troublesome spirits from your computer.

The journey of a human spirit in body is an amazing and challenging journey with many ups and downs. If you have had the unfortunate experience of having a demon or evil spirit occupy your body, you have definitely experienced a tough time. I ask you to look at what you were able to learn for yourself from the experience.

- How did you become wiser?
- How did you become more compassionate and kind to others who are suffering?

- What did you learn about the serenity of a quiet body verses the noise of entities or aliens in your head?

- How will you care for yourself differently?

- What brought the experience to you?

You could ask yourself many more questions to help you synthesize your learning. You can then decide to store your learning up in the akashic records or keep it in your present time mental body. By approaching these challenges as learning experiences, you can wrap them up in a box of learning when you are completely on the other side. It will not define you nor do you need to feel ashamed or embarrassed that you had that journey nor will you have to "wear" that challenge on yourself It will just be your history. You will continue to be very sane, competent and capable, and go on to live a life of learning, joy and exploration.

Chapter 29: Advice From Julie Renee

It's Your Time to Shine Your Miracle Starts Today

This is Julie Renee Doering and I'll meet up with you in your next step.

Julie Renee mentors powerful, ambitious women leaders who refuse to play small, but who are being taken out of the game with exhaustion and "fuzzy brain". She regenerates the brain and gets them back to playing at 100% again.

Books by Julie Renee: The *100% You Formula, Your Divine Human Blueprint*, Awakening the Healthy American and *Balance Your Life Now!*

Julie Renee is the founder and developer of a new spiritual science, the 100% Healthy Human Blueprint. She is the author of the groundbreaking book, *Your Divine Human Blueprint*. Her unique gift of healing defines the energy-science of Cellular Quantum Mechanics. She trains individuals in her "100% You Immersion Program", and sees private VIP clients in her home in northern California.

After launching her first business from her tiny San Francisco studio apartment in 1993, she has prevailed over a challenging history of multiple cancers and five Near-Death experiences. Overcoming tremendous odds, none of her doctors saw a possibility for her to survive her illness. She was repeatedly told she was dying. Unwilling to believe that this was true, even the Angel of Death could not convince her that it was her time to go. She has dedicated her life to the betterment of humankind and the reawakening of humanity to the Divine Human Blueprint.

Recognized for her leadership abilities, she is the recipient of the 2010-2011National Association of Professional Women's "Woman of the Year Award" and the Powerful Women International's "Global Leadership Award" 2012.

Julie Renee has been featured as an expert on CBS, Unity FM, Rock Star Radio, Blog Talk Align, Live 365, Low Down, Spirit Seeker, 11;11 Magazine, Spirit Seeker Magazine, and on various TV shows, including New Era Healing and a Forum on Spirituality. She is a writer for Holistic Fashionista Magazine and Accomplish Magazine. She is also the host of the radio show, 100% Healthy. Additionally, she has both stage and film credits, and is a harpist and singer.

Julie Renee is *the* 100% Healthy Life EXPERT. She helps women succeed in life and business by activating them simply and easily to get to 100% in both health and vitality. An expert meditation instructor, she shares the secrets of altering reality through meditation, and provides an integrated fast track for manifesting, holding and growing abundance, health, beauty, and wealth. Her home activation programs include:

• Look Great Naked – Beautiful From the Inside Out

• Accelerate Wealth 21 – Day Program

• Illumination Rosary for Enlightenment

• The Sound of Truth – Vedic Mantra for transformation

- Your Secret Keys audio series

- Your Divine Human Blueprint home study audio series

- Unlimited Love

As a speaker, she has shared the stage with Marci Shimoff, Jack Canfield, Caterina Rando, James Malinchak, Sean Aston, Stedman Graham, Julie Carrier, Dr Bill Dorfman, Jill Lublin, PJ Van Hulle, and many others.

From farm wife to health activator: Julie Renee started out in Minnesota as a farm wife, attended art school, modeled, waitressed, appeared in 7 films, became a very successful realtor, and finally moved into her passion as a healer in the form of a health activator. She now has over 30 years' experience supporting individuals and groups in Quantum Health Activations, from high-risk pregnancies to life-saving interventions with critically ill individuals. Known as the premier healer for high risk pregnancies, twenty doctors and six midwives sent their most difficult clients to Julie Renee to help them from gestation through the first year after birth. In all, she has assisted 140+ high risk babies to successfully enter this world.

Many years ago, she taught yoga and offered healing massage to people in recovery. She also taught infant massage, worked with insurance companies, and helped injured clients return to living, and hospice clients pass pain-free and without medication as they said good-bye to their loved ones.

Moving deeper into her exploration of regeneration, she developed specialized Jadeite hot stone treatments, accessing the knowledge of the ancient civilizations of the Olmecs and Mayans, who used Jadeite for body initiations and transformations.

As part of a natural progression, Julie Renee moved from physical healing to offering spiritual life coaching for women. Through her clairvoyant gifts, she helped women rapidly shift to move into their next highest step.

For the past 7 years, Julie Renee has been researching and developing programs with the Blueprint, teaching through guidebooks, courses and meditation as a simple way to access the healing gifts and secrets of the Divine Human Blueprint.

Thousands of individuals have created health, wealth and love with Julie Renee's help. Through her extraordinary gifts, she has brought critically ill people back into their lives, restoring health to their cellular and energetic bodies through the Divine Human Blueprint.

Traveling the world, she has studied in India, and is both an ordained minister and a pujari (carrier of the light) in the yogic tradition.

Julie Renee's favorite vacations include repelling down waterfalls, and zip lining and performing daring acts, such as shooting down the longest water slide in Mexico. She loves the ocean, the mountains, and nature, and is a nature girl at heart. You can find her out hiking trails every chance she gets. She challenges herself regularly by repelling, and doing other fun and scary activities that involve hanging from great heights with ropes. Her favorite ice cream is rose petal. She loves mangos and scented flowers.... especially garden roses.

Precious Advice Just for YOU from Julie Renee

Let me help you take

your next step!

You've gotten a lot of great information in this book, and hopefully a lot of value, too. If you're like me, you'll wan to learn how you can take thi work to the next level and ge. skyrocketing with better health, energy, connection and momentum.

Since no two people are exactly alike, I'd like to suggest five choices about ways to take your 100% pursuit into your life. Keep in mind I have been teaching and assisting folks with health for more than two decades and am prolific. I encourage you to explore the www.JulieRenee.com website and discover a wealth of mini-programs and directed meditations if you would like to jump in with baby steps.

If, however, you like to take action in a big way and are ready to have it all, here are the three paths to choose from:

1. **Activate the Program to Help You Clear Hidden Blocks That are Killing Your Business** I created a program to go along with this book, just for you. It gives you a good training and working knowledge as to how to shift the "field of perception" and help you launch into a powerfully successful future.

2. **100% You Immersion Program** Discover the full Divine Human Blueprint for personal and professional use. 12 month training.

566

3. **VIP Mentoring Experience with One-Day Session**
Intimate one-day experience with Julie Renee in her home. Receive 4 hours of directed quantum energy activating shifts in perception, brain, energy and all aspects of the human dynamic. Followed up with 3 months of personalized mentoring and masters programs for full 100% healthy happy results.

Julie Renee can be reached through her website at **www.JulieRenee.com** Or on any of the following social sites.

• Contact me • Youtube

• Facebook • Linked In • Twitter

• Blogtalk Radio • Pinterest

These are the things our attorney wants us to share with you.

The content case studies and examples in this book do not in any way represent the "average" or "typical" member experience. In fact, with any program offering a way to improve health, vitality, wealth and love, we know that some members purchase our systems and never use them, and therefore, get no results from their membership at all. You should assume that you will obtain no results from this program. Therefore, the member case studies we are sharing can neither represent nor guarantee the experience of past, current or future program participants or members. Rather, these unique case studies represent what is possible with our system. Each of these unique case studies, and any and all results reported in these case studies by individual members, are the culmination of numerous variables, many of which we cannot control, including; pre-existing mental, emotional and health conditions, personal incentive, discontinuity of spiritual and energetic conditions and countless other tangible and intangible factors.

Whether this Notice refers to 'you' or 'your' it means you while 'we' or 'our' refers to Gable-Kennedy Inc. dba 100% You.

Any improvements in health, mindset and energy are examples of what we think you can achieve. There are no assurances you'll do as well. If you rely only on the assurances in this book you must accept the risk of not doing as well.

Where specific health activations that have for others returned their health to high function, these examples are used and attributed to the individuals/ participants who have experienced these shifts, through 100% Healthy individual and group programs. There is no assurance you will do as well. If you rely on our 'transformations' you must also assume the risk of not doing as well.

Any representation of improved health, wealth, relationship and mindset in this book, our websites and in our programs are not considered to be average or normal. Likewise any claims or representations from our course participants and students are not considered to be average results.

There can be no assurances that any prior successes, or past results, regarding health, wealth, love and relationship can be used as an indication of future success or results.

Returning health, energy, clarity and ease to the body are based on many factors. We have no way of knowing how well you will do, as we do not know you, your background, your ability to heal, your 'work' ethics or basic health and body care practices. Therefore, we do not guarantee or imply that you will have improvements or achieve better health, wealth, relationships, love, money or any other improvements suggested in this book, on our website or anywhere else. If you rely only on the assurances in this book you must accept the risk of not doing as well.

100% Healthy and 100% You programs are designed for people who are already healthy and want to take their health to the next level. Your health, wealth and love are entirely in your hands. Our programs are meant to be educational in nature and these programs may not be suited for everyone. Making decisions based on any information presented in our products, services or website should be done only with the knowledge that you could experience significant losses or make no improvements at all, or achieve no desired results regarding health, wealth, relationships, and energy.

569

Use caution and seek the advice of qualified professionals. Check with your health care director, therapist or professional business advisor, before acting on this or any information.

Users of our products, services and website are advised to do their own due diligence when it comes to making health decisions and all information, products and services that have been provided should be independently verified by your own qualified professional. Our information, products and services on www.julierenee.com should be carefully considered and evaluated, before reaching a business decision on whether to rely on them.

You agree that our companies are not responsible for the success or failure of your health, wealth or relationship decisions relating to the information presented by www.julierenee.com or our companies' products or services.

Printed in Great Britain
by Amazon.co.uk, Ltd.,
Marston Gate.